Lecture Notes in Artificial Intelligence 5447

Edited by R. Goebel, J. Siekmann, and W. Wahlster

Subseries of Lecture Notes in Computer Science

Hiromitsu Hattori   Takahiro Kawamura
Tsuyoshi Idé   Makoto Yokoo
Yohei Murakami (Eds.)

New Frontiers in Artificial Intelligence

JSAI 2008 Conference and Workshops
Asahikawa, Japan, June 11-13, 2008
Revised Selected Papers

 Springer

Series Editors

Randy Goebel, University of Alberta, Edmonton, Canada
Jörg Siekmann, University of Saarland, Saarbrücken, Germany
Wolfgang Wahlster, DFKI and University of Saarland, Saarbrücken, Germany

Volume Editors

Hiromitsu Hattori
Kyoto University, Graduate School of Informatics
Yoshida-Honmachi, Sakyo-ku, Kyoto 606-8501, Japan
E-mail: hatto@i.kyoto-u.ac.jp

Takahiro Kawamura
Toshiba Corp., Research & Development Center
1, Komukai-Toshiba-cho, Saiwai-ku, Kawasaki 212-8582, Japan
E-mail: takahiro@eel.rdc.toshiba.co.jp

Tsuyoshi Idé
IBM Research, Tokyo Research Laboratory
1623-14 Shimo-tsuruma, Yamato, Kanagawa 242-8502, Japan
E-mail: goodidea@jp.ibm.com

Makoto Yokoo
Kyushu University, Faculty of Information Science and Electrical Engineering
744 Motooka, Nishi-ku, Fukuoka 819-0395, Japan
E-mail: yokoo@is.kyushu-u.ac.jp

Yohei Murakami
National Institute of Information and Communication Technology
3-5 Hikaridai, Seika-cho, Soraku-gun, Kyoto 619-0289, Japan
E-mail: yohei@nict.go.jp

Library of Congress Control Number: Applied for

CR Subject Classification (1998): I.2, H.5.2, I.5, J.1, J.5

LNCS Sublibrary: SL 7 – Artificial Intelligence

ISSN	0302-9743
ISBN-10	3-642-00608-6 Springer Berlin Heidelberg New York
ISBN-13	978-3-642-00608-1 Springer Berlin Heidelberg New York

This work is subject to copyright. All rights are reserved, whether the whole or part of the material is concerned, specifically the rights of translation, reprinting, re-use of illustrations, recitation, broadcasting, reproduction on microfilms or in any other way, and storage in data banks. Duplication of this publication or parts thereof is permitted only under the provisions of the German Copyright Law of September 9, 1965, in its current version, and permission for use must always be obtained from Springer. Violations are liable to prosecution under the German Copyright Law.

springer.com

© Springer-Verlag Berlin Heidelberg 2009
Printed in Germany

Typesetting: Camera-ready by author, data conversion by Scientific Publishing Services, Chennai, India
Printed on acid-free paper   SPIN: 12632589   06/3180   5 4 3 2 1 0

Preface

Artificial intelligence has recently been re-energized to provide the clues needed to resolve complicated problems. AI is also expected to play a central role in enhancing a wide variety of daily activities. JSAI (The Japanese Society for Artificial Intelligence) is responsible for boosting the activities of AI researchers in Japan, and their series of annual conferences offers attractive forums for the exposition of the latest achievements and inter-group communication. In the past, the best papers of the conferences were published in the LNAI series.

This book consists of award papers from the 22nd annual conference of the JSAI (JSAI 2008) and selected papers from the three co-located workshops. Eight papers were selected among more than 400 presentations at the conference and 18 papers were selected from the 34 presentations at the co-located workshops; Logic and Engineering of Natural Language Semantics 5 (LENLS 2008), the 2nd International Workshop on Juris-informatics (JURISIN 2008), and the First International Workshop on Laughter in Interaction and Body Movement (LIBM 2008). The award papers from JSAI 2008 were selected through a rigorous selection process. In the process, papers recommended by session chairs, session commentators, and PC members were carefully reviewed, before the final decision was made.

Papers from the three workshops were selected by the organizers of each workshop based on yet another selection process. On average, half of the workshop papers were selected through discussions among organizers. LENLS 2008 focused on the dynamic semantics of natural language, and, in particular, the interactive turn of formal pragmatics, which takes a formal approach to the interactive quality of pragmatic meanings by making use of game-theoretic, decision-theoretic and utility-theoretic approaches. The aims of JURISIN 2008 included encouraging the discussion of the fundamental and practical issues facing juris-informatics by people from various backgrounds such as law, social science, information and intelligent technology, logic and philosophy, including the conventional AI and law area. LIBM 2008 focused attention on the phenomenon of laughter in interactions and body movements of participants, and emphasized the physical/cognitive factors and conditions socially enact laughing situations or moments.

This book will further the international recognition of the excellent research being performed by the Japanese AI community, and also boost AI research in Japan.

December 2008   Hiromitsu Hattori

Organization

The award papers were selected by the Program Committee of the annual conference of JSAI (Japan Society for Artificial Intelligence) 2008. The paper selection of each co-located international workshop was made by the Program Committee of the respective workshop. Based on the decisions of the paper awards and the paper selections, each chapter was edited by the Program Chairs of the 22nd annual conference of JSAI 2008 and the co-located international workshops. The entire contents and structure of the book were managed and edited by chief editors.

Volume Editors

Primary Volume Editor	Hiromitsu Hattori (Kyoto University, Japan)
Takahiro Kawamura	TOSHIBA Corporation, Japan
Tsuyoshi Idé	IBM Tokyo Research Laboratories, Japan
Makoto Yokoo	Kyushu University, Japan
Yohei Murakami	National Institute of Information and Communications Technology, Japan

Chapter Editors (Program Chairs)

Award Paper Chapter	Makoto Yokoo (Kyushu University, Japan)
LENLS 2008 Chapter	Yasuo Nakayama (Osaka University, Japan)
JURISIN 2008 Chapter	Katsumi Nitta (Tokyo Institute of Technology, Japan)
	Ken Satoh (National Institute of Informatics, Japan)
	Satoshi Tojo (Japan Advanced Institute of Science and Technology, Japan)
LIBM 2008 Chapter	Hitoshi Iida (Tokyo Univeristy of Technology, Japan)
	Masashi Okamoto (Tokyo Univeristy of Technology, Japan)
	Katsuya Takanashi (Kyoto University, Japan)

Table of Contents

Part I: Awarded Papers

Overview of Awarded Papers – The 22nd Annual Conference of JSAI ... 3
Makoto Yokoo

A Japanese Input Method for Mobile Terminals Using Surface EMG Signals 5
Akira Hatano, Kenji Araki, and Masafumi Matsuhara

Evaluation of Similarity Measures for Ontology Mapping 15
Ryutaro Ichise

Network Distributed POMDP with Communication 26
Yuki Iwanari, Yuichi Yabu, Makoto Tasaki, and Makoto Yokoo

Solving Crossword Puzzles Using Extended Potts Model 39
Kazuki Jimbo, Hiroya Takamura, and Manabu Okumura

Socialized Computers and Collaborative Learning 48
Mikihiko Mori, Kokolo Ikeda, Gaku Hagiwara, Masaki Saga, Tetsutaro Uehara, and Hajime Kita

Learning Communicative Meanings of Utterances by Robots 62
Ryo Taguchi, Naoto Iwahashi, and Tsuneo Nitta

Towards Coordination of Multiple Machine Translation Services 73
Rie Tanaka, Toru Ishida, and Yohei Murakami

Ranking Method of Object-Attribute-Evaluation Three-Tuples for Opinion Retrieval 87
Masaaki Tsuchida, Hironori Mizuguchi, and Dai Kusui

Part II: Logic and Engineering of Natural Language Semantics

Overview of Logic and Engineering of Natural Language Semantics (LENLS) 2008 101
Yasuo Nakayama

Multiple Subject Constructions in Japanese: A Dynamic Syntax Account 103
Hiroaki Nakamura, Kei Yoshimoto, Yoshiki Mori, and Masahiro Kobayashi

Topic/Subject Coreference in the Hierarchy of Japanese Complex
Sentences 119
    Alastair Butler, Chidori Nakamura, and Kei Yoshimoto

Japanese Reported Speech: Against a Direct–Indirect Distinction 133
    Emar Maier

The Dynamics of Tense under Attitudes – Anaphoricity and *de se*
Interpretation in the Backward Shifted Past 146
    Corien Bary and Emar Maier

Argumentative Properties of Pragmatic Inferences..................... 161
    Grégoire Winterstein

Prolegomena to Dynamic Epistemic Preference Logic 177
    Satoru Suzuki

Monads and Meta-lambda Calculus 193
    Daisuke Bekki

Part III: Juris-Informatics

Overview of JURISIN 2008... 211
    Katsumi Nitta, Ken Satoh, and Satoshi Tojo

Bootstrapping-Based Extraction of Dictionary Terms from
Unsegmented Legal Text 213
    Masato Hagiwara, Yasuhiro Ogawa, and Katsuhiko Toyama

Computational Dialectics Based on Specialization and Generalization –
A New Reasoning Method for Conflict Resolution 228
    Hiroyuki Kido and Masahito Kurihara

Treatment of Legal Sentences Including Itemized and Referential
Expressions – Towards Translation into Logical Forms 242
    Yusuke Kimura, Makoto Nakamura, and Akira Shimazu

Computing Argumentation Semantics in Answer Set Programming 254
    Toshiko Wakaki and Katsumi Nitta

Part IV: Laughter in Interaction and Body Movement

LIBM 2008 - First International Workshop on Laughter in Interaction
and Body Movement 273
    Hitoshi Iida, Masashi Okamoto, and Katsuya Takanashi

Laughter Around the End of Storytelling in Multi-party Interaction 275
    Mika Enomoto, Masashi Okamoto, Masato Ohba, and Hitoshi Iida

Preliminary Notes on the Sequential Organization of Smile and
Laughter 288
    Hiromichi Hosoma

Laughter for Defusing Tension: Examples from Business Meetings in
Japanese and in English 294
    Kazuyo Murata

Robots Make Things Funnier 306
    Jonas Sjöbergh and Kenji Araki

Laughter: Its Basic Nature and Its Background of Equivocal
Impression 314
    Yutaka Tani

Author Index 331

Part I
Awarded Papers

Overview of Awarded Papers – The 22nd Annual Conference of JSAI

Makoto Yokoo

Faculty of Information Science and Electrical Engineering
Kyushu University
744 Motooka, Nishi-ku
Fukuoka, 819-0395 Japan
yokoo@is.kyushu-u.ac.jp

This chapter features eight awarded papers, selected form JSAI2008 – the 22nd annual conference of Japanese Society of Artificial Intelligence. The conference was held in Asahikawa, Hokkaido from June 11 until June 13, 2008. More than 400 papers were presented in about 80 sessions and 645 people participated in the conference. These awarded papers are truly excellent, as they were chosen out of 400 papers, with the selection rate just about two per cent. Also, the selection involved more than 240 people in total (session chairs, commentators, and program committee members) and rigorous reviews/discussions.

Synopses of the eight papers are as follows.

Hatano *et al.* develop an innovative Japanese input method for mobile terminals. This method uses surface eletromyogram (sEMG) and treat arm muscle movements as input signals. Thus, this method requires no physical keys. Since mobile terminals cannot be equipped with enough keys due to physical restrictions, this method is ideal for using mobile terminals. They show that the recognition rate of their current system is about 80%.

Ichise presents an analysis of similarity measures for identifying ontology mapping. He investigates 48 similarity measures used in previous works. By using discriminant analysis, he extracts 22 similarity measures that are effective for identifying ontology mapping. The extracted measures vary widely in similarity types. This result suggests that for identifying ontology mapping, using several types of similarity is necessary.

Iwanari *et al.* propose a method for introducing communications in the Network Distributed Partially Observable Markov Decision Problems (ND-POMDPs). ND-POMDPs are a popular approach for modeling decision making in teams operating under uncertainty. They extend existing algorithms so that agents periodically communicate their observation/action histories. As a result, agents can reduce the uncertainly about other agents and can avoid the exponential growth in the size of local plans.

Jimbo *et al.* present a system for solving Japanese crossword puzzles. Solving crossword puzzles by computers is a challenging task since it requires logical inference and association as well as vocabulary and common sense knowledge. They use an extension of the Potts model, which is based on the spin model of crystal trellis. Their method can incorporate various clues of solving puzzles and requires less computational cost compared with other existing models.

Mori *et al.* propose a concept called socialized computers (SCs). The SC allows multiple users to access to the computer with multiple mice and keyboards and share information on a single large display. SCs are useful for collaborative learning, a teaching method of asking groups of learners to do tasks collaboratively. They show three application domains of SCs.

Taguchi *et al.* describe a computational mechanism that enables a robot to return suitable utterances to a human or perform actions by learning the meanings of interrogative words (such as "what" and "which"). Their method learns the relationship between human utterances and robot responses that have communicative meanings on the basis of a graphical model of the human-robot interaction.

Tanaka *et al.* propose a context-based coordination framework of multiple machine translation services available on the Web. To realize translations between non-English languages, it is necessary to cascade different translation services by using English as a hub language. To handle inconsistency, asymmetry and intransitivity of word selections between multiple machine translation services, this framework propagates the context among cascaded services by referring to multilingual equivalent terms.

Tsuchida *et al.* propose a ranking method for opinion retrieval that uses a confidence model of opinions as a three-tuple of *object-attribute-evaluation*. The confidence model divides a three-tuple into two pairs, i.e., object-attribute and attribute-evaluation. Furthermore, the confidence model evaluates an opinion simultaneously using syntactic and semantic analyses. Their method improves the precision of the top fifty opinions in the retrieval result.

On behalf of the JSAI 2008 program committee, I would like to thank all the chair persons, commentators, discussants, and attentive audience who contributed to selecting these exiting papers, and the authors who contributed these papers.

JSAI 2008 Program Committee

Makoto Yokoo, Chair
Kazuo Miyashita, Vice-chair
Jiro Araki, Ryutaro Ichise, Tsuyoshi Ide, Atsushi Iwasaki, Michiaki Iwazume,
Yuiko Ohta, Toshihiro Kamishima, Hitoshi Kanoh Takahiro Kawamura,
Tatsuyuki Kawamura, Kazuki Kobayashi, Yuko Sakurai, Ken Sadohara,
Yoshiyuki Nakamura, Hiromitsu Hattori, Masahiro Hamasaki,
Ryouhei Fujimaki, Tohgoroh Matsui, Yohei Murakami, Tomoko Murakami,
Naomi Yamashita, Masaharu Yoshioka

A Japanese Input Method for Mobile Terminals Using Surface EMG Signals

Akira Hatano[1], Kenji Araki[1], and Masafumi Matsuhara[2]

[1] Graduate School of Information Science and Technology,
Hokkaido University, Kita-ku Kita 14 Nishi 9, Sapporo, 060-0814, Japan
{a_hatano,araki}@media.eng.hokudai.ac.jp
[2] Department of Software and Information Science,
Iwate Prefectural University, Iwate, 020-0193, Japan
masafumi@soft.iwate-pu.ac.jp

Abstract. The common use of mobile terminals is for text input. However, mobile terminals cannot be equipped with sufficient amount of keys because of the physical restrictions. To solve this problem we developed an input method using surface electromyogram (sEMG), treating arm muscle movements as input signals. This method involves no physical keys and can be used to input Japanese texts. In our experiments, the system was capable of inputting Japanese characters with a finger motion recognition rate of approximately 80%.

Keywords: input method, surface electromyogram, new generation interfaces, human interface.

1 Introduction

In recent years, mobile terminals have been rapidly miniaturized and improved in performance, and they are often used to input texts. However, such terminals cannot be equipped with sufficient amount of keys because of their physical limitations. Therefore, it is difficult to speed up the input process. There are several studies on effective input methods using only few keys aiming at solving this problem [1,2,3], but the problem of the need for physical keys still remains. Using audio input as a substitute for a physical terminal eliminates the need for physical keys, but introduces new problems, such as recognition accuracy in loud environments and privacy issues.

In this paper, we describe our development of an input method using surface electromyogram (sEMG) which allows treating arm muscle movements as input signals. This method uses no physical keys and enables the input of Japanese characters. EMG signals are electrical signals from a muscle, and are associated with muscle activity. The sEMG signals are measured by receiving signals from a sensor placed on the skin. There have been numerous related studies on muscle fatigue measurement [4], prosthetic hand control [5] and human machine interfaces [6,7,8]. The sEMG signals of hand muscle activities are measured from an area between the wrist and the lower arm, and the user can use the interface without any physical restrictions.

For these reasons, the sEMG should be well-suited as a wearable computer input method. We have been developing a system that recognizes user arm muscle motions using the sEMG signals and translates them to text input [9]. In this paper, we describe a system that recognizes user hand motions using sEMG signals, recognizes 6 different types of input based on those signals and then converts the input into Japanese text in real time. We also introduce the results of an experiment evaluating the number of key presses required to input evaluation texts. Figure 1 shows a screenshot of the system interface.

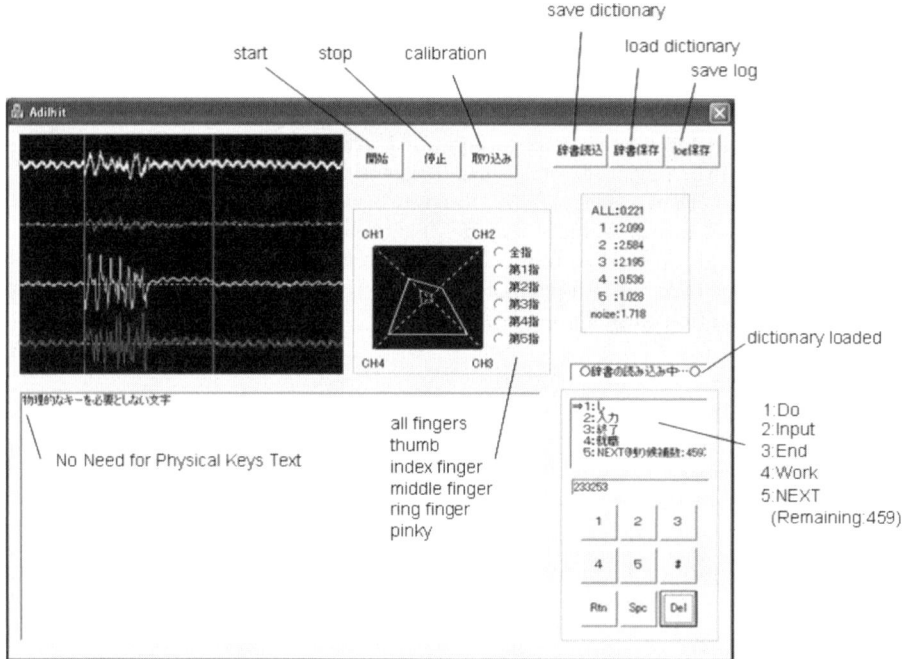

Fig. 1. Screenshot of the system interface

2 System Outline

Figure 2 shows an outline of the experiment system. The sEMG signal processing module uses sensors on the user's arm to capture sequences of arm muscle motions and recognizes finger motions. It then converts the signals to numerical pseudo keys and sends them to the character translation module which shows word candidates corresponding to the input. Selected words are then output in the text box.

The character translation process uses a generic dictionary and a learning dictionary for choosing word candidates. The generic dictionary contains the

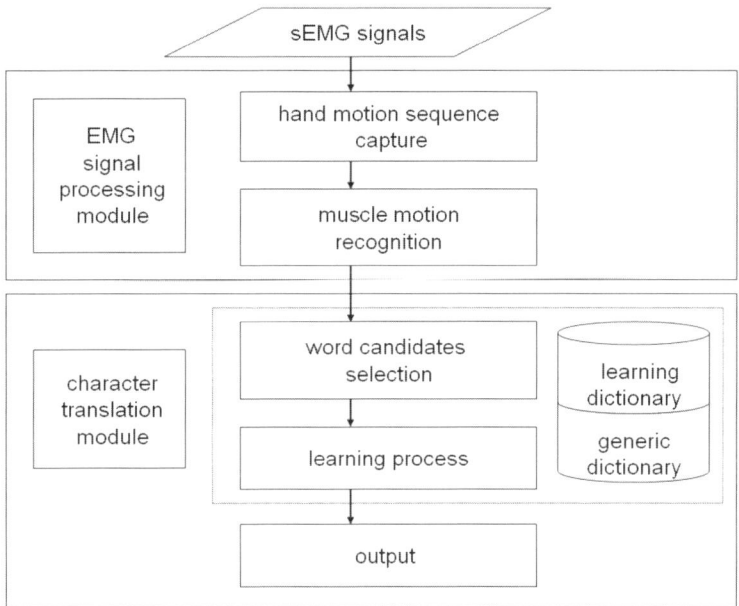

Fig. 2. Outline of the system

10,000 most frequent words from the "Web Japanese N-gram Version 1 [10]". The learning dictionary registers words from the generic dictionary when they are selected by the user. It also keeps information on input frequency, surrounding word n-gram, etc. As it is being updated after every input word, the system can display word candidates adapted to particular users.

3 The EMG Signal Processing Module

In this section we describe the process through which the system recognizes finger flexion using the sEMG signals. In our experiment an sEMG sensor is installed on the flexor digitorum superficialis muscle area and the flexor pollicis longus muscle area that relate to finger flexion as shown in Figure 3. The device for measuring sEMG used in our study is a Personal-EMG [11]. The EMG signal processing module uses four input channels to recognize which finger has been flexed.

3.1 Capturing Hand Motion Sequences

Figure 4 shows the raw sEMG signal difference between a flexed finger and an extended finger. However, the values of the raw sEMG signal oscillate heavily which makes it difficult to tell sequential finger movements apart. To compensate for the oscillations, the system integrates the signal from each of the four channels using the formula shown in (1).

$$S_{x(ch)} = \int_{-0.1(sec)}^{0} \mid e(t+\tau) \mid d\tau \qquad (1)$$

The result of calculating the integral of the sEMG signal is shown in Figure 5. The system captures sequences of hand motions based on intervals of motion/no-motion. If the integrated value in any channel is above a threshold value, the system determines that the user is moving his fingers. Similarly, if the integral value drops below the threshold value, the system determines that the user has stopped moving his fingers. Figure 6 shows an example of a captured hand motion sequence. The system recognizes the interval between the two vertical lines as one motion sequence.

3.2 Recognizing Hand Motions

Once the hand motion sequence has been captured, as described in 3.1, the system determines which finger (or combination of fingers) has been flexed. During its initialization steps, our system collects and stores calibration data for each user. The user is asked to flex each finger one at a time and all fingers at once. The calibration data consists of values for finger flexion for each finger (and all fingers at once) on all four channels, as shown in Table 1. To determine which finger has been flexed, the system first calculates the differences between the two most extreme values from each channel. It then calculates the Manhattan distance between the calculated differences and the flexion values in the calibration data and assigns a hand motion based on the smallest distance. Figure 7 shows the difference values calculated for the signal captured in Figure 6 and Figure 8 shows the calculated Manhattan distance for each hand motion. In this example, the system classifies the hand motion as an all-finger flexion, as it has the smallest Manhattan distance.

4 The Character Translation Module

4.1 Allocation of Japanese Syllables

As before, the system recognizes six types of motions. When inputting characters, finger motions are assigned to pseudo keys. The system assigns thumb flexion

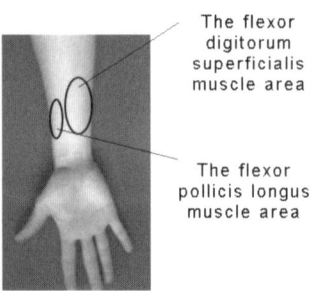

Fig. 3. Measurement points

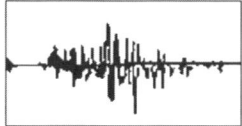 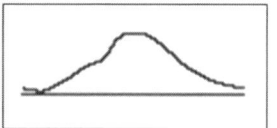

Fig. 4. Raw sEMG signal   **Fig. 5.** Integrated sEMG signal

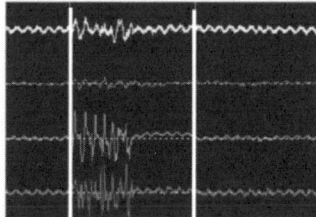

Fig. 6. An example of a captured hand motion sequence

Table 1. Calibration data in experiment

flexion	CH1	CH2	CH3	CH4
Thumb	4.983	4.219	1.545	0.818
Index finger	1.772	2.546	4.878	2.473
Middle finger	1.318	4.299	4.426	1.067
Ring finger	1.208	1.689	4.478	1.768
Pinky	1.248	3.562	1.360	2.898
all fingers	4.470	4.001	3.870	4.236

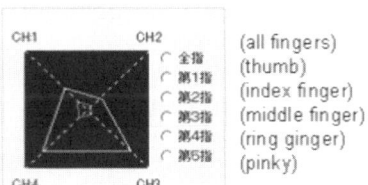

Fig. 7. Amplitude values for each channel

to "key 1", index finger flexion to "key 2", middle finger flexion to "key 3", ring finger flexion to "key 4", pinky flexion to "key 5", and flexion of all fingers to "enter key". The "enter key" is used to display and choose from available word candidates. "Keys" 1 through 5 are used to input Japanese syllables. Japanese syllables consist of one out of five possible vowel sounds and one out of ten possible consonant sounds. Since both the number of vowels in Japanese and the number of input keys are five, each vowel is assigned to a specific key (for example, "key 1" is assigned to vowel "a"). Thus, each key has many syllables assigned to it (for example, "key 1" corresponds to the syllables "a", "ka", "sa",

```
ALL:0.221    (all fingers)
  1 :2.099   (thumb)
  2 :2.584   (index finger)
  3 :2.195   (middle finger)
  4 :0.536   (ring ginger)
  5 :1.028   (pinky)
noise:1.718
```

Fig. 8. Differences between current sequence and model calibration data

"ta", etc.) and the number of times the user has to activate an input key to select one syllable is large. In order to achieve efficient input we use the Number-Kanji Translation method [12], [13]. In this method the user selects a syllable set with a single key press (for example, the syllable set corresponding to "key 1") and disambiguation is left for later. On one hand, the number of key presses is much smaller than that of a general method, such as the letter cycling input used in Japanese cell phones. On the other hand, the number of word candidates gets larger, and displaying a correct word candidate becomes a problem. To solve this problem, the system utilizes two dictionaries, and uses them effectively.

4.2 The Generic and Learning Dictionaries

The generic dictionary contains 10,000 words. These are sorted in descending order of frequency. Word candidates are displayed first in order of the longest match and then in dictionary order (by frequency). When there are word candidates available, the system displays up to four word candidates at a time as shown in Figure 9. The user selects a word candidate using "key 1-4" and accepts the candidate with the "enter key". To display the next 4 candidates the user selects "key 5" followed by the "enter key". Inputting "key 5" and "enter key", the next four word candidates are displayed.

Words selected by the user are removed from the generic dictionary and are saved in the learning dictionary. Words contained in the learning dictionary are preferred over other words when displaying word candidates. In order to sort the words in the learning dictionary we use a Credibility Evaluation Function similar to [9]. Our version of this function is shown in (2).

Fig. 9. The displayed word candidates

$$CEF = \alpha \times ND + \beta \times UN + \gamma \times LN + \delta \times RD \tag{2}$$

There are three changes compared to the method described in [9]. First, we have removed class structures, so all words are now candidates. Second, in order to adopt a method that selects words, two measures were removed from CEF - Frequencies of Correct Translation and Frequencies of Erroneous Translation. Third, the measure Word Uni-gram Frequency (UN), Length of Word Candidate (LN) and Degree of Recency (RD) were added to CEF. ,, and are coefficients. The Degree of Neighboring Character Strings (ND) is calculated from the user's input history of word bi-grams, tri-grams, etc.

5 Evaluation Experiment

In our experiment we evaluate the hand motion recognition rate, the number of key presses and the average rank of the correct word candidate. The documents used in this experiment are author's mobile phone e-mails.

All words in these documents already existed in the the generic dictionary. For evaluating the recognition rate of hand motions and the number of key presses we used 72 e-mail messages (10.3 Japanese characters on average), and for the evaluation of the average rank of the correct word candidate we used 144 e-mail messages. In its initial condition the system's learning dictionary is empty and the coefficients of the CEF are set to =10,=0.1,=10,=0.1 based on previous experimental results.

In the evaluation of the hand motion recognition rate, if the user's finger flexion is the same as what the system recognizes, it counts as a correct recognition, otherwise it counts as a false recognition. In this evaluation, we measure the recognition rate of hand motions only in the Japanese syllables selecting experiment, and not in the word candidates selecting experiment.

In the key presses evaluation, the system counts all key presses. We compare a system using the sEMG signals to a system using mouse clicking to indicate what finger is flexed. When using the sEMG based system, the user uses a mouse button only for deleting words, indicating a false recognition.

When evaluating of the average rank of correct word candidate, 144 e-mail messages were used 36 messages at a time. The results of of the hand motion recognition rate evaluation are shown in Table 2; the results of the number of key presses evaluation are shown in Table 3, and the results of the average rank of the correct word candidate evaluation are shown in Table 4.

6 Results

Table 2 shows that the average hand motions recognition rate is nearly 80%, with a recognition rate for "key 1" of over 95%. The reason for this high recognition rate is that the model-data for thumb flexion (assigned to "key 1") is very different from the other finger, as can be observed in Table 1. In fact, the flexor pollicis longus (the thumb flexion muscle) is quite distant from the flexor

Table 2. Results of the hand motion recognition rate evaluation

	correct recognition	false recognition	recognition rate [%]
1 key	274	10	97
2 key	226	46	83
3 key	205	66	76
4 key	231	120	69
5 key	234	61	79
total	1170	303	79

Table 3. Results of the key presses evaluation

	key 1	key 2	key 3	key 4	key 5	enter key	total
sEMG	338	420	467	423	1442	1801	4891
mouse input	239	245	194	153	1018	1647	3496

Table 4. Results of the average rank of the correct word candidate evaluation

e-mail	average rank	#words in learning dictionaries
1-36	10.7	103
37-72	7.8	156
73-108	8.18	210
109-144	7.25	274

digitorum superficialis (the muscle for flexing the other fingers). In contrast, the reason for the low recognition rate of "key 4" is that the digitorum for flexing the fourth finger is close to the other digitorums.

Table 3 shows that the number of key presses using the sEMG signals (I_{sEMG}) is about 1.4 times higher than while using a mouse button (I_{button}). These numbers include user mistakes. If I_{button} is seen as the number of key presses required when the recognition rate of the sEMG signals is 100%, the recognition rate of all inputs using the sEMG signals (p) can be calculated as follows:

$$p = \frac{I_{button}}{I_{sEMG}} \qquad (3)$$

In our experiment p is about 0.71. Thus the input rate of the system using sEMG is about 70% of the achievable rate. This rate is nearly 10% lower than the recognition rate of hand motions shown in Table 2. The presumed reason for this is that the frequency of using "keys 2-4" when selecting word candidates is larger than the frequency when selecting Japanese syllables, and the recognition rate of "keys 2-4" is lower than that for the other keys.

Table 4 shows that the average rank of the correct word candidate generally decreases, as the number of words in the learning dictionary increases. Therefore we can conclude that the learning dictionary is learning effectively. The system can display up to four word candidates at a time, so a user can usually find the correct input word in the first two candidate lists (on average).

7 Conclusions

We proposed an input system for mobile terminals using sEMG signals. It uses a method that recognizes the flexion if five fingers and uses these as six input "keys". Even with only six keys, the user can still select Japanese syllables effectively using the Number-Kanji Translation method. The system uses two dictionaries in order to solve the problem of increased number of word candidates that arises from the Number-Kanji Translation method.

To evaluate the system we measure the hand motion recognition rate, the number of key presses, and the average rank of the correct word candidate. The evaluation experiment shows that the average recognition rate of hand motions is almost 80% while the number of key presses using the sEMG signals is about 1.4 times higher than while using a mouse button. It also shows that the system learns word usage effectively, since the average rank of the correct word candidate generally decreases.

In the near future, we will experiment with large documents, will make improvements in the EMG signal processing module, and will modify the system to be capable to effectively use linguistic information even when the EMG signal process recognition fails.

References

1. Tanaka-Ishii, K., Inutsuka, Y., Takeichi, M.: Japanese input system with digits –Can Japanese be input only with consonants? In: Human Language Technology Conference, San Diego, USA, pp. 211–218 (2001)
2. Tanaka-Ishii, K., Inutsuka, Y., Takeichi, M.: Entering text using a four button device. In: The 19th International Conference on Computational Linguistics, Taipei, Taiwan, pp. 988–994 (2002)
3. T9. T9 text input home page, http://www.t9.com
4. Yoshida, H., Ujiie, H., Ishimura, K., Wada, M.: The estimation of muscle fatigue using chaos analysis. Journal of the Society of Biomechanisms 28(4), 201–212 (2004) (in Japanese)
5. Suematsu, S., Yokoi, H.: A motion generating system for multi-fingered myoelectric hand. International Congress Series 1291, 257–260 (2006)
6. Calhoun Gloria, L., McMillan Grant, R.: Hands-free input devices for wearable computers. In: Proceedings of Fourth Annual Symposium on Human Interaction with Complex Systems, pp. 118–123. IEEE, Dayton (1998)
7. Costanza, E., Inverso, S.A., Allen, R.: Toward subtle intimate interfaces for mobile devices using an EMG controller. In: Proceedings of the SIGCHI conference on Human factors in computing systems, Portland, Oregon, USA (2005)
8. Aso, S., Sasaki, A., Hashimoto, H., Ishii, C.: Driving Electric Car by Using EMG Interface. In: IEEE International Conferences on Cybernetics Intelligent Systems (CIS). IEEE, CD-ROM (2006)
9. Hatano, A., Araki, K., Masafumi, M.: A Japanese Input Method Using Surface EMG Signals. In: Hokkaido-section Joint Convention of the Institutes of Electrical and related Engineers, Sapporo, Japan, pp. 187–188 (2007)
10. Kudo, T., Kazawa, H.: Web Japanese N-gram Version 1. Gengo Shigen Kyokai

11. Oisaka Electronic Device Ltd. equipment: Personal-EMG,
    http://www.oisaka.co.jp/P-EMG.html
12. Matsuhara, M., Araki, K., Tochinai, K.: Evaluation of Number-Kanji Translation Method using Inductive Learning on E-mail. In: Proceedings of the IASTED International Conference on Artificial Intelligence And Soft Computing, Banff, Canada, pp. 487–493 (2000)
13. Matsuhara, M., Araki, K., Tochinai, K.: Effectiveness for machine translation method using inductive learning on number representation. In: McKay, B., Slaney, J.K. (eds.) Canadian AI 2002. LNCS, vol. 2557, pp. 648–659. Springer, Heidelberg (2002)

Evaluation of Similarity Measures for Ontology Mapping

Ryutaro Ichise

National Institute of Informatics,
Tokyo 101-8430, Japan
ichise@nii.ac.jp

Abstract. This paper presents an analysis of similarity measures for identifying ontology mapping. Using discriminant analysis, we investigated forty-eight similarity measures such as string matching and knowledge based similarities that have been used in previous systems. As a result, we extracted twenty-two effective similarity measures for identifying ontology mapping out of forty-eight possible similarity measures. The extracted measures vary widely in the type in similarity.

1 Introduction

Many people now use the web to collect a wide range of information. For example, when making vacation plans, we check the web for lodging, routes, and sightseeing spots. Because these web sites are operated by individual enterprises, we have to search the sites manually to gather information. In order to solve such a problem, the Semantic Web is expected to become a next-generation web standard that can connect different data resources. On the Semantic Web, the semantics of the data are provided by ontologies for the interoperability of resources. However, since ontologies cover a particular domain or use, it is necessary to develop a method to map multiple ontologies for covering wide domains or different uses. Ichise organized an ontology mapping method for the interoperability of ontologies with a machine learning framework [1]. The framework uses a standard machine learning method with multiple concept similarity measures. Moreover, the paper defines many types of similarity measures, introduced from state-of-the-art systems. Although the system successfully integrates features for ontology mapping from different systems, we still do not know which features are effective for ontology mapping. In this paper, we present an experimental evaluation of a wide range of similarity measures in order to identify effective features for ontology mapping.

This paper is organized as follows. First, we discuss the problem of ontology mapping that we are undertaking and our approach using machine learning with multiple similarity measures. Next, we discuss the similarity measures for ontology mapping. Then, we evaluate the effectiveness of several similarity measures by using real data. Finally, we present our conclusions.

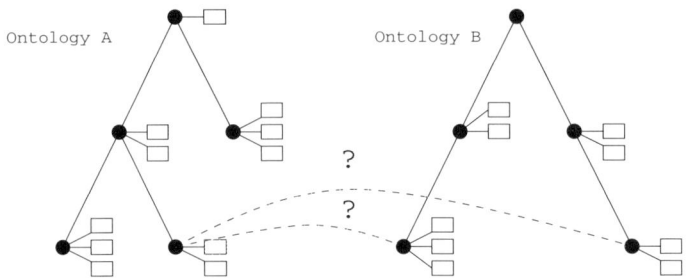

Fig. 1. Problem statement

2 Ontology Mapping

2.1 Problem

In this section, we describe the ontology mapping [2] that we are investigating. When we have many instances of objects or information, we usually use a concept hierarchy to classify them. Ontologies are used for such organization. We assume that the ontologies in this paper are designed for such use. The ontologies used for our paper can be defined as follows:

> The ontology O contains a set of concepts, $C_1, C_2, \ldots, C_n$, that are organized into a hierarchy. Each concept is labeled by strings and can contain instances.

An example of an ontology is shown in the graph representation on the left side of Figure 1. The black circles represent a concept in the ontology and the white boxes represent instances in the ontology. The concepts (black circles) are organized into an hierarchy.

The ontology mapping problem can be stated as follows. When there are two different ontologies, how do we find the mapping of concepts between them? For example, in Figure 1, the problem is finding a concept in ontology B that corresponds to the concept in ontology A. For the concept at the bottom right side of ontology A, a possible mapping in ontology B can be the right bottom concept or the left bottom concept, or there may be others.

2.2 Machine Learning Approach for Ontology Mapping

In order to solve the ontology mapping problem, Ichise proposed to use the machine learning approach with multiple concept similarity measures [1]. In this section, we describe the method to convert the ontology mapping problem into a machine learning framework by using similarity measures.

To solve the ontology mapping problem, we think about the combination of concepts among different ontologies. In this case, the problem can be defining the value of a combination pair. In other words, the ontology mapping problem consists of defining the value of pairs of concepts in a concept pair matrix, as

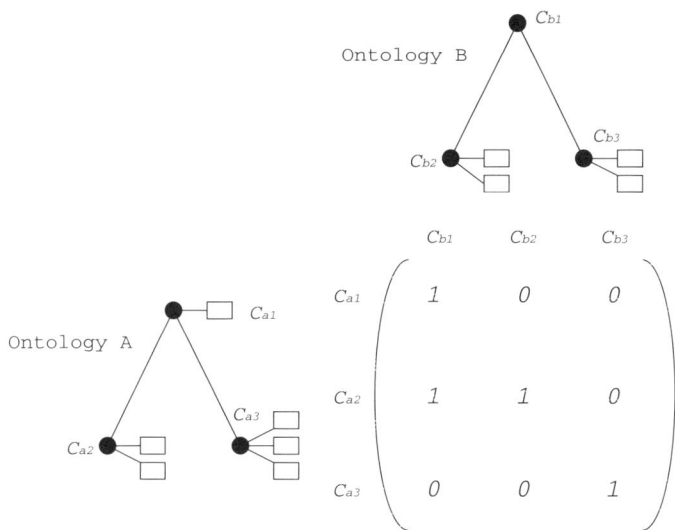

Fig. 2. Mapping matrix

shown in Figure 2. The rows of the matrix illustrate the concepts of Ontology A, that is, C_{a1}, C_{a2} and C_{a3}, and the columns of the matrix illustrate the concept of Ontology B, that is, C_{b1}, C_{b2} and C_{b3}. The values in the matrix represent the validity of the mapping. The value is 1 when two concepts can be mapped and 0 when two concepts cannot be mapped. For example, the second row and third column of the matrix represents the validity of mapping for C_{a2} on Ontology A and C_{b3} on Ontology B. This particular mapping isn't valid because the value in the matrix is 0.

The next question is what type of information is available to compose the matrix? According to our definition of ontologies, we can define a similarity measure of concepts by using a string matching method, such as concept name matching, and so on. However, a single similarity measure is not enough to determine the matrix because of the diversity of ontologies. For example, we can assume the concept of "bank" in two ontologies. The concepts seem to be mapped when we use the string similarity measure. However, when one ontology has a super concept of "finance" and another has that of "construction," these two concepts should not be mapped because each represents a different concept. In such a case, we should also use another similarity measure of the concepts.

From the above discussion, the problem is to define matrix values by using multiple similarity values of the concepts. As a result, we can write the problem in table form, as shown in Table 1. *ID* shown in the table represents a pair of concepts, *Class* represents the validity of the mapping, and the columns in the middle represent the similarity of the concept pairs. For example, the first line of the table represents the ontology mapping for C_{a1} and C_{b1} and has a similarity value of 0.75 for similarity measure 1. When we know some correct mappings, such as $C_{a1} \Leftrightarrow C_{b1}$ and $C_{a1} \Leftrightarrow C_{b2}$, we can use the mapping to determine

Table 1. Description of the ontology mapping problem

ID	Similarity Measure 1	Similarity Measure 2	...	Similarity Measure n	Class
$C_{a1} \Leftrightarrow C_{b1}$	0.75	0.4	...	0.38	1 (Positive)
$C_{a1} \Leftrightarrow C_{b2}$	0.52	0.7	...	0.42	0 (Negative)
...	...	...	...	...	...
$C_{a5} \Leftrightarrow C_{b7}$	0.38	0.6	...	0.25	?
...	...	...	...	...	...

the importance of the similarity measures. Then, we can make a decision on unknown classes such as $C_{a5} \Leftrightarrow C_{b7}$ by using the importance of the similarity measures. The example table shown represents the same problem that occurs in a supervised machine learning framework. Therefore, we can convert the ontology mapping problem into a normal machine learning framework.

3 Similarity Measures of Concepts

Many similarity measures have been proposed for measuring concept similarities. Examples include the string based similarity, graph based similarity, and knowledge based similarity. The string based similarity is widely used for ontology mapping systems. The graph based similarity utilizes the similarity of the structures of ontologies. In this measure, the ontologies are organized as tree structures, and so we can calculate the graph similarity of the ontologies. Examples include Similarity Flooding [3] and S-Match [4]. The knowledge based similarity utilizes other knowledge resources, such as a dictionary and WordNet [5], to calculate similarities.

Usually, ontology mapping systems utilize several types of similarity measures. For example, COMA++ [6] uses a matcher library, which corresponds to multiple similarity measures. However, most systems utilize similarity measures as static values. In other words, these systems do not weight the importance of similarity measures. In this paper, we investigate several of the similarity measures presented in [1] through experiments with real data. Our goal is to identify effective features. In the rest of this section, we discuss some definitions of similarity measures. We used four similarity measures. The similarities are "word similarity," "word list similarity," "concept hierarchy similarity," and "structure similarity." We will discuss these in this order.

3.1 Word Similarity

In order to calculate concept similarity, we introduce four string based similarities and also four knowledge based similarities as base measures.

The string based similarity is calculated for words. We utilize the following similarities:

- prefix
- suffix
- edit distance
- n-gram

The prefix similarity measures the similarity of word prefixes such as Eng. and England. The suffix similarity measures the similarity of word suffixes such as phone and telephone. Edit distance can calculate the similarity from the count of string substitution, deletion and addition. For n-gram, a word is divided into n number of strings, and the similarity is calculated by the number of same string sets. For example, similarity between "word" and "ward" is counted as follows. The first word "word" is divided into "wo, or, rd" for the 2-gram, and the second word "ward" is divided into "wa, ar, rd" for the 2-gram. As a result, we can find the similar string "rd" as the similarity measure for the 2-gram. In our system, we utilize the 3-gram for calculating similarity.

The knowledge based similarity is also calculated for words. We use WordNet as the knowledge resource for calculating similarity. Although a wide variety of similarities for WordNet are proposed, we utilize four:

- synset
- Wu & Palmer
- description
- Lin

The first similarity measure *synset* utilizes the path length of the synset in WordNet. WordNet is organized with synsets. Therefore, we can calculate the shortest path of different word pairs using synsets. The second similarity measure, Wu & Palmer, uses the depth and least common superconcept (LCS) of words [7]. The similarity is calculated in the following equation:

$$similarity(W_1, W_2) = \frac{2 \times depth(LCS)}{depth(W_1) + depth(W_2)}$$

W_1 and W_2 denote word labels for a concept pair, the depth is the depth from the root to the word and LCS is the least common superconcept of W_1 and W_2. The third similarity measure, *description*, utilizes the description of a concept in WordNet. The similarity is calculated as the square of the common word length in the descriptions of each word of a pair. The last similarity measure is proposed by Lin [8]. This measure is a calculation using a formula similar to that of Wu & Palmer except it uses information criteria instead of depth.

3.2 Word List Similarity

In this section, we extend the word similarity measures presented in the previous section. Word similarity measures are designed for words, but the measures are not applicable to a word list such as "Food_Wine." Such a word list can usually be used as a concept label. If we divide such words by a hyphen or underscore, we can obtain a word list. We define two types of similarities for a word list: *maximum word similarity* and *word edit distance*.

Let us first explain the maximum word similarity. When we use the combination of words in both lists, we can calculate the similarity for each pair of words by word similarity measures. We use the maximum value for word pairs in the word list as the maximum word similarity. In our paper, since we define eight word similarities (stated in the previous section), we can obtain eight maximum word similarities.

The second similarity measure, word edit distance, is derived from the edit distance. In the edit distance definition, similarity is calculated by each string. We extend this method, considering words as strings. Let us assume two word lists, "Pyramid" and "Pyramid, Theory." It is easy to see the two lists are very similar. If we consider one word as a component, we can calculate the edit distance for the word lists. In this case, "Pyramid" is the same in both word lists, so we can calculate the word edit distance as 1. Furthermore, if we assume "Top" and "Pyramid, Theory," the word edit distance is 2. As such, we can calculate the similarity by the word distance. However, another problem occurs for similar word lists. For example, when we assume "Social, Science" and "Social, Sci," the similarity is difficult to determine. The problem is the calculation of similarity for "Science" and "Sci, " that is, whether the two words are the same word. If we decide the two words are the same, the word edit distance is 0, but if not, the word edit distance is 1. In order to calculate the similarity of the words, we utilize the word similarity measure. For example, if we use the prefix as the word similarity measure, we can consider the two words as the same for calculating the word edit distance. However, if we use the synset as the word similarity measure, we cannot consider the two words as the same because "sci" is not in WordNet. From the above discussion, we can define the word edit distance for the eight word similarity measures. As a result, we define sixteen similarity measures for word lists, which include eight maximum word similarities and eight word edit distance similarities.

3.3 Concept Hierarchy Similarity

In this section we discuss the similarity for the concept hierarchy of an ontology. As we discussed in Section 2, ontologies are organized as concept hierarchies. In order to utilize the similarity of a concept hierarchy, we introduce similarity measures for concept hierarchies. The concept hierarchy similarity measure is calculated for the path from the root to the concept. Let us explain by the example shown in Table 2. We assume the calculation of the path "Top / Social_Sci" in ontology A and "Top / Social_Science" in ontology B. For calculation of the similarity, we divide the path into a list of concepts, as shown in the middle column of Table 2. Then, the similarity is calculated by the edit distance if we consider the concept as a component. For example, the concept "Top" is the same in both ontologies, but the second concept is different. Then, the edit distance for the path is 1. However, how do we decide whether the concept is the same or not? To determine this, we divide the concept into the word list for calculating the similarity by using the word list similarity. In this case, if "Social_Sci" and "Social_Science" are considered as a similar concept using the

Table 2. Examples for concept hierarchy similarity calculation.

	Path	Path list	Word list
Ontology A	Top / Social_Sci	{Top, Social_Sci}	{Top}, {Social, Sci}
Ontology B	Top / Social_Science	{Top, Social_Science}	{Top}, {Social, Science}

word list similarity, the edit distance is 0; if the two concepts are not considered as a similar concept using the word list similarity, the edit distance is 1. In other words, we calculate the edit distance with the right-hand lists in Table 2. As a result, we can calculate the concept hierarchy similarity by using the edit distance of the path. Because we can use any word list similarity measures for deciding the similarity of the word list, we obtain sixteen concept hierarchy similarity measures.

3.4 Structure Similarity

In this section, we define the similarity measures that use the structure of ontologies. In the previous section, we defined similarity using the concept hierarchy. However, a similarity can contain the similarity of a parent. We utilize the parent concept label for calculating similarity. This similarity is one of the variations of structure similarities, because it measures the neighborhoods on the graphs. Because the similarity is calculated by word list similarity, we can obtain 16 similarity measures for parents.

4 Evaluation of Similarity Measures

4.1 Internet Directory Data

In order to evaluate the effectiveness of similarity measures for the ontology mapping problem, we conducted an analysis of 48 similarity measures, which include 16 word list similarity measures, 16 concept hierarchy similarity measures, and 16 structure similarity measures. In our paper we used real Internet directory data, provided by the Ontology Alignment Evaluation Initiative (OAEI)[1] for the 2005 campaign. The data is constructed from three Internet directories, Google, Yahoo, and Looksmart, and contains simple relationships of class hierarchies. The data includes 2265 pairs of ontologies written in OWL format, and only one correct matching answer, which was verified by a human. Unfortunately, since the data has some format errors, we used 2193 pairs of ontologies and the correct mapping for the analysis. The data has positive (correct) mappings, and negative mappings are not available. We created negative mappings, as follows:

1. We choose the concept C_s, which is in the source ontology and has correct mappings.

---
[1] http://oaei.ontologymatching.org/

2. We randomly choose concept C_t, which is in the target ontology. If it is the correct mapping of C_s, then we again choose a concept in the target ontology.

As a result, the mapping pair produced by the above algorithm is relatively negative, not positive. We utilized the positive mappings and negative mappings for our experiments.

4.2 Analysis Method and Results

We conducted discriminant analysis for the 48 similarity measures to test the contribution of each similarity measure. In the analysis, we utilize the forward selection method, which takes, in order, the most effective explanatory variable into the discriminant. We utilize 5% as the level of significance when the variable is selected.

As a result, we obtained 22 similarity measures out of 48 possible similarity measures, as shown in Table 3. We consider those similarity measures as effective measures for identifying ontology mappings. On the left side of the table, *comparison target* denotes the type of objects compared in the ontologies. In this field, we have three values: "concept," "concept hierarchy," and "structure." The values come from comparison between concept labels defined in Section 3.2, comparison between concept hierarchies defined in Section 3.3, and comparison between structures defined in Section 3.4. *Word list method*, shown in the center of Table 3, denotes the type of word list similarity measure used. The value in this field has a "maximum word similarity" or "word edit distance," as defined in Section 3.2. *Base method*, shown on the right side of Table 3, denotes the base methods for comparing the similarity of words. There are eight possible values in this field: "prefix," "suffix," "edit distance," "n-gram," "synset," "Wu & Palmer," "description," and "Lin," as defined in Section 3.1.

When we examine the comparison target in Table 3, we can see the balanced results, which has 7 concepts, 8 concept hierarchies, and 7 structures. Although most previous systems for ontology mapping usually utilize the concept comparison, it is not enough to produce a good result. According to the results in Table 3, the other comparison targets, such as structure comparison and concept hierarchy comparison, are important for predicting the ontology mappings. However, when we examine the ranking of effective features, we see many features related to the comparison between concept hierarchies in the higher ranking of the list. Therefore, we can verify that the comparison between concept hierarchies is important for identifying a rough sketch of mappings, and the other comparisons are important for detail mappings.

Next, when we examine the word list method in Table 3, we see that the number of word edit distances is slightly larger than the number of maximum word similarities. The number of word edit distances is 13, and 9 for the maximum word similarity. However, the maximum word similarity appears in higher ranking of the list. Therefore, we can conclude that the maximum word similarity is effective for identifying rough mappings, but, the word edit distance is necessary to identify detail mappings.

Table 3. Effective similarity measures for ontology mapping

Comparison target	Word list method	Base method
structure	maximum word similarity	edit distance
concept	maximum word similarity	edit distance
concept hierarchy	word edit distance	Lin
concept hierarchy	maximum word similarity	edit distance
concept hierarchy	word edit distance	description
concept hierarchy	maximum word similarity	description
concept hierarchy	word edit distance	prefix
concept hierarchy	maximum word similarity	Lin
concept hierarchy	maximum word similarity	synset
structure	maximum word similarity	Wu & Palmer
concept	word edit distance	n-gram
concept	maximum word similarity	Wu & Palmer
structure	word edit distance	Lin
concept hierarchy	word edit distance	Wu & Palmer
concept	word edit distance	Wu & Palmer
structure	word edit distance	description
structure	word edit distance	suffix
structure	word edit distance	synset
concept	maximum word similarity	description
concept	word edit distance	edit distance
concept	word edit distance	prefix
structure	word edit distance	prefix

Finally, when we examine the base methods in Table 3, we can see balanced results: three prefixes, one suffix, four edit distances, one n-gram, two synsets, four Wu & Palmer's, four descriptions, and three Lin's. We can see from the results that all measures are necessary features for ontology mapping, because all methods appear in the list. In addition, we analyzed the measures for string-based similarity and knowledge-based similarity, which are discussed in Section 3.1. That list has 9 string based similarity measures and 13 knowledge based similarity measures. The number of knowledge based similarity measures are slightly larger then that of the string based similarity measures. The string based similarity measures are very popular in ontology mapping systems, but the knowledge based similarity measure is more effective for predicting the ontology mapping.

We define 48 similarity measures in this paper, but only 22 measures among them are effective for ontology mapping. The 22 measures consist of all the similarity measures defined in Section 3. The results indicate that there are no single definite method for identifying ontology mappings, and it is necessary to combine multiple methods for solving the ontology mapping problem.

We tested the obtained discriminant, which consists of 22 similarity measures. The results are shown in Figure 3. Group 1 and Group 2 denote positive examples (mapping) and negative examples (not mapping), respectively. The x-axis indicates the discriminant value and the y-axis indicates the percentage of examples. The accuracy is 73.78%. We understand that the problem is very difficult,

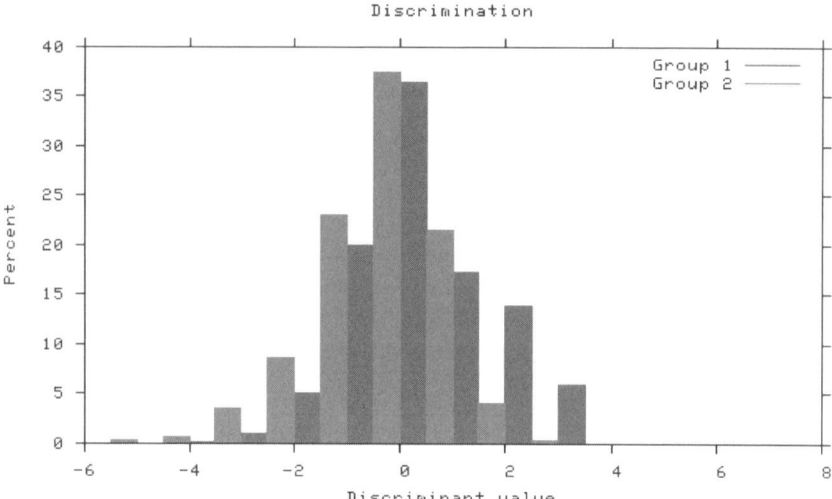

Fig. 3. Results of discrimination for ontology mapping

because the discrimination area in Figure 3 is very close between both groups. In addition, since the accuracy is not very high with the assumption of linear separation, we have to consider introducing a nonlinear learning method and more features, other than those discussed in this paper.

5 Conclusions

In this paper, we investigated effective features for deciding ontology mappings. We introduced several similarity measures and many types of similarities such as "word list similarity, " "concept hierarchy similarity" and "structure similarity." We analyzed these measures by discriminant analysis. As a result, we extracted 22 effective similarity measures out of 48 possible similarity measures. However, the extracted measures, which are effective for ontology mapping, vary widely in the type in similarity. Therefore, the experimental results suggest that for identifying ontology mapping it is necessary to use several types and compositions of similarity measures.

In our future work, we plan to extend the current research. In this work, we used 48 similarity measures introduced from previous research. However, there are still many other types of similarity measures for ontology mapping, such as instance based similarity measures [9]. In addition, Pedersen et al. proposed another measurement of word similarity [10]. We have to investigate such similarity measures, too. Furthermore, we would like to consider changing the learning methods. In this work, we utilized discriminant analysis for evaluating similarity measures. Since the performance was limited, the ontology mapping problem can be considered a nonlinear separation problem. Therefore, we would like to investigate several machine learning methods, including nonlinear machine learning methods, such as support vector machines (SVM) [11], to improve performance.

References

1. Ichise, R.: Machine learning approach for ontology mapping using multiple concept similarity measures. In: Proceedings of the 7th IEEE/ACIS International Conference on Computer and Information Science, pp. 340–346 (2008)
2. Euzenat, J., Shvaiko, P.: Ontology Matching. Springer, Heidelberg (2007)
3. Melnik, S., Garcia-Molina, H., Rahm, E.: Similarity flooding: A versatile graph matching algorithm and its application to schema matching. In: Proceedings of the 18th International Conference on Data Engineering, San Jose, CA, pp. 117–128 (February 2002)
4. Giunchiglia, F., Shvaiko, P., Yatskevich, M.: S-match: an algorithm and an implementation of semantic matching. In: Bussler, C.J., Davies, J., Fensel, D., Studer, R. (eds.) ESWS 2004. LNCS, vol. 3053, pp. 61–75. Springer, Heidelberg (2004)
5. Fellbaum, C.: Wordnet: An Electronic Lexical Database. MIT Press, Cambridge (1998)
6. Aumueller, D., Do, H.H., Massmann, S., Rahm, E.: Schema and ontology matching with COMA++. In: Özcan, F. (ed.) Proceedings of the ACM SIGMOD International Conference on Management of Data, pp. 906–908. ACM, New York (2005)
7. Wu, Z., Palmer, M.: Verb semantics and lexical selection. In: Proceedings of the 32nd Annual Meeting of the Association for Computational Linguistics, New Mexico State University, Las Cruces, New, Mexico, pp. 133–138 (1994)
8. Lin, D.: An information-theoretic definition of similarity. In: Proceedings of the 15th International Conference on Machine Learning, pp. 296–304. Morgan Kaufmann, San Francisco (1998)
9. Ichise, R., Takeda, H., Honiden, S.: Integrating multiple internet directories by instance-based learning. In: Proceedings of the 18th International Joint Conference on Artificial Intelligence, pp. 22–28 (2003)
10. Pedersen, T., Patwardhan, S., Michelizzi, J.: Wordnet: similarity - measuring the relatedness of concepts. In: Proceedings of the 19th National Conference on Artificial Intelligence, pp. 1024–1025 (2004)
11. Cristianini, N., Shawe-Taylor, J.: An Introduction to Support Vector Machines and Other Kernel-based Learning Methods. Cambridge University Press, Cambridge (2000)

Network Distributed POMDP with Communication

Yuki Iwanari, Yuichi Yabu, Makoto Tasaki, and Makoto Yokoo

Kyushu University
Fukuoka, 819-0395 Japan
{iwanari@agent.,yabu@agent.,
tasaki@agent.,yokoo@}is.kyushu-u.ac.jp

Abstract. While Distributed POMDPs have become popular for modeling multiagent systems in uncertain domains, it is the Network Distributed POMDPs (ND-POMDPs) model that has begun to scale-up the number of agents. The ND-POMDPs can utilize the locality in agents' interactions. However, prior work in ND-POMDPs has failed to address communication. Without communication, the size of a local policy at each agent within the ND-POMDPs grows exponentially in the time horizon. To overcome this problem, we extend existing algorithms so that agents periodically communicate their observation and action histories with each other. After communication, agents can start from new synchronized belief state. Thus, we can avoid the exponential growth in the size of local policies at agents. Furthermore, we introduce an idea that is similar the Point-based Value Iteration algorithm to approximate the value function with a fixed number of representative points. Our experimental results show that we can obtain much longer policies than existing algorithms as long as the interval between communications is small.

1 Introduction

Distributed Partially Observable Markov Decision Problems (Dis-POMDPs) are emerging as a popular approach for modeling sequential decision making in teams operating under uncertainty [1,2,3]. The uncertainty is due to the nondeterminism in the outcomes of actions and the limited observability of the world state. Unfortunately, as shown by Bernstein *et al.* [1], the problem of finding an optimal joint policy for a distributed POMDP is NEXP-Complete if no assumptions are made about the domain conditions.

To address this significant computational complexity, Networked Distributed POMDPs (ND-POMDPs) [4], a model motivated by domains such as distributed sensor nets, distributed UAV teams, and distributed satellites, was introduced. These domains are characterized by teams of agents coordinating with strong locality in their interactions. For example, within a large distributed sensor net, only a small subset of sensor agents must coordinate to track targets. By exploiting the locality, LID-JESP [4] (locally optimal) and SPIDER [5] (globally optimal), which are leading algorithms in this area, can scale-up in the number of agents. However, these approaches cannot handle run-time communication among agents. A consequence of this shortcoming is the exponential growth in the size of local policies.

To overcome this problem, we provide extensions of these algorithms called LID-JESP-Comm and SPIDER-Comm by introducing the run-time communication scheme presented in [3]. More specifically, agents periodically exchange observation and action histories with each other. Compared to other approaches such as [6,7,8], the advantage of using this scheme is that it allows the agents to build a new joint policy from a new synchronized belief state, i.e., instead of having one huge policy tree, an agent has multiple smaller policy trees.

Though this approach reduces the size of policies, it creates an exponential number of synchronized belief states after communication. To overcome this problem, we introduce an idea that resembles the Point-based Value Iteration (PBVI) algorithm [9] for single agent POMDPs. Instead of computing optimal policies for all the synchronized belief states, we compute optimal policies (and corresponding value vectors) only for a set of of representative belief points. Thus, we approximate the value function over the entire belief set by these value vectors, i.e., for any given belief point, we use the policy corresponding to the value vector that yields the highest value.

We develop two new algorithms based on this idea, i.e., LID-JESP-Comm and SPIDER-Comm (extensions of LID-JESP and SPIDER respectively). Since communication introduces inter-dependencies among agent policies, these algorithms lose some of the merits of the original algorithms. In LID-JESP-Comm, to update the policy of an agent, we need to consider the policies of all the other agents. SPIDER-Comm cannot provide global optimality, because it requires the enumeration of all joint policies. Despite these disadvantages, our experimental results show that these algorithms can obtain much longer policies than existing algorithms within a reasonable amount of time.

2 Model: Networked Distributed POMDP

We follow the networked distributed POMDP (ND-POMDP) model [4] as a concrete description of a Dis-POMDP. It is defined for a group of n agents as tuple $\langle S, A, P, \Omega, O, R, b \rangle$, where $S = \times_{1 \leq i \leq n} S_i \times S_u$ is the set of world states. S_i refers to the set of local states of agent i and S_u is the set of unaffectable states. Unaffectable state refers to that part of the world state that cannot be affected by agent actions. $A = \times_{1 \leq i \leq n} A_i$ is the set of joint actions, where A_i is the set of actions for agent i.

ND-POMDP assumes transition independence, i.e., the transition function is defined as $P(s, a, s') = P_u(s_u, s'_u) \cdot \prod_{1 \leq i \leq n} P_i(s_i, s_u, a_i, s'_i)$, where $a = \langle a_1, \ldots, a_n \rangle$ is the joint action performed in state $s = \langle s_1, \ldots, s_n, s_u \rangle$ and $s' = \langle s'_1, \ldots, s'_n, s'_u \rangle$ is the resulting state. $\Omega = \times_{1 \leq i \leq n} \Omega_i$ is the set of joint observations where Ω_i is the set of observations for agent i. Observational independence is assumed in

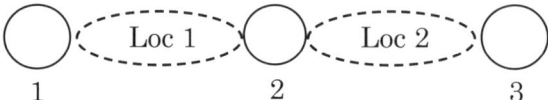

Fig. 1. A 3-chain sensor configuration

ND-POMDPs i.e., the joint observation function is defined as $O(s', a, \omega) = \prod_{1 \leq i \leq n} O_i(s'_i, s'_u, a_i, \omega_i)$. where s' is the world state that results from the agents performing a in the previous state, and ω is the observation received in state s'. Reward function R is defined as $R(s,a) = \sum_l R_l(s_{l1}, \ldots, s_{lr}, s_u, \langle a_{l1}, \ldots, a_{lr} \rangle)$, where each l could refer to any subgroup of agents and $r = |l|$. Based on the reward function, an interaction hypergraph is constructed. Hyper-link l exists between a subset of agents for all R_l that comprise R. The interaction hypergraph is defined as $G = (Ag, E)$, where agents Ag are the vertices and $E = \{l | l \subseteq Ag \wedge R_l$ is a component of $R\}$ are the edges. The distribution over the initial state b is defined as $b(s) = b_u(s_u) \cdot \prod_{1 \leq i \leq n} b_i(s_i)$, where b_u and b_i refer to distribution over the initial unaffectable and agent i's belief states, respectively. Each agent i chooses its actions based on its local policy π_i that maps its observation history to an action. The goal in ND-POMDP is to compute joint policy $\pi = \langle \pi_1, \ldots, \pi_n \rangle$ that maximizes the team's expected reward over finite horizon T starting from belief state b.

Distributed sensor networks are a large, important class of domains that motivate our work. This paper focuses on a set of target tracking problems that arise in certain types of sensor networks [4]. Figure 1 shows a specific problem instance within this type that consists of three sensors. Here, each sensor node can scan in one of four directions: North, South, East or West (see Figure 1). To track a target and obtain associated reward, two sensors with overlapping scanning areas must be coordinated by simultaneously scanning the same area. In Figure 1, to track a target in Loc 1, sensor 1 needs to scan 'East' and sensor 2 needs to scan 'West' simultaneously. We assume two independent targets and that each target's movement is uncertain and unaffected by the sensor agents. Based on the area it is scanning, each sensor receives observations that can have false positives and false negatives. Sensors' observations and transitions are independent of each other's actions. Each agent incurs a scanning cost whether the target is present or not, but no cost if it is turned off. There is a high reward for successfully tracking a target.

3 Existing Algorithms

3.1 LID-JESP

The locally optimal policy generation algorithm called LID-JESP (Locally interacting distributed joint search for policies) is based on DBA [10] and JESP [3]. In this algorithm, each agent tries to improve its policy with respect to its neighbors' policies in a distributed manner similar to DBA.

Initially each agent i starts with a random policy and exchanges its policies with its neighbors. It then computes its local neighborhood utility with respect to its current policy and its neighbors' policies. The local neighborhood utility of agent i is defined as the expected reward for executing joint policy π accruing due to the hyper-links that contain agent i. Agent i then tries to improve upon its current policy by computing the local neighborhood utility of agent i's best response to its neighbors' policies. Agent i then computes the gain that it can make to its local neighborhood utility, and exchanges its gain with its neighbors. If i's gain is greater than any of its neighbors' gain, i changes its policy and sends its new policy to all its neighbors. This process of trying to improve the local neighborhood utility is continued until the joint policies reach an equilibrium.

3.2 SPIDER

The key idea in SPIDER [5] is avoiding the computation of expected values for the entire space of joint policies by utilizing the upper bounds on the expected values of policies and the interaction structure of agents. SPIDER has a pre-processing step that constructs a Depth First Search tree (DFS tree) that allow links between ancestors and children. SPIDER places agents with more constraints at the top of the tree. This tree governs how the search for the optimal joint policy proceeds in SPIDER.

In Figure 2, we show a snapshot of search trees in the SPIDER algorithm. A rectangle indicates an agent, and a tree within a rectangle indicates an agent's policy. In this example, each agent has a policy with $T = 2$. Each rounded rectangle (search tree node) indicates a partial/complete joint policy. The heuristic or actual expected value for a joint policy is indicated in the top right corner of

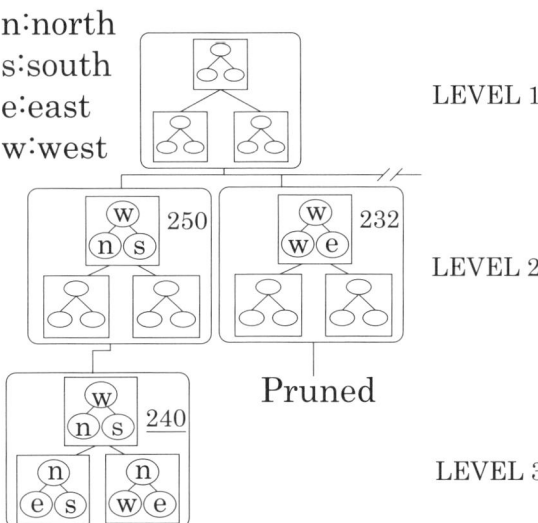

Fig. 2. Execution of SPIDER

the rounded rectangle. If the number is underlined, the actual expected value of the joint policy is provided. SPIDER begins with no policy assigned to any of the agents (shown in level 1 of the search tree). Level 2 of the search tree indicates that the joint policies are sorted based on upper bounds computed for the root agent's policies. Level 3 shows one SPIDER search node with a complete joint policy (a policy assigned to each agent). The expected value for this joint policy is used to prune the nodes in level 2 (those with upper bounds < 240). When creating policies for each non-leaf agent i, SPIDER potentially performs two steps:

STEP 1 Obtaining upper bounds and sorting. In this step, agent i computes the upper bounds on the expected values of the joint policies corresponding to each of its policies and the fixed ancestor policies. An MDP-based heuristic (more details will be explained later) computes these upper bounds on the expected values. All the policies of agent i are then sorted based on these upper bounds in descending order.

STEP 2 Exploring and pruning. Exploring implies computing the best response joint policy that corresponds to the fixed ancestor policies of agent i. This is performed by iterating through all policies of agent i and summing two quantities for each policy: (i) the best response for all of i's children; (ii) the expected value obtained by i for fixed policies of ancestors. Pruning refers to avoiding the exploration of all policies at agent i using the current best expected value as *threshold*. A policy need not be explored if its upper bound is less than the *threshold*. For example, if the best response policies from the leaf agents yield an actual expected value of 240, a policy with upper-bound 232 is pruned (see Figure 2).

4 Communication in ND-POMDP

We introduce the run-time communication scheme presented in [3] to ND-POMDPs as follows.

- In the initial state, agents have a synchronized belief state. Each agent has a local plan for subsequent k steps[1].
- Each agent executes its local plan for k steps. Then, agents go through the *communication phase*.
- During the *communication phase*, agents communicate their observation/action histories with each other. By exchanging the observation and action histories with each other, they have common knowledge on the observation/action histories of all agents. Thus, they can update their beliefs and reach a a new synchronized belief state.
- Each agent chooses a new plan prepared for that new synchronized belief state.

---
[1] For simplicity, we assume one communication phase occurs exactly once after k non-communication steps. Extending the algorithms to the cases where one communication phase occurs *at least* once within k steps is rather straightforward.

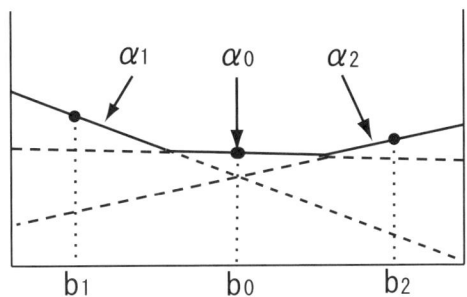

Fig. 3. Value function and α vectors

Thus, we use multiple small policy trees with a constant depth k instead of one huge policy tree whose size is exponential to the length of the time horizon.

However, the number of joint (small) policies grows exponentially to the length of the time horizon. To overcome this problem, we introduce an idea that resembles the Point-based Value Iteration (PBVI) algorithm [9] for single agent POMDPs. More specifically, we use a fixed number of *representative belief points* and compute the k-step optimal joint policy for each representative belief point. By using a fixed number of representative belief points, the obtained policy can be suboptimal. However, as shown in [9], we can bound the the difference between the obtained approximated policy and the optimal policy.

Let us assume we fix one particular k-step joint policy π. The expected reward of π starting from one particular belief state b is represented as a weighted linear combination of the expected reward for each state (Figure 3). More specifically, assume that possible states are $\{s_1, s_2, \ldots\}$ and a belief state $b = \langle b(s_1), b(s_2), \ldots \rangle$. The expected reward for joint policy π starting from b, denoted as $ER(b, \pi)$, can be represented as:

$$b(s_1) * ER(\langle 1, 0, \ldots \rangle, \pi) + b(s_2) * ER(\langle 0, 1, 0, \ldots \rangle, \pi) + \ldots$$

Here, we call the vector $\langle ER(\langle 1, 0, \ldots \rangle, \pi), ER(\langle 0, 1, \ldots \rangle, \pi), \ldots \rangle$ as α vector. The expected reward starting from belief state b is obtained by calculating the inner product of the belief state and the α vector. Since the optimal reward of the entire belief space is obtained by taking the maximal value for all possible joint polices, it is clear that the optimal reward satisfies piece-wise linear, convex (PWLC) property.

We approximate this optimal reward for the entire belief space (value function) using these α vectors of representative belief points (Figure 3).

4.1 ND-POMDP-Comm Algorithm (the Mechanism)

Next, we describe the details of algorithm in ND-POMDP with communication. We employ the following notation to denote the policies and the expected values:

$\pi^* \Rightarrow$ optimal joint policy of all agents.
$\pi^{i,*} \Rightarrow$ joint policy computed before searching for the policy of agent i.
$\pi^{j+} \Rightarrow$ joint policy of agents searched for after j.
$\pi_i \Rightarrow$ local policy of agent i.
$v[\boldsymbol{\alpha}, b] \Rightarrow$ the expected value for $\boldsymbol{\alpha}$ given belief state b.
$\hat{v}[\pi^{i,*}||\pi_i] \Rightarrow$ upper bound on the expected value given $\pi^{i,*}$ and π_i.

We need to find a joint policy for each representative point after each communication phase. If there are $|B|$ representative points and c communication phases, we need to find $c|B|$ joint policies for belief points after communication and one joint policy for the initial belief state.

Figure 4 shows the local policy given $k = 2$. First, our algorithm computes the joint policy for each of the representative points after the last communication phase, i.e., the joint policy for time steps 7-8 (Figure 4). This results in three policies: π_{20}, π_{21}, and π_{22}. Our algorithm computes the α-vectors for these joint policies.

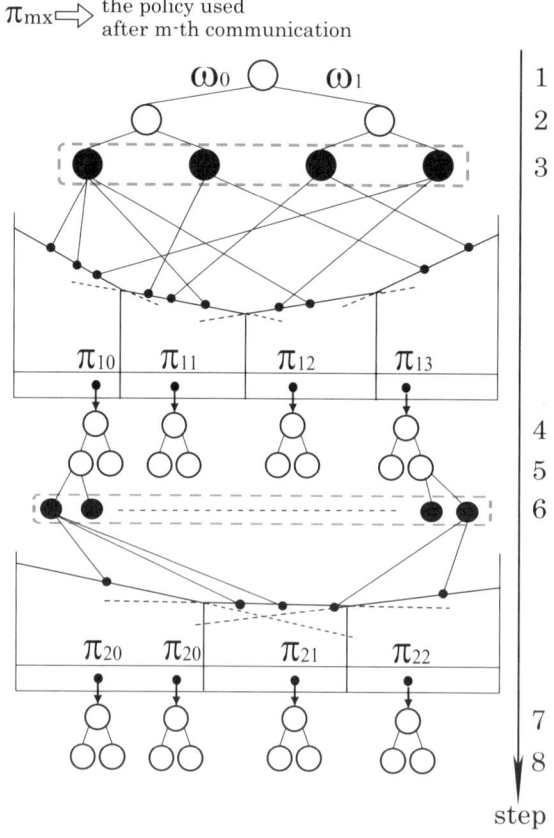

Fig. 4. Policy obtained by LID-JESP-Comm or SPIDER-Comm

Algorithm 1. ND-POMDP-Comm($k, CommPhase$)

1: initialize $\boldsymbol{\alpha}^*, \pi^* \leftarrow null$
2: $B \leftarrow$ BeliefExpansion(b_{init})
3: **while** $CommPhase \geq 0$ **do**
4:    **for all** $b \in B$ **do**
5:       $\langle \pi^*[b, CommPhase], \boldsymbol{\alpha} \rangle \leftarrow$
      FINDPOLICY($b, root, null, -\infty, k, \boldsymbol{\alpha}^*$)
6:       $\boldsymbol{\alpha}^*[CommPhase] \leftarrow \boldsymbol{\alpha}^*[CommPhase] \| \boldsymbol{\alpha}$
7:    $CommPhase = CommPhase - 1$
8: **return** π^*

Next, it computes a joint policy for time steps 4-6. A rectangle (represented by dashed lines) indicates the communication phase and lines from filled circles indicate the transitions to synchronized belief states after communication. The policies generated are π_{10}, π_{11}, π_{12}, and π_{13}. The algorithm computes the α-vectors for these joint policies. Finally, it determines the joint policy for the initial belief state.

Algorithm 1 provides the pseudo code for ND-POMDP with communication. This algorithm outputs a joint policy π^*. $CommPhase$ represents the number of communication phases. In line 2, a set of representative belief points is generated using the method described in the next subsection. Then, a joint policy is calculated for each representative belief point $b \in B$, and the obtained joint policy is stored in $\pi^*[b, CommPhase]$ (lines 5-7). In each action phase, FINDPOLICY function finds a joint policy and its α-vector, and utilizes two new algorithms based on LID-JESP-Comm or SPIDER-Comm.

4.2 Belief Point Selection

The way to choose representative belief points can affect the solution quality. We consider the following two methods. We assume that initial belief state b_{init} is always included in representative belief points B.

Random Belief Selection (RA). In this method, we sample belief points from uniform distribution over the entire belief space.

Stochastic Simulation with Exploratory Action (SSEA). This method is based on the algorithm presented in [9]. We gradually expand B by adding new reachable belief points after k actions and communication. More specifically, we stochastically run k actions in the forward trajectory from the belief points already in B and obtain several candidates. ¿From these candidates, we select belief points that improve the worst-case density, i.e., we choose the point farthest from any point already in B.

4.3 LID-JESP with Communication

LID-JESP with Communication (LID-JESP-Comm) performs the following procedure:

(i) For each representative point, we find the joint equilibrium policy (where each policy of an agent is the best response for other agents' policies) for k steps after the last communication using LID-JESP [4].

(ii) Then, for each representative point, we find the joint equilibrium policy for k steps after the second to the last communication. For the current k steps, we need only the policies of neighbors to evaluate the expected reward. On the other hand, to evaluate the expected reward after communication, we consider the policies of non-neighbors and obtain the probability distribution of the new synchronized belief states. For each new synchronized belief state, we use the best expected reward for the joint policies obtained in (i).

(iii) Then, we find the joint equilibrium policy for k steps after the third to the last communication, and so on.

4.4 SPIDER with Communication

Next, we describe the details of SPIDER with Communication (SPIDER-Comm). SPIDER can obtain global optimal joint policies by exploiting the locality of agent interaction. However, communication phase invalidates the locality in interaction that original SPIDER was relying on. In essence, previously independent agents (on different hyperlinks) are not interdependent. More specifically, a new synchronized belief state (and the expected reward after communication) depends on all agents' policies. In SPIDER-Comm, we utilize a greedy method i.e., when finding a best response policy for agent i in the DFS tree, we don't enumerate the combinations of the joint policies of different subtrees, while we enumerate the combinations within a subtree. Thus, although the SPIDER-Comm cannot guarantee to find the global optimal joint policy, it can utilize the locality of interaction and obtain a reasonable policy within a reasonable amount of time.

Algorithm 2 provides a pseudo code for procedure **FINDPOLICY** for SPIDER-Comm, which finds a joint policy and its α-vector. First, we store all possible local policies in Π_i (line 2). If i is a leaf agent, the local policies of all agents in its subtree are already assigned. SPIDER-Comm obtains an exact value for the subtree (and ancestors) and new synchronized belief states after communication (assuming default policies are used by the agents whose policies are not assigned yet), and chooses the best one (lines 3-9). On the other hand, if i is not a leaf agent, SPIDER-Comm performs the following procedure: (a) sorts policies in descending order based on heuristic values (line 12), (b) recursively calls **FINDPOLICY** for the next agent and calculates the best response policies for each local policy of agent i as long as the heuristic evaluation of the policy is better than the solution found so far (line 17), (c) maintains the threshold, the best solution found so far (lines 18-21).

Heuristic Function. In SPIDER-Comm, we need to construct a heuristic function that estimates the expected reward for the current k steps and after communication.

Algorithm 2. FINDPOLICY$(b, i, \pi^{i,*}, threshold, k, \boldsymbol{\alpha}^*)$

1: $\hat{\boldsymbol{\alpha}} \leftarrow null, \hat{\pi}^* \leftarrow null$
2: $\Pi_i \leftarrow$ GET-ALL-POLICIES(k, A_i, Ω_i)
3: **if** IS-LEAF(i) **then**
4:    **for all** $\pi_i \in \Pi_i$ **do**
5:       $\boldsymbol{\alpha}_i \leftarrow$ GETVECTOR$(i, \pi_i, \pi^{i,*}, \boldsymbol{\alpha}^*)$
6:       **if** $v[\boldsymbol{\alpha}_i, b] > threshold$ **then**
7:          $\hat{\pi}^* \leftarrow \pi_i$
8:          $threshold \leftarrow v[\boldsymbol{\alpha}_i, b]$
9:          $\hat{\boldsymbol{\alpha}} \leftarrow \boldsymbol{\alpha}_i$
10: **else**
11:    $children \leftarrow$ CHILDREN(i)
12:    $\hat{\Pi}_i \leftarrow$ UPPER-BOUND-SORT$(b, i, \Pi_i, \pi^{i,*}, \boldsymbol{\alpha}^*)$
13:    **for all** $\pi_i \in \hat{\Pi}_i$ **do**
14:       **if** $\hat{v}[\pi^{i,*}||\pi_i] < threshold$ **then**
15:          Go to line 22
16:       **for all** $j \in children$ **do**
17:          $\langle \pi^{j+}, \boldsymbol{\alpha}_i \rangle \leftarrow$
            FINDPOLICY$(b, j, \pi^{i,*}||\pi_i, threshold, k, \boldsymbol{\alpha}^*)$
18:          **if** $v[\boldsymbol{\alpha}_i, b] > threshold$ **then**
19:             $\hat{\pi}^* \leftarrow \pi_i || \pi^{j+}$
20:             $threshold \leftarrow v[\boldsymbol{\alpha}_i, b]$
21:             $\hat{\boldsymbol{\alpha}} \leftarrow \boldsymbol{\alpha}_i$
22: **return** $\langle \hat{\pi}^*, \hat{\boldsymbol{\alpha}} \rangle$

In [5], the MDP heuristic function is introduced. More specifically, the subtree of agents is a Dis-POMDP in itself. Thus, we can construct a centralized MDP corresponding to the (subtree) Dis-POMDP and obtain the expected value of the optimal policy for this centralized MDP. The advantage of the MDP heuristic is that it is admissible, i.e., it never under-estimates the optimal value. Thus, the SPIDER is guaranteed to find an optimal joint policy.

However, if we assume the subtree is solved by a centralized MDP (in which the current state is fully observable), we cannot estimate the new synchronized belief state after communication. Thus, we assign default policies to agents whose policies are not assigned yet and estimate the new synchronized belief state after communication assuming these agents use the default policies. We can use these default policies also for evaluating the expected reward for the current k steps. In this case, the heuristic function is no longer admissible, but it can prune more nodes and the run-time can be reduced. We will evaluate this trade-off in the next section.

5 Experimental Results

Our experiments were conducted on the example of the sensor network domain described in Section 2. We use three different topologies of sensors shown in Figure 5. Figure 5 (i) shows the example where there are three agents and two

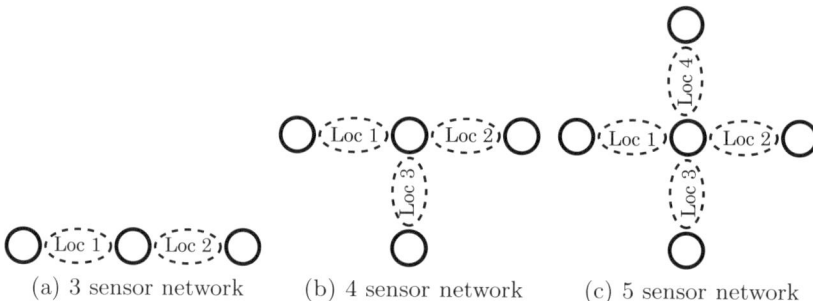

Fig. 5. Sensor net configurations

Table 1. Run time (msec) /expected value for SPIDER and SPIDER-Comm ($T = 3$)

	SPIDER	SPIDER-Comm
runtime [msec]	20797	390.00
value	141.90	87.05

targets. Target 1 is either absent or in Loc1, and target 2 is either absent or in Loc2. Thus, there are 4 unaffectable states. Each agent can perform turnOff, scanEast, or scanWest. Agents receive +45 as an immediate reward for finding target 1, +35 for finding target 2, and −5 for failing to find any target. Figure 5 (ii) shows the example where there are four agents and three targets, and (iii) shows the example where there are five agents and four targets.

We have compared two alternative methods for selecting representative points, i.e., RA or SSEA. We found that SSEA dominates RA, especially when the number of representative points is small. Thus, we use SSEA for selecting representative points in the following experiments.

Next, we evaluate the runtime and expected reward of SPIDER-Comm and LED-JESP-Comm. Figure 6 (a) provides runtime comparisons between SPIDER-Comm and LID-JESP-Comm that for $k = 2$ and $c = 1$ (c is the number of communications). In Figure 6, SPIDER-Comm (Default policy) indicates that SPIDER-Comm uses default policies both for the heuristic function for the current k steps and for estimating the belief states after communication. SPIDER-Comm (MDP+Default policy) indicates that SPIDER-Comm uses the MDP heuristic function for the current k steps and default policies for estimating the belief states after communication. The X-axis denotes the number of agents, while the Y-axis indicates the amount of time taken to compute the solution. SPIDER-Comm (MDP+Default policy) obtains runtime improvements over other methods in 3 agents configuration, while, in 4 and 5 agents configurations, SPIDER-Comm (Default policy) obtains runtime improvements over other methods. In Figure 6 (b), We evaluate the expected reward of SPIDER-Comm and LID-JESP-Comm in the same setting as Figure 6 (a). In 3 agents configuration, all methods obtain the same expected values. While, in 4 and 5

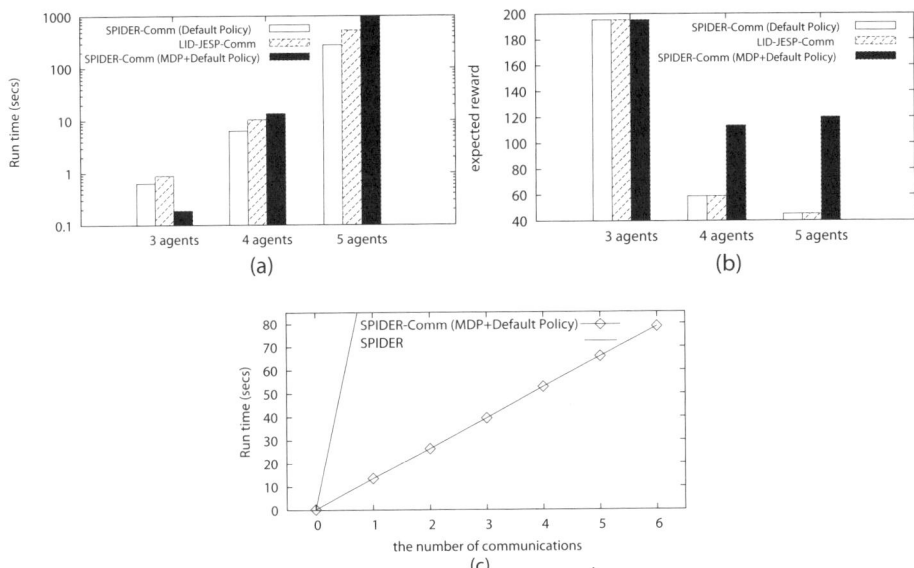

Fig. 6. Runtime (a) and expected reward (b) of SPIDER-Comm and LID-JESP-Comm, and runtime (c) of SPIDER-Comm by increasing the number of communications

agents configurations, SPIDER-Comm (MDP+Default policy) obtains significantly better expected reward over other methods.

Finally, we evaluate the run-time of SPIDER and SPIDER-Comm (MDP+Default policy) by increasing the number of communications c for $k = 2$ in 4 agents configuration (Figure 6 (c)). When $c = 6$, the total time horizon is 20. We have obtained similar results for the run-time of other methods. We can see that our newly developed methods can obtain policies even if the length of the time horizon is large, as long as the interval between communications is small. For the original SPIDER, the maximal length of the time horizon is at most 4, and for LID-JESP, the maximal length is around 6.

6 Conclusion

In this paper, we extended ND-POMDP so that agents can periodically communicate their observation and action histories with each other, and developed two new algorithms: LID-JESP-Comm and SPIDER-Comm. To address the problem that the number of new synchronized belief states after communication will grow exponentially, we introduced an idea similar to the PBVI algorithm. Our experimental results show that these algorithms can obtain much longer policies than existing algorithms within a reasonable amount of time. Our future works include introducing a more flexible communication scheme, such as varying the interval between communications, introducing partial communications, etc.

References

1. Bernstein, D.S., Zilberstein, S., Immerman, N.: The complexity of decentralized control of markov decision processes. In: Proceedings of the 16th Conference on Uncertainty in Artificial Intelligence (UAI 2000), pp. 32–37 (2000)
2. Szer, D., Francois Charpillet, S.Z.: MAA*: A heuristic search algorithm for solving decentralized POMDPs. In: Proceedings of the 21st Conference on Uncertainty in Artificial Intelligence (UAI 2005), pp. 576–590 (2005)
3. Nair, R., Roth, M., Yokoo, M., Tambe, M.: Communication for improving policy computation in distributed pomdps. In: Proceedings of the Third International joint Conference on Autonomous Agents and Multiagent Systems (AAMAS 2004), pp. 1096–1103 (2004)
4. Nair, R., Varakantham, P., Tambe, M., Yokoo, M.: Networked distributed POMDPs: A synthesis of distributed constraint optimization and POMDPs. In: Proceedings of the Twentieth National Conference on Artificial Intelligence (AAAI 2005), pp. 133–139 (2005)
5. Varakantham, P., Marecki, J., Yabu, Y., Tambe, M., Yokoo, M.: Letting loose a SPIDER on a network of POMDPs: Generating quality guaranteed policies. In: Proceedings of the 6th International Joint Conference on Autonomous Agents and Multi-agent Systems (AAMAS 2007), pp. 822–829 (May 2007)
6. Goldman, C.V., Zilberstein, S.: Optimizing information exchange in cooperative multi-agent systems. In: Proceedings of the Second International Joint Conference on Autonomous Agents and Multi-agent Systems (AAMAS 2003), pp. 137–144 (2003)
7. Roth, M., Simmons, R., Veloso, M.: Exploiting factored representations for decentralized execution in multiagent teams. In: Proceedings of the 6th International joint conference on Autonomous agents and Multi-agent Systems (AAMAS 2007), pp. 457–463 (2007)
8. Shen, J., Becker, R., Lesser, V.: Agent interaction in distributed pomdps and its implications on complexity. In: Proceedings of the fifth international joint conference on Autonomous agents and multiagent systems (AAMAS 2006), pp. 529–536 (2006)
9. Pineau, J., Gordon, G., Thrun, S.: Anytime point-based approximations for large POMDPs. Journal of Artificial Intelligence Research 227, 335–380 (2006)
10. Yokoo, M., Hirayama, K.: Distributed breakout algorithm for solving distributed constraint satisfaction problems. In: Proceeding of the Second International Conference on Multiagent Systems (ICMAS 1996), pp. 401–408 (1996)

Solving Crossword Puzzles Using Extended Potts Model

Kazuki Jimbo[1], Hiroya Takamura[2], and Manabu Okumura[2]

[1] Tokyo Institute of Technology, Department of Computer Science
[2] Tokyo Institute of Technology, Precision and Intelligence Laboratory

Abstract. Solving crossword puzzles by computers is a challenging task in artificial intelligence. It requires logical inference and association as well as vocabulary and common sense knowledge. For this task, we present an extension of the Potts model. This model can incorporate various clues for solving puzzles and require less computational cost compared with other existing models.

1 Introduction

The crossword puzzle is one of the most famous puzzles in the world. Solving crossword puzzles automatically by computers is a challenging task in artificial intelligence and is more difficult than solving other logical puzzles. One has to use his or her linguistic knowledge, world knowledge, and logical and association inference when solving crossword puzzles, while one does not have to use them when solving sudoku or other logical puzzles. There are strict rules on sudoku or other logical puzzles and one can verify that his or her solution is correct by checking whether the solution follows the rules completely. On the other hand, rules on crossword puzzles are not strict because of the diversity of human language expressions. One cannot verify that his or her solution is correct by simply checking whether the solution follows the rules.

In this writing, we introduce an extended Potts model for solving Japanese crossword puzzles. Using this model, one can incorporate various clues for solving crossword puzzles. Moreover, this model requires less computational cost compared with other existing models.

2 Related Work

Keim *et al.* constructed Proverb, a system which solves American-style crossword puzzles in English automatically [2]. Proverb divides the process of solving crossword puzzles into two steps: generating a list of candidate answers for each clue using many language resources and algorithms, and finding the best solution combining the candidate answers for the clues. In the first step, they used a database which contains more than 350,000 clue-answer pairs from 5,133 puzzles. In American-style crossword puzzles, this database of clue-answer pairs is very useful because clues in American-style crossword puzzles are usually short and the same clue-answer pair can be found many times in different puzzles. In the second step, they used Shazeer *et al.*'s algorithm [1], which finds the optimal answer from the list of candidate answers. This algorithm recursively updates the weight of each candidate so that the expected number of correct answers will be maximized. Additionally, it finds all feasible combinations of candidate answers, and then calculates the score of each feasible combination using the weights of candidate answers. The combination with the maximum score should be the solution.

This algorithm is computationally complex because it needs to find all feasible combinations of candidate answers. Moreover, this algorithm outputs no solutions if there is no feasible combination of candidate answers. On the other hand, the extended Potts model, which we propose in this writing, is computationally less complex. Additionally, our model outputs a solution even if there are no feasible combinations.

Sato attempted to automatically solve crossword puzzles in Japanese [3]. His system also divides the solving process into two steps as in Proverb. Clues of Japanese crossword puzzles tend to be longer and hence more difficult than those of English ones. In order to tackle the difficulty, he classified the clues according to how their answers would be found. The algorithm used in his second step is Shazeer's, the same one as in Proverb.

Ernandes *et al.* constructed a crossword solver named WebCrow [4]. The system uses the World Wide Web as a knowledge base.

3 The Proposed Model for Solving Crossword

3.1 Solving Crossword Puzzles

The process of automatically solving crossword puzzles by computers is divided into two steps: making a list of candidate answers for each clue and finding the correct combination of answers from the lists.

The first step is to create a list of candidate answers for each clue. This step is to answer some quizzes. Each crossword puzzle contains one grid and some clues. A clue is a hint which represents one word in the puzzle grid. Clues are often so ambiguous that one clue can represent more than one word. That is why most algorithms create a list of candidate answers for each clue, instead of a unique answer. In this step, the system searches linguistic resources or World Wide Web, retrieves candidate answers, and calculates their confidence scores. These candidate answers are inputs to the next step. This first step is similar to the question answering task.

The second step is to find the correct combination of answers from the lists. The combination should satisfy the following constraint: if two words cross each other, they should have the same character at the crossing point. Violation of this constraint means that at least one of the two words is incorrect.

3.2 Candidate Answer Detection

In this section, we explain how to detect the candidate answers and their scores from clues of crossword puzzles. We introduce two types of methods: the method exploiting dictionaries as in Sato [3] and the method exploiting the World Wide Web as in Ernandes [4].

We use multiple methods to generate candidate answers. First, the system extracts content words from each clue. We refer to those content words as *keywords*. Next, the system applies multiple methods independently to each keyword and extracts candidate answers. Finally, the system merges all the extracted candidates into one list. We describe the details of these methods below.

Dictionary-based method. First, we explain methods using dictionaries.

Japanese-Japanese dictionary: This method looks up each keyword in a Japanese-Japanese dictionary (Iwanami Japanese dictionary), and returns the words found in the glosses (i.e., definition sentences) as candidates. The score is the number of the words found.

Japanese-Japanese dictionary (inverted): This method searches a Japanese-Japanese dictionary (Iwanami Japanese dictionary) for the entry words whose glosses contain the keyword. The candidate answers are those entry words. The score is the number of the keywords in the glosses.

Japanese-Japanese dictionary (filling-in): The filling-in method attacks filling-in clues, which contain a blank, such as "___ bon-ni kaerazu (It's no use crying over spilt ___)." Only in this method, instead of extracting keywords in preprocessing, we take the clue as a pattern including blanks. Then, the method searches a Japanese-Japanese dictionary (Iwanami Japanese dictionary) for expressions matching the clue pattern. The candidate answers are the found expressions. The score is the number of the matched expressions in the dictionary.

Thesaurus: This method returns the words categorized as in the same semantic group as the keyword, which is given by a thesaurus (*Bunrui Goihyo*, Word List by Semantic Principles). The score is the depth of the most specific ancestor shared by the keyword and the candidate words.

Thesaurus (antonym): This method finds antonyms of keywords from a thesaurus (Kadokawa thesaurus). The score is the number of the found descriptions on the antonym information in the thesaurus.

Web-based method. Second, we explain methods using the World Wide Web. Dictionary-based method has an advantage that we can obtain reliable answers from high-quality linguistic resources, but also has a disadvantage that we cannot obtain an answer if the knowledge is not contained in the resources. We expect that we can obtain answers for more various questions by using huge amount of information on the World Wide Web.

Search by keyword: For each clue, we create a query for web search (Yahoo! JAPAN) by listing keywords. The words in the snippets of the top 50 results retuned by the search engine with the query are used as candidates. The score is the number of the words found in the snippets.

Filling-in pattern match: This method is a variation of 'Japanese-Japanese dictionary (filling-in)' method above. This method uses the World Wide Web instead of the dictionary.

For each filling-in clue, we create a query of web search (Yahoo! JAPAN) consisting of the expression around the blank. Then, the method searches the snippets of the top 50 results for expressions matching the clue pattern. The score is the number of the found expressions in the 50 snippets.

Candidate merging. After obtaining the lists of candidate answers by the above methods, the system merges these lists into one. If more than one method generate the same candidate, the score for the candidate the merged list is the sum of the scores given by each method.

This merged list contains words of various parts of speech. However, most of the words used as answers of crossword puzzles are nouns. Therefore, the candidate words with other parts of speech than noun are excluded from the list.

3.3 Finding the Best Combination

Generally, more than one answer candidates will be found for each clue. The correct solution of the puzzle may consist of words without the highest scores in the candidate lists. In other words, the highest-scored words may not be in the best combination. Then, it is important how to find the best combination from the candidate lists. We use the extended Potts model for this purpose, which is described below.

Originally, the Potts model is used for describing behaviors of spins on crystal trellis in the domain of statistical dynamics. This model is used for describing states of nodes on the problem concerned with network [6].

For graph (or network) $G(V, E)$, $c_i \in \{1, \ldots, n\}$ represent states of nodes $v_i \in V$ The weight between v_i and v_j is represented by w_{ij}. L is the set of indices for the observed nodes, $a_i \in \{1, \ldots, n\}$ is the state of each observed variable indexed by i.

Let $H(\mathbf{c})$ denote an energy function, which indicates a state of the whole network:

$$H(\mathbf{c}) = -\beta \sum_{ij} w_{ij}\delta(c_i, c_j) + \alpha \sum_{i \in L} -\delta(c_i, a_i), \qquad (1)$$

where β is a constant called *the inverse-temperature*, and α is a positive constant representing a weight on labeled data. Function δ returns 1 if two arguments are equal to each other, 0 otherwise. The state is penalized if $c_i (i \in L)$ is different from a_i. Using $H(\mathbf{c})$, the probability distribution of the network is represented as

$$P(\mathbf{c}) = \frac{\exp(-H(\mathbf{c}))}{Z}, \qquad (2)$$

where Z is a normalization factor. One can estimate the state of this network at $\hat{\mathbf{c}}$ which maximizes $P(\hat{\mathbf{c}})$.

However, it is computationally difficult to exactly estimate the state of this network. A mean-field approximation method described by Nishimori [5] can be applied in order to avoid this difficulty. In the method, $P(\mathbf{c})$ is replaced by factorized function $\rho(\mathbf{c}) = \prod_i \rho_i(c_i)$, where $\rho_i(c_i)$ corresponds to the probability that the state of node v_i is c_i. Then we can obtain the function with the smallest value of the variational free energy:

$$F(\mathbf{c}) = \sum_{\mathbf{c}} P(\mathbf{c})H(\mathbf{c}) - \sum_{\mathbf{c}} -P(\mathbf{c}) \log P(\mathbf{c}) \quad (3)$$

$$= -\alpha \sum_i \sum_{c_i} \rho_i(c_i)\delta(c_i, a_i) \quad (4)$$

$$-\beta \sum_{ij} \sum_{c_i, c_j} \rho_i(c_i)\rho_j(c_j) w_{ij} \delta(c_i, c_j) \quad (5)$$

$$-\sum_i \sum_{c_i} -\rho_i(c_i) \log \rho_i(c_i). \quad (6)$$

By minimizing $F(\mathbf{c})$ under the condition that $\forall i, \sum_{c_i} \rho_i(c_i) = 1$, we obtain the following fixed point equation for $i \in L$:

$$\rho_i(c) = \frac{\exp(\alpha\delta(c, a_i) + \beta \sum_j w_{ij}\rho_j(c))}{\sum_n \exp(\alpha\delta(n, a_i) + \beta \sum_j w_{ij}\rho_j(n))}. \quad (7)$$

The fixed point equation for $i \notin L$ can be obtained by removing $\alpha\delta(c, a_i)$ from above. This fixed point equation is solved by an iterative computation.

We convert the crossword puzzle into a problem of finding a state of the network modeled by a variant of the Potts model. As pointed out by Shazeer et al. [1], crossword puzzles can be described by a graph as follows:

Node: Blank for answer of a clue
State: Selected answer of a clue
Edge: Crossing of down and across blanks (nodes)

However, the original Potts model cannot be applied straightforwardly for solving crossword puzzles in two reasons. First, in the Potts model, the value of energy function is low and the probability of combination is high, if the states of nodes connected with an edge are the same. However, in crossword puzzles, crossing blanks does not mean that the blanks have the same answer, while the character at the crossing point has to be shared by the blanks. Second, in the task of solving crossword puzzles, a list containing weighted multiple candidate words is given for each clue.

Now, we define the extended Potts model, which is applicable to the task of solving crossword puzzles. First, we define the energy function $H_{\text{cross}}(\mathbf{c})$ as

$$H_{\text{cross}}(\mathbf{c}) = -\beta \sum_{ij} M_{ij}(c_i, c_j) + \alpha \sum_i -S_i(c_i) \quad (8)$$

while M_{ij} is a function which indicates whether the words in two nodes v_i and v_j satisfy the constraint, and S_i is the normalized score of node v_i in the candidate list. When the states of v_i and v_j are c_i and c_j respectively, $M_{ij}(c_i, c_j) = 1$ if the two nodes have the same character at the crossing point, or the two nodes do not cross, and $M_{ij}(c_i, c_j) = 0$ otherwise. The score S_i satisfies $\forall i, \sum_c S_i(c) = 1$.

Then, we derive the probability of state vector $P_{\text{cross}}(\mathbf{c})$ and the free energy $F_{\text{cross}}(\mathbf{c})$ in the task of solving crossword puzzles from the energy function H_{cross} as follows:

$$P_{\text{cross}}(\mathbf{c}) = \frac{\exp(-H_{\text{cross}}(\mathbf{c}))}{Z}, \tag{9}$$

$$F_{\text{cross}}(\mathbf{c}) = \sum_{\mathbf{c}} P_{\text{cross}}(\mathbf{c}) H_{\text{cross}}(\mathbf{c}) \tag{10}$$

$$- \sum_{\mathbf{c}} -P_{\text{cross}}(\mathbf{c}) \log P_{\text{cross}}(\mathbf{c}) \tag{11}$$

$$= -\alpha \sum_i \sum_{c_i} \rho_i(c_i) S_i(c_i) \tag{12}$$

$$- \beta \sum_{ij} \sum_{c_i, c_j} \rho_i(c_i) \rho_j(c_j) M_{ij}(c_i, c_j) \tag{13}$$

$$- \sum_i \sum_{c_i} -\rho_i(c_i) \log \rho_i(c_i), \tag{14}$$

while Z is the normalization factor and $\rho_i(c_i)$ is the probability that the state of node v_i is c_i. Note that $\forall i, \sum_{c_i} \rho_i(c_i) = 1$.

Minimizing $F_{\text{cross}}(\mathbf{c})$ on the condition that $\forall i, \sum_{c_i} \rho_i(c_i) = 1$, we obtain the equation

$$\rho_i(c) = \frac{\exp(\alpha S_i(c) + \beta \sum_j \sum_{c_j} M_{ij}(c, c_j) \rho_j(c_j))}{\sum_n \exp(\alpha S_i(n) + \beta \sum_j \sum_{c_j} M_{ij}(n, c_j) \rho_j(c_j))}. \tag{15}$$

We can minimize $F_{\text{cross}}(\mathbf{c})$ by updating ρ_i recursively using this equation. In our experiments, we iteratively update ρ_i until the value of the energy function $H_{\text{cross}}(\mathbf{c})$ converges. After the convergence of $H_{\text{cross}}(\mathbf{c})$, we select the word c_i which maximizes value of $\rho_i(c_i)$ for each clue v_i and output all c_i as the final solution.

In this writing, we call this model the extended Potts model. The constraints in the puzzle are embedded in this model as penalty factors. That is why this model outputs a solution even if there are no feasible combinations.

In this writing, we compare two initial values of ρ_i: score-based initial value $\rho_i(c_i) = S_i(c_i)$ and random initial value satisfying $\rho_i(c_i)$ ($0 \leq \rho_i(c_i) \leq 1$) and $\sum_{c_i} \rho_i(c_i) = 1$.

Annealing process can be applied to the Potts model. Annealing process is a process which increases the inverse temperature β by $\Delta\beta > 0$ after every convergence of ρ and executes the iterative updating again. In the extended

Potts model, large β emphasizes the constraints. However, the scores of words tend to be neglected in this case. On the other hand, large α emphasizes the scores of words. However, the constraints tend to be neglected in this case.

Annealing process first computes the state of the network emphasizing the scores of words by setting β small. After that, the process sets β slightly larger and computes the state again. These two computations are iterated by turns until convergence.

4 Experiments

We conducted some experiments in order to test the performance on real crossword puzzles. To measure the performance of our method, we used the word accuracy, which indicates the ratio of the correct words to all words for clues. This measure is also used by [1] and [3].

4.1 Data Set

We tested the performance using 15 puzzles from http://cross.matrix.jp/. The size of all these puzzles is 7x7 letters. The maximum, minimum, and average number of clues in each puzzle are 22, 18, and 20.5, respectively.

4.2 Experiments

We tried search for the optimal solution using candidate answers that we obtained by the methods in section 3.2. In this section, we used candidate answers from all the methods including Web-based ones, unless otherwise noted.

Variation of parameters. We conducted the experiments with various parameter values. We adjusted the parameters α and β in range of 0–100000, executed the iterations without annealing, and calculated the word accuracy. The values of the parameters which give the best performance are ($\alpha = 1000$, $\beta = 2$) with the score-based initialization (14.9 % correct), and ($\alpha = 1000$, $\beta = 2$) and ($\alpha = 500$, $\beta = 5$) with the random initialization (13.0 % correct). Table 1 shows the variation of the word accuracy for fixed $\alpha = 1000$ and various β.

The word accuracy with the score-based initialization is higher than that with the random initialization in most cases.

Next, we conducted the same experiment over the candidates from only dictionary-based methods. The word accuracy without the Web-based methods is much lower than that with the Web-based methods.

Table 1. The word accuracy (%) for fixed $\alpha = 1000$ and various β

Initial value	\multicolumn{9}{c}{β}								
	0	1	2	5	10	20	30	40	50
Score	12.3	13.0	**14.9**	14.0	11.7	13.3	9.1	8.8	10.1
Random	11.9	11.4	11.4	12.3	11.7	**13.0**	11.4	7.8	9.4

Table 2. The word accuracy (%) with annealing

β Initial value	Δβ 0.01	0.05	0.1	0.5	1	2	5	Without annealing
2 Score	14.0	14.0	15.3	14.0	14.0	14.0	—	14.9
2 Random	10.7	12.0	11.7	11.4	12.7	10.1	—	11.4
10 Score	13.6	13.0	13.3	14.0	14.3	13.6	14.3	11.7
10 Random	11.4	11.4	12.7	13.0	12.3	10.7	12.7	11.7

Annealing. We compared results with and without annealing, in $\alpha = 1000$, which gives high performance in the above experiment. We tested both the score-based initialization and the random initialization. The increment $\Delta\beta$ in one annealing step is set in range of 0.01–5. We executed them with β from 0 to 2 and from 0 to 10. Table 2 shows the result.

In most cases, annealing increases the word accuracy. However, how to decide the parameter values is also important when we employ annealing, because the word accuracy also depends on the parameter value.

Comparison with related work. We conducted another experiment for comparing Shazeer et al.'s method [1] and our method. The computer used in this experiment has 2.66 GHz x 2 dual core CPU and 2 GB memory. We compared only execution time.

Shazeer et al.'s method takes more than 3 days for one puzzle, while our method takes 15.47 seconds in average for one puzzle with 10 times annealing. This result shows that our method using the extended Potts model is quite effective to shorten the execution time. Additionally, the execution time tends to be long if the number of candidates increases.

5 Conclusion

We proposed to use the extended Potts model for automatically solving crossword puzzles. Our method is much faster than existing methods. However, the maximum word accuracy was around 15 %. This is because the method for candidate answer detection is too rough. Consequently, the inaccurate result made a bad effect on the solution of optimization problems. Therefore, our future work will include making the candidate answer detection more accurate. For this work, question answering technology can be applied.

Moreover, the extended Potts model has some parameters. How to decide the values of these parameters is also an open problem.

References

1. Shazeer, N.M., Littman, M.L., Keim, G.A.: Solving Crossword Puzzles as Probabilistic Constraint Satisfaction. In: Proceedings of the sixteenth national conference on Artificial intelligence and the eleventh Innovative applications of artificial intelligence conference innovative applications of artificial intelligence, pp. 156–162 (1999)

2. Keim, G.A., Shazeer, N., Littman, M.L., Agarwal, S., Cheves, C.M., Fitzgerald, J., Grosland, J., Jiang, F., Pollard, S., Weinmeister, K.: PROVERB : The Probabilistic Cruciverbalist. In: Proceedings of the Sixteenth National Conference on Artificial Intelligence, pp. 710–717 (1999)
3. Sato, S.: Solving Japanese Crossword Puzzles. IPSJ SIG Notes, NL-147-11, 69–76 (2002) (in Japanese)
4. Ernandes, M., Angelini, G., Goli, M.: WebCrow: a WEB-based system for CROss-Word solving. In: Proceedings of the Twentieth National Conference of Artificial Intelligence, pp. 1412–1417 (2005)
5. Nishimori, H.: Statistical Physics of Spin Glasses and Information Processing. Oxford University Press, Oxford (2001)
6. Wu, F.-Y.: The Potts model. Reviews of Modern Physics 54(1), 235–268 (1982)

Socialized Computers and Collaborative Learning

Mikihiko Mori[1], Kokolo Ikeda[1], Gaku Hagiwara[2], Masaki Saga[2], Tetsutaro Uehara[1], and Hajime Kita[1]

[1] Academic Center for Computing and Media Studies, Kyoto University
[2] Graduate School of Informatics, Kyoto University

Abstract. Collaborative Learning, a teaching method of asking groups of learners to do tasks collaboratively attracts attention for its effectiveness of acquiring various skills. Recognizing the limit of current design of personal computer (PC) for collaborative use in face-to-face environment, this paper proposes a computer system called Socialized Computer (SC) as an extension of or alternative to PC. The SC allows multiple users access to the computer with multiple mice and keyboards, and share information on a single large display. In this paper, the authors introduce the concepts of the SC, give overview of the related works, discusses implementation issues. Further, three application developed along the concept of the SC and results of experiments using them are also shown.

1 Introduction

Along with the remarkable progress in Information and Communication Technologies, computers are widely used in people's life in various styles such as personal computing, mobile computing, embedded computing etc. Among such styles of computing, personal computing plays a key role in supporting creative work of people. Further, combining computers with the Internet, it also supports people in communication and collaborative work with their distant partners.

Current style of personal computing owes the design Personal Computer (PC) whose origin is *Alto*, an epoch making development at Xerox PARC[5]. Since then, development of hardware and software for PC has made remarkable progress, and PC has been powerful in computing power, large in storage capacity, small in size, and cheap in cost. Currently, many people use PCs for their business, hobby and daily life. While the PC made remarkable progress, the basic concept of PC is not changed since development of Alto. That is, the commonly accepted characteristics of PC such as WIMP architecture (windows, icons, menus and pointer), and collaboration and sharing information over a high-speed network that connects PCs are all demonstrated in Alto.

In school education, the impact of personal computing has two effects. One is *to teach personal computing* as a basic skill of contemporary world. In Japan, subject *Information* that teaches computer and information literacies has been introduced as a compulsory course at high schools in the current national curriculum since 2003.

The other one is *teaching using PCs*, that is, to enhance teaching with the help of computers. While there have been vast amount of effort of introducing computers into the classroom, however, their use was quite limited[1]. The reasons of the limited success may be the cost of introducing computers in the classroom, lack of adequate software and content, or lack of specialists. We propose another hypothetical reason. It is mismatch between the concept/architecture of PC and characteristics of teaching/learning in classroom. In classroom, people's activities are more social and collaborative using rich media such as verbal and non-verbal communication sharing dynamic writing/drawing on blackboard in the face-to-face environment. Recently, social and collaborative aspects in learning has been paid more attention as an effective way of learning as *Collaborative Learning*. PC designed for personal use of computer may fail in supporting such social activities effectively. Takada et al. has pointed out that students sharing a same PC for collaborative work are split into single operator and the other spectators[14].

Based on this hypothesis, we has been started study of extending the concept of PC to more social media that matches collaboration in the face-to-face environment[2], and as an alternative style of computers, we have proposed the concept of *Socialized Computer* (SC) which provides an environment for cooperative/collaborative work by giving multiple uses some control of the computer which has one display to share information among the users. From the technical point of view, SC belongs to the category called Single Display Groupware (SDG). However, we named our concept Socialized Computer to put more stress on contrast with the Personal Computer, current dominant style of computer rather than groupware.

This paper is organized as follows. In Section 2, we make an overview of collaborative learning that motivates our study. In Section 3, we introduce the concept of SC, review related work such as SDG, and discuss some implementation issues of SC. In Section 4, three example applications of SC are shown with experimental results using them. Section 5 is conclusion of this paper.

2 Collaborative Learning

Conventionally, education mainly focuses on learning of concepts and skills by an individual learner. That is, a learner acquires knowledge individually through lectures given by instructors, or self-learning using various learning materials. However, as shown in the discussion of *the legitimate peripheral participation*[6], a novel view of learning attracts attention. It considers learning as participation to society, and is called *the social constructivism*. With such a view of learning, *collaborative learning* in which the learners work together for a common task is considered an effective teaching method[4].

Collaborative learning is expected to have the following four advantages than individual learning:

- It motivates the learners more by existence of other learners. The learners are motivated by awareness of others in repulsive, sympathizing or competing sense.
- It gives the learners more variety of learning styles. Through collaboration with others, learners exchange and share their learning styles.
- It gives the learners opportunities of learning social interaction. Through experience of collaboration, the learners acquire skills for collaboration such as task division, role taking, reporting and discussion.
- It gives the learners opportunities of refining their knowledge by externalizing their own comprehension. Each learner obtain feedback to refine his/her knowledge through explanation of his/her knowledge and comprehension to the other collaborators.

While collaborative learning over network is also investigated, collaboration in face-to-face environment is more effective to handle complex tasks, and hence the primal matter to be considered. We are trying to support such face-to-face collaboration by designing adequate computing environment.

3 Socialized Computer

3.1 The Concept of Socialized Computer

Since development of Alto at Xerox PARC, PC has brought about revolutionary changed to personal creative activities at office, home and other fields. With PC, personal activities are supported by its computing power, digital storage, communication over network, and services behind the network.

As for collaborative work, support by computers are also investigated as CSCW (Computer Supported Cooperative Work) and CSCL (Computer Supported Cooperative Learning). However, currently available CSCW/CSCL technologies usually assume personal work with PC as its basis, and seek collaboration in the virtual space through the PCs as channels. It enables collaboration among distant people, or people working different time. However, if collaboration is done in a face-to-face environment, its support by current PC-based CSCW/CSCL is quite restrictive, because PCs separete real and virtual spaces.

Socialized computer (SC) proposed in this paper aims to provide a computer supported environment connecting real and virtual spaces more seamlessly. SC consists of computer (CPU/memory/network), multiple mice or other pointing devices and keyboards to allow several users to access the computer in parallel, and a (large) display to share information among the users. A reference device of SC is a conventional blackboard which can be seen commonly in classrooms. A blackboard can be used by several people in parallel, and information on the blackboard is shared by the people. Thus, collaboration is well supported by the blackboard.

3.2 Related Work

There have been proposed many systems that support collaboration in distributed or co-present situation. *Croquet*[10] is a system to support collaboration between users through a peer-to-peer architecture. It provides us with a distributed multi-user social experience that enhances online teaching and learning. However, when we think about daily activities at schools or offices, we find that collaboration frequently occurs in co-present or face-to-face situations, and to support such collaborations is an important issue.

Tabletop computers have developed for such purpose along with increasing computing power. In Xerox PARC's *Colab project*[11], participants are seated around a table arranged workstations, and interact with each other using table-centered affordances. The *iRoom project*[8] supported interactions more directly on tables and vertical surfaces. These Tabletop computers, however, aren't suitable for classroom situations because collaboration occurs in classroom situations which requires very flexible and seamless usage of computers.

Stewart et al. proposed *Single Display Groupware*[12] which is a model for supporting collaborative work sharing single output channel e.g., display. SDG users can not only operate single system cooperatively, but also can break into personal work and can take over. *Caretta*[13] which is categorized as a kind of SDG integrates personal and shared spaces to support face-to-face collaborations. It uses PDAs and sensing board to link the shared space and personal spaces. While PDAs support users easily displaying personal work spaces without disturbance by other users, it decreases an advantage of SDG in flexibility and easiness to set up. Pawar et al. have developed software that allows multiple mice pointer to share the monitor for educational content in developing countries[7]. Ueda has also developed *Multi-mouse middleware toolkit* (MMTk) which enables to use multiple mice in applications coded specially for that environment[16]. Similar middleware named *SDGToolkit* has been developed by Tse and Greenberg[15]. Huttcrcr et al. proposed *Groupware Windowing System* (GWWS)[3], and *MPX* which is an implementation of GWWS for X Window System is available by downloading it. *Virtual Network Computing* is popular implementation to share mouse cursor[9]. Although VNC can make users sharing desktop, VNC cannot show different mouse cursors for each user.

From the technical point of view, SC belongs to the category called SDG. However, we named our concept Socialized Computer to put more stress on contrast with the PC, current dominant style of computer, and as extention of or alternative to PC. Concerning hardware of current PC, mice and keyboards with USB interface enable to connect multiple mice and keyboards to a single computer, and large high-resolution flat panel display, or multiple display gives a large screen for collaborative work. In development of SC, we are planning to use only such common hardware considering its usage in school education.

3.3 Implementation Issues of Socialized Computer

As stated in the previous section, hardware of current PC is usable also for SC. However, as for software, current operating systems or window systems such as

Microsoft Windows, Apple Mac OS, or X-window are all designed for single user, or multiple users operating in separate GUI environments.

Hence, we need to reconstruct software to support multiple and simultaneous access by users to realize SC. In implementation of SC, there can be several strategies with trade off between freedom as SC and availability of existing (application) software:

System reimplementation: The whole window system is implemented from scratch to identify the multiple mice and keyboards, and to give adequate control of computer to all the such devices independently. Because of the altered window system, all the current application software have to be modified to use. MPX belongs to this strategy.

Application-layer implementation: By intervening at the device driver level from an application software, and reconstructing GUI inside the application, SC is implemented as an application software on an existing OS or window system. As same as the system reimplementation strategy, existing application is not available on SC, and all the needed application software have to be made from scratch. MMtk and SDGToolkit are middleware developed for applications along this strategy.

Pseudo pointing device: This strategy is to write an application program with transparent window that lays over the screen, and shows a cursor for pseudo pointing device on the window. No or limited control to the computer is given to the pseudo pointing device. All the existing application only with the authentic pointing device is available without any change. Pseudo pointing device can be implemented using mouse of other PC that sends the information of mouse over network to the SC. 'Dummy Mouse' described in next section belongs to this strategy.

4 Example Applications and Experiments

In this section, we introduce three applications developed under the concept of SC, and some experimental results using them.

The proposal of SC requires reconstruction of the whole GUI of the current PC developed for personal use, and since behavior of the users in the environment of multiple access to a shared display has not yet been understood well, to implement the whole framework of the SC is very difficult task. Hence, as a research strategy, we are developing particular applications under the concept of SC separately. Through the experience of using such applications, we will accumulate the knowledge of behaviors of the users in such computing environment, its effectiveness, guidelines of GUI design, and ways for facilitating users in educational usages.

4.1 Teaching Web Browser Usage with Dummy Mouse

Teaching usage of GUI-based application software is a typical task found in the course using computer, e.g., computer literacy courses. Because current GUI-based application requires complex mouse button operation (press right or left button, single or double click, drag and drop etc.), and exploration of hierarchical menu containing vast items, to teach usage of the software to novice is very laborsome task requiring collaboration of an instructor and a learner.

Dummy Mouse System. To examine the teaching under multiple mouse environment, we have implemented a tool of pseudo pointing device type called *Dummy Mouse*. Dummy Mouse requires two PCs, the primary PC and the secondary PC which are mutually connected by a network. The secondary PC sends the position and status of button of its mouse to the primary PC via network. On the primary PC, usual Windows OS and applications are working with its local mouse and keyboard, and additionally the secondary mouse cursor is displayed using the information obtained from the secondary PC as pseudo pointing device. No control on the primary PC is given to the pseudo pointing device. To make identification of the two pointers easier, the secondary pointer is shown with bigger cursor on the primary PC.

Experimental Setup. We conducted a experiment to find effectiveness and problems of a multiple cursor environment and to investigate how people collaborate each other in a shared display environment. The asked task was to teach the usage of Firefox, a tab-browser. The experiment was conducted by pairs of subjects. One subject of a pair took the role of an instructor and was given the mouse of the secondary PC, i.e., pseudo pointing device on the primary PC, and the other took the role of a learner who used the local mouse that could operate the primary PC.

The teaching task consisted of the following subtasks to teach:

1. How to carry out tab-browsing
2. How to configure the interface of the tab-browser
3. How to configure the function of the tab-browser
4. How to install ad-on tools and how to use them

Subjects were three graduate students and three undergraduate students of Kyoto University. They were grouped into three pairs, and three students having enough experience of using the tab-browser took the role of the instructors, and those having few experiences took the role of the learners as shown in Table 1.

Table 1. Profile of Subject Groups on the Experiment for Dummy Mouse

		Grade	Major	Experience of tab-browser
Pair 1	Instructor	Graduate	Informatics	Enough
	Learner	Undergraduate	Engineering	None
Pair 2	Instructor	Graduate	Informatics	Enough
	Learner	Undergraduate	Economics	None
Pair 3	Instructor	Graduate	Informatics	Enough
	Learner	Undergraduate	Law	None

In the experiment, at first, subjects were explained the task and shown sample setting of the tab-browser which had been set up in advance. During the experiment, subjects' behavior was recorded by video. Each pair was asked to carry out the task for 30 minutes, and then subjects were interviewed with questions asking overall impressions, the effectiveness and difficulties of a multiple cursor environment and so on.

Since the purpose of the experiment was to observe the behavior of the subjects, and to ask them impression of multiple mouse cursor environment as much as possible with the limited number of subjects and time, no control experiment was carried out.

Observations. While the experience was carried out in quite simple environment, we could find many implications to develop SC. The interesting findings are mainly related to the social aspect of operation of the multiple cursors by different persons. Although all participants showed positive opinion for the multiple pointer environment, concrete findings were as follows:

- The frequency of appearance of demonstrative pronoun in verbal action: All the pairs frequently used demonstrative pronouns to interact with each other instead of using the actual names of e.g. menu items of the software. In interviews, all subjects told that by using demonstrative pronouns, they could understand the other's intension sufficiently with combination of the movement of mouse pointer. We found some characteristic sentence structure in verbal actions which consists of almost demonstrative pronoun. For example, one participant said "Bring it here like this."
- Pointer movement in the case that subjects used demonstrative pronoun: We observed some gestures using mouse pointer to send particular message to the other subjects. If an instructor wanted to emphasize the important point, he draw a circle with mouse pointer quickly, or move it back and forth laterally with uttering "This!!" strongly. These emphasizing actions occurred in all the pairs of subjects. One participant moved his pointer like pulling the learner's one.
- Pointer movement in the case that the distance between pointers was close: We observed some characteristic movements when a pointers came close each other. Each pointer was suddenly stand back or jiggly movement was shown. These were recognized as actions to identify the ownership of each pointer. The instructor of the Pair 1 told that he sometimes kept the distance between the pointers to confirm which his pointer was.

While, the Dummy Mouse provided the users with quite restrictive collaborative environment, the results showed it has promising effect for collaboration, especially asymmetric work like teaching task for existing software developed on conventional OS. We also tried preliminary experiment of more than two pointers/users environment. In such trial, we found that users felt limitation of screen size and confusion of ownership of their pointers.

4.2 Collaborative Painting with Multi-mouse Paint Tool

In elementary school, collaborative painting or drawing of one (usually large) picture in a group is often carried out as an activity in classroom. Similar activities using computer may have some advantages such as saving works on disk, colorful painting without painting material. Recent reduction of cost for large flat panel display enlarges possibility of such computer-assisted work. However, ordinary PC environment can hardly support such works because of its design.

Multi-Mouse Paint Tool. We have created multi-user single display paint program called *Multi-Mouse Paint Tool* (MMPT) to investigate collaborative painting on one display. See Fig. 1. MMPT is developed as an application-layer implementation utilizing SDG Toolkit[15]. MMPT is developed assuming elementary school children as main users, and simple and intuitive painting tools such as pens of several colors and an eraser are implemented. These tools are placed in the tool box at the bottom of the screen,

To investigate the relationship between painting tools and collaboration in doing task, tools such as pens and an eraser can work in two modes. One is exclusive mode, in which each tool can be used exclusively by one user. If one user selects a particular tool, other users have to wait until he/she returns the tool to the tool box. In order to find the place to return the tool, each box is

Fig. 1. An Example Screenshot of Multi-Mouse Paint Tool

Table 2. Profile of Subject Groups on the Experiment for Multi-Mouse Paint Tool

	Grade	Sex	Use of Computer
Group 1	4th	Male	Few
	4th	Male	Frequently
	4th	Male	Usually
Group 2	5th	Male	Few
	5th	Female	Frequently
Group 3	4th	Male	Frequently
	5th	Male	Few
	6th	Male	Usually
Group 4	6th	Female	Frequently
	6th	Female	Usually
	6th	Female	Usually

labeled its name. The other mode is non-exclusive mode, in which any user can use any tool simultaneously.

Experimental Setup. We conducted an experiment on collaborative painting using MMPT. For the purpose of comparing simultaneous painting in a group with/without restriction of operation in painting, we conducted experiments in the following three modes:

Single user mode: this mode enabled only one user to operate. As well as ordinary painting software, this mode offered one operative mouse. Every user could paint when he/she took the operative mouse.
Non-exclusive mode: in this mode, every user could paint simultaneously with any tool.
Exclusive mode: in this mode, every user could draw simultaneously, but they could use particular tool exclusively.

In the experiment, every group of subjects were asked to paint one picture for every mode. During the experiment, we recorded the screen periodically and the subjects' behavior by video. At the end of the experiment, we conducted interview to the subjects and ask to answer a questionnaire.

Subjects were 11 elementary school children. Group of subjects, and their grades, sex, and experience of using computer is shown in Table 2.

Every group tried every modes, whose orders were shuffled to cancel order effects. Because of limited available time for experiment, Group 2 did not try the single user mode. To give motivation of painting, and to encourage painting in limited time, we chose greeting pictures for a new year as the theme, and we showed six pictures containing illustrations of mouse, pine tree, bamboo and blooming plum, which were traditional motifs for new year greeting in Japan. To make painting picture easier, pen tablets were used instead of mice for all the subjects and modes.

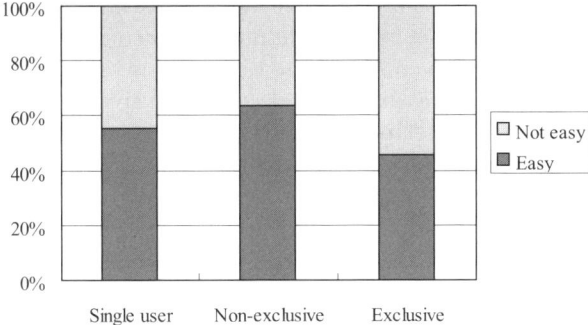

Fig. 2. The result of the question asking easiness to use Multi-Mouse Paint Tool for each mode

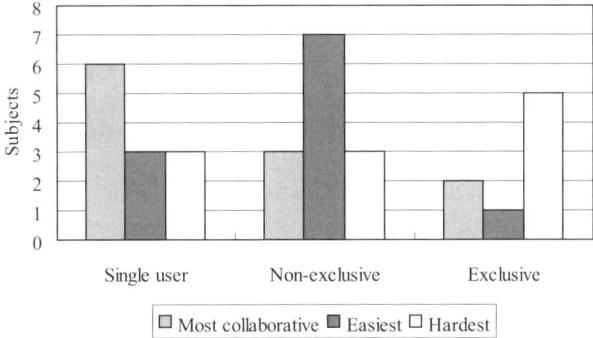

Fig. 3. The result of the question asking the easiest mode, the hardest mode and the most collaborative mode

Experimental Results and Discussions. Figure 2 is the result of the question asking subjects whether MMPT was easy or not. The results shows subjects answered "Easy" were more than those answered "Not easy" in single user, and non-exclusive modes, and the percentage of "Easy" in non-exclusive mode is higher than the single user mode. In contrast, in the exclusive mode, the number of subjects answered "Easy" was less than those answered "Not easy". In the interviews, a subject said, "everyone can use tablet pens in exclusive mode, but I couldn't use the pen when I want." The answer indicates that they felt inconvenience not by limitation of physical devices but by limitation of software resource on the screen.

We also asked to the subjects the easiest mode, the hardest mode and the most collaborative mode among the three modes. Figure 3 shows result. The result shows that the single user mode was most collaborative, and the non-exclusive mode was the easiest, and the exclusive the hardest. Concerning collaboration, from the interview, it was found that handing over the physical tablet pen made the subjects felt collaborative. At the same time, some subjects complained that they had to wait while another were using the tablet pen and that they had nothing to do while waiting. non-exclusive mode was evaluated at easiest mode. From the comment of the subjects, it might mean they could paint independently. Although the color pens in exclusive mode were similar to restriction of physical pen in single user mode, the subjects selected exclusive mode as the hardest one. Mismatch of plural tablet pens in physical space and exclusive use of pen in virtual space might make the subjects feel more inconvenient.

From the observation of the behavior, the subjects in non-exclusive mode tended to concentrate on their own work independently because MMPT kept them free from restriction of on-screen pens. In the single user mode and exclusive mode, we observed that some subjects imitated actions of others because the subjects had chances to see the actions of others at the time for waiting. In some cases, subjects interfered with another's works when the other came in the subjects' work area when the other did it maliciously or not. Subjects interfered with another's works when the other negated the subject's works. The interference continued until the end of the experiment when it happened.

The results indicate that there is a trade-off relation between usability of painting and opportunities of collaboration. Usability of painting environment relates how users work independently, and opportunities of collaboration relates the resource restriction by which users were force to interact other users. As Stewart et al. indicated that new conflicts and frustrations may arise between users when they attempted simultaneous incompatible actions[12], we observed interferences in the wake of "simultaneous incompatible actions". Since overlapping is not only on a screen but also on a desk on which mice stay, overlapping on the desk may cause interferences. Thus, we have to pay attention to design of SC in consideration of overlap of individuals' personal spaces and shared spaces both on desks and screens.

4.3 Multi-mouse Quiz System

Quiz is a typical tool in teaching and learning. It gives chances not only to develop intellectual curiosity but also to keep motivation of learning and to enhance the learned knowledge. We attempt to quiz school students about their studying topics for the purpose of giving the opportunity to acquire knowledge and to be interested in the topics in classroom. Yatani et al. has reported that to make quizzes and to answer quizzes are effective on collaborative learning [17]. As well as painting, to use computer for quiz has various advantages, it is expensive to give simultaneous access to computers to all the students in classrooms.

In order to make several learners to play quiz simultaneously, and to enhance collaboration in thinking the answer to the quiz, we have constructed multi-answerer quiz program called *Multi-Mouse Quiz System* (MMQS) aiming at elementary school children as users. MMQS is developed also as an application-layer implementation utilizing SDG Toolkit [15]. Current version is a prototype to figure out necessary requirements in facilitation of learning using the MMQS.

Figure 4 (a) shows the start screen of waiting for entries. Three mouce cursors are represented with the arrows of the same shape at this time. When any one click the "Start" button, the screen changes to registration screen shown in

Socialized Computers and Collaborative Learning   59

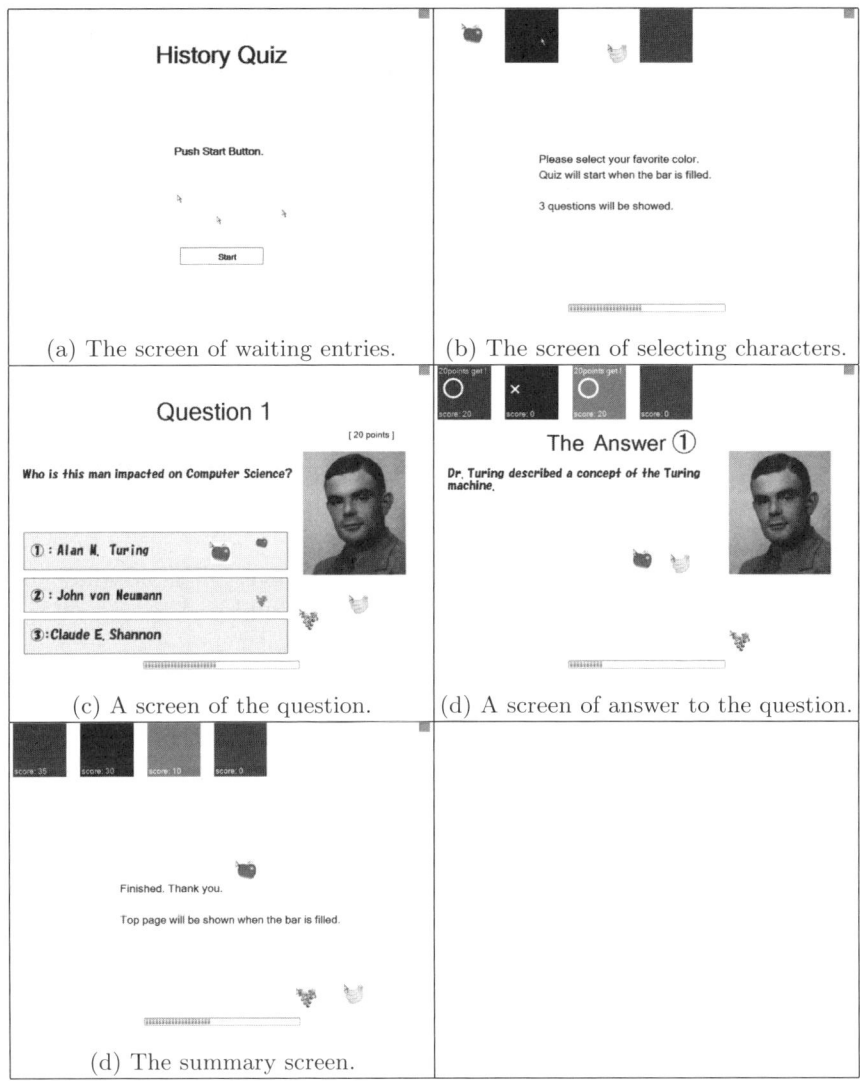

Fig. 4. Multi-Mouse Quiz System

Fig. 4 (b) . the entries have to choose favorite color among the four colors shown in the top of screen within the prescribed time. The progress bar displayed at the bottom shows the passed time. When an entry chooses one color, mouse cursor is changed to preset characters having the selected color. After the set period, the screen changes to first question screen shown in Fig. 4 (c). All the entries can retry selection of the alternative choice as answer until prescribed time has passed. After the set period, the screen changes to an answer screen that shows the correct answer and descriptions with scores for every entries as shown in Fig.

4 (d). After the periods, the system displays the next question and then displays its answer. After all the questions is finished, the system shows summary screen shown in Fig. 4 (e).

Synchronization of behaviors of multiple users, or control of screen change is one important design issue in SC. In this application, except for start of the quiz, all the screen changes are driven not by users' actions but by preset timers. Preliminary experiments were carried out two times at Kyoto University Museum in July, 2008 as one activity of outreach program of the museum held in every Saturday. Subjects were visitors of the museum, and mostly, elementary school children and their parents. Through this experiments, we observed interesting social activities among the subjects as well as hints to improve the system.

5 Conclusion

Recognizing the limit of current design of personal computer (PC) for collaborative use in face-to-face environment, especially collaborative learning in education, this paper proposes a conceptual design of computer called Socialized Computer (SC) as an extension of, or alternative to the PC. The SC allows multiple users to access the computer with multiple mice and keyboards, and share information on a single large display. We discussed implementation strategies for SC considering compromise with current OS, window systems and applications developed on it. We also showed three applications developed along the concept of the SC, and some experimental results of using them. In future study, we extend our activity to develop more applications, to accumulate findings from them, and to propose more concrete design of SC as well as to study of collaborative learning utilizing the developed softwares.

References

1. Cuban, L.: Oversold And Underused: Computers in the classroom. Harvard University Press (2001)
2. Hagiwara, G., Ikeda, K., Mori, M., Uehara, T., Kita, H.: On Socialization of Personal Computing. In: Proc. The Fifth International Conference on Creating, Connecting and Collaborating through Computing (C5 2007), pp. 62–65 (2007)
3. Hutterer, P., Thomas, B.H.: Groupware Support in the Windowing System. In: Piekarski, W., Plimmer, B. (eds.) Proc. 8th Australasian User Interface Conference (AUIC 2007), Balarat, Vic, Australia (January 2007)
4. Johnson, D.W., Johnson, R.T., Smith, K.A.: Active Learning: Cooperation in the College Classroom. Interaction Book Co. (1991)
5. Kay, A., Goldberg, A.: Personal Dynamic Media, pp. 31–41. IEEE Computer, Los Alamitos (1977)
6. Lave, J., Wenger, E.: Situated Learning, Legitimate Peripheral Participation. Cambridge University Press, Cambridge (1991)
7. Pawar, U.S., Pal, J., Toyama, K.: Multiple Mice for Computers in Education in Developing Countries. In: 1st Int. Conf. ICT and Development, UC Berkeley (May 2006)

8. Rekimoto, J.: Pick and drop: Adirect manipulation technique for multiple computer environments. In: UIST, pp. 31–39 (1997)
9. Richardson, T., Stafford-Fraser, Q., Wood, K.R., Hopper, A.: Virtual Network Computing 2(1), 33–38 (1998)
10. Smith, D.A., Kay, A., Raab, A., Reed, D.P.: Croquet — A Collaboration System Architecture. In: Proc. the First Conference on Creating, Connecting, and Collaborating through Computing (C5 2003), pp. 2–10. IEEE Computer Society Press, Los Alamitos (2003)
11. Stefik, M., Bobrow, D., Learning, S., Tartar, D.: WYSIWIS revised: early experiences with multiuser interfaces. ACM Trans on Info. Systems 5(2), 147–167 (1987)
12. Stewart, J., Bederson, B., Druin, A.: Single Display Groupware: A model for co-present collaboration. In: Human Factors in Computing Systems (CHI 1999), pp. 286–293. ACM Press, New York (1999)
13. Sugimoto, M., Hosoi, K., Hashizume, H.: Caretta: A system for Supporting Face-to-Face Collaboration by integrating Personal and Shared Spaces. In: Proc. CHI 2004, Vienna, Austria, pp. 41–48. ACM Press, New York (2004)
14. Takada, H., Kita, H.: Creativity Education by Distance Learning Connecting Kyoto University and UCLA. In: Proc. World Conference on Educational Multimedia, Hypermedia and Telecommunications (July 2005)
15. Tse, E., Greenberg, S.: Rapidly Prototyping Single Display Groupware through the SDGToolkit. In: Proc. Fifth Australasian User Interface Conference. The CRPIT Conferences in Research and Practice in Information Technology Series, vol. 28, pp. 101–110. Australian Computer Society Inc. (2004)
16. Ueda, M.: MMTk Multi-mouse middleware. Takeuchi Laboratory, Graduate School of Information Science and Technology, University of Tokyo (2006), http://www.nue.ci.i.u-tokyo.ac.jp/~masa-u/mmtk/
17. Yatani, K., Onuma, M., Sugimoto, M., Kusunoki, F.: Musex: A System for Supporting Children's Collaborative Learning in a Museum with PDAs. J. IEICE Trans. Inf. & Syst. J89-D-I(10), 773–782 (2003) (Japanese Edition)

Learning Communicative Meanings of Utterances by Robots

Ryo Taguchi[1], Naoto Iwahashi[2,3], and Tsuneo Nitta[4]

[1] Nagoya Institute of Technology
Gokiso-cho, Showa-ku, Nagoya, Aichi, 466-8555 Japan
taguchi.ryo@nitech.ac.jp
[2] National Institute of Information and Communications Technology,
[3] Advanced Telecommunications Research Institute International
2-2-2 Hikaridai, Seika-cho, Soraku-gun, Kyoto, 619-0288 Japan
naoto.iwahashi@atr.jp
[4] Toyohashi University of Technology
1-1 Hibariga-oka, Tempaku-cho, Toyohashi-city, Aichi, 441-8580 Japan
nitta@tutkie.tut.ac.jp

Abstract. This paper describes a computational mechanism that enables a robot to return suitable utterances to a human or perform actions by learning the meanings of interrogative words, such as "what" and "which." Previous studies of language acquisition by robots have proposed methods to learn words, such as "box" and "blue," that indicate objects or events in the world. However, the robots could not learn and understand interrogative words by those methods because the words do not directly indicate objects or events. The meanings of those words are grounded in communication and stimulate specific responses by a listener. These are called communicative meanings. Our proposed method learns the relationship between human utterances and robot responses that have communicative meanings on the basis of a graphical model of the human-robot interaction.

Keywords: Language Acquisition, Human-Robot Interaction, Machine Learning.

1 Introduction

To achieve language-mediated interactions with humans, robots must have much knowledge including names of objects and events, grammar, and traditions. The research into language acquisition by robots is intended to make robots acquire knowledge through interaction. Previous studies have proposed methods based on inductive learning using sets of pairs in which each pair consisted of a word sequence and visual information about its meaning [1,2,3,4,5,6]. By using these methods, robots correctly learned meanings of words referring to names of objects and features (e.g, "box" and "blue") and phrases referring to motions (e.g, "move onto" and "jump over").

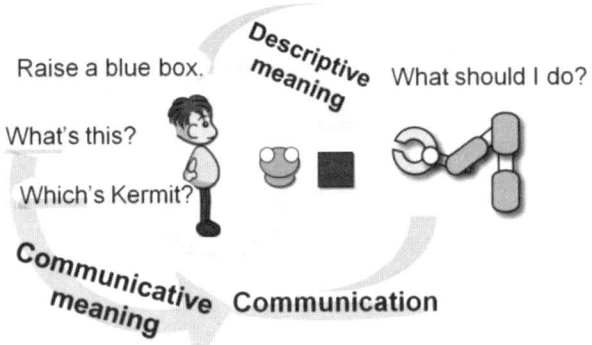

Fig. 1. Descriptive meanings and communicative meanings

On the other hand, in everyday situations, words that do not directly indicate objects and events, such as interrogatives (e.g, "what" and "which") and interjections (e.g., "hello" and "bye"), are also used. They stimulate specific responses by a listener. A robot can infer what a user is directing his/her attention to by understanding descriptive meanings that are grounded in objects or events, (see Fig. 1). Moreover, by understanding communicative meanings that are grounded in communication, the robot can appropriately respond to the user. For example, when the user says "What's this?", the robot needs to infer what should be returned. Human utterances generally include both descriptive and communicative meanings. However, previous studies have treated only descriptive meanings, yet communicative meanings have been given implicitly. Achieving natural and rich communication requires learning and understanding the two types of meanings.

This paper proposes a computational model that integrates both types of meanings and enables a robot to learn the relationship between user utterances and robot responses as communicative meaning.

2 Setting for Learning

The spoken-language acquisition task discussed in this paper was set up as follows. A camera and a robot arm with a hand were placed next to a table. A user and the robot saw and moved objects (e.g. stuffed toys) on the table as shown in Fig. 2.

First, the robot learned 14 words referring to objects (e.g, "Kermit," "red," and "small") and 7 phrases referring to motions (e.g., "move onto" and "move over") [6].

Second, the robot learned communicative meaning of words and user action. In this learning, the user asked the robot to move an object with a specific trajectory or asked a question about an object or a motion. User utterances were simple without particles and conjugation. For example, when the user wanted to ask the robot to put the left frog onto the blue box in Fig. 1, he said in

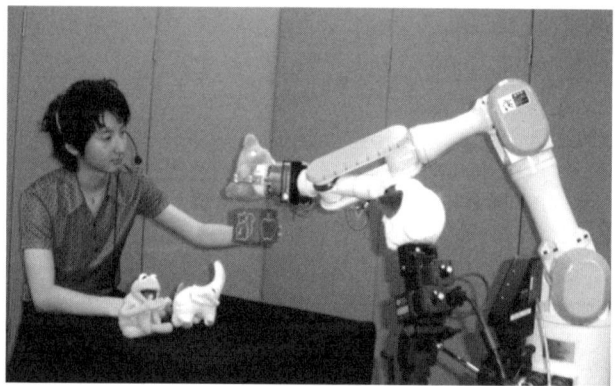

Fig. 2. Interaction between user and robot

Japanese "KERMIT AOI HAKO NOSETE". Each of the words in the utterance can be translated into English as "KERMIT BLUE BOX MOVE ONTO." In the descriptions that follow, Japanese utterances in the experiments are translated literally into English and written with capital letters to improve the readability of this paper.

When the user wanted to know the name of an object, he pointed at it and said "WHAT?" Moreover, when he did not know which is "KERMIT," he said "KERMIT WHICH?" The user asked such simple questions and more complicated questions. For example, he moved Kermit onto an object and asked a question about the name of the object by saying "KERMIT WHICH MOVE ONTO?"

When the robot received a user utterance, it inferred the user intention and returned an utterance or an action as a response to the user. If the robot responded incorrectly, the user slapped the robot hand and demonstrated an appropriate response. Through such interactions, the robot was able, incrementally and online, to learn communicative meaning included in user utterances and actions.

3 Learning Method

3.1 Shared Belief Function

The dynamical graphical model that represents the interaction between a user and the robot is shown in Fig. 3. This model was made by extending the model proposed by previous studies [6]. A user utterance and behavior at time t are denoted by S_{1t} and B_{1t}, respectively. A robot utterance and behavior as a response to the user are denoted by S_{2t} and B_{2t}, respectively. Behavior B_{1t}/B_{2t} consists of behavior content B_{C1t}/B_{C2t} ("POINTING," "MOVING," or "NULL") and target object B_{O1t}/B_{O2t}. Namely, $B_{1t} = (B_{C1t}, B_{O1t})$ and $B_{2t} = (B_{C2t}, B_{O2t})$. Their utterances and behaviors S_{1t}, B_{1t}, S_{2t} and B_{2t} are directly observed. When the user moves an object, the robot detects trajector object O_{Tt}, which is moving,

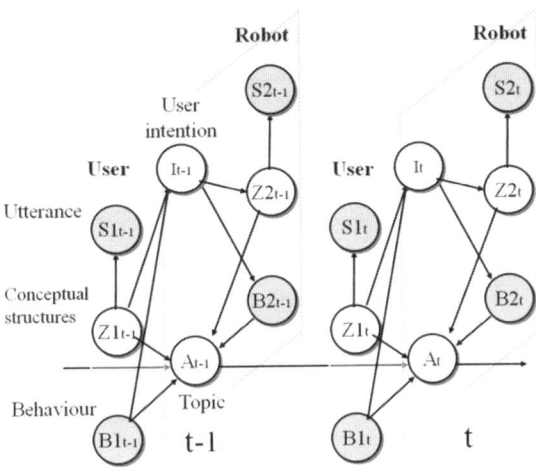

Fig. 3. Dynamical graphical model of human-robot interaction. Gray nodes represent information that can be directly observed.

and its trajectory U_t. Moreover, it infers landmark object O_{Lt}, which is a reference point of the motion, from the trajectory U_t or user utterances. If the user utters words without moving it, the robot infers the desired motion (O_{Tt}, O_{Lt}, and U_t) from the utterance S_{1t}, user behavior B_{1t}, and previous objects O_{Tt-1} and O_{Lt-1}. In this paper, the authors call a combination of them a topic $A_t = (O_{Tt}, O_{Lt}, U_t)$. Conceptual structure Z_{1t}/Z_{2t} represents words in a user/robot utterance, and relationships between them and topic A_t. For instance, when the user says "WHAT RED BOX MOVE ONTO?" (which means "What moved onto the red box?"), conceptual structure $Z_{1t} = (Z_{T1t}, Z_{L1t}, Z_{M1t}, Z_{I1t})$ is

$$\begin{bmatrix} Z_{T1t} \ (trajector) & : (Null) \\ Z_{L1t} \ (landmark) & : RED, BOX \\ Z_{M1t} \ (motion) & : MOVE-ONTO \\ Z_{I1t} \ (interrogative) & : WHAT \end{bmatrix},$$

where the righthand column contains the spoken word subsequences referring to a trajector object, a landmark object, a motion, and an interrogative. Note that conceptual structure Z_{1t} must be inferred because the robot cannot know directly what each word indicates.

Topic A_t is inferred from conceptual structures Z_{1t}, Z_{2t}, behaviors B_{1t}, B_{2t} and previous topic A_{t-1}. This means the user and robot exchanges utterances about a common topic. The previous topic A_{t-1} is used to infer the next topic A_t as a context. User intention I_t as well as topic A_t has the role of the middle node that connects a user's conceptual structure Z_{1t} and behavior B_{1t} to a robot's conceptual structure Z_{2t} and behavior B_{2t}, respectively. This means that a robot's response is generated on the basis of a user's utterances and behaviors. In this paper, translating user input Z_{1t} and B_{1t} into a user intention

I_t is called communicative meaning. A response constraint is a user intention I_t that constrains robot's responses S_{2t} and B_{2t}. The robot inferred topic (A_t), user intention (I_t), and its own responses (S_{2t}, B_{2t}) from the user's utterance Z_{1t} and behavior B_{1t} by maximizing the following function:

$$\begin{aligned}\Psi(S_{1t}, B_{1t}, A_t, S_{2t}, B_{2t}) = \max_{A_t, S_{2t}, B_{2t}} \Big\{ &\gamma_1 \log p(S_{1t}|Z_{1t}; L, G) \\
&+ \gamma_2 \log p(O_{Tt}|Z_{T1t}; L) + \gamma_2 \log p(O_{Lt}|Z_{L1t}; L) \\
&+ \gamma_2 \log p(U_t|Z_{M1t}, O_{Tt}, O_{Lt}; L) \\
&+ \gamma_3 \log p(O_{Tt}, O_{Lt}|Z_{M1t}; R) \\
&+ \gamma_4 \log p(O_{Tt}, O_{Lt}|B_{1t}, A_{t-1}; H) \\
&+ \gamma_5 \log p(I_t|Z_{1t}, B_{1t}; CM) \\
&+ \gamma_6 \log p(Z_{2t}, B_{2t}|I_t; RC) \\
&+ \gamma_1 \log p(S_{2t}|S_{2t}; L, G) \\
&+ \gamma_2 \log p(O_{Tt}|Z_{T2t}; L) + \gamma_2 \log p(O_{Lt}|Z_{L2t}; L) \\
&+ \gamma_2 \log p(U_t|Z_{M2t}, O_{Tt}, O_{Lt}; L) \\
&+ \gamma_3 \log p(O_{Tt}, O_{Lt}|Z_{M2t}; R) \\
&+ \gamma_4 \log p(O_{Tt}, O_{Lt}|B_{2t}, A_{t-1}; H) \Big\}\end{aligned} \quad (1)$$

where $LCGCHCRCCM$, and RC are model parameters of a lexicon, grammar, behavioral context, motion-object relationship, communicative meaning, and response constraint, respectively. A set of weighting coefficients to regulate each influence is $\Gamma = \gamma_1, \gamma_2, \gamma_3, \gamma_4, \gamma_5, \gamma_6$ [6]. We call this function Ψ, the shared belief function. A graphic representation of this function is given in Fig. 3. The function represents the user's utterance-action and robot's response. Lexicon L, grammar G, behavioral context H, motion-object relationship R, and weighting coefficients Γ (other than γ_5 and γ_6) were learned on the basis of [6]. Here γ_5 and γ_6 were given manually. Communicative meaning CM and response constraint RC are described in the following section.

3.2 User Intention and Communicative Meaning

3.2.1 Model of User Intention

In this paper, we assume that user intention I_t means "I would like the robot to express I_{At} by using I_{Ot}." I_{At} is called robot's attention and I_{Ot} is called output modality. Robot's attention I_{At} takes one of the topic elements: "TRAJECTOR", "LANDMARK," and "TRAJECTORY." Output modality I_{Ot} takes one of the three values: "SPEECH", "ACTION," and "INACTION". For example, when a user said "KERMIT WHAT MOVE ONTO?" the true intention was that "I would like the robot to express the landmark object (I_{At} = LANDMARK) by speech (I_{Ot} = SPEECH)." The model of user intention I_t is shown in Fig. 4. User intention I_t was inferred from phrase structure Y_{1t}, interrogative word Z_{I1t}, and behavior content B_{C1t}. Phrase structure Y_{1t} that expresses presences of words in $Z_{T1t}, Z_{L1t}, Z_{M1t}$, and Z_{I1t} was used in place of Z_{1t} because

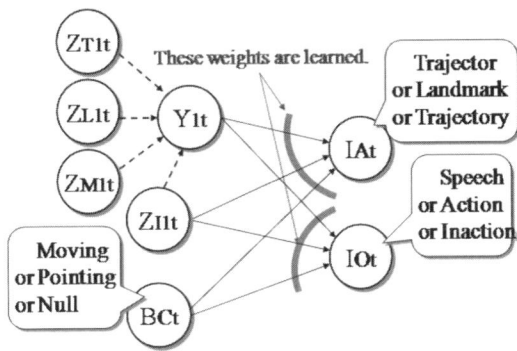

Fig. 4. Graphical model of user intention

the user's conceptual structure Z_{1t} is too complicated to learn communicative meaning effectively. Moreover, target object B_{O1t} depending on actually placed objects was not used for the same reason.

3.2.2 Response Constraint

We assumed that the robot responded with certainty on the basis of an inferred intention, and the response constraint was given manually. Specifically, if I_{Ot} was "SPEECH" and I_{At} was "LANDMARK", the robot determined Z_{L2t}, which is a word referring to a landmark object, and uttered it by using the shared belief function. If I_{At} was "TRAJECTOR" or "MOTION," the robot determined Z_{T2t} or Z_{M2t} and uttered those words. As I_{Ot} was "ACTION" and I_{At} was "MOTION," the robot moved an object on the basis of inferred topic A_t. As I_{Ot} was "ACTION" and I_{At} was "TRAJECTOR" or "LANDMARK," the robot pointed at the object indicated by I_{At}.

3.2.3 Learning Communicative Meaning

If the robot responded incorrectly, the user slapped the robot's hand and demonstrated an appropriate response. For example, if the user said "WHICH KERMIT?" and the robot said "KERMIT", the user pointed at Kermit after slapping its hand. The robot inferred Z_{2t} from the response and learned the conditional probabilities $p(I_{At}|Y_{1t}, Z_{I1t}, B_{C1t})$ and $p(I_{Ot}|Y_{1t}, Z_{I1t}, B_{C1t})$. The robot must learn all of the combinations of Y_{1t}, Z_{I1t}, and B_{C1t} for making a appropriate response. The calculation was approximated to enable the robot to learn with fewer samples as follows.

$$p(I_{At}|Y_{1t}, Z_{I1t}, B_{C1t})$$
$$\approx w_{A1} p(I_{At}|Y_{1t}) + w_{A1} p(I_{At}|Z_{I1t}) + w_{A1} p(I_{At}|B_{C1t}) \qquad (2)$$

$$p(I_{Ot}|Y_{1t}, Z_{I1t}, B_{C1t})$$
$$\approx w_{O1} p(I_{Ot}|Y_{1t}) + w_{O1} p(I_{Ot}|Z_{I1t}) + w_{O1} p(I_{Ot}|B_{C1t}) \qquad (3)$$

The probabilities $p(I_{At}|Y_{1t})$, $p(I_{At}|Z_{I1t})$, $p(I_{At}|B_{C1t})$, $p(I_{Ot}|Y_{1t})$, $p(I_{Ot}|Z_{I1t})$, $p(I_{Ot}|B_{C1t})$, weighting coefficient w_{A1}, w_{A2}, w_{A3}, w_{O1}, w_{O2}, and w_{O3} were estimated by the EM algorithm. Initially, $p(I_{At}|Y_{1t}, Z_{I1t}, B_{C1t})$ was a rectangular distribution, and $p(I_{Ot}|Y_{1t}, Z_{I1t}, B_{C1t})$ output "INACTION," which means the robot did nothing.

This paper assumes that words referring to objects or motions are learned beforehand. The words that were newly taught in the following experiments were considered as interrogative words. That is, a class of each word was given. Word class determination is a topic for future work.

4 Experiments

4.1 Experimental Conditions

The experiment was executed to confirm the validity of the proposed method. Seven objects were prepared, and three of them were put on the table. They were replaced by three new objects after the robot returned a correct response or the user demonstrated it. Motions fell into six categories: "MOVE OVER," "MOVE ONTO," "MOVE CLOSE TO," "MOVE AWAY," "MOVE UP," and "MOVE-CIRCLE."

User utterances came in three types: (1) Requests for Moving, (2) Questions with "WHAT" and (3) Questions with "WHICH".

(1) Requests for Moving were intended to make the robot move an object. The utterances had four types of phrase structures: "T-L-M," "T-M," "L-M," and "M." T, L, and M denote the presences of phrases referring to a trajector object, a landmark object, and a motion, respectively. For example, an utterance of "T-L-M" is "SMALL ELMO RED BOX MOVE ONTO."

(2) Questions with "WHAT" were intended to make the robot utter an object name. The object was indicated by a user utterance or pointing. The utterances with "WHAT" had four types of phrase structures: "I (+P)," "T-I-M (+M)," "I-L-M (+M)," and "I-M (+M)." "I" denotes an interrogative word. "(+P)" denotes that a user points at an object. "(+M)" denotes that a user moves an object. Thus, "I (+P)" means that a user points at an object and says "WHAT?" "I-L-M (+M)" means that a user moves an object and utters an interrogative word, words referring to the landmark object and a word referring to the motion. The correct response to "I-L-M (+M)" and "I-M (+M)" was to say the name of the trajector object. The correct response to "T-I-M (+M)" was to say the name of the landmark object.

(3) Questions with "WHICH" were intended to make the robot point at an object. The utterances had four types of phrase structures: "T-I," "T-I-M (+M)," "I-L-M (+M)," and "I-M (+M)." For example, an utterance of "T-I" was "ELMO WHICH?" that meant "Which is Elmo?" The correct response to "T-I" was to point at the object that was indicated by the user utterance. In the cases of "I-L-M (+M)" and "I M (+M)," the correct response was to point at the trajector object. In the case of "T-I-M (+M)," it was to point at the landmark object.

Twenty utterances each for types (1), (2), and (3) were prepared, and a total of sixty samples for the learning were given to the robot in the above order.

4.2 Experimental Results

The robot's responses in the experiment are shown in Fig. 5. The x-axis indicates time. The phrase structure of the utterance actually given by the user at each time is written under the axis. The y-axis represents types of responses. Gray boxes represent the correct responses to user utterances, and black circles represent the robot's actual responses. Black circles on gray boxes mean the robot correctly responded. The others mean the robot's response was incorrect, and the user taught a correct response.

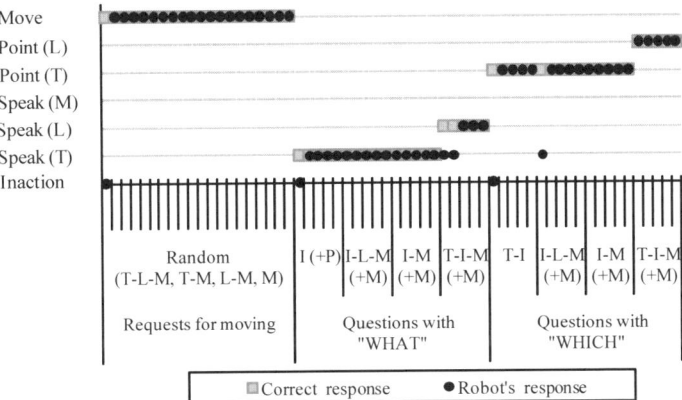

Fig. 5. Responses of robot to user utterances

4.2.1 Responses to Requests for Moving

At first, the robot did nothing because the initial $p(I_{Ot}|Y_{1t}, Z_{I1t}, B_{C1t})$ was set to output "INACTION." Then, the user taught the robot a correct response by moving the object. In the next turn, the robot correctly moved the object in accordance with the user's utterances. Utterances for requests had four types of phrase structures; however, the robot correctly responded regardless of the differences between these structures.

4.2.2 Responses to Questions with "WHAT"

When the user pointed at an object and said "WHAT?", after only one learning, the robot correctly responded as well as responding to motion requests. Then, the robot correctly responded to utterances of phrase structures "I-L-M (+M)" (e.g, "WHAT RED BOX MOVE ONTO?") and "I-M (+M)" (e.g, "WHAT MOVE ONTO?"). The robot always uttered the name of a trajector object when a user's utterance included "WHAT." This means the robot acquired a generalized response. However, the generalization caused wrong responses to "T-I-M(+M)." For example, when the user said "ELMO WHAT MOVE ONTO," the robot said "ELMO." The robot corrected the errors by learning correct responses twice.

4.2.3 Responses to Questions with "WHICH"

In the case of phrase structures "T-I" (e.g, "ELMO WHICH?"), the robot learned correct responses from only one example. However, unlike the previous case, the robot returned an incorrect response to "I-L-M(+M)." For example, the robot uttered the name of the trajector object when the user said "WHICH RED BOX MOVE-ONTO?" The reason was that the robot had already learned the response (that was to utter the object's name) to "I-L-M (+M)" through learning the response to "WHAT." After being taught to point at an object, the robot became capable of correctly responding to different phrase structures.

4.2.4 Change in Weighting Coefficients Caused by the Learning

As shown in Fig. 6, the change in the weighting coefficients (w_{A1}, w_{A2}, w_{A3}, w_{O1}, w_{O2} and w_{O3}), which were used for calculating $p(I_{At}|Y_{1t}, Z_{I1t}, B_{C1t})$ and $p(I_{Ot}|Y_{1t}, Z_{I1t}, B_{C1t})$, explains the generalization. The weights did not change until the middle stage of learning about questions with "WHAT" because Y_{1t}, Z_{I1t}, and B_{C1t} achieved correct responses. When "ELMO WHAT MOVE ONTO?", which caused two failures, was learned, first w_{A1}, w_{A2}, and w_{A3} were changed, and w_{A1} became the highest. This means the robot learned to determine attention I_{At} in accordance with phrase structure Y_{1t}. On the other hand, w_{O1}, w_{O2}, and w_{O3} were changed when "WHICH RED BOX MOVE ONTO?" was learned. As mentioned above, the robot responded with no distinction between "WHAT" and "WHICH" before learning this utterance. However, weight w_{O2} became the highest by learning it. This means the robot learned to determine the output modality I_{Ot} in accordance with interrogative words Z_{I1t}. That is, the robot learned that "WHAT" requested the robot to utter words and

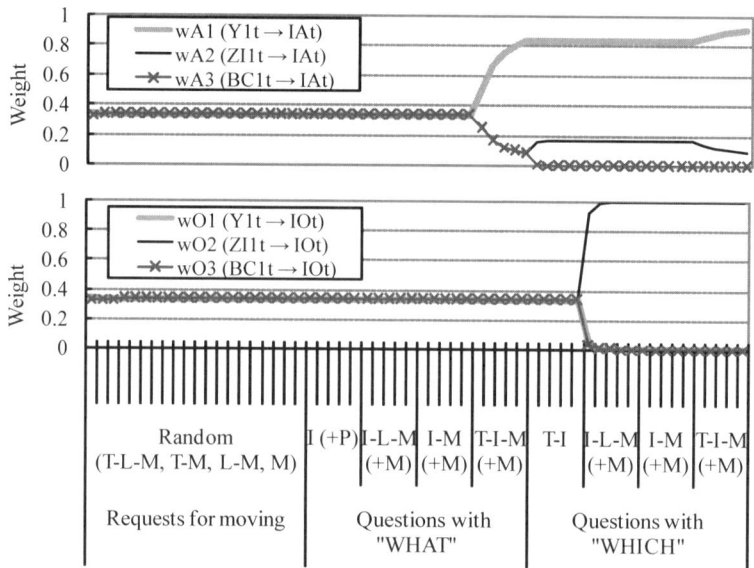

Fig. 6. Change in weighting coefficients

"WHICH" requested the robot to point at an object. By learning the weighting coefficients, the robot became capable of suitably responding to new questions such as "WHICH MOVE ONTO?" and "ELMO WHICH MOVE ONTO?"

4.2.5 Response Correct Rate

The percentage of correct responses of $p(I_{At}|Y_{1t}, Z_{I1t}, B_{C1t})$ and $p(I_{Ot}|Y_{1t}, Z_{I1t}, B_{C1t})$ is shown in Fig. 7. In each stage of learning, twelve different combinations of Y_{1t}, Z_{I1t} and B_{C1t}, which corresponded to all assumed requests and questions, were input. For each input, I_{At} and I_{Ot} were inferred as follows.

$$\tilde{I}_{At} = \arg\max_{I_{At}} p(I_{At}|Y_{1t}, Z_{I1t}, B_{C1t}) \qquad (4)$$

$$\tilde{I}_{Ot} = \arg\max_{I_{Ot}} p(I_{Ot}|Y_{1t}, Z_{I1t}, B_{C1t}) \qquad (5)$$

The percentage of correct responses was calculated from $\tilde{I}_{At}$ and $\tilde{I}_{Ot}$. For comparison, results of the combination model that normally calculated $p(I_{At}|Y_{1t}, Z_{I1t}, B_{C1t})$ and $p(I_{Ot}|Y_{1t}, Z_{I1t}, B_{C1t})$ by combining Y_{1t}, Z_{I1t} and B_{C1t} are also shown. This result shows the generalization capability of the proposed model was higher than that of the combination model. Moreover, it shows the correct responses were maintained even if new samples were learned.

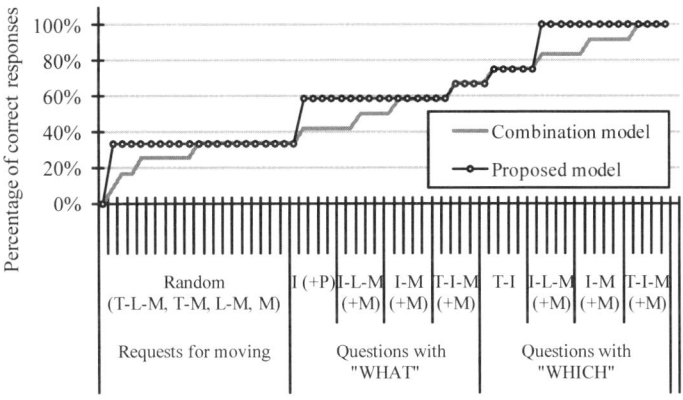

Fig. 7. Percentage of correct responses

5 Conclusion

This paper proposed a computational model that integrates descriptive meanings and communicative meanings and that enables a robot to learn the probabilistic relationship between a user's utterances and robot's responses as communicative meanings. In the experiment, the robot learned the meanings of interrogative words and the meanings of phrase structures of user utterances, and became capable of returning appropriate utterances and actions to the user. The experiment of inverting roles of the robot and the user is a topic for future work.

Acknowledgments. This work was supported by a research grant from the National Institute of Informatics.

References

1. Regier, T.: The Human Semantic Potential: Spatial Language and Constrained Connectionism. MIT Press, Cambridge (1996)
2. Akaho, S., Hasegawa, O., Yoshimura, T., Asoh, H., Hayamizu, S.: Concept acquisition from multiple information sources by the EM algorithm. IEICE Trans. J80-A(9), 1546–1553 (1997)
3. Steels, L., Kaplan, K.: AIBO's first words: the social learning of language and meaning. Evolution of Communication 4(1), 3–32 (2001)
4. Roy, D., Pentland, A.: Learning Words from Sights and Sounds: A Computational Model. Cognitive Science 26(1), 113–146 (2002)
5. Yu, C., Ballard, D.: On the Integration of Grounding Language and Learning Objects. In: Proc. 19th National Conference on Artificial Intelligence (AAAI), pp. 488–494 (2004)
6. Iwahashi, N.: Robots That Learn Language: A Developmental Approach to Situated Human-Robot Conversations. In: Sankar, N. (ed.) Human-Robot Interaction, pp. 95–118. I-Tech Education and Publishing (2007)

Towards Coordination of Multiple Machine Translation Services

Rie Tanaka[1,2,*], Toru Ishida[1,2], and Yohei Murakami[2]

[1] Department of Social Informatics, Kyoto University, Kyoto, 6068501, Japan
[2] National Institute of Information and Communications Technology (NICT), Kyoto, 6190289, Japan

Abstract. Machine translation services available on the Web are getting increasingly popular. Multiple translation services are often combined for intercultural communication. Furthermore, since English is most frequently used as a hub language, it is often necessary to cascade different translation services to realize translations between non-English languages. As a result, the word sense is often changed because of the inconsistency, asymmetry, and intransitivity of word selections between machine translation services. Therefore, we propose a context-based coordination framework in which the context is propagated among cascaded translation services by referring to multilingual equivalent terms. By considering machine translation services as black boxes, we achieve substantial quality improvements through Web service coordination.

Keywords: Context-based coordination, Web services, Machine translations, Service composition architectures.

1 Introduction

The number of languages used in Web pages has increased rapidly in recent times. Of all Internet users, people who use English on the Internet now comprise 30%; Asian languages, including Chinese, Japanese, and Korean, 26%; European languages, excluding English, 25%; and all other languages, 20% [1]. This trend necessitates translation between non-English languages in addition to between English and non-English languages. For example, the EU, which has 23 official languages, stipulates that all official documents need to be translated to all official languages. The publisher has to translate a new document to the remaining 22 languages before publishing it.

In a separate development, the number of online translation services available on the Web has also increased rapidly. This development enables people to access machine translation services easily and encourages intercultural communication

---

[*] This author now works for C&C Innovation Research Laboratories, NEC Corporation. This collaborative research was conducted between NICT and Kyoto University when the author was affiliated to both institutes.
[1] The latest estimation of Internet users by language, carried out in May 2008 by Internet World Stats; see: http://www.internetworldstats.com/stats7.htm

and collaboration among people with different first languages. However, it is almost impossible to develop translation services between every two languages. To cover all pairs among n languages, the development of $n(n-1)$ direct machine translation services is required, which is costly and probably impossible.

For translations between languages for which no direct translation services are available, the most practical solution would be to combine multiple machine translation services to achieve this. Since English is a hub language for the development of translation services or other resources such as bilingual dictionaries, which are developed between English and non-English languages, translation between various languages can be achieved by using English as an intermediate language; in particular, a combination of translation services via English is essential to translate Asian languages into European ones, excluding English. In fact, the development of machine translators for conducting translations between Asian languages is insufficient, and a combination of translators via English is required for even Asian languages.

In view of the increasing language resources such as machine translators or bilingual dictionaries, the Language Grid Project [Ishida 06] practices activities that require the application and coordination of such resources, for overcoming the language and cultural barriers and realizing worldwide intercultural collaboration. As an example of such activities, in a junior high school where many foreign students study with Japanese students, the communication between Japanese teachers and foreign students in the Japanese language class and between Japanese teachers and the parents of the foreign students are supported by machine translators and collaboration tools. Japanese-Portuguese translation for Brazilian students in this school is achieved by combining Japanese-English and English-Portuguese translators, because there are few direct Japanese-Portuguese translators available.

2 Necessity of the Coordination of Composite Web Services

The impact of machine translators on communication has already been analyzed in the course of the activities of the Language Grid Project, and it was realized that problems in the communication process occur when multiple translators are combined [Yamashita and Ishida 06]. Even in combining multiple machine translators, there are initial problems pertaining to the consistency of input and output data type of each translator. However, cascaded machine translators often lead to mistranslations even if all the machine translators are combined correctly. Since how each machine translator analyzes and selects the translated words for the input sentence is not considered by the other translators in the combination, the sense of the translated sentence can change in the process of the cascaded translations. Such a change is caused by inconsistent word selections. An analysis in Yamashita and Ishida revealed that there are two phenomena that cause mistranslations: *asymmetry* and *inconsistency* of word selections. In machine translation-mediated communication, the echoing of a statement is disrupted by asymmetries, and the formation of referring expressions of the same object is disrupted by inconsistencies; this means that confirmation or agreement is difficult to achieve. For example, in Japanese-German-Japanese translation (often referred to as back translation), "octopus" is translated to "squid," which is an obvious error. Moreover, such problems are not limited to communication. When translating sentences by multi-hop translation using cascading multiple translators, we may not be able to achieve the correct translation results because the sense of the words may change.

We aim to resolve these problems by not just combining multiple machine translation services but also by coordinating them with the context of the sentences. In the field of machine translation, researchers in natural language processing use linguistic annotation to embed the lexical and syntactic information of a source sentence into the translated sentence [Kanayama and Watababe 03]. However, since the users of online translation services cannot manipulate the translation process of the underlying system and are also unaware of the functioning of the translation services, they must await the application of the proposed technology to all translation services. A more practical solution would be to coordinate the existing machine translation services. Mistranslation results when the context of the target sentence is not retained during sequential translation. Thus the context-based coordination of Web services is required to keep a consistent sence of the sentence.

The primary focus of several researches in the field of Web service composition has been the automation of the service composition ([Hassine et al. 06], [Traverso and Pistore 04] and [Wu et al. 03]). *WS-BPEL* (Web Services Business Process Execution Language)[2], one of the specifications for Web service composition, can combine Web services by matching input and output data types. On the basis of the previous researches that utilized planning technologies, the consistency of the input and output of Web services is guaranteed [Liu et al. 07]. However, the primary concern in the composition of machine translation services is not the issue of their combination by inspecting the input and output data types. The *WS-Coordination* (Web Services Coordination)[3] specification propagates the service ID or the port to other services as a "CoordinationContext." This idea can be extended to the context propagation across translation services. This study refers to such technologies and addresses the following issues.

Developing multilingual equivalent terms
In order to maintain the consistency of the sense of each translated sentence generated in each language, we propose a method to obtain multilingual equivalent terms in all the languages used. Equivalent terms among more than two languages are developed manually among some parts of the languages. Therefore, this research aims to automatically generate multilingual equivalent terms from the existing language resources.

Coordinating translation services by propagating the context
Maintaining consistency in the sense of the translated sentence is achieved by extracting the context of the sentence or the document containing it,

---
[2] http://www.ibm.com/developerworks/library/ws-bpel/
[3] http://www-106.ibm.com/developerworks/library/ws-coor

propagating the context among the translation services, and enabling these services to select the translated words that suit the propagated context. This study assumes that the context has already been extracted by some method and focuses on the coordination by propagating the extracted context.

This research does not propose a new machine translation technology. Instead, it aims to substantially improve the translation quality by realizing the context-based coordination of Web services, while considering the internal translation process of each translation service as a black box. The advantage of this approach is that high-quality translations can be achieved from the existing services without modifying their internal coding system.

3 Issues and Analysis of Composite Machine Translation Services

3.1 Examples of Issues in Machine Translation-Mediated Communication

Problems occurring in cascaded machine translators are classified into three categories: inconsistency, asymmetry, and intransitivity of word selections. *Inconsistency* is the phenomenon in which the translated words of the same source word vary in different sentences. *Asymmetry* is the phenomenon in which the back-translated word is different from the source word. These issues are also addressed by Yamashita and Ishida [Yamashita and Ishida 06]. *Intransitivity* is the phenomenon in which the word sense differs across machine translators. Fig. 1 illustrates some examples of the problems in combined machine translation services. All the sentences in this paper are presented in English; the original Japanese and German sentences are indicated in parentheses.

Fig. 1(a) illustrates an example of inconsistency in word selection. The English word "paper" is translated to the Japanese word for "thesis" (ronbun) in case 1, while it is translated to "paper" (kami) in case 2. An example of asymmetry in word selection is presented in Fig. 1(b). In the first step of the machine translation-mediated communication, the Japanese word for "party" (pa-thi-), which means a social gathering, is translated to English correctly. However, when an English user subsequently uses the word "party," it is translated to the Japanese word for "political party" (tou). This mistranslation occurs because the English word "party" can mean both. An example of intransitivity in word selection is presented in Fig. 1(c). The Japanese word for "fault" (ketten), which implies a weakness in character, is translated to English correctly; however, it is mistranslated to the German word for "responsibility" (Schuld) because the intermediate English word "fault" has several meanings, and the English-German translator does not have any knowledge pertaining to the context of the preceding Japanese-English translation.

The example including both asymmetry and intransitivity is presented in Fig. 1(d). This is an example of a Japanese-German back translation generated by combining Japanese-English, English-German, German-English, and

⟨ Case 1 ⟩
  Source sentence (English): Please add that picture in this paper.
  ⇒ Translation (Japanese): Please add that picture in this thesis.
              (douzo, sono shashin wo kono ronbun no naka ni tsuika shinasai.)
⟨ Case 2 ⟩
  Source sentence (English): Please send me this paper.
  ⇒ Translation (Japanese): Please send me this paper.
              (douzo, kono kami wo watashi ni okuri nasai.)

(a) Inconsistency in word selection

Japanese user (Japanese): We had a party yesterday.
              (kinou watashi tachi ha pa-thi- wo sita.)
⇒ Translation (English): There was a party yesterday.
English user (English): How was the party?
⇒ Translation (Japanese): How was the political party?
              (tou ha doudesita ka?)

(b) Asymmetry in word selection

Source sentence (Japanese): Her fault is a big problem.
              (kanojo no ketten ha ookina mondai da.)
⇒ Translation (English): Her fault is a big problem.
⇒ Translation (German): Her responsibility is a big problem.
              (Ihre Schuld ist ein großes Problem.)

(c) Intransitivity in word selection

Source sentence (Japanese): Please get an octopus for the dinner of today.
              (kyo no yusyoku no tame ni tako wo katte kite kudasai.)
⇒ Translation (English): Please get octopus for today's dinner.
⇒ Translation (German): Please get cephalopods* for the dinner of today.
              (Besorge Tintenfisch für das Abendessen von heute bitte.)
⇒ Translation (English): Please procure squid for the dinner of today.
⇒ Translation (Japanese): Please procure squid for the dinner of today.
              (douzo, kyo no dina no tame ni ika wo nyusyu sinasai.)

* "cephalopod" is a type of animal such as squid, octopus, etc.

(d) An example including both asymmetry and intransitivity in word selection

Fig. 1. Issues in composite machine translation services

English-Japanese translation services. Back translation is frequently used to examine the quality of translation. In order to translate between various languages, in many cases, we have to combine several translation services. In Fig. 1(d), first, the Japanese source word for "octopus" (tako) is translated correctly to the English word "octopus" by Japanese-English translation. Second, in the English-German translation, the translated German word for "cephalopod" (Tintenfisch)—meaning a type of animal such as octopus, squid, and nautilus—is selected. Although this selection of words is not necessarily incorrect, it results in the inappropriate selection of the English word "squid" by extracting the meaning of squid in the next step of the cascaded translation. Therefore, the back-translated Japanese word "squid" (ika) is different from the source word "octopus" (tako).

Although the technology to select the most appropriate words for the source sentence is important, if these phenomena occur in situations such as a multi-hop translation or a translation-mediated chat, it becomes difficult to continue with the conversation. Inconsistency and asymmetry can occur in various situations besides conversations. Moreover, it can be stated that all problems depicted in Fig. 1 result from inconsistency in word selection.

3.2 Analysis of an Issue

Fig. 2 is the conceptual picture illustrating how each translated word was selected in the example shown in Fig. 1(d). The words are presented in circles, and concepts, in squares. This conceptual picture is obtained using bilingual dictionaries. For instance, the Japanese-English dictionary describes the Japanese word for "octopus/kite/etc." (tako) as a type of animal as well as a type of toy, and the English word "octopus" is shown as the translated word for "tako" as a type of

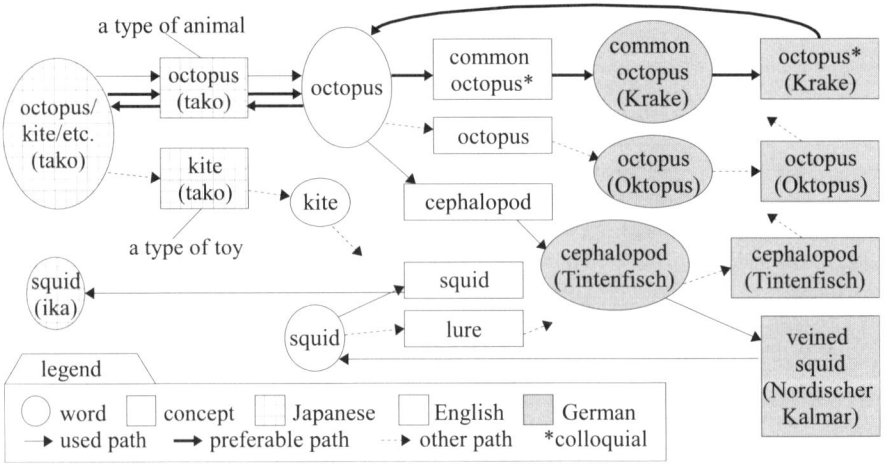

Fig. 2. Conceptual picture illustrating the translation of the word "octopus"

animal. Parts of words and concepts related to the translation in the above example are selected from the Japanese-English, English-German, German-English, and English-Japanese dictionaries and are shown in Fig. 2. The solid arrows indicate the path consisting of words and concepts routed in each translation, and the bold arrows indicate the preferable path. Although the translated words are directly combined with the source words within the actual translation services, it is supposed that such selections of words and concepts are done conceptually.

In Fig. 1(d), in the English-German and German-English translations, the concept of "cephalopod" was selected for the English word "octopus"; the German word "cephalopod" (Tintenfisch) was selected for the concept; and the concept of "veined squid" (Nordischer Kalmar), which is a type of squid, was selected for the German word. As a result, the meaning of the translated words was changed from octopus to squid. In contrast, in the path indicated by bold arrows, the meaning was kept consistent. In order to realize such consistent selection, a translation mechanism that considers the correspondence across all languages—and not just between two languages—is required.

4 Framework of Context-Based Coordination

We propose a framework in which each translation service propagates a context-referring multilingual dictionary, as shown in Fig. 3. The usual translation services output translated sentences by referring only to the input sentences. Such services are wrapped in such a way that they generate translated sentences as outputs after considering the context of the input sentence in addition to the sentence itself, and output both translated sentences and the contexts of them. The composition of such wrapped services enables the generation of translated sentences within the propagated context. Since different translation services handle different languages, a multilingual dictionary is required when interpreting the propagated context. Multilingual dictionaries consist of multilingual equivalent terms, and each translated word in each language is obtained for a single word. The information regarding the equivalent terms in the multilingual dictionaries facilitate the interpretation of the context. The following sections describe the method of generating multilingual equivalent terms and present the overview of the framework of coordinating the translation services with these terms.

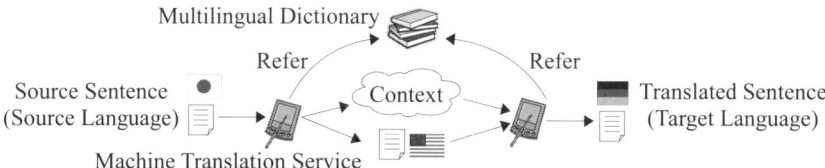

Fig. 3. Overview of the context-based coordination of translation services

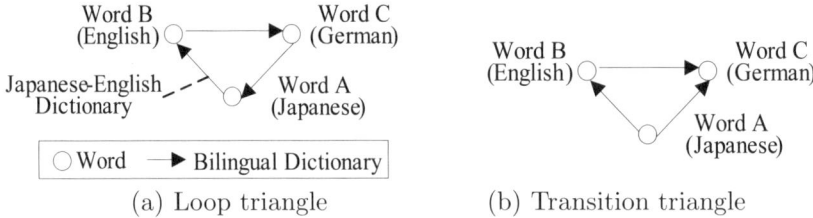

Fig. 4. Two types of the shapes of triples

5 Generating Multilingual Equivalent Terms

The set of equivalent terms can be generated by analyzing generic bilingual dictionaries. Multilingual equivalent terms can also be developed manually, as in the case of EuroWordNet [Vossen 1998]. In addition, there is a multilingual dictionary that includes a few thousand basic words in twenty-six languages [Bergman 1981]. However, it is costly difficult to manually develop multilingual dictionaries that include all words in all languages required for regular conversations. Hence, we require an automated method to develop such a dictionary.

In the previous work on this subject, the concepts in different languages were matched using bilingual dictionaries [Tokunaga and Tanaka 1990]. We extend this idea and formulate a method to generate a set of trilingual equivalent terms (hereafter referred to as a *triple*). We represent the mapping of words belonging to different languages in the form of a graph: a word is represented as a vertex, and a mapping in bilingual dictionaries is represented as a directed edge. If the graph contains a triangle, the three words are considered to be equivalent terms.

Fig. 4 presents the two types of triangles, namely, *loop* and *transition* triangles. The loop triangle is formed by beginning from a source language, looking up dictionaries three times, and returning to the source language. The transition triangle is formed by starting from a source language and looking up dictionaries to locate the transitive and direct routes between the source and target languages. It is easy to generate a triple from such triangles.

Example 1 (A loop triangle representing the sense of "sky")
Fig. 5 illustrates an example of a loop triangle, beginning with the Japanese word for "sky/heaven/midair" (sora). Words such as "sky" and "air" are extracted as the translated words by looking up a Japanese-English dictionary. The German word for "sky/heaven" (Himmel) is obtained by looking up the word "sky" in an English-German dictionary. Since the Japanese word for "sky/heaven/midair" (sora) is extracted from a German-Japanese dictionary, {sky/heaven/midair (sora), sky, sky/heaven (Himmel)} is considered as a triple. Continuing this process further yields the triple {sky/heaven/midair (sora), air, midair (Luft)}.

In the related research field of dictionary formulation, Tanaka and Umemura proposed a method for developing a bilingual dictionary by using a third language as an intermediate [Tanaka and Umemura 94]. This study addresses the

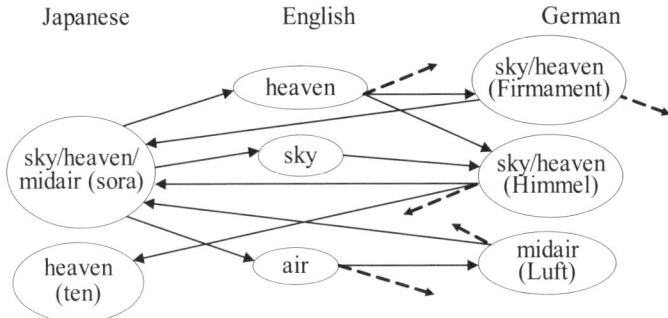

Fig. 5. Example of a loop triangle representing the sense of "sky"

problems in automatically generating a new bilingual dictionary by combining the existing dictionaries. Our research focuses on the method of obtaining more reliable equivalent terms when dictionaries for each pair of languages are available; moreover, our research differs from that of Tanaka and Umemura in terms of its assumption and objective. In order to develop composite machine translation services even when a sufficient number of dictionaries are not available, the methods proposed by them are required to obtain the equivalent terms.

6 Context-Based Coordination with Propagated Context

6.1 Method of Achieving Context-Based Coordination

The detailed process of coordinating with the propagated context is illustrated in Fig. 6, and the algorithm corresponding with the process, in Fig. 7. Machine translation services are considered as black boxes receiving input sentences and outputting translated sentences. Coordination can be realized by extracting the

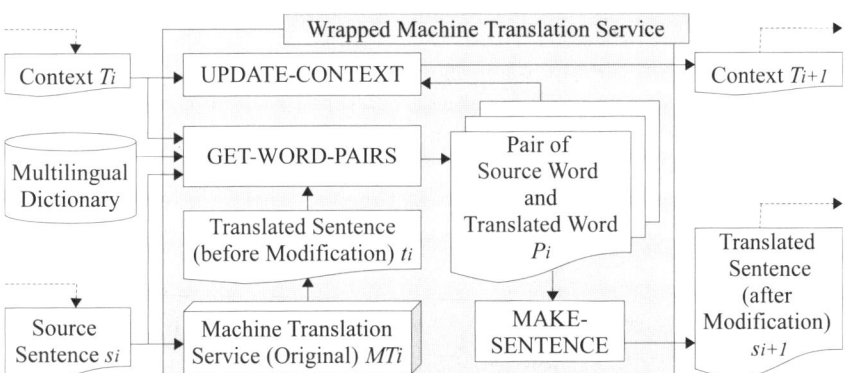

Fig. 6. Detailed process of coordination

Algorithm. COORDINATE-TRANSLATION-SERVICES(MT, s_1) **return** s_{n+1}

1:    MT /* An ordered list of cascaded machine translation services combined ($MT = \{MT_1, MT_2, ..., MT_n\}$) */
2:    s_i /* Original input sentence of MT_i */
3:    t_i /* Output sentence of MT_i ($t_i \neq s_{i+1}$) */
4:    $MT_i = (s_i, t_i)$ /* An original machine translation service; a set of pairs of s_i and t_i */
5:    T_i /* A set of n-tuples $(w_1, ..., w_n)$, where w_k is included in $s_k (k \leq i)$; All n-tuples are registered in n-Lingual Dictionary */
6:    P_i /* A set of pairs (o_i, o_{i+1}), where $o_i \in s_i$ and $o_{i+1} \in s_{i+1}$, modified translated word of o_i */
7:
8:    $T_1 \leftarrow \{(w_1, ..., w_n) | w_1 \in s_1\}$
9:    **for each** MT_i **in** MT **do**
10:       $t_i \leftarrow MT_i(s_i)$
11:       $P_i \leftarrow$ GET-WORD-PAIRS(s_i, t_i)
12:       $s_{i+1} \leftarrow$ MAKE-SENTENCE(P_i)
13:       $T_{i+1} \leftarrow$ UPDATE-CONTEXT(T_i, P_i)
14:    **end loop**
15:    **return** s_{n+1}

Fig. 7. Algorithms for the coordination of translation services with the context

inappropriately translated words in the output sentences of the translation services by referring to the propagated context and replacing these words with the appropriate ones. The translation service and the process of extracting words and modifying them are wrapped as a new translation service. Wrapped services are connected in runtime. The *context* in Fig. 6 refers to the meaning of the source sentence or of the document including the sentence (this type of context is generally referred to as "context"). The latter type of context, that is, the meaning of the document, enables the consistent translation in not only one sentence but also across whole documents or a sequence of sentences in chats.

In the translation processes within the wrapped service, the original translation service translates the input sentence first. In the algorithm shown in Fig. 7, the ith translation service MT_i is defined as a set of pairs of the source sentence s_i and the translated sentence t_i, and the translated sentence without any check or modification is obtained (in line 10). Then, each translated word in t_i is examined, and if its meaning is inappropriate in the propagated context, it is replaced by an appropriate word, and the pairs of source words and modified translated words are generated. This sequence of processes is represented by "GET-WORD-PAIRS" (in line 11). Thereafter, the modified translated sentence s_{i+1}, which is the input sentence of the next service, is generated by the "MAKE-SENTENCE" process. The context T_i is updated by the "UPDATE-CONTEXT" process, in which the modified translated words are used.

In this algorithm, the context is represented by a set of n-tuples, which is a set of equivalent terms in n languages, and each word in one n-tuple is in each language. For example, 3-tuple (triple) in Japanese, English, and German is represented as {octopus(tako), octopus, octopus(Krake)}. For instance, the meaning of a sentence can be represented by a set of the meanings of the words included in it. The multilingual translation with the propagated context is realized by using a set of n-tuples as a context, in which one of the words in each n-tuple is included in the source sentence, as each n-tuple has the same meaning of the words in the source sentence. At the beginning of the translation, n-tuples including words of the source sentence are set as T_1. There can be multiple n-tuples including the same source word, and if a word is not included in T_i, it is replaced by using one of the candidate n-tuples selected in some way, and the context T_i is narrowed down after the translation so as to include the used translated words. There are many ways of selection, for instance, by referring to the term frequency or the priority of the words. This is the simplest method of maintaining the context, and if some methods of extracting the context from the translated sentence—a technology used in the field of natural language processing—are available, we can obtain more natural results of translation.

6.2 Example of Coordination and Evaluation

We implemented the multilingual dictionary by using the method proposed in Section 5 and executed context-based multilingual translation by referring to the algorithm presented in Section 6.1. In the development of a dictionary and the implementation of translation, we used existing reliable dictionaries such as the Oxford dictionaries and the existing machine translation services available on the Web. We used Japanese, English, and German and limited the parts of speech of words to be modified to nouns.

Example 2 (Translation of a sentence shown in Fig. 1(d))
Table 1 shows an example of a translation of the sentence shown in Fig. 1(d) with the propagated context. In this example, the simplest representation of the context is used, where the context is a set of triples in Japanese, English, and German. This table only shows the triples related to the translation of the word "octopus" (tako). At first, before beginning a translation, a set of triples including the source words in the Japanese source sentence is set as the context T_1. The Japanese word "tako" has several meanings as shown in Fig. 2, and both triples—meaning of the animal and the toy—are included in T_1. The word "cephalopod" (Tintenfisch), which resulted in a mistranslation, is not included in T_1, because the English word "octopus" is not provided as the translated word of "cephalopod" (Tintenfisch) in many German-English dictionaries; moreover, the triple {octopus (tako), octopus, cephalopod (Tintenfisch)} is not obtained by using our method of generating the set of triples.

In the first Japanese-English translation, the source sentence s_1 = "Please get an octopus for the dinner of today" (kyo no yusyoku no tame ni tako wo katte kite kudasai) is translated to English. The corresponding source words and translated words can be obtained, for instance, by conducting a morphological analysis and using a bilingual dictionary, and the pair of "octopus" (tako) and

Table 1. Example of coordinated translation

First translation: Japanese to English

Sentence	s_1 = Please get an octopus for the dinner of today. (kyo no yusyoku no tame ni tako wo katte kite kudasai.) → t_1 = Please get octopus for today's dinner.
Translation	octopus (tako) → octopus
Modification	(none)
Context	T_1 = {{octopus (tako), octopus, common octopus (Krake)}, {octopus (tako), octopus, octopus (Oktopus)}, {kite (tako), kite, kite (Drachen)}...}
Result	s_2 = Please get octopus for today's dinner.

Second translation: English to German

Sentence	s_2 = Please get octopus for today's dinner. → t_2 = Please get cephalopods for the dinner of today. (Besorge Tintenfisch für das Abendessen von heute bitte.)
Translation	octopus → cephalopod (Tintenfisch)
Modification	octopus → common octopus (Krake)
Context	T_2 = {{octopus (tako), octopus, common octopus (Krake)}, {octopus (tako), octopus, octopus (Oktopus)}}
Result	s_3 = Please get common octopus for the dinner of today. (Besorge Kraken für das Abendessen von heute bitte.)

Third translation: German to English

Sentence	s_3 = Please get common octopus for the dinner of today. (Besorge Kraken für das Abendessen von heute bitte.) → t_3 = Please procure octopus for the dinner of today.
Translation	octopus (Kraken) → octopus
Modification	(none)
Context	T_3 = {{octopus (tako), octopus, common octopus (Krake)}}
Result	s_4 = Please procure octopus for the dinner of today.

Fourth translation: English to Japanese

Sentence	s_4 = Please procure octopus for the dinner of today. → t_4 = Please procure octopus for the dinner of today. (douzo, kyo no dina no tame ni tako wo nyusyu sinasai.)
Translation	octopus → octopus (tako)
Modification	(none)
Context	T_4 = {{octopus (tako), octopus, common octopus (Krake)}}
Result	s_5 = Please procure octopus for the dinner of today. (douzo, kyo no dina no tame ni tako wo nyusyu sinasai.)

"octopus" is obtained. Since the English word "octopus" is included in T_1, it is considered as the correct word and no modification is executed. After all the translated words are determined, the context T_1 is updated to T_2, so as to include the triples including the word "octopus" (tako) and "octopus" only. The triples including the word "kite" (tako) are eliminated in this step.

In the second English-German translation, the source sentence $s_2 =$ "Please get octopus for today's dinner" is translated as "Please get cephalopods for the dinner of today" (Besorge Tintenfisch für das Abendessen von heute bitte). When examining the pair of "octopus" and "cephalopod" (Tintenfisch), the German word is considered to be inappropriate because it is not included in the context T_2. It is replaced by the word included in T_2, namely, "common octopus" (Krake), assuming that the first triple {octopus (tako), octopus, common octopus (Krake)} is selected. The translated sentence is revised as "Please get common octopus for the dinner of today" (Besorge Kraken für das Abendessen von heute bitte). The context T_2 is narrowed down to T_3. The third and fourth translation processes are executed in the same manner by checking whether the translated words are included in the context and modifying them if necessary.

We conducted a preliminary evaluation of the quality of the Japanese-German back translation by using the cascade of Japanese-English, English-German, German-English, and English-Japanese translations. The above example is one of the outputs of the cascaded translation services. We verified the sense of the Japanese source sentence and the back-translated sentence and confirmed that the quality of the translated sentence was improved considerably by comparing it with the translated sentence obtained without context-based coordination.

7 Conclusion

This study addressed the issues of cascaded multiple machine translation services and the *inconsistency*, *asymmetry*, and *intransitivity* in word selection among these services, and proposed a method for their coordination with the context to overcome these issues. Considering the internal translation process of each machine translation service as a black box, an improvement in translation quality was realized. The major aspects of our proposed method are summarized below.

Developing multilingual equivalent terms
In order to examine whether the sense of a translated sentence is different from that of the source sentence, the equivalent terms in all languages are required. We regarded the contents of bilingual dictionaries as the data of the bilingual equivalent terms and proposed a method of combining such data to obtain equivalent terms in more than two languages.

Coordinating translation services by propagating the context
In order to maintain the consistency of the sense of the translated sentence, we proposed a framework of coordination of the translation services wherein these translation services were considered as black boxes, and the obtained results of the translation were verified and modified outside them.

This improvement is significant in the domain of intercultural collaboration, which employs the technology of natural language processing or machine translation. Moreover, it will play an important role in the field of Web service composition, which is required in various areas, as well as in the technologies of each Web service.

References

[Ishida 06] Ishida, T.: Language Grid: An Infrastructure for Intercultural Collaboration. In: IEEE/IPSJ Symposium on Applications and the Internet (SAINT 2006), keynote address, pp. 96–100 (2006)

[Yamashita and Ishida 06] Yamashita, N., Ishida, T.: Effects of Machine Translation on Collaborative Work. In: International Conference on Computer Supported Cooperative Work (CSCW 2006), pp. 515–523 (2006)

[Kanayama and Watababe 03] Kanayama, H., Watanabe, H.: Multilingual Translation via Annotated Hub Language. In: MT-Summit IX, pp. 202–207 (2003)

[Hassine et al. 06] Ben Hassine, A., Matsubara, S., Ishida, T.: A constraint-based approach to horizontal web service composition. In: Cruz, I., Decker, S., Allemang, D., Preist, C., Schwabe, D., Mika, P., Uschold, M., Aroyo, L.M. (eds.) ISWC 2006. LNCS, vol. 4273, pp. 130–143. Springer, Heidelberg (2006)

[Traverso and Pistore 04] Traverso, P., Pistore, M.: Automated composition of semantic web services into executable processes. In: McIlraith, S.A., Plexousakis, D., van Harmelen, F. (eds.) ISWC 2004. LNCS, vol. 3298, pp. 380–394. Springer, Heidelberg (2004)

[Wu et al. 03] Wu, D., Parsia, B., Sirin, E., Hendler, J., Nau, D.S.: Automating DAML-S Web Services Composition Using SHOP2. In: Fensel, D., Sycara, K.P., Mylopoulos, J. (eds.) ISWC 2003. LNCS, vol. 2870, pp. 195–210. Springer, Heidelberg (2003)

[Liu et al. 07] Liu, Z., Ranganathan, A., Riabov, A.V.: A Planning Approach for Message-Oriented Semantic Web Service Composition. In: AAAI 2007, pp. 1389–1394 (2007)

[Vossen 1998] Vossen, P. (ed.): EuroWordNet: A Multilingual Database with Lexical Semantic Networks. Kluwer, Dordrecht (1998), http://www.hum.uva.nl/~ewn/

[Bergman 1981] Bergman, P.M.: The Concise Dictionary of Twenty-Six Languages in Simultaneous Translations. Avenel Books, New York (1981)

[Tokunaga and Tanaka 1990] Tokunaga, T., Tanaka, H.: The Automatic Extraction of Conceptual Items from Bilingual Dictionaries. In: PRICAI 1990, pp. 304–309 (1990)

[Tanaka and Umemura 94] Tanaka, K., Umemura, K.: Construction of a Bilingual Dictionary Intermediated by a Third Language. In: COLING 1994, pp. 293–303 (1994)

Ranking Method of Object-Attribute-Evaluation Three-Tuples for Opinion Retrieval

Masaaki Tsuchida, Hironori Mizuguchi, and Dai Kusui

Common Platform Software Research Laboratories, NEC Corporation.
8916-47, Takayama-cho, Ikoma, Nara, 630-0101, Japan
{m-tsuchida@cq,hironori@ab,kusui@ct}.jp.nec.com

Abstract. In this paper, we propose a ranking method for opinion retrieval that uses a confidence model of opinion as a three-tuple of *object-attribute-evaluation*. The confidence model has two characteristics for calculating confidence scores. One, the model divides a three-tuple of an opinion into two pairs: object-attribute and attribute-evaluation. Two, the confidence model evaluates an opinion simultaneously using syntactic and semantic analyses. Our experiments show that our method improves the precision of the top fifty opinions in search results by ranking based on our confidence compared with random ranking.

Keywords: opinion retrieval, opinion confidence, ranking.

1 Introduction

Due to the Internet's ubiquity, people feel comfortable posting messages on web sites, especially on their own weblogs. The popularity of weblog services continues to rise, and currently a huge amount of weblog articles is available. If a system were to automatically extract opinions from such documents, we could exploit these opinions for such various purposes as consumer purchase assistance, marketing research, and risk management.

In our previous work, we developed a system that automatically extracts and retrieves opinions from weblog articles by defining an opinion as an (*Object, Attribute, Evaluation*) three-tuple relation with subjectivity [7,8]. *Object* refers to the brand or service names. *Attribute* is a property or a part of an Object, and *Evaluation* is the positive/negative expression that judges the Attribute of the Object. For example, "The [Attribute: design] of [Object: iPhone] is [Evaluation: good]."

In this system, when a user gives a keyword (an object), it works as follows: i) the system searches for the keyword position using a full text index and ii) extracts the attribute-evaluation pairs located close to the keyword (more specifically within n characters). All attribute-evaluation pairs were extracted beforehand by a classification approach by machine learning and stored in the database as a back-end process.

However, not all of the extracted attribute-evaluation pairs are correct; some contain extraction errors. In addition, even if the distance between the keyword and the attribute-evaluation pair is small, it is not always true that the attribute-evaluation pair semantically indicates the keyword. Therefore, without a ranking strategy, the system might offer users incorrect opinions on the top level of the search results.

In this paper, we propose a ranking method that gives confidence scores of extracted opinions for opinion retrieval. The confidence is the degree of the likelihood of an extracted opinion.

Implementation might seem very simple using the output of the subjectivity classification model [8] (learned by Support Vector Machine (SVM) [1] using the contextual features of attribute-evaluation pairs) to extract attribute-evaluation pairs.

However, this simple approach has three problems. First, the system does not consider the semantic preferences between an attribute and an evaluation. For example, "[attribute: design] - [evaluation: beautiful]" is better than "[attribute: design] - [evaluation: delicious]" with regard to semantic preference, because "beautiful" is a much more natural linguistic expression than "delicious" to evaluate "design." Second, the system fails to consider whether the extracted attribute is an attribute of the object, because it merely extracts an object-attribute relation when the number of characters between an object and an attribute is less than a pre-defined threshold. Third, the system does not consider whether an extracted object-attribute pair is actually related to the text. For instance, extracting "iPhone - design - bad" from "iPhone's design is good, but my cellphone's design is bad" is wrong.

Considering these three problems, we designed our method to score high confidence when an opinion has both high syntax and semantics scores. *Syntactic confidence* is calculated based on i) the distance between an object and an attribute in the text and ii) the output value of the subjectivity classification model to extract an attribute-evaluation pair. *Semantic confidence* is calculated using a word co-occurrence probability. Our system estimates the co-occurrence probability of two words using many extracted word co-occurrences from a large corpus.

Subsequently, we describe an overview of our previous opinion retrieval system [8] in Section 2. In Section 3, we explain our method to score opinion confidence, and in Section 4, we evaluate our method with an experiment and describe the evaluated results. In Section 5, we discuss problems of our method and improvements. Finally, we conclude and summarize our paper in Section 6.

2 Opinion Retrieval System: eHyouban

Our previous opinion retrieval system named eHyouban [8] can be divided into a back-end and a front-end. Fig. 1 shows the architecture of eHyouban, which can retrieve the opinions of arbitrary objects (given by users as keywords) from weblog articles in Japanese.

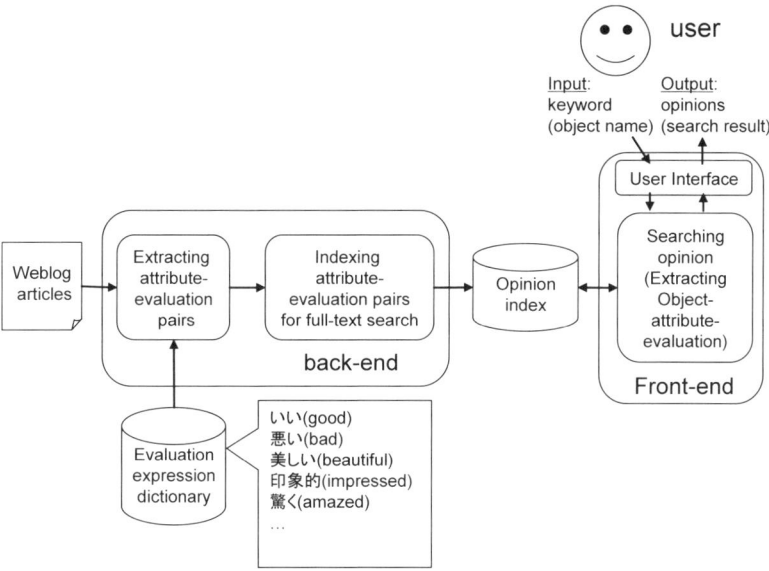

Fig. 1. System architecture

2.1 Back-End System

A back-end system i) extracts attribute-evaluation pairs as opinion candidates from weblog articles (*Extracting attribute-evaluation pairs*) and ii) makes an index (*Opinion Index*) of extracted pairs for full-text searches (*Indexing attribute-evaluation pairs for full-text search*).

i Extracting attribute-evaluation pairs: This module's purpose is to extract subjective attribute-evaluation pairs from a given text. The module consists of three steps:

1. Extraction of attribute and evaluation candidates
2. Detection of related attributes to each evaluation candidate to extract attribute-evaluation pair candidates
3. Determination of subjectivity of each attribute-evaluation pair candidate extracted in Step 2

First, the system extracts attribute and evaluation candidates using evaluation-expression and noun dictionaries. *The evaluation-expression dictionary* contains about 13,000 linguistic expressions used for the evaluation of things, including "good", "bad", "beautiful", and so on. Basically, except for pronouns, we assume that all nouns are attribute candidates.

Second, the system detects the best related attribute candidate based on the syntax for each evaluation candidate. For this problem, we employed a tournament model [4,5], which is a selection method that plays a tournament to select the best candidate. It uses a binary classifier that decides the winner between two candidates.

Third, the system judges the subjectivity of each extracted attribute-evaluation pair by a binary classifier learned by SVM, because an opinion requires subjectivity. For example, in the following two sentences, "EVAL" means the evaluation of an attribute-evaluation pair, and "ATTR" means the attribute of an attribute-evaluation pair.

S1. I want a portable information device of [EVAL: good] [ATTR: design].
S2. My portable information device has a [EVAL: good] [ATTR: design].

"design-good" in Sentence 1 is not an opinion because it has no subjectivity. "design-good" in Sentence 2 is an opinion. Therefore, in other words, the purpose of the third step is to remove not-subjective pairs extracted in Step 2, as in the former example.

ii Indexing attribute-evaluation pairs for full-text search: This module's purpose is to make an index of attribute-evaluation pairs for opinion retrieval with which users can retrieve opinions of an arbitrary object.

We suppose that an object is written near the front of an attribute-evaluation pair. This supposition is based on our observation in a previous work [7], where we showed that the precision of opinion extraction improved as the system limited the opinion candidates at a small distance between an object and an attribute.

According to this supposition, the system creates an inverted index from the front $N(=50)$ characters of each attribute-evaluation pair. Therefore, for searchable opinions, an object always exists at the front of the attribute-evaluation pair, and the distance between them is always below the N characters.

2.2 Front-End System

A front-end system consists of a user interface (Fig. 2) and an opinion search module (*Searching Opinion*). The user interface accepts the user query and sends it to the opinion search module as an object. The opinion search module retrieves the opinions of the object input by a user with an *opinion index* created by the back-end system. We employed a general method for a full-text search based on an inverted index. The opinion search module returns opinions written about an input object as search results to the user interface, which displays them.

Fig. 2. Image of user interface

3 Calculation Method of Opinion Confidence

3.1 Opinion Confidence Model

We can divide an object-attribute-evaluation three-tuple as an opinion into object-attribute and attribute-evaluation relations. We can also divide opinion confidence (C_{oae}) into *object-attribute relation confidence* (C_{oa}) and *attribute-evaluation relation confidence* (C_{ae}):

$$C_{oae} = C_{oa}(o,a,S)C_{ae}(a,e,S). \quad (1)$$

o, a, and e show object, attribute, and evaluation, respectively. S shows a sentence set extracted by the system that had o-a-e three-tuple as an opinion.

Moreover, we divided each above opinion confidence into *syntactic confidence* and *semantic confidence*.

- Syntactic confidence: the likelihood degree of opinion in the syntactic viewpoint
- Semantic confidence: the likelihood degree of opinion in the semantic viewpoint

Next we describe how to divide confidence into syntactic and semantic elements with an example.

S1. I went to a famous [o: restaurant], because I wanted to eat a [e: delicious] [a: dish].
S2. I went to a [o: restaurant], and ate a [e: delicious] [a: dish] for lunch.
S3. I went to a [o: electronics store] and ate a [e: delicious] [a: dish] for lunch.

Syntactic confidence is a measure of the correctness of the three-tuple to be evaluated of its syntactic viewpoints for the differences between S1 and S2. Both S1 and S2 include a three-tuple of restaurant, dish, and delicious. However, S1, which is not an opinion, shows a request. As described, whether the three-tuple is a opinion or not can be determined by syntactic dependency even if the three-tuple is the same.

Semantic confidence is a measure of the correctness of a three-tuple to be evaluated by its semantics viewpoint for the difference between S2 and S3. S2 and S3 have approximately the same syntax. However, since "dish" is rarely an attribute of "electronics store" in S3, this "dish" must have been eaten at a restaurant en route.

Finally, opinion confidence is as follows. C_{sem} and C_{syn} show semantic and syntactic confidence, respectively:

$$C_{oae} = C_{oa}(o,a,S)C_{ae}(a,e,S)$$
$$C_{oa}(o,a,S) = C_{sem_{oa}}(o,a)C_{syn_{oa}}(o,a,S)$$
$$C_{ae}(a,e,S) = C_{sem_{ae}}(a,e)C_{syn_{ae}}(a,e,S)$$

3.2 Calculation Method

In this section, we describe a method to calculate the four confidences explained in the previous section. Each confidence is calculated as follows:

1. $C_{sem_{oa}}$: co-occurrence probability of an object and an attribute calculated from the search result set
2. $C_{syn_{oa}}$: distance between an object and an attribute in the text
3. $C_{sem_{ae}}$: co-occurrence probability of an attribute and an evaluation estimated from a large and pre-collected number of modification relations between an noun and an evaluation expression
4. $C_{syn_{ae}}$: output value of subjectivity classification model (learned by SVM using contextual features of attribute-evaluation pairs) to extract attribute-evaluation pairs

Semantic confidence of object-attribute: $C_{sem_{oa}}(o, a)$: The basis concept for this confidence is that a co-occurrence word of an object with high frequency is an attribute because it has high relevance to the object. Therefore, the system calculates this confidence as the co-occurrence probability of an object and an attribute. To be more precise, it is calculated by expression 2. "A" is a set of attributes contained in the opinions of "o(object)." "$freq(x)$" is a function to return the frequency of "x" in the opinions of "o." We applied logarithmic transformation to the frequency to reduce its influence:

$$C_{sem_{oa}}(o, a_i) = \frac{\ln(freq(a_i) + 1)}{\sum_k \ln(freq(a_k) + 1)} \quad (2)$$

$$a_i, a_k \in A, (1 \leq i, k \leq n)). \quad (3)$$

The system calculates the co-occurrence probability of an object and an attribute using the search results at each time, because preparing all the co-occurrence probabilities of potential objects and attributes is difficult.

Semantic confidence of attribute-evaluation: $C_{syn_{oa}}(o, a, S)$: Our intuition for this confidence is that an object and an attribute are related when the distance between them in the text is small. Therefore, this confidence is calculated as a multiplicative inverse of the distance between an object and an attribute. More precisely, it is calculated by expression 4. $length(o, a, S)$ is a function that returns the number of characters between object "o" and attribute "a" in "S." We applied logarithmic transformation to the distance to reduce its influence:

$$C_{syn_{oa}}(o, a, S) = \frac{1}{\ln(length(o, a, S) + 1) + 1}. \quad (4)$$

Generally, better methods exist to calculate this confidence using linguistic information such as dependence analysis and anaphora resolution. However, this process should be light because the system calculates this confidence in real-time every search. Therefore, we counted the number of characters as a light process.

Semantic onfidence of object-attribute: $C_{sem_{ae}}(a, e)$: We consider this confidence to be high if the pair of evaluation and attribute expressions is typically used. With a back-end system, we can easily collect many noun-evaluation modification relations from a large text corpus such as the Web. Therefore, this confidence is a co-occurrence probability estimated from a large number of noun-evaluation modification relations. More precisely, it is calculated by expression 5. We employed PLSI [2], which is a method to estimate each parameter $(p(z_k), p(a_i|z_k), p(e_j|z_k))$:

$$C_{sem_{ae}}(a_i, e_j) = \sum_k p(z_k)p(a_i|z_k)p(e_j|z_k) \tag{5}$$

$$a_i \in A, (1 \leq i \leq n) \tag{6}$$

$$e_j \in E, (1 \leq j \leq m) \tag{7}$$

$$z_k \in Z, (1 \leq k \leq l). \tag{8}$$

"E" is a set of evaluations contained in the collected noun-evaluation modification relations. "A" is a set of nouns contained in the collected noun-evaluation modification relations. "Z" is a set of latent common classes of elements of both "E" and "A." $p(z)$ is the occurrence probability of "z." $p(a|z)$ is the occurrence probability of attribute "a" from class "z." $p(e|z)$ is the occurrence probability of evaluation "e" from class "z."

$C_{sem_{ae}}(a_i, e_j)$ becomes high when "a_i" and "e_j" well occur from the same latent class. Intuitively, $p(a|z)$ and $p(e|z)$ become high when "a" and "e" have similar words in the modification relations. For the property, the system gives co-occurrence probabilities of "a" and "e" even if "a" and "e" have never occurred in the collected modification relations.

Syntactic confidence of attribute-evaluation: $C_{syn_{ae}}(a, e, S)$: We employed an output value of the subjectivity classification model to the extracted attribute-evaluation pairs, because its model is learned by SVM based on syntactic features. SVM's features include: i) a binary value that determines whether the attribute evaluations have a modification relation; ii) the number of bunsetsus[1] between the attributes and evaluations; iii) a binary value that determines whether the attributes and evaluations exist in the same sentence; iv) morpheme information of the attribute's bunsetsus; v) morpheme information of the evaluation's bunsetsus; vi) morpheme information of the dependent bunsetsus for evaluation; and vii) morpheme information of the dependent bunsetsus to the attributes. Here, this morpheme information means the original form, its part of speech, and its written form.

In our method, the system applies the sigmoid function to the output value (distance from the separating SVM's hyperplain) because the sigmoid function (expression 10) gives a good approximation of the probability from the output value of SVM that was confirmed experimentally [3]:

---

[1] *Bunsetsu* is a phrasal unit in Japanese that consists of at least one content word and zero or more functional words.

$$C_{syn_{ae}}(a_i, e_j, S) = sigmoid(F(f(a_i, e_j, S))) \tag{9}$$

$$sigmoid(x) = \frac{1}{1+e^{-x}}. \tag{10}$$

$f(a_i, e_j, S)$ is a function to return a feature vector of attribute "a_i" - evaluation "e_j" pair from "S." $F(x)$ is a subjectivity classification model learned by SVM.

4 Experiment

4.1 Purposes and Methods

The purpose of this experiment was to evaluate the confidence calculated by our proposed method by ranking the opinion retrieval tasks. We experimented with two methods for two different sub-purposes.

In the first experiment, we evaluated the precision of the top fifty ranked opinions of three keywords to judge the effectiveness of our proposal. In the second experiment to evaluate the effectiveness of syntactic confidence (C_{syn}) and semantic confidence (C_{sem}), we evaluated both the precision and the average precision of the top fifty opinions ranked by independence by combining the syntactic and semantic confidences. Average precision, which is often used for evaluating methods or models for retrieval experiments [6], is computed as high since relevant documents (correct answers) are in the higher ranks.

Experimental Data and Setting: We used the same experimental data set as in the first and second experiments. The document set is a set of weblog articles written from March 1st to 31st in 2008 in Japan collected by our crawler. We acquired three fifth ranking keywords from each ranking of movie, cellphone, and digital camera as retrieval target objects to exclude arbitrariness. [2]

To calculate the co-occurrence probability of the attribute-evaluation, we collected noun-evaluation expression modification relations from one million weblog articles. The low frequency modification relation became noise when PLSI estimated the parameters and modification relations were excluded that occurred only one time. Finally, the system had 86,119 modification relations, 16,173 noun, and 4,450 evaluation expressions. The number of latent classes as parameters in PLSI is 20, which was determined by a pilot experiment that used different keywords from the three keywords.

4.2 Experimental Results

First Experiment: We show the experimental results in Table 1. "Random" means the precision of the fifty opinions sampled randomly from the search results. Correspondingly, "Ranking" means the precision of the top fifty opinions ranked by our confidence method.

As Table 1 shows, we confirmed the effectiveness of our proposed method, because precision improved with all keywords.

---

[2] We acquired a movie from http://movie.goo.ne.jp/ranking/boxoffice/, and cellphones and digital cameras were acquired from http://kakaku.com.

Table 1. Precision of 50 opinions for ranking and random sampling

Keyword	Ranking	Random	# of opinions
EOS5D [digital camera]	**0.30**	0.24	70
F905i [cellphone]	**0.66**	0.62	171
Kurosagi (NTM) [movie]	**0.78**	0.46	2341

Table 2. Precision of top 50 opinions ranked by each confidence

Keyword	Syntax	Semantics	Combination (proposal)
EOS5D [digital camera]	0.28	**0.30**	**0.30**
F905i [cellphone]	**0.72**	0.66	0.66
Kurosagi (NTM) [movie]	0.76	0.60	**0.78**

Table 3. Average Precision of top 50 opinions ranked by each confidence

Keyword	Syntax	Semantics	Combination (proposal)
EOS5D [digital camera]	**0.55**	0.37	0.45
F905i [cellphone]	**0.81**	0.65	0.74
Kurosagi (NTM) [movie]	0.73	0.78	**0.89**

Table 4. Expected value of average precision from top 50 opinions precision ranked by each confidence

Keyword	Syntax	Semantics	Combination (proposal)
EOS5D [digital camera]	0.33	0.35	0.35
F905i [cellphone]	0.74	0.68	0.68
Kurosagi (NTM) [movie]	0.77	0.62	0.79

Table 5. Difference between average precision and expected value of average precision for each confidence

Keyword	Syntax	Semantics	Combination (proposal)
EOS5D [digital camera]	+0.22	+0.02	+0.10
F905i [cellphone]	+0.07	-0.03	+0.06
Kurosagi (NTM) [movie]	-0.04	+0.16	+0.10

Second Experiment: We show the experimental results in Tables 2 and 3. "Syntax" means ranking only by syntactic confidence (C_{syn}). "Semantic" means ranking only by semantic confidence (C_{sem}). "Combination" denotes ranking by our confidence method that combined syntactic and semantic confidences. The values in Table 2 are precision, and those in Table 3 are average precision.

In Tables 2 and 3, we found a disagreement over the best result of confidence among the keywords. In fact, the proposed method is not the best among each confidence from this result, but we confirmed that all confidences are better than random by comparing Tables 1 and 2.

To quantify the goodness of the ranking measure of each confidence, we calculated the expected value of average precision when assuming the occurrence probability of the correct opinion is the precision in Table 2. The confidence is better as a ranking measure if the difference between an expected value and the actual measurement of average precision is larger. The expected value of average precision is calculated by expression 11. $N(=50)$ is the number of documents of the search result. $R(N \times precision)$ is the number of relevant documents in the search result:

$$\frac{R - 1 + N^{-1} \sum_{i=1}^{N} \frac{N-R}{i}}{N - 1}. \tag{11}$$

We show the experimental results in Table 5, where each value is the difference between an actual value in Table 3 and an expected value in Table 4. A negative value shows that random sampling is better than ranking by our confidence. As Table 5 shows, only "combination" had all positive values. Therefore, a combination of two confidences is better than a single confidence, a syntactic or a semantic confidence.

5 Discussion and Future Work

In evaluation experiments, we confirmed that the precision of the high ranked opinions in search results was improved by the ranking of our proposed confidence. However, we also confirmed that the precision of opinion retrieval was not improved by the simple combination of syntax and semantic confidences. Given this factor, we discuss an effective combination method of syntactic and semantic confidences in this section.

In the components of confidence, only the semantic confidence of an object-attribute pair fundamentally depends on the retrieval result (equals the search keyword). This is because only the semantic confidence of an object-attribute pair is calculated from the entire search result.

The co-occurrence probability of an object-attribute as semantic confidence is not effective when the number of search results is insufficient. The reliability of the parameters estimated from a small amount of data in general is low, because the parameters overfit the input data.

Conversely, the semantic confidence of an object and an attribute is effective when the number of search results is adequate. Actually, from Tables 2 and 3, we can confirm that the average precision and the precision of "Kurosagi," which had many searched opinions, was improved by semantic confidence.

We consider a method to change the combination weight between syntactic and semantic confidences when the number of searches is better than the uniform combination weight between the two confidences. Concretely, the method makes the combination weight of the syntactic confidence higher than the semantic ones when the searched opinions are few. By contrast, the method raises the combination weight of the semantic confidence higher than the syntactic ones when there are many searched opinions. The method is most likely the linear sum with the weight of each confidence. In the case of a sum, scores must be regularized to absorb the difference of the distribution and the scale of each confidence. However, based on a regularization method, retrieval speed might be reduced for processing. In future work, we will verify the effect of changing weight based on the number of search results, and the influence on the retrieval speed will be verified at the same time.

6 Conclusion

In this paper, to improve the precision of opinion retrieval by ranking, we proposed a method to calculate the confidence of each searched opinion. Our method divides an object-attribute-evaluation three-tuple as an opinion into object-attribute and attribute-evaluation relations. In addition, the confidence of the opinion is calculated by determining all syntactic and semantic confidences. In syntactic confidence, i) the syntactic confidence of the object-attribute relation is calculated by the number of characters between an object and an attribute, and ii) the syntactic confidence of the attribute-evaluation relation is calculated by the output value of the subjectivity classification model [7] (learned by SVM [1] using the contextual features of attribute-evaluation pairs).

In semantic confidence, iii) the semantic confidence of the object-attribute relation is a co-occurrence probability of the object-attribute relation calculated from searched opinions, and iv) the semantic confidence of the attribute-evaluation is the co-occurrence probability of the attribute-evaluation to be estimated by PLSI [2] from a large amount of collected modification relations of noun-evaluations.

As a result of the evaluation experiments, we confirmed that the precision of the high ranked opinions in the retrieval result is improved by ranking based on the confidence of opinions calculated by our proposed method. Moreover, we confirmed that our confidence was better than using each syntactic and semantic confidence independently by evaluating the difference between the expected and the actual values of average precision.

In future work, we will verify the effect of changing weight based on the number of search results. In addition, to improve the opinion extraction performance, we will develop an opinion extraction method to apply the idea of confidence.

References

1. Cortes, C., Vapnik, V.: Support-Vector Networks. Machine Learning 20(3), 273–297 (1995)
2. Hofmann, T.: Probabilistic Latent Semantic Indexing. In: Proceedings of SIGIR 1999, pp. 50–57 (1999)
3. Platt, J.: Probabilistic Outputs for Support Vector Machines and Comparisons to Regularized Likelihood Methods. Advances in Large Margin Classifiers, pp. 61–74 (1999)
4. Iida, R., Inui, K., Takamura, H., Matsumoto, Y.: Incorporating Contextual Cues in Trainable Models for Coreference Resolution. In: Proceedings of the EACL Workshop on The Computational Treatment of Anaphora, pp. 23–30 (2003)

5. Iida, R., Kobayashi, N., Inui, K., Matsumoto, Y., Tateishi, K., Fukushima, T.: A Machine Learning-Based Method to Extract Attribute-Value Pairs for Opinion Mining. In: Information Processing Society of Japan SIGNL Note 165(4), 21–28 (2005) (in Japanese)
6. Kishida, K.: Property of average precision as performance measure for retrieval experiment. Information Processing Society of Japan Transactions on Databases 43(SIG2), 11–26 (2002) (in Japanese)
7. Tsuchida, M., Mizuguchi, H., Kusui, D.: Opinion Extraction by Identifying Object-attribute-evaluate Relations. In: Proceedings of The 13th Annual Meeting of The Association for Natural Language, pp. 412–415 (2007) (in Japanese)
8. Tsuchida, M., Mizuguchi, H., Kusui, D.: On-Demand Reputation Analysis System from Weblogs: eHyouban. In: Proceedings of The 14th Annual Meeting of The Association for Natural Language, pp. 899–902 (2008) (in Japanese)

Part II
Logic and Engineering of Natural Language Semantics

Overview of Logic and Engineering of Natural Language Semantics (LENLS) 2008

Yasuo Nakayama

Graduate School of Human Sciences, Osaka University
1-2 Yamada-oka, Japan 565-0871
nakayama@hus.osaka-u.ac.jp

LENLS (Logic and Engineering of Natural Language Semantics) is an annual international workshop focusing on dynamic aspects of the formal treatment of natural languages. This workshop is organized as a satellite of the Japanese Society for Artificial Intelligence Conference. The fifth LENLS was held at Asahikawa Tokiwa Citizens Hall, Asahikawa, Japan, June 9-10 in 2008. The special topic of the 2008 conference was the *interactive turn in formal pragmatics*, which takes a formal approach to the interactive quality of pragmatic meanings via various formal approaches. However, the focus of this workshop also included more general topics such as the following:

- Formal Semantics of Natural Language (especially dynamic approaches)
- Dynamic Syntax and Labeled Deductive Systems of Natural Language
- Dynamic (Epistemic) Logics and Natural Language Semantics/Pragmatics
- Coalgebraic Logics and Natural Language Semantics/Pragmatics
- Category-Theoretic Semantics of Natural Language
- Type-Theoretic Semantics of Natural Language
- Substructural Logics of Natural Language
- Extensions of Lambek Calculi including Combinatory Category Grammars and Type-Logical Grammars
- Other Mathematical Theories of Information Structures of Natural Language Discourse
- Natural Language Processing based on Dynamic Semantics, Dynamic Syntax, or Formal Pragmatics.

In the workshop, two invited talks and twelve contributed talks were given by logicians, computer scientists, computer linguists, and philosophers. It was a very interesting and exciting workshop where fruitful discussions took place among participants from various research fields. This chapter comprises seven revised extended papers that are selected from the fourteen papers presented in the workshop.

The first two papers deal with dynamic aspects of the *parsing* of complex sentences in Japanese. The paper "Multiple Subject Constructions in Japanese: A Dynamic Syntax Account" by Hiroaki Nakamura *et al.* proposes an incremental parsing device building up semantic structures for multiple subject constructions in Japanese which are represented by the logic of finite trees. They argue that subjects are licensed not by argument structures of verbs but by open propositions in Japanese stative sentences. "Topic/Subject Coreference in the Hierarchy of Japanese Complex Sentences" by Alastair Butler *et al.* addresses the coreference of topicalized and untopicalized subjects in Japanese complex sentences which is known to depend on the type of subordinate clause head and topicalization of the matrix subject. To deal with this problem, they apply Scope Control Theory, a semantic theory using operator-variable dependencies.

The third and the fourth papers use extensions of Discourse Representation Theory (DRT), a theory in dynamic semantics proposed by H. Kamp, as the formal framework. The paper "Japanese reported speech: Against a direct-indirect distinction" by Emar Maier proposes a unified analysis of speech reports in which a general mechanism of mixed quotation replaces the classical two-fold distinction, the direct-indirect distinction. He shows that speech reporting follows Kaplan's semantics of indirect discourse except for the parts that consist of mixed quotation. "The dynamics of tense under attitudes: Anaphoricity and *de se* interpretation in the backward shifted past" by Corien Bary *et al.* proposes an extension of DRT to resolve the tension created by the independently motivated anaphoric and *de se* aspects of tense interpretation. In this new framework, updates of the common ground are accompanied by updates of each relevant agent's complex attitudinal state.

The fifth paper "Argumentative Properties of Pragmatic Inferences" by Grégoire Winterstein deals with pragmatic inferences. It shows how the argumentative approach to pragmatics, proposed by J. C. Anscombre and O. Ducrot, provides a straightforward explanation for the licensing of adversaives when reinforcing some implicatures. He provides a solution in an argumentative framework and extends his observations to cases including an overt restriction rather than implicatures.

The sixth and the seventh papers are strongly formal. The paper "Prolegomena to Dynamic Epistemic Preference Logic" by Satoru Suzuki proposes a new version of sound and complete dynamic epistemic preference logic. This new framework can deal with a wide range of decision problems. In "Monads and Meta-Lambda Calculus", Daisuke Bekki defines a new framework *Meta-Lambda Calculus* that is an extension of the typed lambda calculi with meta-constructions, whose categorical semantics is defined by means of a hom-functor from a Cartesian closed category to *Set*. He proves that both normal and meta beta-conversions are sound in this categorical semantics.

This workshop is organized by Daisuke Bekki (Ochanomizu University), Eric McCready (Aoyama Gakuin University), Yoshiki Mori (Tsukuba University), Norihiro Ogata (Osaka University), Katsuhiko Yabushita (Naruto University), Tomoyuki Yamada (Hokkaido University), Kei Yoshimoto (Tohoku University), and myself (Osaka University). In early September 2008, we received word that Mr. Ogata, one of the organizing committee, had passed away in the previous month. We, the organizers, were surprised by this sad news, because he had not shown any sign of illness before. Since Mr. Ogata initiated the first LENLS in 2004, he had been playing the central role in the organizational activities of LENLS. His death is a great loss for our activities of formal semantics in Japan. Mr. Ogata was not only scientifically very talented but also always very helpful for organizing meetings related to formal semantics and dynamic syntax. We, the members of the organizing committee, would like to thank him for all he has done to activate formal semantics in Japan.

Multiple Subject Constructions in Japanese: A Dynamic Syntax Account

Hiroaki Nakamura[1], Kei Yoshimoto[2], Yoshiki Mori[3], and Masahiro Kobayashi[4]

[1] Department of Liberal Arts, Japan Coast Guard Academy, 5-1, Wakaba-cho,
Kure City, Hiroshima 737-8512, Japan
hiroaki-nakamura@ax2.mopera.ne.jp
[2] Graduate School of International Cultural Studies,Tohoku University
kyoshimoto@mail.tains.tohoku.ac.jp
[3] Doctoral Program in Linguistics and Literature, Graduate School of Humanities and Social
Sciences, University of Tsukuba
mori@lingua.tsukuba.ac.jp
[4] University Education Center, Tottori University
kobayashi@uec.tottori-u.ac.jp

Abstract. Though Multiple Subject Constructions have long received much attention mainly from syntactic points of view because they show distinctive features of languages like Japanese, a unified treatment which tries to translate MSCs into appropriate semantic representations/logical forms has not been proposed yet. This study presents how logical structures of MSCs are built up in a time-linear parsing perspective. We highlight an important semantic feature of a set of common nouns often called relational nouns which enables the layers of predication to be formed in MSCs. This group of nouns inherently have an extra variable inside, which can be bound by the preceding subjects in MSCs. We argue that subjects are licensed not by argument structures of verbs but by open propositions in Japanese stative sentences, and show that our analysis can account for some asymmetries in extraction constructions, such as relative and cleft constructions.

Keywords: Multiple Subject Construction, relational noun, major subject, Dynamic Syntax, time-linear parsing.

1 Introduction: Multiple Subject Constructions in Japanese

In this study[1], we will present how to translate the so-called Multiple Subject Constructions (hereafter, MSC) into semantic representations. It is important to establish the mechanism of translating all syntactic constructions, not fragments, of one language into some kind of logical forms to prove a grammar formalism to be both syntactically and semantically sound. We may safely say that any framework with a syntax/semantic interface does not seem to be well-established without such mechanism. Taking MSCs as an example, we explore how a grammar formalism can parse

---

[1] We are deeply grateful to Ruth Kempson and Norry Ogata for their warm encouragement and valuable suggestions from which this study has benefited immensely.

sentences in a incremental fashion, and build up interpretations for them. MSCs, where more than one nominative-marked noun phrases occur in a single sentence, have long been a central object of theoretical and empirical studies, due to their outstanding characteristics from a typological perspective. Japanese MSC are illustrated in (1) (see also Kuno 1973, Sugimoto 1990):

(1) a. Syusyoo-no   byojoo-ga   saikin omo-i.
       Prime-Minister-GEN condition-NOM recently serious-PRES
       'The Prime Minister's condition of the desease is recently serious.'
    b. Syusyoo-ga   saikin   byojoo-ga   omo-i.
       Prime Minister-NOM recently condition-NOM serious-PRES
    c. Sono jisyo-ga   hotondo-no gakusei-ga   riyoosuru.
       the dictionary-NOM   most-GEN   student-NOM   use-PRES
       'The dictionary is the one the most of students are using.'
    d. Kono settyakuzai-ga kawa-ga   yoku tuku.
       this cement-NOM   leather-NOM   fast stick-PRES
       'This cement is the one by which we can stick leather to something.'

The MSC in (1b) is often said to be derived from the non-MSC in (1a). For instance, Hasegawa (1999) proposes the analysis in which the derived subject, called the 'major subject', moves up from its original position in the specifier of the following subject by NP-movement.

(2) [IP Neko-ga$_j$ [IP [NP t_j karada-ga]$_i$ [AP t_i yawaraka-$_i$]].
        cat-NOM   body-NOM   pliant-PRES

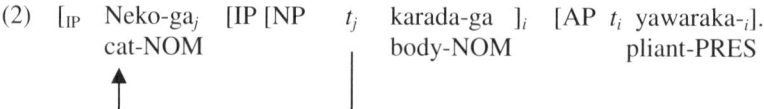

'Lit. Cats are such that their bodies are pliable.'

She argues that the new subject *Neko-ga* raises to the higher [Spec,IP] position to get the nominative case licensed by the INFL. Incidentally, she also suggests that the nominative NP gets an interpretation as the subject of the derived predicative phrase (i.e., the lower IP) due to its higher position. However, it remains unclear how to construct the semantic interpretation she argues from structure (2), reflecting the new predication relation between the major subject and the remaining part of the sentence. We present the formal method to parse MSCs as in (1) to construct the logical forms in terms of the syntax-semantics interface, which are represented by a modal logic of finite trees (LOFT), and how it extends to relativization of MSCs.

In MSCs involving subjectivization of the possessors of following subjects, a remarkable semantic property of the following subjects must be taken into account in the analysis. Observe sentence (3).

(3) Kono atari-wa   subete-no kawa-ga   kakoo-ga   suisin-ga fukai.
    here-Top   all-GEN river-NOM   mouth-NOM   depth-NOM deep-PRES
    'Lit.: In this region, all rivers are such that their river mouths are deep.'

The values of the second and third subjects in (3) obligatorily covary with the value of the first subject. This property of following subjects in MSCs shows a sharp contrast in interpretation with normal sentences with more than one arguments like (4), the preferred reading of which is that the nominative object takes scope over the preceding subject.

(4) Siken-de-wa   dono gakusei-mo   aru mondai-ga   tokenakatta.
    exam-in-Top   every student-NOM   a certain question-NOM   solve-Cannot-Past
    'In the math exam, every student couldn't solve a certain problem.'

The object NP *aru mondai* 'a certain problem' takes wide scope with respect to the universally quantified subject *dono gakusei* 'every student' in (4), so this sentence should be true if there was at least one question in the math exam which could not be solved by all the students. On the other hand, in MSC (3) we do not have the interpretation that at least one river mouth all the rivers have in common is deep in this district.

In this study, we also attend to long-distance dependency phenomena involving MSCs, in which non-arguments are allowed to be extracted, unlike in English:

(5) a. saikin   byojoo-ga   omoi   syusyo
       recently condition-NOM serious   prime minister
       'prime minister whose condition of the disease is serious.
   b. toshin-ni   kumanezumi-ga ooino   Tokyo-da
      downtown-IN black rats-NOM many-exist-TOP Tokyo-BE-Pres
      'Tokyou in the down town of which there are many black rats
(6) a. Saikin byojyo-ga   omoi-no-wa   syusyo-da.
       Recently condition-NOM serious-N.-Top prime-minister-BE-Pres
       'It is the prime minister whose condition of the disease is serious.'
   b. Toshin-ni   kumanezumi-ga ooi-no-wa Tokyo-da.
      downtown-IN black-rats-NOM many-N.-Top Tokyo-BE-Pres
      'It is in Tokyo that there are many black rats in the downtown.

On the other hand, the following subjects cannot be extracted, as shown in (7) and (8).
(7) a. *[Syusyo-ga   saikin   omoi]   byojyo
        prime-minister-NOM recently serious-Pres   condition
    b. *[Tokyo-ga   kumanezumi-ga ooi]   toshin-bu
        Tokyo-NOM   black-rats-NOM many-BE-Pres   downtown
    cf. Tokyo-de kumanezumi-ga ooi]   toshin-bu
        Tokyo-IN   black-rats-NOM many-BE-Pres   downtown
(8) a. *[Syusyo-ga   saikin   omoi-no-wa]   byojyo-da
        prime-minister-NOM recently serious-N.-TOP condition-BE-Pres
    b. *[Tokyo-ga   kumanezumi-ga   ooi-no-wa]   toshinbu-da.
        Tokyo-NOM   black-rats-NOM   many-BE-N.-TOP downtown-BE-Pres

We will offer an explanation to such surprising asymmetry in extractability between major and non-major subjects in MSCs. Especially, we will explore the nature of indefinites which seem to play a crucial role in forming the layers of predication in a sentence projected from a single verb.

2 Dynamic Syntax

We adopt the Dynamic Syntax model (Kempson, et al. 2001, Cann, et al. 2005) as a framework of description. In Dynamic Syntax, syntactic properties of expressions are defined as a set of actions to parse input sentences and construct partial trees representing their semantic contents strictly on left-to-right basis. No syntactic representation is needed in any component of grammar, and syntactically ill-formed information simply cause parsing actions to abort. Various forms of underspecification are permitted in the course of parsing input sequences and building logical forms. Initial underspecification must be resolved during the construction process of semantic trees step by step. There are many competing actions at each stage of parsing, and pragmatic factors are relevant for choice of transition possibilities (Sperber and Wilson, 1986). Each node of a partial tree is decorated by formulae called Declarative Units (DUs) comprising first-order predicates. The decoration of each node includes a Formula value (Fo) representing semantic content and a Type value (Ty) with a form of typed lambda calculus. For instance, a root node eventually becomes a propositional node of type t with a Fo value representing the logical meaning of an input sentence.

Let us take sentence (9) to show an example of parsing in DS. Parsing of input sequences is reflected in the process of semantic structure building, which is defined in terms of transitions between partial trees. The interpretation process starts with the introduction of the root node with a requirement (represented by '?') and proceeds by unfolding and decorating the tree node by node, as information from the words progressively enables a tree to be constructed. A structures given at each step is represented as a pointed partial tree in which the pointer $\Diamond$ indicate a node under development.

(9) John upset Mary.

The root node decorated with a requirement of propositional formula of type t is expanded into the subject of type e and the predicate phrase of type $e \rightarrow t$ by the transition rules called INTRODUCTION and PREDICTION.[2] Notice that the pointer is at the subject node now.

(10)

$?Ty(t)$ $\rightarrow$ $?Ty(t)$

$?Ty(e), \Diamond$ $?Ty(e \rightarrow t)$ John $?Ty(e \rightarrow t)$

After *John* is scanned, the requirement of noun is satisfied and removed, and the pointer moves to the predicate node of type $(e \rightarrow t)$. Then, the verb *upset* is parsed and the predicate phrase is constructed according to its lexical specification as in (11):

(11)

	IF	$?Ty(e \rightarrow t)$	Predicate trigger
	THEN	go$<\uparrow_1>?Ty(t)$;	Go to propositional node
		put($Tns(PAST)$);	Tense Information
		go($<\downarrow_1>?Ty(e \rightarrow t)$);	Go to predicate node
upset		make($<\downarrow_1>$);	Make functor node
		put(Fo(Upset'),$Ty(e \rightarrow (e \rightarrow t))$),$[\downarrow]\perp$);	Annotation
		go($<\uparrow_1>$);	Go to mother node
		make($<\downarrow_0>$);	Make argument node
		go($<\downarrow_0>$);	Go to argument node
		put($?Ty(e)$)	Annotation
	ELSE	Abort	

Fo(Upset') in the decoration is precisely expressed via a lambda operator specifying the number and type of its arguments, and as the order of combination (i.e.,

---

[2] Transition rules generally have the following form as schematically shown below:
    Input Tree Description

    Output Tree Description

They are general rules to build up structures top-down, universally available and optional.

Fo($\lambda y. \lambda x$[Upset'(x,y)]). More importantly, the actions specified in the lexical information in (11) do participate in construction of the semantic representation. After processing *Mary*, the accumulation of information is carried out by the COMPLETION/ELIMINATION rules (see Kempson et al. 2001, Cann, et al. 2005), all the requirements are removed, and the pointer moves back to the top node, resulting in the formula 'Upset'(Mary')(John')'.

(12)

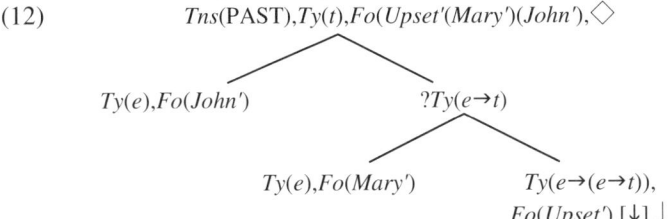

The concept of structural underspecification is central to the explanation of Dynamic Syntax. Let us introduce another aspect of such underspecification, by using an example of Scrambling in Japanese, as in (13):

(13) Mary-o   John-ga   home-ta.
      Mary-ACC   John-NOM   praise-PAST
      'Mary, John praised.'

Because the word-order is relatively free in Japanese, the INTRODUCTION rule cannot be invoked for introducing the subject and predicate in parsing (12). Japanese noun phrases actively contribute to tree growth and verbal templates are simply unified with trees already constructed when verbs are finally processed. Noun phrases are incrementally processed by Local *Adjunction as if they formed a flat structure. By Local *Adjunction an noun phrase with an arbitrary role projects an (initially) unfixed node decorated with a modality $<\uparrow_0\uparrow_*>$ indicating an underspecified modal relation pointing to some node that dominates the current node. Local *Adjunction is defined as in (14):[3]

(14) Local *Adjunction   (Cann et al. 2005:236)
$$\{ ... \{Tn(a), ..., ?Ty(t), \Diamond \} ... \}$$

$$\{...\{Tn(a), ?Ty(t)...\}...\{...\{<\uparrow_0\uparrow_1^*>Tn(a), ?Ty(e), ?\exists x.Tn(x), \Diamond\}...\}$$

A locally scrambled NP is introduced into the tree, with a locally unfixed node decorated by $?Ty(e)$.

(15) $Tn(0), ?Ty(t), \Diamond$ $Tn(0), ?Ty(t)$
                                      $\longrightarrow$ |
                                                                |
                                                   $<\uparrow_0\uparrow_*>Tn(0), ?Ty(e), ? \exists x.Tn(x)$
                                                                  Mary

---

[3] The underspecified modal relation indicated by $<\uparrow_*>$ is defined over the reflexive, transitive closure of the mother relation as shown in (ia) and its obverse, $<\downarrow_*>$, over the daughter relation as in (ib).
 (i) a. $<\uparrow_*>\alpha$ =def $\alpha \lor <\uparrow><\uparrow_*>\alpha$
     b. $<\downarrow_*>\alpha$ =def $\alpha \lor <\downarrow><\downarrow_*>\alpha$
 A modality like $<\uparrow_*>?Ty(t)$ holds just in case either the current node is decorated by $?Ty(t)$ or some node dominating the current node is so decorated.

The dotted line indicates that the introduced position is currently unfixed and must be resolved within the local domain given by the propositional template of a verb introduced later. Next, the accusative marker -o is scanned and it induces the action defined in (16). The overt case markers serve as output filters and also play more constructive roles in the process of structure-building.

(16)
-o | IF $Ty(e)$
   | THEN IF $<\uparrow_*>(Tn(a) \wedge ?Ty(t))$
   | THEN $put(?<\uparrow_0>Ty(e \rightarrow t))$
   | ELSE Abort
   | ELSE Abort

The introduced NP must be interpreted within the local clause due to the locality restriction defined by Local *Adjunction. Then the unfixed node of the scrambled object NP simply identified with the object argument node of the propositional template of the verb *homer-*, and the pointer moves back to the local $Ty(t)$-node.

The subject *John-ga* is processed in a similar way, initially introduced as an unfixed node with the local relation to the dominating type-t-requiring node, which is fixed by the action depicted by its case specification. The application of MERGE is not imposed here because the fixed node is vacuously be duplicated by the associated argument node, creating one and the same tree relation. Finally, we get the tree representation like (17):

(17)

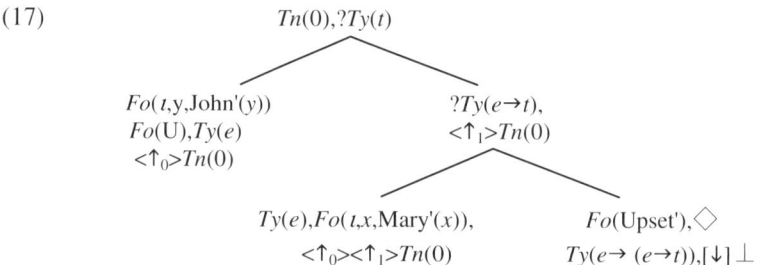

The ELIMINATION rule applies to compile the sentence meaning, yielding the formula Fo(Upset'(Mary')(John')), the same result as in (12) in English.

Here we should introduce another important device necessary to deal with relative clauses of MSCs later, in which we again have recourse to underspecification of tree positions. A relation between a head noun and relative clause is called LINK relation in DS. A semantic tree for a relative clause (a LINKed structure) is projected by LINK Adjunction Rule defined in (18):

(18)
⌐──────── head ────────┐
        $\{...\{Tn(a),Fo(\alpha),Ty(e),\Diamond\}...\}$
──
$\{...\{Tn(a),Fo(\alpha),Ty(e)\}...\{, \{<L_{-1}>Tn(a),?Ty(t),\ ?<\downarrow*>Fo(\alpha)\ ,\Diamond\}$
                                                    └─Formula Requirement─┘

        head   LINKed node

Suppose that the parser is processing sentence *A man who Sue likes smokes* and *a man* is already introduced in the tree. The LINK Adjunction rules applies, imposing the requirement to find a copy of this variable somewhere inside it. The newly introduced node, with the modality $<\uparrow_*><L^{-1}>$, constructed by the lexical actions of the relative pronoun is unfixed initially, and its decorations provide updates to the object node with the requirement ?Ty(e) in the MERGE process.

(19)
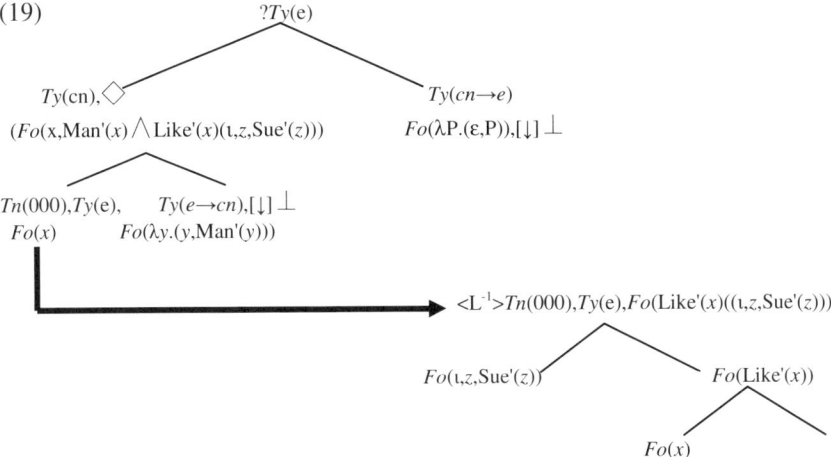

The new modality <L> and its inverse modality <L^{-1}> are introduced, with the former pointing to the newly built (relative clause) structure and the latter pointing back to the node of the head noun variable. The point is that a LINKED tree must have a requirement to find the copy of a head noun, so the interpretation involves a kind of anaphora resolution. Relative clauses are interpreted by one of the LINK Evaluation rules, and we indicate the version for restrictive construal for relative clauses.

(20) LINK Evaluation 2 (Restrictive construal):
$$\{... \{Tn(a),?Ty(cn)...\}, \{<\uparrow_0>Tn(a),Fo(x),Ty(e)\},$$
$$\{<\uparrow_1>Tn(a),Fo(\lambda X.(X,\psi(X)),Ty(e{\to}cn)\}...\}$$
$$\{<L^{-1}><\uparrow_0>Tn(a),Fo(\varphi),Ty(t),\Diamond\}$$

$$\{...\{Tn(a),Fo(x,\varphi \wedge \psi(x),Ty(cn),...,\Diamond\}, \{<\uparrow_0>Tn(a),Fo(x),Ty(e)\},$$
$$\{<\uparrow_1>Tn(a),Fo(\lambda X.(X,\psi(X))),Ty(e{\to}cn)\}...\}$$
$$\{<L^{-1}><\uparrow_0>Tn(a),Fo(\varphi),Ty(t)\}$$

As the interpretation for the common noun *man who Sue likes* shows, the conjoined restrictor Man'(x) $\wedge$ Like'(x)(ι,z,Sue'(z)) is derived by (20), and finally, the interpretation of the noun phrase should be represented as formula Fo(ε,x,Man'(x) $\wedge$ Like'(x)(ι,z,Sue'(z)), as shown in (21):

Finally, let us touch on the treatment of quantification in Dynamic Syntax very briefly. Because noun phrases always appear without articles in Japanese, quantifier construal is crucial for interpretations of all indefinite NPs. Quantified noun phrases are represented in terms of the epsilon calculus (see Kempson et al. 2001, Cann et al. 2005, Kempson and Meyor-Viol 2004 for detailed discussion). Indefinites show quite different behaviors from universal quantifiers and in general scope freely (i.e., not clause bound). Dynamic Syntax assumes that all noun phrases including quantified expressions project the structure of type *e*, indefinites share some property with anaphoric expressions, and try to model the choice of dependency of indefinites using the notion of epsilon term and quantified NP representations are formed by variable-binding operators. For instance, *a man* is represented as in (21):

(21) $(\varepsilon, x, \text{Man}'(x)) = \exists x.\text{Man}'(x)$

The structure of Quantified NPs have the three parts:
1. The Binder (e.g. ε) indicating a mode of quantification
2. The Variable (e.g. x) indicating a variable bound by the binder
3. The Restrictor (e.g. Man'(x)) indicating the binding domain of a variable

In addition, a sequence of scope statement is accumulated during the construction process to characterize relative scope among quantified terms, as in (22):

(22) $x < y$

where x and y are arbitrary variables of type *e* stating that the quantifier binding *x* has scope over the quantifier binding *y*. The scope relation in a clause is defined in the linear order of variables in the sequence of scope statements, which should also includes the index of evaluation for ψ, $S_i:\psi$, with S_i is taken to be a temporal index of a clause. The scope of indefinites is determined by the free choice mechanism, where every indefinite must take narrow scope. When an indefinite is interpreted with a wide scope over other quantified terms, its scope is taken to be dependent on the term S_i (which is associated with the tense specification of a clause). For example, observe sentence (23):

(23)   Every dog ate a biscuit.
       every dog = $(\tau, x, \text{Dog}'(x))$ a biscuit = $(\varepsilon, y, \text{Biscuit}'(y))$
       $\psi = \text{Ate}((\tau, x, \text{Dog}'(x))(\varepsilon, y, \text{Biscuit}'(y)))$

If the scope relation is defined as $<_B = \{<S_i, x, y>\}$, then we get the final representation like (24a) and if defined as $<_B \{<S_i, y, x>\}$, we eventually get (24b).

(24) a. $\forall x(\text{Dog}(x) \rightarrow \exists y(\text{Biscuit}(y) \wedge \text{Ate}(x,y)))$
     b. $\exists y(\text{Biscuit}(y) \wedge (\forall x(\text{Dog}(x) \rightarrow \text{Ate}(x,y))))$

In (24b), the indefinite should pick up some referent in the speaker's mind. With these basic assumptions in Dynamic Syntax, let us turn to the syntax/semantics of MSCs.

3   Layers of Predication in MSC

As we have already seen, Japanese subjects are licensed by open propositions in stative sentences.[4] We want to explore a syntactic/semantic analysis reflecting the following intuitions on MSCs. Observe the sentences in (25):

(25) a. <u>Neko-wa/$^?$-ga</u> [$_\alpha$ karada-ga yawarakai]   (Assertive sentence)
         Cat-Top   body-Nom   Be_pliant-Pres
         'Lit. As for cats, their bodies are pliant.'
     b. <u>Nani-ga/*-wa</u>   [$_\alpha$ karada-ga yawarakai-no]? (Interrogative sentence)
         what-Nom/-Top   body-Nom   Be_pliant-Q

First, MSCs must convey kind/individual-level interpretations (which should also be represented somehow in the semantics), and the subjects of these kinds of predicates

---

[4] Even in English, we often find sentences which seem to be simply licensed by predicate phrases with gaps, not by the propositional templates (argument structures) of predicates:
   (i) a. This violin [is easy to play the sonata with e].
       b. This book [is said to be worth reading e].
       c. This wall [seems to need repainting e].

exhibits strong tendency to get marked by the topic marker -*WA*, not by the nominative *GA* in declarative sentences. The nominative major subject in (25a) must be taken as foci and receive exhaustive-listing reading (see Kuno 1973) and usually becomes acceptable only in embedded clauses. On the other hand, interrogative words never get marked as topic, so MSCs are obligatory in questions. The point is that the structures indicated by [$_\alpha$ ...] have something in common.[5] Second, we want to capture the structural symmetry observed in the examples below.

(26) a. Neko-ga [$_\alpha$ karada-ga yawarakai] (= (2))
    b. [$_\alpha$ karada-ga   yawarakai]   neko
        body-Nom Be_pliant-Prescats
        'cats whose bodies are pliant'
    cf.   [karada-ga   yawarakai]   no-wa   neko-da.
        body-Nom Be_pliant-Pres Gen-Top cat-be-Pres
        'It is the cats whose bodies are pliant.'
    c. Major Subject [OPEN PROPOSITION] head of relative clause
          ↑licensing the major subject↑   ↑licensing the relative head↑

It is clear that the major subject *Neko-ga* and the head of the relative clause are both licensed by the "embedded" sentence, in which the argument structure of the verb *yawarakai* is fully saturated, but it has a "gap" in the possessor position of the subject. It should be noticed that all MSCs in (1) have an open position somewhere in the predicative sentences following the major subjects.

   A purely syntactic approach will find much difficulty in associating these subjects and their corresponding 'gaps' occurring anywhere inside "predicative clauses" but we assume that the open propositions indicated by the brackets denote (enduring/inherent) properties the referents of subjects should have, so the predication relations between the major subjects and the open propositions must be established during the construction process of their semantic representations. The predicative propositions must contain at least one gap somewhere inside them, but there is no restriction on the positions of gaps. Observe the following sentences.

(27) a. Tokyo-ga   [$_{PredP}$[*e* tosibu]-ni   kumanezumi-ga ooi].
      Tokyo-NOM   downtown-IN blackrats-NOM many-BE-Pres
    b. Kono naifu-ga [$_{PredP}$ [*e* sentan]-de   enpitsu-ga/-o   kezurer-u].
      this knife-NOM   edge-WITH   pencil-NOM/-ACC sharpen-CAN-Pres
      'This knife is such that they can sharpen points of pencils with its edge.'

If there is no gap inside a clause following the major subject, the derived MSC is ungrammatical.

(28) a. Tanaka-sensei-ga   [$_{PredP}$ deshi-tati-ga   yuusyu-da].
      Tanaka-Mr.-Nom   [student-Pl.Nom   excellent-Be-Pres
      'Lit. Mr. Tanaka is such that his students are excellent.'
    b.*Tanaka-sensei-ga [$_{PredP}$ gengogakusya-ga   yuusyu-da].
      Tanaka-Mr.-NOM   linguist-Nom   excellent-Be-Pres

---

[5] Here we do not intend to argue that the predicative clauses following the topic and major subject project the same structure. Rather, we assume that the syntactic structures of the two clauses should be distinguished in principle, but we leave this question open.

Because the factor causing the difference in grammaticality between (28a) and (28b) is only the meaning of the second subject, we should examine the semantic difference among common nouns more carefully. While nouns like *linguist* simply denotes a set of individuals, *students* in this context denotes relations between individuals, or in other words, functions from individuals to sets, which take particular individuals to return individuals who stand in the teacher-student relation to the former. Let us define the meaning of relational noun *student* as $\lambda y.\lambda x.$Student-of$(y)(x)$ (for discussion, see Vikner & Jensen 1999, Barker 1995, Asudeh 2003, Jacobson 1999, 2000, Partee & Borschev 2000, Nakamura 2002). Relational nouns tend to get bound by other terms in the local domain. In languages like English, this binding is immediately done by the preceding possessors within NPs, whereas, in Japanese, the possessor variable binding can be delayed. So major subjects can bind the possessor variables contained in the following subjects via predication after subjectivization applies to the former. We do not mean to argue that there is syntactic connectivity between a major subject and the corresponding gap. Our proposal is that the semantic relation between the major subject and its gap within the predicative proposition can be established in the course of building the semantic representation of a MSC, given the notion of initial underspecification and subsequent resolution during the process of constructing an interpretation.

Let us start with an assumption that an open proposition predicated of a MSC subject have a <u>requirement to find the copy of the subject</u>, and this requirement can be resolved step-by-step in the course of parsing on line during left-to-right processing. To construct a semantic representation for (26a), the position for the major subject *Neko* 'cats' is constructed as an unfixed node by Local *Adjunction in (14) exactly as we expect in projecting unfixed nodes for ordinary argument NPs in Japanese sentences, but it should be noticed that the major subject can NOT be directly associated with any argument node of the propositional template of the verb *yawarakai* 'pliable' though Cann, et al. (2005) argues that 'it is the verbs that which project a full predicate-argument structure whose argument values can be identified directly from context' (p. 230). Here the parser must leave the tree node relation unfixed. As a first approximation, let us assume that we have two different lexical entries for the nominative marker *-GA,* one for regular subjects and the other for major subjects, which is defined in (29). The latter does not fix a subject node for *Neko-ga* after processing of the nominative marker, and simply return the pointer to a local type-t-requiring node with a requirement of its copy in a subsequent structure, as in (30):[6]

(29)
-ga | IF $Ty(e)$, Fo(α)
      | THEN IF $<\uparrow_0\uparrow_1^*>(Tn(a) \wedge Ty(t))$
      | THEN put(?$\exists x.Tn(x)$);
      | go($<\uparrow_0\uparrow_1^*>$); put(?$<\downarrow_*>Fo(\alpha)$);
      | ELSE Abort
      | ELSE Abort

---

[6] Notice that the lexical actions of regular nominative and other case markers does not return the pointer-return to a local *$Ty(t)$ node. This process is ensured by Completion. See Cann, et al. 2005:237 for discussion.

Multiple Subject Constructions in Japanese: A Dynamic Syntax Account   113

(30) $Tn(0), ?Ty(t), ?(\downarrow *)Fo(\tau,x,\text{Neko}'(x)), \diamondsuit$

          $<\uparrow_0\uparrow_1^*>Tn(0), ?Ty(e)$
          $?\exists x.Tn(x)), Fo(\tau,x,\text{Neko}'(x))$

Then, the second subject *karada* 'body' is introduced, again, by Local *Adjunction, which project the complex internal structure with an extra node for a possessor variable by lexical actions defined in its entry as in (31):

(31) *karada* 'body'

IF	$?Ty(e)$
THEN	make($<\downarrow_1>$);go($<\downarrow_1>$);put($Ty(cn\rightarrow e),Fo(\lambda P.(\varepsilon.P)),[\downarrow]\bot$;
	go($<\uparrow_1>$);make($<\downarrow_0>$;go($<\downarrow_0>$);put($?Ty(cn)$);
	make($<\downarrow_1>$);go($<\downarrow_1>$);put($?Ty(e\rightarrow(e\rightarrow cn)),Fo(\lambda x(x,\lambda y(y,\text{Karada}'(x,y)))$;
	make($<\downarrow_1>$);go($<\downarrow_1>$);put($Ty(e\rightarrow cn),Fo(\lambda y.\text{Karada}'(y))[\downarrow]\bot$;
	go($<\uparrow_1>$);make($<\downarrow_0>$);go($<\downarrow_0>$);freshput($x,Fo(x)$)
	go($<\uparrow_0>$);go($<\uparrow_1>$);make($<\downarrow_0>$);go($<\downarrow_0>$);put($?Ty(e)$), freshput($z,Fo(z)$);
ELSE	Abort

The partial tree constructed at present should be something like (32):

(32)

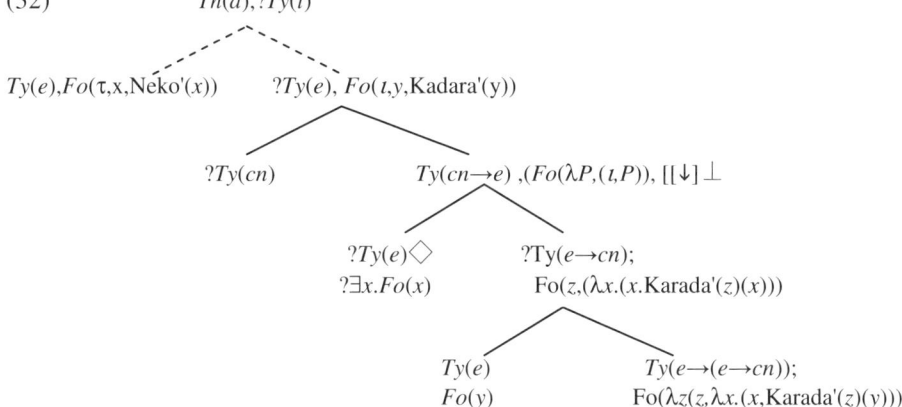

The higher type-*e*-requiring node is constructed by the lexical specification for the relational noun *karada* 'body', which is roughly a function of type ($e\rightarrow(e\rightarrow cn)$) from possessors to their bodies. In the non-MSC counterpart in (33), the possessor argument marked with genitive case fills the position corresponding to the first *e*.

(33)   [NP Neko-no   karada-ga]   yawarakai.
            Cat-Gen   body-Nom   pliant-Pres.
       'Cats' bodies are pliant.'

In the tree for MSC (32), however, the node currently under development has no formula value, which is provided from the copy of the major subject passed down the tree, step by step until this open node is projected. This process must be distinguished from the scrambling of an possessor argument to the sentence-initial position, which is ungrammatical as seen in the degraded status of sentence *Neko-no totemo karada-ga yawarakai* (here the adverb is inserted to cut the constituency between the possessor and possessee arguments) because the possessor argument is not subjectivized. The nominative marker requires expressions it marks to stand in a predication relation to predicative phrases (in MSCs, the latter must refer the former's permanent or stable attributes). Though the particle *GA* of the second subject fixes its tree node relation, as the ordinary GA or other case markers. However, the derivation suggested above requires multiple application of Local *Adjunction at the same $Ty(t)$ node, and this is what Dynamic Syntax disallows, because more than one node with the same tree relation cannot be distinguished. In (32), there are two unfixed nodes, the major subject and the regular subject node, are both unfixed in a local type-t-requiring tree, and the derivation aborts by definition.

Another motivation to have recourse to a different computational rule, Generalized Adjunction, comes from our intuition that MSCs project complex structures, while non-MSCs like (32) do not. Finally, we hope to capture a parallelism between MSCs and its relativized counterparts we will discuss in the next section. First, the major subject is introduced, as before, but the requirement to find a copy is not imposed on the type-t-requiring node. The next step is to introduce a kind of embedded clause into the structure by Generalised Adjunction defined in (34):

(34)   Generalised Adjunction (Cann, et. al 2005:242)

$$\frac{\{...\{Tn(a), ..., ?Ty(t), \Diamond\}...\}}{\{...\{Tn(a),..., ?Ty(t)\}, \{<U>Tn(a), ?\exists x.Tn(x),...,?Ty(t), \Diamond\}...\}}$$

(34) is the rule to introduce a clause under the current type-t-requiring node. $<U>$ is defined as the reflexive transitive closure of the union of the inverse($<L^{-1}>$) and mother($<\uparrow>$) relation. In tree-diagrams, this tree relation is indicated by a dotted line, to distinguish it from the dashed line indicating the relation established by Local *Adjunction. After processing of the major and regular subject, (34) yields the interim transition as shown in (35):

(35)

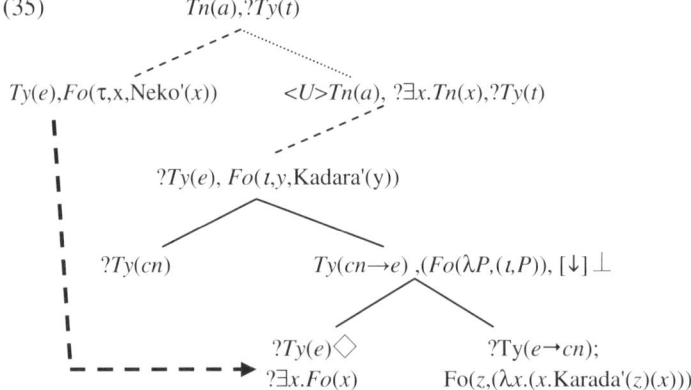

The partial structure is not ruled out by the prohibition of multiple application of the same Adjunction Rule at one time because one unfixed node is constructed by Local *Adjunction, while the other (type-t-requiring) node by Generalised Adjunction. Local *Adjunction may apply to construct another unfixed node for the following subject *karada* 'body', as shown in (31). The major subject node and the possessor node of the following subject is identified by the step of Merge (indicated by the heavy dashed line in (31)), which is here a step of structural abduction which is required as a meta-level process of reasoning (see Cann, et al. 2005:256 for discussion).

Because this is a pragmatic and system-external step, its application may be rejected.[7] After the predicate *yawarakai* 'pliable' is processed, the higher $Ty(t)$-requiring and adjoined $Ty(t)$-requiring nodes are identified because they are eventually interpreted to refer to one and the same node. In effect, the application of Generalized Adjunction makes a vacuous contribution to the semantic representation. Finally, the complete semantic tree for MSC (26b) should be something like (36):

(36)

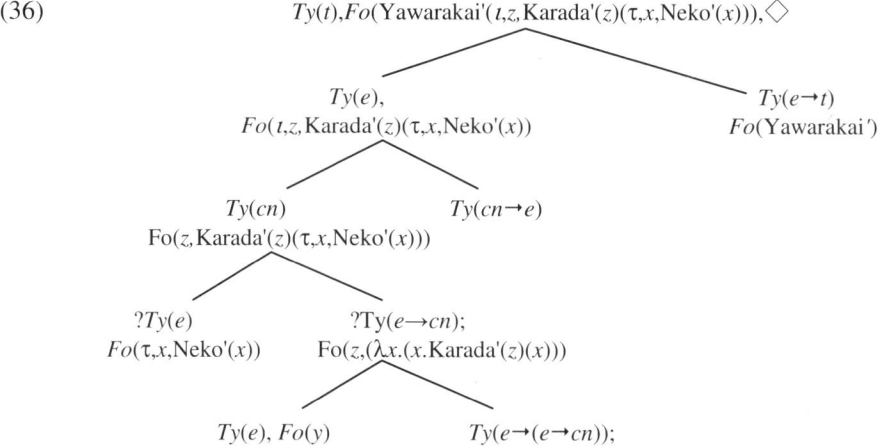

It should be noticed that the construction process proposed here can be repeatedly applied. We can easily build the semantic representations for MSCs with more than two subjects in a simple clause, as in (3), which reflect the intuition of native speakers concerning the presence of the layers of predication in MSCs in the parsing process.

4 Relative Clause Formation of MSCs

In this section, we discuss relativization from MSCs where preceding major subjects can be extracted, while following subjects cannot, as shown in (5) and (7). In Japanese, any argument, adjunct or possessor can be relativized even in non-stative sentences. Note that the argument structures of the embedded predicates are fully saturated in these examples. Such unbounded dependency must be problematic for any syntactic theory proposed so far. In our analysis of MSCs in the preceding section suggests that major subjects are licensed by open propositions with unfixed nodes, which can in turn license the construction of relative clauses.

Another fact to be explained is the asymmetry in extractablity between major and regular subjects. Once subjectivization is invoked to raise a possessor to the major subject position to form the layers of predication, the remaining second or third

---

[7] For instance, observe the difference in acceptability of (ib) and (28a):
(i) a. Tanaka-sensei-no   aiken-ga   makkuro-da.
       Tanaka-Mr.-Gen   pet-dog-Nom   inky-black-Be-Pres
       'Mr. Tanaka's pet dog is inky black.'
    b.*Tanaka-sensei-ga   aiken-ga   makkuro-da.
       Tanaka-Mr.-Nom   pet-dog-Nom   inky-black-Be-Pres

subject must be stuck in a kind of 'island' formed by possessor extraction. How can our analysis account for the difference in grammaticality between (6a, 7a) and (6b, 7b)? First, let us consider how to build a semantic representation for a relative clause of a MSC. In parsing sentence (26b), the propositional node of the relative clause is introduced by Generalized Adjunction in (34). This weak rule merely introduce a type-t-requiring node (which may be an embedded clause or a relative clause) into the emergent structure. Then Local Adjunction constructs another kind of unfixed (type-e-requiring) node. The lexical specification of the relational noun *karada-ga* 'body' projects the structure with its possessor node open:

(39)   Parsing of *Karada-ga*

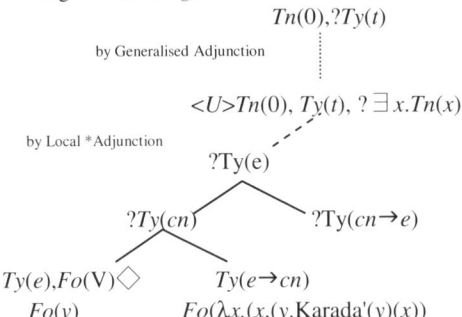

The metavariable decorating the open type-e-requiring (possessor) node of the relational noun in (39) cannot be replaced with any formula. Hence, a fresh variable is constructed by the step of abduction to instantiate the metavariable, satisfying its formula requirement. The abduction process allows the propositional formula to be projected, and Completion and Elimination pass up this fresh variable to the local type-t-requiring node, and this variable is copied over to the new structure into which the head noun is introduced by the LINK Adjunction rule for Japanese in (40).

(40) LINK Adjunction (Japanese) (Cann, et al. 2005:274)

$$\{...\{Tn(n), Ty(t), ..., \Diamond\}...\{<\uparrow_*>Tn(n), Fo(x), Ty(e)...\}\}$$

$$\{...\{Tn(n), Ty(t),...\}...\{<\uparrow_*>Tn(n), Fo(x), Ty(e), ...\}\},$$
$$\{\{<L>Tn(n), Fo(x), Ty(e)\}, \{<\downarrow_0><L>Tn(n)\},$$
$$\{<\downarrow_0><\downarrow_0><L>Tn(n), <U>Tn(n), ?\exists x.Tn(x), \Diamond\}\}$$

Due to lack of space, we show only the tree resulting from the parsing of the relative clause *Karada-ga yawarakai neko* 'cats whose bodies are pliant' in (41) on the next page.

If the second subject is extracted from the relative clause in an MSC as in (7), there is no fresh variable left within the LINKed structure, the copy of which should be carried over, and (40) cannot apply to construct a term corresponding to the head noun. On the other hand, in successful parsing of the relative clause with the major subject extracted, as in (41), the evaluation rule can derive the proper interpretation like $\lambda x.(x, \lambda y.(y, \text{Neko}(x) \wedge (\text{Pliant}'(\text{Body}'(y))(x)))$.

Finally, let us turn to the general issue of what role subjectivization plays in Japanese grammar. Recall that an MSC only carries an kind-level or individual-level interpretation, referring to the predication of an enduring inherent property of entity/entities denoted by a major subject. We, therefore, posit the presence of a generic operator, indicated by Gen, in MSCs. Observe the examples below.

(41)
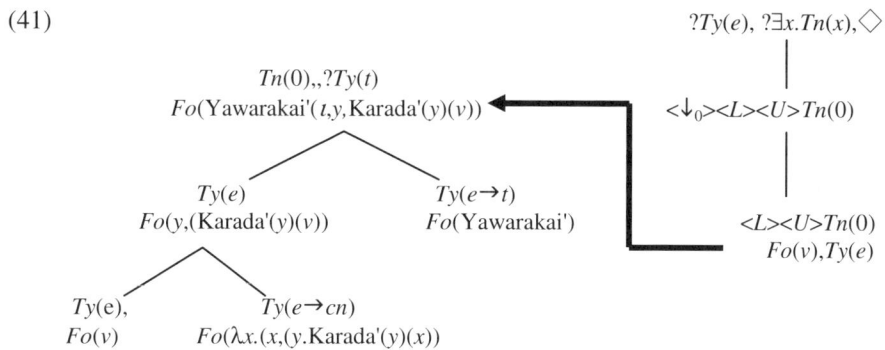

(42) a. [$_{NP}$ Neko-no   karada-ga] yawarakai.
           cat-Gen   body-Nom   pliable-Be-Pres
     b. [$_{NP}$ Neko-ga]$_i$ [e_i karada-ga]   yawarakai.
           cat-Nom   body-Nom   pliable-Be-Pres
     c. [$_{NP}$ [$_S$ e_i karada-ga   yawarakai]   neko$_i$]-ga ...
                      body-Nom   pliable-Be-Pres   cat-Nom

As mentioned above, the value of *karada* 'body' must co-vary with the value of *neko* 'cat' in all the examples in (42). However, we should form different restrictors from quantified nouns of these sentences:

(43) a. $Gen\ x(\exists y(Cat'(x) \wedge Body'(x,y)) \rightarrow Pliable'(y))$
     b. $Gen\ x(Cat'(x) \rightarrow \exists y(Body'(x,y) \wedge Pliable'(y)))$
     c. $\lambda P.Gen\ x(\exists y\ (Cat'(x) \wedge Pliable'(Body'(x,y))) \rightarrow P(x))$

As for quantification concerning MSCs, we speculate that subjectivization is the device to take some predicate out of the restrictor to make it a new restrictor, and assemble the remaining elements into a new nuclear scope probably with internal structure, while relativization is the device to expand the restoricter, as can be seen from the analysis so far, but we do not discuss the interesting interaction between subjectivization and quantification any further.

5 Conclusion

In this paper, we explored an incremental parsing device building up semantic structures for multiple subject constructions in Japanese which are represented by the logic of finite trees. In Japanese stative sentences, argument structures (propositional templates) of predicates do not play any role for licensing of major subjects. Subjectivization of an arbitrary element in a stative clause is licensed by establishing a predication relation between a major subject and an open proposition, where pragmatic contexts should be taken into account. We have also shown how the layers of predication is constructed in a MSC projected from a single predicate, focusing on the semantic property of relational nouns which introduces an extra argument node into the structure. This construction process is not reflected in the semantic representation itself, but in sequences of transitions. The semantic properties of following subjects also provide an account to the asymmetry in applicability of relative clause formation in MSCs. Possibilities of establishing predication and relativization for MSCs have also given compelling evidence for our proposal. Many striking typological properties of MSCs have been clarified from a dynamic processing perspective following from general principles of left-to-right parsing and monotonic tree growth assumed in the Dynamic Syntax framework.

References

1. Asudeh, A.: The Resumptive Puzzle of Relational Nouns. Ms (2003)
2. Barker, C.: Possessive Descriptions. Center for the Study of Language and Information, Stanford (1995)
3. Cann, R., Kempson, R., Marten, L.: The Dynamics of Language. Academic Press, Amsterdam (2005)
4. Diesing, M.: Indefinites. MIT Press, New York (1992)
5. Engdahl, E.: Relational Interpretation. In: Kempson, R. (ed.) Metal Representation: The Interface between Language and Reality, pp. 63–82. Cambridge University Press, London (1988)
6. Hasegawa, N.: Seisei-Nihongogaku Nyuumon. Taisyuukan, Tokyo (1999)
7. Jacobson, P.: Towards a Variable-Free Semantics. Linguistics and Philosophy 22, 117–184 (1999)
8. Jacobson, P.: Paycheck Pronouns, Bach-Peters Sentences, and Variable-free Semantics. Natural Language Semantics 8, 77–155 (2000)
9. Kempson, R.: Japanese Scrambling as Growth of Semantic Representation. King's College, London (manuscript, 2003)
10. Kempson, R., Cann, R., Kiaer, J.: Topic, Focus and the Structural Dynamics of Language. Ms. King's College, London (2003)
11. Kempson, R., Meyer-Viol, W.: Indefinites and Scope Choice. In: Reimer, M., Bezuidenhout, A. (eds.) Descriptions and Beyond, pp. 553–583. Oxford U.P., London (2004)
12. Kempson, R., Meyer-Viol, W., Gabbay, D.: Dynamic Syntax: The Flow of Language Understanding. Blackwell, London (2001)
13. Kuno, S.: The Structure of the Japanese Language. MIT Press, Cambridge (1973)
14. Mihara, K.: Nihongo-no Tougo-Kouzou: Seisei-bunpou Riron-to Sono Ouyou. Syoohakusya, Tokyo (1994)
15. Morikawa, M.: A Parametric Approach to Case Alternation Phenomena in Japanese. Hituzi Syobo (1993)
16. Nakamura, H.: Tajuusyugo-koobun-no Hasei-to Kaisyaku, Nihongo-kagaku 12, 72–94, Kokuritsu-Kokugo Kenkyusyo, Tokyo (2002)
17. Partee, B., Borschev, B.: Genitives, Relational Nouns, and the Argument-Modifier Distinction. In: Fabricius-Hansen, C., Lang, E., Maienborn, C. (eds.) ZAS Papers in Linguistics, vol. 17, pp. 177–201 (2000)
18. Sperber, D., Wilson, D.: Relevance: communication and Cognition, 2nd edn. Blackwell, Oxford (1986/1995)
19. Sugimoto, T.: Nihon-go no Daisyugo to Syudai. Kyusyu Daigaku Kougakubu Kiyou 3, 165–182 (1990)
20. Vikner, C., Jensen, P.A.: A Semantic Analysis of the English Genitive. Interaction of Lexical and Formal Semantics. Ms. Copenhagen (1999)

Topic/Subject Coreference in the Hierarchy of Japanese Complex Sentences

Alastair Butler[1], Chidori Nakamura[2], and Kei Yoshimoto[3]

[1] Japan Society for the Promotion of Science
6 Ichibancho, Chiyoda-ku, Tokyo 102-8471 Japan
ajb129@hotmail.com
[2] International Center, Iwate University
3-18-8 Ueda, Morioka, Iwate 020-8550 Japan
chidori@iwate-u.ac.jp
[3] Center for the Advancement of Higher Education, Tohoku University
Kawauchi 41, Aoba-ku, Sendai 980-8576 Japan
kyoshimoto@mail.tains.tohoku.ac.jp

Abstract. This paper addresses coreference of topicalized and untopicalized subjects in Japanese complex sentences which is known to depend on the type of subordinate clause head and topicalization of the matrix subject. We provide an account based on Scope Control Theory, a semantic theory using operator-variable dependencies, which explains the above-mentioned issue as part of regularities deriving from the hierarchical structure in Japanese sentences.

1 Introduction

It has been known in the circle of traditional studies of Japanese grammar that the reference of the subject in a subordinate clause depends on both the topicalization of the matrix subject and the type of subordinate clause head. While the traditional research remained descriptive in terms of this kind of linguistic data, syntactic rules have been proposed by Yoshimoto (1998) which constrain different levels of the sentential hierarchy to share semantic information. In this paper, we provide an account directly based on semantics using operator-variable dependencies which lead to regularities found throughout the Japanese grammar including the topic/subject coreference.

The organization of this paper is as follows. Section 2 gives an outline of the linguistic data we are going to deal with. In section 3, we provide an introduction to the semantic system to be employed in the following sections, i.e. Scope Control Theory (SCT). The fourth section illustrates how simple sentences in Japanese are represented as SCT expressions. Section 5 shows how SCT explains the observed linguistic data. Section 6 concludes the paper.

2 Topic and Subject in Complex Sentences

Different types of subordinate clause in Japanese impinge on subject coreference in complex sentences. In the following examples,

(1) a. **Tarō$_i$ ga** [ϕ_i uwagi o nui]$_A$ de hangā ni kake- ta.
NAME NOM (SBJ) jacket ACC take off SUCC hanger LOC hang PST
'Taro took off his jacket and hung it on a hanger.'
b. **Tarō$_i$ wa** [ϕ_i uwagi o nui]$_A$ de hangā ni kake- ta.
NAME TOP (SBJ) jacket ACC take off SUCC hanger LOC hang PST
'Taro took off his jacket and hung it on a hanger.'

the obligatorily omitted subject of the subordinate clause headed by *de* (i.e., an allomorph of *te* (SUCCESSIVE)) is identical with that of the matrix clause, irrespective of whether the latter is suffixed by a topic marker *wa* or not.

By contrast, the subject of a subordinate clause introduced by a postposition *to* (SUCCESSIVE) is influenced by the topicalization of the matrix subject for its reference.

(2) a. [**Tarō$_i$ ga** uwagi o nugu]$_B$ *to* ϕ_j hangā ni kake- ta.
NAME NOM jacket ACC take off SUCC (SBJ) hanger LOC hang PST
'After Taro had taken off his jacket, someone hung it on a hanger.'
b. **Tarō$_i$ wa** [ϕ_i uwagi o nugu]$_B$ *to* hangā ni kake- ta.
NAME TOP (SBJ) jacket ACC take off SUCC hanger LOC hang PST
'After Taro had taken off his jacket, he hung it on a hanger.'

In (2a), the omitted matrix subject and the one in the subordinate clause can in general refer to different denotations. In (2b), where the matrix subject is topicalized and the subordinate subject is zero-pronominalized, both of them share the same reference (Mikami 1970). Note that different syntactic structures are assigned to the two sentences: while the subject NP is included in the Level B subordinate clause in (2a), the topicalized subject lies outside its scope in (2b), following Minami's (1974) hierarchical syntactic structure.

Lastly, in a subordinate clause headed by *kara* (CAUSAL) as below, the subject has a denotation independent of that of the matrix subject.

(3) a. [**Tarō$_i$ ga** uwagi o nui- da]$_C$ *kara* ϕ_j hangā ni kake-
NAME NOM jacket ACC take off PST CAUS (SBJ) hanger LOC hang
ta.
PST
'Since Taro took off his jacket, someone hung it on a hanger.'
b. [**Tarō$_i$ wa** uwagi o nui- da]$_C$ *kara* ϕ_j hangā ni kake-
NAME TOP jacket ACC take off PST CAUS (SBJ) hanger LOC hang
ta.
PST
'Since Taro took off his jacket, someone hung it on a hanger.'

The observed fact is no isolated linguistic data; it forms part of regularities found throughout Japanese sentences. As Minami (1974) has made clear, subordinate clauses in Japanese behave differently according to whether various constituents can occur within them. This finding has been developed into the layered structure of the Japanese sentence in general, which consists of Levels A, B, C, and D, with the outer levels enclosing the inner ones. The schema given below illustrates how the sentence in Japanese is composed hierarchically. The whole sentence is obtained by recursively adding different levels of case phrases (CPs), adverbial phrases (APs) including subordinate clauses, and predicate constituents (PCs), i.e. auxiliary verbs and modal particles, to the main verb (MV).

(4) $[AP^* \; [AP^* \; [AP^* \; CP^* \; [AP^* \; CP^* \; MV]_A \; \text{-}PC^*]_B \; \text{-}PC^*]_C \; \text{-}PC^*]_D$

Heterogeneous linguistic facts have been discussed in relation to the four-level hierarchy. For instance, interpretation of tenses in complex sentences is determined by the hierarchical level the subordinate clause belongs to, tense of the matrix sentence, and Aktionsarten (dynamic or stative) of the predicates (Yoshimoto 1998). Furthermore, focus, or that part of sentence new information can fall on, can be affected by the Minami hierarchy, as has been studied by Takubo (1987).

3 Scope Control Theory

Scope Control Theory (SCT; Butler 2007) is a small logical language which attempts to approximate the dependency structures in natural languages by fine-grained and restricted scope management. With SCT, dependencies are established as operator-variable dependencies. The influence of a scope varies depending on its placement within the hierarchical structure of an overall expression.

SCT, under the influence of the Sequence Semantics by Vermeulen (1993, 2000), makes extensive use of sequences and operations on sequences. Below are the important notations:

(5) i. $\vec{x}$: a sequence of x's.
 ii. $[x_0, \ldots, x_{n-1}]$: a sequence with n elements.
 iii. $(.)_i$: the i-th element of a sequence, e.g., $([x_0, \ldots, x_{n-1}])_i = x_i$ for $0 \leq i < n$.
 iv. $|.|$: the sequence length, e.g., $|[x_0, \ldots, x_{n-1}]| = n$.
 v. $\text{cons}(y, [x_0, \ldots, x_{n-1}]) = [y, x_0, \ldots, x_{n-1}]$.
 vi. $\text{snoc}(y, [x_0, \ldots, x_{n-1}]) = [x_0, \ldots, x_{n-1}, y]$.

The binding names of SCT expressions are linked to scope sequences via scope sequence assignments.

(6) A scope sequence assignment, g, is a mapping that assigns a (possibly empty) sequence of predicate logic variable names to each SCT name: $g : Name \rightarrow Var^*$.

Meanings of SCT operators are explained in terms of $\texttt{pop}$ and $\texttt{shift}$ operations on scope sequence assignments. Let SSA be the set of scope sequence assignments; x, y, z be variables representing SCT names; and $op \in \{\texttt{cons}, \texttt{snoc}\}$. We define $\texttt{pop}_x \subseteq SSA \times SSA$ and $\texttt{shift}(op)_{x,y} \subseteq SSA \times SSA$ as follows:

(7) $(g, h) \in \text{pop}_x$ iff
- $g(x) = \text{cons}((g(x))_0, h(x))$ and
- $h(y) = g(y)$ whenever $y \neq x$.

(8) $(g, h) \in \text{shift}(op)_{x,y}$ iff $\exists k$:
- $(h, k) \in \text{pop}_y$ and
- $g(x) = op((h(y))_0, k(x))$ and
- $g(z) = k(z)$ whenever $z \neq x$.

These basic operations are illustrated in (9), moving from g to h. Boxed letters represent scopes while unboxed letters represent SCT names.

(9)
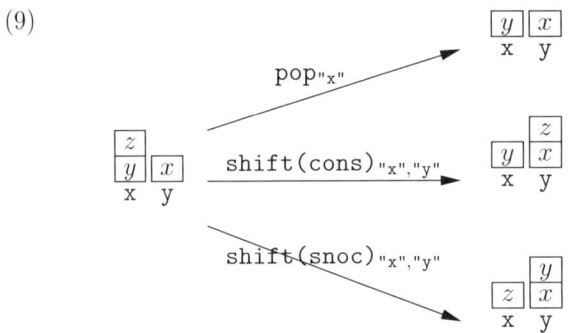

Assignment operations can be repeated n times when augmented with a positive superscript n, e.g. (10).

(10) $(\begin{array}{c}\boxed{y}\\\boxed{x}\\\overrightarrow{x\ y}\end{array}, \begin{array}{c}\boxed{y}\\\boxed{x}\\\overleftarrow{x\ y}\end{array}) \in \text{shift}(\text{snoc})^2_{\text{"x","y"}}$

The building blocks of SCT expressions are six operators.

(11) i. Use (x,e) adds to an x usage count, helping to ensure the SCT expression is well-formed.
  ii. Hide (x,e) terminates an x usage count.
  iii. T(x,i) builds a term, which is the i-th element of the scope sequence assigned to x.
  iv. Close (x,e) creates a fresh scope for x based on usage count.
  v. Lam (x,y,e) shifts a scope's binding name from x to y.
  vi. Rel $(\vec{x}, \vec{y}, r, \vec{e})$ builds a relation r with a sequence of arguments $\vec{e}$, changing the assignment for each argument based on $\vec{x}$ and $\vec{y}$.

Usage counts over e, $x(e)$, return a count of the number of times Use $(x,\#)$ occurs in e outside the scope of any Hide $(x,\#)$. This is used to check the well-formedness of SCT expressions.

(12) i. $x(\text{Use }(y,e)) = \begin{cases} x(e) + 1 & \text{if } x = y \\ x(e) & \text{otherwise} \end{cases}$

ii. $x(\text{Hide } (y,e)) = \begin{cases} 0 & \text{if } x = y \\ x(e) & \text{otherwise} \end{cases}$

iii. $x(\text{T } (y,i)) = 0$

iv. $x(\text{Close } (y,e)) = x(e)$

v. $x(\text{Lam } (y,z,e)) = x(e)$

vi. $x(\text{Rel } (\vec{y},\vec{z},r,\vec{e})) = \sum_{i=0}^{|\vec{e}|-1} x(\vec{e}_i)$

SCT evaluation takes the form of a translation from SCT expressions into expressions of predicate logic notation. The translation procedure for each operator is shown below. This is presented as a function $(g,e)^\circ$ that takes expression e and scope sequence assignment g and returns a predicate logic formula or *, the latter signaling failure of the translation.

(13) i. $(g,\text{Use } (x,e))^\circ$
 - return $(g,e)^\circ$

ii. $(g,\text{Hide } (x,e))^\circ$
 - return $(g,e)^\circ$

iii. $(g,\text{T } (x,i))^\circ$
 - return $(g(x))_i$, provided $i < |g(x)|$
 - otherwise return *

iv. $(g,\text{Close } (x,e))^\circ$
 - if $x(e) = 0$ return $(g,e)^\circ$
 - else $\exists h : (h,g) \in \text{pop}_x^{x(e)}$ return $\exists (h(x))_0...(h(x))_{x(e)-1}(h,e)^\circ$, provided $(h,e)^\circ \neq *$
 - otherwise return *

v. $(g,\text{Lam } (x,y,e))^\circ$
 - $\exists h : (g,h) \in \text{shift}(\text{cons})_{x,y}$ return $(h,e)^\circ$
 - otherwise return *

vi. $(g,\text{Rel } (\vec{x},\vec{y},r,\vec{e}))^\circ$
 - return $r((0,g,\vec{x},\vec{y},\vec{e})^\circ,...,(|\vec{e}|-1,g,\vec{x},\vec{y},\vec{e})^\circ)$, provided for $0 \leq i < |\vec{e}|$, $(i,\vec{x},\vec{y},\vec{e})^\circ \neq *$
 - otherwise return *

 — $(n,g,\vec{x},\vec{y},\vec{e})^\circ$
 - if $|\vec{x}| = 0$ return $(g,\vec{e}_n)^\circ$
 - else $\exists h_0...h_{|\vec{x}|} : h_0 = g$ and for $0 \leq i < |\vec{x}|$, $(h_i, h_{i+1}) \in$
 $(\text{pop}_{\vec{x}_i}^{|h_i(\vec{x}_i)|-\sum_{k=0}^n \vec{x}_i(\vec{e}_k)}; \text{shift}(\text{snoc})_{\vec{x}_i,\vec{y}_i}^{|h_i(\vec{x}_i)|-\sum_{k=n}^{|\vec{e}|-1}\vec{x}_i(\vec{e}_k)})$
 return $(h_{|\vec{x}|},\vec{e}_n)^\circ$
 - otherwise return *

The Rel operator constrains the number of scopes available for any name to match the usage count in order to check the scope-use balance. See the next section.

In order to bridge the gap between SCT and natural language expressions, we adopt notation as syntactic sugar introduced by let. The definition of enriched SCT notation by let can be translated into the pure λ-calculus as follows:

(14) let $v \ x_1 \ldots x_n = B$ in $E \equiv (\lambda E)(\lambda x_1 \ldots x_n.B)$

By means of this notation, we can define a general encoding for an intransitive verb (e.g., *smiles*) as a one place relation linked to the most recent "x" binding, i.e. the leftmost element of the sequence of scopes for "x".

(15) `Rel (nil, nil, "smiles", [T ("x", 0)])`

The above SCT expression can be simplified by using `let`:

(16) `let vi s = Rel (nil, nil, s, [T ("x", 0)])`

This makes possible an alternative notation for the intransitive verb as follows:

(17) `vi "smiles"`

4   Parsing of Simple Sentences

What corresponds to existential quantification in predicate logic can be achieved in SCT by combining `Hide`, `Close`, and `Use` operators. Thus, an enriched notation `exists` can be defined as follows.

(18) `let exists name f =`
     `Hide (name, Close (name, Use (name, f)))`

A sentence with existential quantification (19a) is given the SCT expression in (19b) by supplying `exists` with a binding name and an expression for the intransitive verb:

(19) a. Someone smiles.
     b. `exists "x" (vi "smiles")`

(20) gives the translation of (19) against the empty scope sequence assignment λ, which is exactly the predicate logic formula standardly assigned to sentence (19a).

(20) $(\lambda,$ `exists "x" (vi "smiles")`$)^\circ = \exists x \mathrm{smiles}(x)$

The figure in (21) illustrates how (20) is evaluated step by step based on the SCT operators.

(21) `Hide "x"`
       $\overline{x}$ `Close "x"`
        |

      `Use "x"`
        $\boxed{x}$ `Rel [], [], "smiles"`
         x
         |
        $\boxed{x}$ `T("x", 0)`
         x

Hide ("x", f) terminates any count for occurrences of Use ("x", #) in f. If the whole expression presented here is embedded under another exists "x" # environment, then the latter will not interfere with the former. This is an analogue of insensitivity of a variable in predicate logic bound by an embedded quantifier to the binding by an embedding one. Close ("x", f) opens a fresh scope on the "x" sequence as represented by $\boxed{x}$ in the diagram. Use ("x" #) is specified here for usage counts and has no effect on the assignment. Lastly, vi "smiles" gives the smiles relation, with its argument being bound by the frontmost scope of "x", or the topmost scope on the "x" stack, i.e., $\boxed{x}$ in (21).

We introduce a scope name "ga" that stands for the grammatical relation subject to which evaluation is made sensitive. We also require "wa" bindings to deal with topicalized sentences. We define (22) to check for the presence of "ga" bindings.

(22) let check name f =
     Hide (name, Rel ([name], ["c"], "∧", [f]))

We also need a base form for predicate relations. The simplest possible form is the following:

(23) let rel s l = Rel (nil, nil, s, l)

Next, we define predicate forms for "ga" and "wa" bindings:

(24) let rga s = check "ga" (Use ("ga", rel s [T ("ga", 0)]))
(25) let rwa s = check "ga" (rel s [T ("wa", 0)])

Let us see how rga prescribes the requirement for one and only one "ga" binding based on the check definition in (22) using Rel. (26a) is an ungrammatical sentence with duplicated indefinite NPs as subjects.

(26) a. ***Dareka ga   dareka ga**   ki-ta.
         someone NOM someone NOM   come-PST
         ('Someone someone came.')
     b. exists "ga" (exists "ga" (rga "kita"))

SCT ascribes this ungrammaticality to the failure of evaluation for the corresponding SCT expression (26b). The embedded predicate rga "kita" is equivalent to the following *plain* expression:

(27) Hide ("ga",
        Rel (["ga"], ["c"], "∧",
          [Use ("ga",
            Rel (nil, nil, "kita", [T ("ga", 0)] ...)

When this is evaluated, the two occurrences of exists "ga" in (26b) have introduced two "ga" scopes. That is, $|g(\text{"ga"})| \geq 2$. The argument Use ("ga", Rel #) in (27) needs to be evaluated against an assignment h, which must meet the conditions below following the translation of Rel explained in (13.vi):

(28) $(g, h) \in (\text{pop}_{\text{"ga"}}^{|g(\text{"ga"})|-\text{"ga"}(\text{Use}(\text{"ga"}, \text{Rel \#}))};$
$\qquad \text{shift}(\text{snoc})_{\text{"ga"},\text{"c"}}^{|g(\text{"ga"})|-\text{"ga"}(\text{Use}(\text{"ga"}, \text{Rel \#}))})$

Since `"ga"(Use ("ga", Rel #)) = 1`, the above specification means that $g(\text{"ga"})$ must be popped $|g(\text{"ga"})| - 1$ times and `shift(snoc)`-moved $|g(\text{"ga"})| - 1$ times. It can be easily shown that it is impossible if $|g(\text{"ga"})|$ is two or larger. In this manner, using `Rel`, `rga` keeps well-balanced a newly introduced scope for `"ga"` and the evaluation of the predicate based on it.

We also need `np`, which takes a binding name as a parameter and includes the act of combining a restriction `f` and a nuclear scope `f'`.

(29) `let np name f f'=`
`    Rel (nil, nil, "∧", [Lam (name, "h", f), f'])`

In addition, the environment of the restriction is changed by shifting the binding of the name given to `np` to an `"h"` binding. This added detail gives a uniform way to link material in the restriction—namely, link material to the open `"h"` binding—no matter what the binding name of the noun phrase in the containing clause happens to be. This lets us form nominals in a uniform way with `n`, (30).

(30) `let n s = rel s [T ("h", 0)]`

From (30), it follows that, apart from requiring an `"h"` binding, nominals place no further constraints on the environment in which they are evaluated.

Based on having `np`, we can provide codings for the nominative case marker *ga* and topic marker *wa* as infix operators `ga` and `wa`, which connect the expression for the subject NP and that for the predicate as follows:

(31) a. `let f ga f' = exists "ga" (np "ga" f f')`
     b. `let f wa f' = np "wa" f f'`

Note that while (31a) opens a fresh `"ga"` binding, (31b) presupposes that there already exists an open `"wa"` binding in the context.

Now, let us see how the building blocks we have introduced work together, as we provide parsed forms for sentences with and without a topic. In the following pair of sentences, one with the nominative case marker *ga* and the other with the topic marker *wa*,

(32) a. Tarō **ga** ki- ta.
         NAME NOM come PST
         'Taro came.'
     b. Tarō **wa** ki- ta.
         NAME TOP come PST
         'Taro came.'

the sentence with an untopicalized subject (32a) is given an SCT notation (32a'). In this coding, `rga` (see (24)) checks whether there exists one and only one `"ga"` binding, based on which the evaluation of a predicate is made. `ga` (see (31a))

first mimics existential quantification by opening a fresh "ga" binding; then
it combines a nominal restriction, material from its left, and a nuclear scope,
material from its right. The evaluation of (32a′) is the predicate logic formula
(32a″). (32a‴) diagrams the process of evaluation.

(32) a′. n "Taro" ga rga "kita"
     a″. $\exists x(\text{Taro}(x) \wedge \text{kita}(x))$
     a‴.

```
                          Hide "ga"
                    ga h    Close "ga"
                       |
                    Use "ga"
                 [y]      Rel nil, nil, "∧"
                ga h
              /        \
         [y]   Lam "ga", "h"      Hide "ga"
        ga h                   [y]   Rel ["ga"], ["c"], "∧"
         |                    ga h
       [y]  Rel nil, nil, "Taro"    |
      ga h                       Use "ga"
         |                    [y]   Rel nil, nil, "kita"
       [y]  T("h", 0)         ga h
      ga h                       |
                              [y]   T("ga", 0)
                             ga h
```

An SCT encoding (32b′) is assigned to the sentence with a topicalized subject
(32b). rwa (see (25)) requires one "wa" binding and no open "ga" binding. wa (see
(31b)) combines a restriction with a nuclear scope similarly to ga, but linking to
an already open "wa" binding. Working together as in (32b′), the two operators
lead to an evaluation (32b″), an open formula with a free variable x bound in
the context. Note that the predicate 'kita' is interpreted here in terms of the
value of the "wa" binding.

(32) b′. n "Taro" wa rwa "kita"
     b″. $\text{Taro}(x) \wedge \text{kita}(x)$
     b‴.

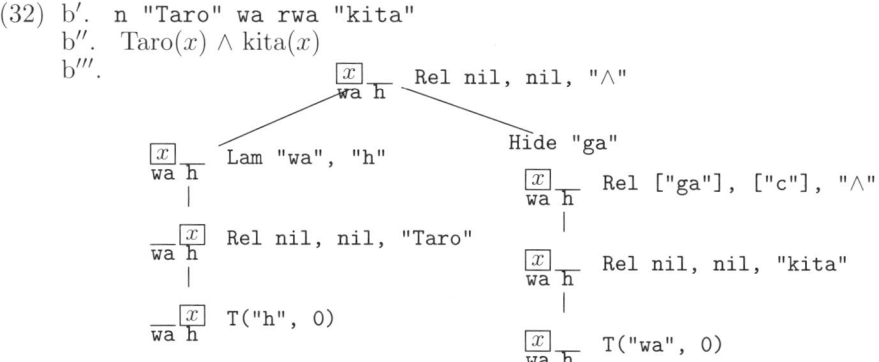

5 Parsing of Complex Sentences

Coordination is introduced by an infix operator coord defined as (33). First
this forms a subordinate clause consisting of a clause f and a relation name

s corresponding to the subordinate clause head, and then combines it with a matrix clause f'. The result is an s-relation that combines f and f'.

(33) let (f coord s) f' = Rel (nil, nil, s, [f, f'])

Level A subordinate clauses exclude subject. This fact is captured by assigning the following forms to this type of subordinate clause.

(34) a. (rga # coord #)
     b. (rwa # coord #)

(1a′) is the SCT expression obtained as a result of parsing (1a). This has essentially the same structure as the parsing (32a′) for the *ga*-marked simple sentence (32a), the only distinction being the duplication of '(rga ...)' subexpressions, which is caused by the constraint assigned to *de*. (1a″) is the evaluation. Note that both predicates "uwagi o nui" and "hanga ni kaketa" share the same referent in their argument positions, which is equivalent to that for the argument of 'Taro'. Likewise, (1b′) and (1b″) are a topicalized version of (1a′) and (1a″). (35) illustrates how the evaluation of (1a′) is derived.

(1) a. **Tarō$_i$ ga** [ϕ_i uwagi o nui]$_A$ de hangā ni kake- ta.
    NAME NOM (SBJ) jacket ACC take off SUCC hanger LOC hang PST
    'Taro took off his jacket and hung it on a hanger.'
    a′. n "Taro" ga ((rga "uwagi o nui" coord "de")
        (rga "hanga ni kaketa"))
    a″. $\exists y(\text{Taro}(y) \wedge \text{de}(\text{uwagi\_o\_nui}(y), \text{hanga\_ni\_kaketa}(y)))$
    b. **Tarō$_i$ wa** [ϕ_i uwagi o nui]$_A$ de hangā ni kake- ta.
    NAME TOP (SBJ) jacket ACC take off SUCC hanger LOC hang PST
    'Taro took off his jacket and hung it on a hanger.'
    b′. n "Taro" wa ((rwa "uwagi o nui" coord "de")
        (rwa "hanga ni kaketa"))
    b″. $\text{Taro}(x) \wedge \text{de}(\text{uwagi\_o\_nui}(x), \text{hanga\_ni\_kaketa}(x))$

(35)
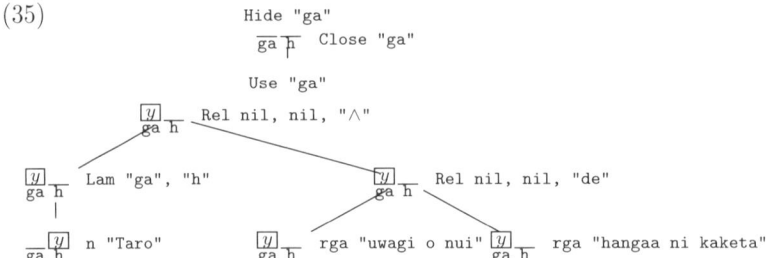

The Level B subordinate clause including *to* has no constraints on its form:

(36) (# coord #)

Topic/Subject Coreference in the Hierarchy of Japanese Complex Sentences   129

(2a′) is the parsing of (2a), a complex sentence with a *ga*-marked subordinate clause introduced by *to*. *To* allows the subordinate clause to open a fresh "ga" binding independent of that of the main clause, as stipulated by ga. The latter clause is construed as one with an omitted topic. This brings about the translation (2a″) in which the argument of the main predicate 'hanga_ni_kaketa' is bound by a free variable x in distinction from the existentially quantified variable y for the subordinate predicate. By contrast, (2b′) is the result of parsing the *wa*-marked complex sentence (2b). rwa attached to both predicates "uwagi o nugu" and "hanga ni kaketa" makes their interpretation sensitive to the value of the "wa" binding, which is given by the context. See the evaluation (2b″). Note also that an alternative parsing (2b‴) with an equivalent evaluation is possible. Contrast the evaluation derivations (37a) for (2a′) and (37b) for (2b′).

(2) a. [**Tarō**$_i$ **ga**   uwagi o   nugu]$_B$ *to* ϕ_j hangā ni   kake- ta.
       NAME NOM jacket ACC take off SUCC (SBJ) hanger LOC hang PST
       'After Taro had taken off his jacket, someone hung it on a hanger.'
   a′. ((n "Taro" ga (rga "uwagi o nugu")) coord "to")
       (rwa "hanga ni kaketa")
   a″. to($\exists y(\mathrm{Taro}(y) \wedge \mathrm{uwagi\_o\_nugu}(y))$, hanga_ni_kaketa($x$))
   b. **Tarō**$_i$ **wa** [ϕ_i uwagi o   nugu]$_B$ *to*   hangā ni   kake- ta.
       NAME TOP (SBJ) jacket ACC take off SUCC hanger LOC hang PST
       'After Taro had taken off his jacket, he hung it on a hanger.'
   b′. ((n "Taro" wa (rwa "uwagi o nugu")) coord "to")
       (rwa "hanga ni kaketa")
   b″. to((Taro(x) $\wedge$ uwagi_o_nugu(x)), hanga_ni_kaketa(x))
   b‴. n "Taro" wa ((rwa "uwagi o nugu") coord "to")
       (rwa "hanga ni kaketa"))

(37a)

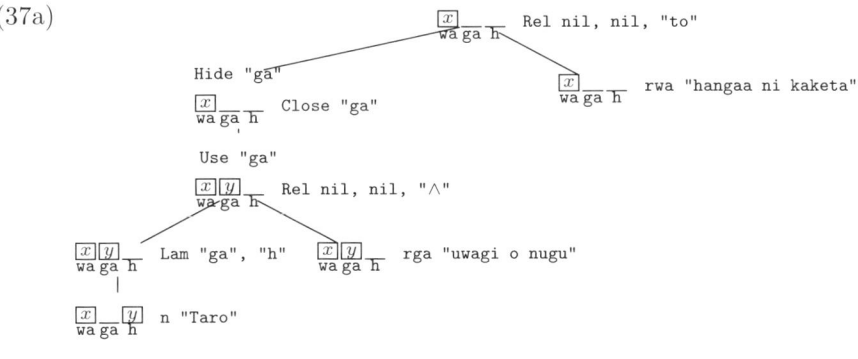

(37b)

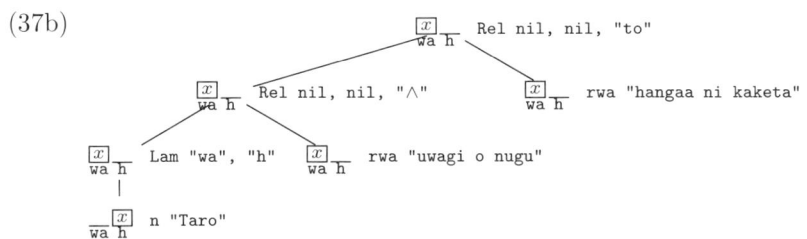

As a matter of fact, there exist exceptions in terms of reference of an omitted subject within a Level B subordinate clause.

(38) a. **Tarō**$_i$ **wa** [ϕ_j naguru]$_B$ *to* sugu naku.
NAME TOP (SBJ) hit SUCC soon cry
'Taro cries out as soon as we/one hit(s) him.'
b. **Haruko**$_i$ **wa** [ϕ_j samuku naru]$_B$ *to* gakkō ni ko- naku
NAME TOP (SBJ) cold become SUCC school GOAL come- NGT
naru.
become
'Haruko stays away from school when it is cold.'

However, in such cases with matrix and omitted subordinate subjects that are not identical, the referents of the embedded subject are quite limited: the speaker, people including the speaker, indefinite pronouns, the weather, the temperature, etc. Therefore, we take these interpretations as caused by some special contexts that trigger pragmatic rules to link between the subordinate subject and the contextually salient referent. By default, an omitted subordinate subject is identified with the topic as stipulated above.

(3a′,b′) are SCT notations resulting from parsing (3a,b). The subordinate clauses are just like independent simple sentences, with the exception that they are embedded in `levelc`, an operator which opens a fresh `"wa"` binding. `levelc` is defined as (39a) using the recursive `cleanup` that in turn is stipulated as (39b).

(39) a. `let levelc n f = cleanup n "wa" (exists "wa" f)`
b. `letrec cleanup n name f =`
      `(case n`
        `of 0 => check name f`
        `| n => Lam (name, "c", cleanup (n-1) name f)`
      `)`

`cleanup` shifts the frontmost scope of `name` to `"c"` n times and terminates with a call to `check`. Based on this, evaluation of `levelc` can only succeed provided all inherited values on the `"wa"` stack are removed, making the fresh `"wa"` binding that is added the only `"wa"` binding. This brings about a topicalized subject closed in the local Level C clause to which constituents in the matrix clause are inaccessible. The translations are (3a″,b″), in both of which a free variable is assigned to the argument of the matrix predicate. The process of evaluation for (3b′) is given in (40).

(3) a. [**Tarō**$_i$ **ga** uwagi o nui- da]$_C$ *kara* ϕ_j hangā ni kake-
NAME NOM jacket ACC take off PST CAUS (SBJ) hanger LOC hang
ta.
PST
'Since Taro took off his jacket, someone hung it on a hanger.'
a′. `(levelc 1 (n "Taro" ga (rga "uwagi o nuida")) coord "kara") (rwa "hanga ni kaketa")`

a″. kara($\exists y \exists z$(Taro(z) $\wedge$ uwagi_o_nuida(z)), hanga_ni_kaketa(x))
b. [**Tarō**$_i$ **wa** uwagi o nui- da]$_C$ *kara* ϕ_j hangā ni kake-
   NAME TOP jacket ACC take off PST CAUS (SBJ) hanger LOC hang
   ta.
   PST
   'Since Taro took off his jacket, someone hung it on a hanger.'
b′. (levelc 1 (n "Taro" wa (rwa "uwagi o nuida")) coord
    "kara") (rwa "hanga ni kaketa")
b″. kara($\exists y$(Taro(y) $\wedge$ uwagi_o_nuida(y)), hanga_ni_kaketa(x))

(40)

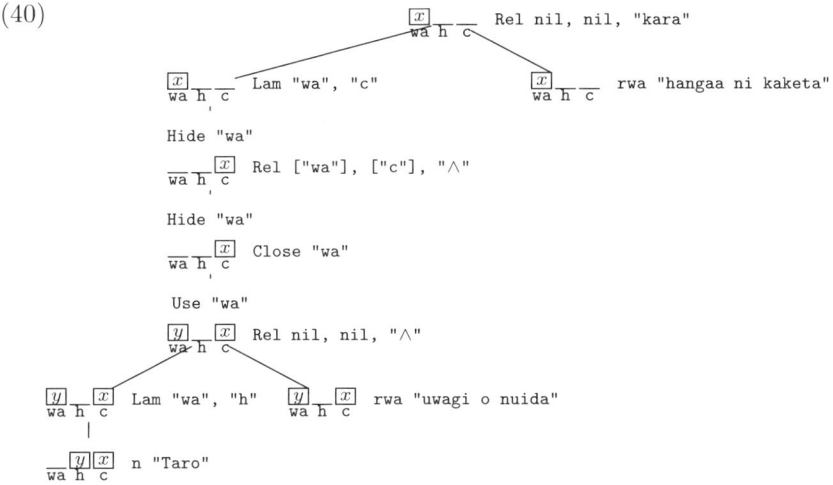

6 Conclusion

We have seen how the topic/subject reference in the three types of subordinate clause in Japanese is interpreted differently according to the management of scopes triggered by the postpositions *ga* and *wa* and the subordinate clause head particles, supplemented by constraints assigned to the latter. The distinction between NPs with and without a topic marker has been accounted for in terms of different domains in which scopes for `"ga"` and `"wa"` are bound. Essentially the same semantics-based approach can be applied to heterogeneous linguistic data including those concerning tenses and focus of question and negation in complex sentences, those which so far have been investigated syntactically.

References

Butler, A.: Scope Control and Grammatical Dependencies. Journal of Logic, Language and Information 16, 241–264 (2007)
Mikami, A.: Bumpō Shōron-Shū. Kurosio Syuppan, Tokyo (1970)
Minami, F.: Gendai Nihongo no Kōzō. Taishukan, Tokyo (1974)
Takubo, Y.: Tōgo Kōzō to Bunmyaku Jōhō. Nihongo-gaku 6(5), 37–48 (1987)

Vermeulen, C.F.M.: Sequence Semantics for Dynamic Predicate Logic. Journal of Logic, Language and Information 2, 217–254 (1993)

Vermeulen, C.F.M.: Variables as Stacks: A Case Study in Dynamic Model Theory. Journal of Logic, Language and Information 9, 143–167 (2000)

Yoshimoto, K.: Tense and Aspect in Japanese and English. Peter Lang, Frankfurt am Main (1998)

Japanese Reported Speech: Against a Direct–Indirect Distinction*

Emar Maier

ILLC/University of Amsterdam
emar.maier@gmail.com
www.ru.nl/ncs/~emar/

Abstract. English direct discourse is easily recognized by, for example, the lack of a complementizer, the quotation marks (or the intonational contour those induce), and verbatim ('shifted') pronouns. Japanese employs the same complementizer for all reports, does not have a consistent intonational quotation marking, and tends to drop pronouns where possible. Some have argued that this shows no more than that many Japanese reports are ambiguous. These authors claim that, despite the lack of explicit marking, the underlying distinction is just as hard in Japanese as it is in English. On the basis of a number of 'mixed' examples, I claim that the line between direct and indirect *is* blurred and I propose a unified analysis of speech reporting in which a general mechanism of mixed quotation replaces the classical two-fold distinction.

1 Introduction

There is an obvious contrast between:

(1)   a.   Taro said that I would go to Tokyo
       b.   Taro said: "I will go to Tokyo"

The first is an example of indirect speech, in which I report what Taro said on an earlier occasion in my own words; the second is a direct report, where I report Taro by quoting his words verbatim. From these informal characterizations it follows that in (1a) the pronoun *I* is used by (and refers to) me, whereas in (1b) it refers to Taro, which makes these reports semantically incompatible.

There is an ongoing debate about the direct–indirect distinction in Japanese, where, in a colloquial setting, a sentence like (2) can mean both (1a) and (1b) (Hirose, 7:224):

(2)   Taroo-wa boku-ga Tookyoo e   iku to   itta
       Taro-Top I-Nom   Tokyo   to go   Comp said

---

* I thank the Japanese friends I used as informants for valuable suggestions along with their judgments: Mana Kobuchi-Philip, Yurie Hara, Hidetoshi Shiraishi, and Katsuhiko Yabushita. Further thanks go to Jennifer Spenader and the participants and organizers of LENLS 2008 in Asahikawa. This research is supported by the Netherlands Organisation of Scientific Research (NWO), grant 446-07-004.

The received view now seems to be that Japanese reports like (2) are simply ambiguous between direct and indirect. Instead, the current paper offers more Japanese data to argue against the notion of a categorical direct–indirect distinction. I present an alternative in which mixed quotation allows one to 'shift' parts of any report complement. But first we take a closer look at this traditional distinction between direct and indirect speech.

2 Distinguishing Indirect and Direct Speech

The difference between direct and indirect speech is marked in a number of different ways in different languages. Let's go through a couple of the better known ones.

Syntax. English indirect discourse is usually marked by a complementizer *that*; in Dutch, such a complementizer and an additional change in word order are obligatory; in German, indirect discourse requires changes in both word order and mood of the verb. A distinguishing feature of direct speech syntax is its 'syntactic opacity' (Oshima 13), i.e. it blocks movement, (3), quantifying in, (4), and NPI licensing, (5) (Anand and Nevins 2):

(3) a. What did Taro say he had seen?
     b. *What did Taro say: "I have seen"?

(4) a. There's something that Taro says he likes
     b. *There's something that Taro says: "I like"

(5) a. Nobody said they had seen anything
     b. ??Nobody said "we saw anything"[1]

Orthography/intonation. In written languages, direct speech is usually marked with quotation marks. In spoken language this direct speech marking surfaces as a distinct intonational contour (Potts 15).

Semantics/pragmatics. As noted above, reporting someone's words in indirect speech requires adjusting the original utterance's indexicals to the reporting context. To report the same as (1b) in indirect speech, Taro's *I* would have to be changed to *he*. In English, the same holds for indexicals like *tomorrow* and the present tense. Note however the cross-linguistic variation: in Russian, the present tense is not adjusted, while in Amharic even first person forms can apparently be retained (Schlenker 17).

These and other characteristics give the impression of a "binary, categorical distinction" where "a direct report is about a relation between an agent and a linguistic object while an indirect report is about a relation between an agent and a proposition" (Oshima 13:23). This traditional explanation of the direct–indirect distinction seems to rest on a fundamental distinction between

---

[1] The sentence as a whole is grammatical, and likely true. It does not however report the same as (5a).

two functions of language: words can be used to refer to the world (*use*), but also to refer to words and other linguistic items (*mention*). Before arguing against it, let me first clarify the supposed link between indirect–direct and use–mention.

3 Modeling the Indirect–Direct Distinction as Use vs. Mention

Modeltheoretically, language *use* is what's captured by the familiar Fregean semantics. A proper analysis of indirect speech reporting and indexicality requires Kaplan's two-dimensional version, which analyzes indirect *saying that* as an intensional operator. *x says that* φ means that x uttered some sentence that expressed the same proposition as that expressed by φ in the current report context.

Mention requires the addition of a separate expression type (u) and domain (D_u) of utterances to our models (Potts 16). Mentioning is modeled as an operator ⌜ ⌝, the formal counterpart of (pure) quotation, that turns any utterance into a term of type u referring to that utterance. Strictly speaking, D_u contains phonetic or alphabetic surface representations of utterances (say, finite strings of symbols in a finite alphabet). The formal quotational language, $\mathcal{QL}$, consists of triples containing a linguistic object ($\in D_u$), a semantic type, and a standard logical representation:[2]

(6)   a.   notation: fool' := $\langle \mathbf{fool}, et, \lambda x[\mathtt{fool}(x)] \rangle \in \mathcal{QL}$
   semantics: $[\![\text{fool'}]\!]$ = the set of fools $\subseteq D_e$
b.   notation: ⌜fool⌝ := $\langle \text{'fool'}, u, \ulcorner\mathbf{fool}\urcorner \rangle \in \mathcal{QL}$
   semantics: $[\![\ulcorner\text{fool}\urcorner]\!] = \mathbf{fool} \in D_u$

This logic of mention extends to a straightforward semantics of direct speech: Simply analyze 'say' in its direct discourse sense as a transitive verb that takes as direct object a term of type u, and analyze quotation marks as mention, capturing the traditional view of direct discourse being a relation between an individual and an utterance.

To summarize, the direct–indirect discourse distinction can be cached out formally in an intensional logic with a mention operator. Indirect discourse saying translates as say$_{id}$', an operator of type $(st)et$, as in (7a), while direct discourse translates as say$_{dd}$', an operator of type uet, as in (7b):

(7)   a.   Taro said I'm going to Tokyo
  ⤳ say$_{id}$'(taro')($^\wedge$go_tokyo'(i'))
b.   Taro said: "I will go to Tokyo"
  ⤳ say$_{dd}$'(taro')(⌜I will go to Tokyo⌝)

The distinguishing characteristics of direct and indirect speech listed in the first section all follow from this semantics.

---

[2] The last two slots may be empty, to allow for quotations of speech errors, meaningless sounds or ungrammatical utterances (Maier 11): misunderestimate $\approx \langle \mathbf{misunderestimate}, eet, - \rangle$, grrr $\approx \langle \mathbf{grr}, -, - \rangle$.

Syntax. Direct speech's 'verbatimness' with respect to clause structure and word order, among other things, follows from the fact that in (7b) it is the original utterance itself that is the object of the say$_{dd}$ relation. The fact that mentioning turns the quote into a referential term of type u with no internal semantic structure, explains the syntactic opacity with respect to movement and NPI licensing.

Orthography/intonation. The various forms of quotation marking in direct speech fall out as simply the linguistic realization of the mention operator, ⌜ ⌝.

Semantics/pragmatics. Indexical adjustment in indirect speech follows from the Kaplanian semantics of indirect speech where we have to match the proposition that was expressed in the reported context with the proposition expressed by the complement clause in the reporting context.

4 Challenging the Indirect–Direct Distinction: The Case of Japanese

Despite this apparent success of a rather simple semantics, Maier (11) challenges the strict indirect–direct distinction by pointing out that even English direct discourse is semantically somewhat transparent. This claim is backed by the observations that (i) anaphoric and elliptical dependencies can cross direct discourse boundaries (as in *"My girlfriend bought me this tie," said John, but I don't think she did*, from Maier 2007), and (ii) a direct report comes with a rather strong (but cancellable) implicature that the corresponding indirect version is also true (for example, the direct (1b) implies that Taro said that he will go to Tokyo).

For so-called mixed quotation (Cappelen and Lepore 4), consisting of an indirect report in which only a certain part is directly quoted, Maier's (2007) case is strengthened by additional syntactic/semantic evidence. But, focusing on genuine direct discourse, it may well be possible to get around both of the transparancy arguments by adding a distinct pragmatic mechanism that leaves the separation of direct and indirect discourse intact at the semantic level.[3] In the remainder of this paper I present some further evidence against the direct–indirect distinction.

4.1 A Rumor about Japanese Speech Reporting

As "rumor has it that there is no such [direct–indirect] distinction in Japanese" (Coulmas 5:53) I turn to that language in hope to seal the fate of the classical

---
[3] I know of no actual proposal to this effect, but I envisage a kind of system that takes the strictly separatist semantics of direct speech as mention and combines it with a strengthening mechanism that adds the corresponding indirect version of a direct report, the *use* inference, to the semantic representation. Assuming that the resolution of ellipsis and anaphora triggered by the following discourse apply after pragmatic strengthening of a direct report, would derive (i) as well.

report distinction. My ultimate goal is to replace it with an analysis of speech reports as indirect discourse (analyzed as section 3's say$_{id}$) with optional mixed quotation of any notable parts. Unfortunately, some work remains to be done as Coulmas continues the sentence quoted above by remarking that the rumor about Japanese is "obviously not true."

Let's reconstruct how the rumor might have started originally. Recall our enumeration of the ways in which direct and indirect discourse can be kept apart. First, syntactically, Japanese does not distinguish direct and indirect discourse by a special complementizer. The marker *to* is used for all speech reporting. Tense and word-order are consistently retained in speech reports, nor is there a special mood for indirect discourse. Then, ortographically, direct discourse in written text may often be recognizable from the quotation marks, but in colloquial spoken language these may go unnoticed.[4]

So, of the previously listed tests for distinguishing the two modes we are left with indexical adjustment and syntactic transparency as indicators of indirectness. Unfortunately, these characterictics are invisible in a single given sentence itself, so less useful for the task of classifying reports that are not otherwise marked. In addition, the clearest examples of indexicals, person pronouns, tend to be dropped in colloquial Japanese. For these reasons our current test battery will indeed fail to classify many reports as either direct or indirect. Following Coulmas, this is the source of our rumor.

So what does this mean for the interpretation of Japanese reports? Given a strict, logical direct–indirect separation (Coulmas, Hirose, Oshima *op. cit.*), many reports must be simply ambiguous between the two distinct logical forms demonstrated in (7). So, even with overt pronouns, we will often have to rely on the context to disambiguate. A case in point is (2), where taken on its own perhaps no more than a slight pause distinguishes the readings (1a) and (1b).[5] Presumably, the context will favor one of these readings, so, as Coulmas rightly observes, this syntactic/semantic ambiguity need not hinder communication, yet a genuine ambiguity it is nonetheless.

Separatists, like Coulmas, Hirose and Oshima, point out that, to facilitate contextual disambiguation, Japanese can rely on a very rich repertoire of what Hirose (7) calls "addressee-oriented expressions." These include particles like *yo* and *ne*, imperatives, and honorifics like the polite *-masu* verb forms. Like traditional indexicals, the meanings of such expressions are tied to the actual utterance context (Potts and Kawahara 14) and "semantically presuppose the existence of an addressee" (Hirose 7) in that context. For speech reporting this means that such expressions can only occur in direct speech, or else, when they

---

[4] One informant speaks of a distinct quotation intonation, another of a short pause after the quote should clarity demand it. Further research is required, but it seems that the intonational clues in Japanese are more subtle than in English. Note that even in English colloquial speech quotation may go unmarked.

[5] If the report was made in Tokyo, *kuru* ('come') could be used to indicate indirect discourse, though *iku* ('go') would still be compatible with indirect discourse too, as indirect discourse is known to shift the indexical goal parameter of *come/go* in Japanese. More on this below.

do occur embedded in an indirect report, apply only to the actual reporter and her relation to her addressee. Unfortunately for the separatist's cause, this prediction is not borne out, as I show next.

4.2 Neither Direct Nor Indirect: The Data

Take the embedded honorific -*masu* form in:

(8)   kare wa   watashi ga   matta machigaimashita to   iimashita
        he   *Top*   *I*   *Nom again was.wrong-Polite Comp said-Polite*
        a.   'He said: "I was wrong again"'
        b.   'He said that I was wrong again'   [(Coulmas 5:57)]

The embedded first person pronoun could well be the reported speaker's, as in the direct reading (8a), but, according to Coulmas, it could also refer to the reporter, in which case we should be dealing with indirect discourse, (8b). The question is, who is being polite to whom with *machigaimashita*? Unless it's a direct quote it must refer to the context of the report, but the reporter has already expressed his politeness to his addressee sufficiently in the matrix verb. Coulmas claims that even in the indirect reading, (8b), it could indicate politeness of the reported speaker, apparently contradicting the indexical addressee-orientation of -*masu*. For now let's use the term 'shifting' for the phenomenon of (arguably) addressee-oriented expressions used in (arguably) indirect speech and interpreted with respect to the reported context/speech act.

Shifted addressee-orientation in indirect speech is not restricted to the occasional embedded -*masu* form (as Coulmas seems to suggest). Here is an example of what Kuno (10) would call 'blended quasi-direct discourse' with an imperative. My boss tells me:

(9)   asatte   made ni kono shigoto-o yare
        day after tomorrow until   *this*   *work-Acc do-Imp-Impolite*
        'Finish this work in two days!'

If I want to report this to you the next day, I might say:

(10)   ashita   made ni sono shigoto-o yare   to   jooshi-ni
        tomorrow until   *that work-Acc do-Imp Comp boss-by*
        iwaremashita
        was told-Polite
        'I was told by the boss that I should finish that work by tomorrow'

The adjustment of the indexicals (*asatte* to *ashita*; *kono* to *sono*) clearly indicate indirect speech. On the other hand, the impolite imperative form *yare* is strictly addressee-oriented and as such indicates direct speech. To see this last point, note that in Japanese, as in English, imperatives simply do not embed under indirect reports at all:

(11)   *The boss said that finish that work!

It may not be technically impossible to devise a system that allows indirect discourse to shift the relevant addressees for the examples in (8) en (10). Discussing an example like (10) Oshima for instance argues that

> Except for the imperative form, what Kuno calls blended discourse has all the characteristics of indirect discourse. For example, a wh-phrase in a 'quasi-direct quote' can take matrix scope:
>
> (12)   Taro$_i$-wa [yatu$_i$-no uti-ni   nanzi-ni   ko-i]   to
>   *Taro-Top he-Gen   house-Dat what.time-Dat come-Imp Comp*
>   it-ta   no ka?
>   *say-Past Q Q*
>   'What time did Taro$_i$ say, [come to his$_i$ house]?'
>
> [(Oshima 13:13)]

According to Oshima we're dealing with indirect discourse, we just need to add some shiftable parameters to the semantics of the imperative form to account for this non-addressee-oriented interpretation.

I argue that the phenomenon is much more widespread, so a more general shifting or mixing mechanism would be less *ad hoc*. Note for instance that it's not just the imperative force that is shifted in (10), the honorific marking of *yare*, impolite, is also shifted, as it is not something I, the reporter, would dare say to you. In fact, such boldness would even directly contradict the matrix verb's politeness marking. Oshima himself also provides two more classes of speaker/addressee-oriented expressions that retain their original form inside an otherwise indirect report: deictic predicates and empathy-loaded expressions.

As an example of a deictic predicate, take *iku* 'go', indicating movement away from the context's speaker:

(13)   kinoo,   Matsushima-kun-wa [kyoo boku-no uti-ni   ik-u]   to
       yesterday Matsushima-Top   today I-Gen   home-Dat go-Pres Comp
       it-ta
       say-Past
       'Yesterday, Matsushima said that he would go to my home today.'
       [(Oshima 13:15)]

As the reported movement is toward the speaker's own house, we'd expect *kuru* ('come'), so we're dealing with a perspective shift here.

As an example of an empathy-loaded expression, finally, take *yaru* 'give', indicating the speaker empathizes more with the giver than with the receiver:

(14)   kinoo,   Matsushima-kun-wa boku-ni [kyoo boku-ni purezento-o
       yesterday Matsushima-Top   I-Dat   today I-Dat   gift-Acc
       yaru]   to   itta
       give-Pres Comp say-Past

'Yesterday, Matsushima said to me that he would give me a gift today.' [(Oshima 13:16)]

Here too we have an indexical, speaker-oriented expression embedded in an indirect report, and interpreted with respect to the reported rather than the actual speech context.

5 Towards a Unified Analysis: Mixed Quotation in Speech Reporting

The problem separatists have in dealing with the examples above is an apparent shifting and mixing of perspectives in indirect speech. There are ways to deal with such indirect shifting, but they involve a substantial overhaul of the semantics of indirect speech reporting or of indexicality/addressee-orientation (cf. Schlenker's analyses of indexical shifting in Amharic). I claim that we need not go there, we already have everything we need with (i) Kaplan's (1989) classic semantics of indexicals and indirect speech and (ii) an account of mixed quotation. Both of these mechanisms are independently motivated and relatively uncontroversial, but the second one may need some explanation.

5.1 Geurts and Maier's Presuppositional Account of Mixed Quotation

My preferred semantic analysis of mixed quotation is Geurts and Maier's (2005) presuppositional account. In that framework, quotation marks trigger the presupposition that someone used precisely the words mentioned within them (necessitating an underlying mention logic, as developed above in 3 already) to express something, while that something is left embedded in an indirect report, as in (15) (the ∂ symbol marks a presupposition).

(15) Quine says that quotation "has a certain anomalous feature"
 $\rightsquigarrow$ Quine said that quotation has ∂[the property he refers to as ⌜has a certain anomalous feature⌝]

For those interested in, but unfamiliar with, the DRT formalization of this idea, let me go over the basics. The uninterested reader can safely skip the rest of this subsection.

To formalize the presupposition *the property he refers to as* ⌜*has a certain anomalous feature*⌝, we need not only a device to mention the quoted expression, but also to relate it to its utterer (as in say$_{dd}$, section 3) and to the object, property, quantifier etc. that the utterer used it to mean. The type of this third argument depends on the category of the quoted expression as it fits in the sentence, i.e. in (15) it's a property (et). We'll call this new three place relation refer. Otherwise, the DRS just represents an indirect report, using the Kaplanian monster-free say$_{id}$ from section 3 above.

More specifically, after some trivial resolutions the DRS representing (15) is:

(16)
$$\text{say}_{id}(x) : \begin{array}{|c|} \hline x \\ \text{quine}(x) \\ \hline \begin{array}{|c|} \hline y \\ \text{quotation}(y) \\ P(y) \\ \hline P \\ \hline \end{array} \\ \text{refer}(x, \ulcorner\text{has a certain anomalous feature}\urcorner, P) \\ \hline \end{array}$$

Now, the remaining presupposition searches the global context for a speech event of Quine uttering the mentioned phrase to bind to. If that fails, an appropriate antecedent will be accommodated. In any case, we get an output DRS as in (17), that states that Quine uttered "has a certain anomalous feature" to refer to some property (not otherwise specified), and says$_{(id)}$ that quotation has that property:

(17)
$$\begin{array}{|c|} \hline x\ P \\ \text{quine}(x) \\ \text{refer}(x, \ulcorner\text{has a certain anomalous feature}\urcorner, P) \\ \hline \text{say}_{id}(x) : \begin{array}{|c|} \hline y \\ \text{quotation}(y) \\ P(y) \\ \hline \end{array} \\ \hline \end{array}$$

In this way we get an account of the hybrid use/mention character of mixed quotation. The analysis suggests an extension to direct discourse, analyzing it as mixed quotation of an entire sentence (i.e. type t rather than et). This would effectively blur the line between direct and indirect discourse. The following picture emerges: to report another's speech there is only indirect discourse, within which the device of mixed quotation can be used to mimic a particular phrase of the reported speech act verbatim.[6] Direct discourse, in this picture, is merely a limiting case of mixed quotation. The aim of the current paper is to present independent evidence for this blurring of the direct–indirect distinction.

For more details and a comparison with Potts' (16) related framework, I refer the reader to Geurts and Maier (6) and Maier (11).

5.2 Shifting Amharic *I* and English Expressives with Mixed Quotation

The presuppositional semantics of mixed quotation can be and has been applied to account for some aspects of shiftiness in indirect discourse. Maier (12), for in-

---

[6] The reporter can have a variety of reasons for wanting to do this: he may not have understood the original words, the words may be meaningless, the reporter may be uncomfortable using the phrase, may want to liven up his whole report, may consider that phrase exceptionally well put, etc.

stance analyzes Amharic *I* as mixed quoted, rather than meddling with Kaplan's semantics:

(18)   jon ǰəgna nə -ññ   yɨl   -all
       john hero be -1.sg say.3.sg -Aux.3.sg
       'John says that he is a hero'   [(Schlenker 17)]
      ⇝ John said that "I" am a hero
      ⇝ John said that ∂[the person he refers to as ⌜I⌝] is a hero
                                                                            [(Maier 12)]

After presupposition resolution, we get that John used the first person pronoun to refer to someone and says that that person is a hero. Assuming that John uses the first person pronoun to refer to himself,[7] we get the intended reading, without changing Kaplan's classic semantics of indexicals and indirect speech.

The lack of overt quotation marks around the first person in Amharic can be no counterargument, as we have already seen that overt quotation marking may be absent even in full-blown direct discourse, in colloquiual spoken Japanese at least. At the subclausal level we also find naming constructions where overt quotation marks are lacking consistently, even in writing (though they are required semantically):

(19)   My name is Emar

The fact that the Amharic first person is not a word but an inflection on the verb need not worry us either, the theory predicts that any morpheme[8] can be mixed quoted.

Perhaps even closer to the current data set is Anand's (2007) suggestion to treat apparently shifted expressives like *that bastard* in (20) as mixed quoted:

(20)   My father screamed that he would never allow me to marry that bastard Webster   [(Kratzer 9)]
      ⇝ My father screamed that he would never allow me to marry "that bastard Webster"   [≈(Anand 3)]
      ⇝ My father screamed that he would never allow me to marry ∂[the individual he refers to as ⌜that bastard Webster⌝]

Anand argues that the quotational shift analysis of 'non-speaker-oriented expressives' is empirically superior to Potts' analysis that meddles with the Kaplan's contexts by adding a 'expressive judge' parameter.

---

[7] I ignore the very general problem of translation from Amharic to English, as that is a problem for any account of quotation and should eventually be accommodated in the mention logic.

[8] Even 'anything with a compositional contribution to the truth-conditions' (Maier 12). This includes subconstituent quotations such as *John said the stalag"mites" were falling down* (cf. Maier 12) and superconstituent quotations such as *Mary said the dog ate "strange things, when left to its own devices"* (from Abbott 2005, analyzed in terms of quote-breaking by Maier 11).

I claim that in both cases of shiftiness in reports the mixed quotation analysis is simpler and more compatible with tried and tested semantic theory than the alternatives: Schlenker's monsters, which overturn Kaplan's famous prohibition thereof and even threaten the notion of rigidity,[9] in the case of Amharic shifted *I*; and the *ad hoc* addition of shiftable expressive judges to the utterance context (cf. Anand 3), in the case of expressive shift.

5.3 Mixed Quotation in Japanese and beyond

My analysis of the Japanese data is now easily stated. The examples in 4.2 appear to mix direct and indirect discourse because they do; they are indirect reports with a mixed quoted phrase. Let's go through a couple of our examples.

The intended 'indirect' reading (8b) of (8), the report with the embedded *-masu* form, corresponds to a logical form where that form (and perhaps some more, but not the first person pronoun) is mixed quoted:

(21)   kare wa   watashi ga   "matta machigaimashita"   to   iimashita
       he Top   I   Nom   again was.wrong-Polite   Comp   said-Polite
       ≈ 'He said that I was "wrong again"'[10]   [cf. (8)]
       ⤳ he said that I was ∂[what he referred to as ⌜wrong again⌝]

Note again that this involves quotation marks that are invisible on the surface. I have defended this assumption for Amharic briefly above. In fact, I share it with direct–indirect separatists like Coulmas, who appeals to them to get the other reading, (8a). For us, that so-called direct discourse reading brings nothing new, the only difference with (21) is that the first person pronoun is now also part of the mixed quote, which presumably now covers the whole clause:

(22)   He said that "I was wrong again"

The next two examples, (10) and (12), feature (invisible) mixed quoted imperatives:

(23)   ashita   made ni sono shigoto-o   "yare"   to   jooshi-ni
       tomorrow until   that work-Acc do-Imp Comp boss-by
       iwaremashita
       was told-Polite

---

[9] Schlenker argues that his system upholds Kaplan's fundamental distinction between rigid/directly referential and descriptive terms, but this is much less clear in e.g. Von Stechow's (18) related account where shifted indexicals correspond to mere bound variables.

[10] My English translation's quotation does not include the *was*, which is included in the Japanese version. In English it would sound strange to include the auxiliary because of the clash of third vs. first person inflection. Note also that the inclusion of the past tense morpheme in both Japanese and English is not theoretically necessary; the theory predicts that it should also be possible to mix-quote just the politeness morpheme, for instance.

≈ 'I was told by the boss that I should "finish!" that work by tomorrow'
[cf. (10)]

The quotation marks correctly defer the impolite imperative force to the reported speaker, the boss.[11]

To get a fully unified account of shifting through mixed quotation, the logical form of (13), finally, requires mixed quotation of *iku* ('go'), which yields the interpretation *Matsushima said he would do ∂[what he referred to as ⌜go⌝] to my house*. And similarly for (14). Of course, on the basis of only these particular examples we cannot discard the possibility that *iku* and *yaru* are simply descriptive terms that can be freely shifted by binding to any salient reference point. To decide between these alternative analyses, shifting by quotation or by binding, the behavior of the predicates in non-report clauses is crucial: if they can shift their reference point there as well the predicate is not truly context-oriented and quotation is not needed. If shifts occur only in reports, however, the by now properly motivated mixed quotation mechanism can take care of the perspective shifting without added semantic machinery. To determine which way to go with the predicates at hand more empirical research is required.

I have provided a principled account of shifting without complicating our contexts or the semantics of indexicals and reports. We have essentially given up the two-fold direct–indirect distinction. In fact, we have given up the whole notion of direct discourse: speech reporting follows Kaplan's semantics of indirect discourse except for the parts (in some cases the whole clause, or more) that are mixed quoted. These quoted parts are automatically (by presupposition resolution) deferred to the reported speaker. For Japanese in particular, this means we can keep the intuitive analysis of speaker/addressee-oriented expressions as indexicals, so that indeed in reported speech "addressee-oriented expressions are, by definition, used only as public expressions [= direct discourse/quotation]." What we reject is the, often implicit, assumption that "phrases and sentences containing addressee-oriented expressions are also adressee-oriented, functioning as public expression [= direct discourse]." (Hirose 7:227)

References

Abbott, B.: Some notes on quotation. In: de Brabanter, P. (ed.) Hybrid Quotations. Belgian Journal of Linguistics, vol. 17, pp. 13–26. John Benjamins, Amsterdam (2005)

Anand, P., Nevins, A.: Shifty operators in changing contexts. In: Young, R. (ed.) Proceedings of SALT XIV. Cornell, NY (2004)

Anand, P.: Re-expressing judgment. Theoretical Linguistics 33, 199–208 (2007)

Cappelen, H., Lepore, E.: The varieties of quotation. Mind 106, 429–450 (1997)

Coulmas, F.: Direct and indirect speech: general problems and problems of Japanese. Journal of Pragmatic 9, 41–63 (1985)

---

[11] Spelling out the whole story here requires that we settle on a proper semantics of imperatives, a rather tricky but independent problem that I cannot go into here.

Geurts, B., Maier, E.: Quotation in context. In: de Brabanter, P. (ed.) Hybrid Quotations. Belgian Journal of Linguistics, vol. 17, pp. 109–128. John Benjamins, Amsterdam (2005)

Hirose, Y.: Direct and indirect speech as quotations of public and private expression. Lingua 95, 223–238 (1995)

Kaplan, D.: Demonstratives. In: Almog, J., Perry, J., Wettstein, H. (eds.) Themes from Kaplan, New York, pp. 481–614. Oxford University Press, Oxford (1989)

Kratzer, A.: Beyond ouch and oops: How descriptive and expressive meaning interact. In: Cornell Conference on Theories of Context Dependence (1999)

Kuno, S.: Blended quasi-direct discourse in Japanese. In: Poser, W. (ed.) Papers from the Second International Workshop on Japanese Syntax, Stanford, CSLI, pp. 75–102 (1988)

Maier, E.: Mixed quotation: between use and mention. In: Proceedings of LENLS 2007, Miyazaki, Japan (2007)

Maier, E.: Quotation marks as monsters, or the other way around? In: Aloni, M., Dekker, P., Roelofsen, F. (eds.) Proceedings of the Sixteenth Amsterdam Colloquium, Amsterdam. ILLC, pp. 145–150 (2007)

Oshima, D.: Perspectives in Reported Discourse. PhD thesis, Stanford (2006)

Potts, C., Kawahara, S.: Japanese honorifics as emotive definite descriptions. In: Watanabe, K., Young, R.B. (eds.) Proceedings of the 14th Conference on Semantics and Linguistic Theory, pp. 235–254. CLC Publications, Ithaca (2004)

Potts, C.: Lexicalized intonational meaning. In: Kawahara, S. (ed.) University of Massachusetts Occasional Papers 30. GLSA, Amherst (2005)

Potts, C.: The dimensions of quotation. In: Barker, C., Jacobson, P. (eds.) Direct Compositionality, pp. 405–431. Oxford University Press, Oxford (2007)

Schlenker, P.: A plea for monsters. Linguistics and Philosophy 26, 29–120 (2003)

von Stechow, A.: Binding by verbs: Tense, person and mood under attitudes. In: Kadowaki, M., Kawahara, S. (eds.) Proceedings of NELS 33, pp. 379–403. GLSA, Amherst (2002)

The Dynamics of Tense under Attitudes – Anaphoricity and *de se* Interpretation in the Backward Shifted Past[*]

Corien Bary[1] and Emar Maier[2]

[1] Radboud University Nijmegen
[2] ILLC/University of Amsterdam
www.ru.nl/ncs/~corien/
www.ru.nl/ncs/~emar/

Abstract. This paper shows that both anaphoricity and egocentric *de se* binding play a crucial role in the interpretation of tense in discourse. It uses the English backwards shifted reading of the past tense in a mistaken time scenario to bring out the tension between these two features. We provide a suitable representational framework for the observed clash in the form of an extension of DRT in which updates of the common ground are accompanied by updates of each relevant agent's complex attitudinal state.

1 Introduction

The challenge of this paper is to deal with the interpretation of the embedded past tense in past-under-past sentences like (1):

(1)   Sam said that she was in London.

This sentence has two readings, a *simultaneous* reading, where Sam said *I am in London*, and a *backward shifted* reading, where she said *I was in London*. We show that the interpretation of the embedded past tense on the latter reading combines two independent features of tense interpretation: anaphoricity and *de se* binding. There is however a tension between these two features: anaphoricity means that the interval introduced by the tense morpheme is bound to a salient past time, whereas *de se* interpretation implies that it is trapped by the local now. In other words, the interpretation of tense seems to be both "wide" and "narrow" at the same time.

Current frameworks tend to focus on one of these features at a time and are unable to deal with the combination of the two. In this paper, we propose a new dynamic framework to solve this problem.

---

[*] We thank Nick Asher, Rob van der Sandt, and Hans Kamp for insightful comments. We also thank the organizers and audience of LENLS 2008, Asahikawa. Emar Maier is supported by the Netherlands Organisation for Scientific Research (NWO), grant 446-07-004.

The paper is organized as follows. In section 2 we formulate the challenge. We establish two distinct features of tense interpretation in general, anaphoricity in 2.1 and *de se* binding in 2.2, and show that the two come together in the case of the backward shifted interpretation of sentences like (1) (2.3). In section 3 we present an analysis that resolves the tension.

2 Challenge: Two Distinct Features of Tense Interpretation

2.1 Anaphoricity

On the basis of examples like (2) and (3), Partee (12) argues that tenses behave like pronouns, in that both are anaphoric:

(2)   Sheila owns a donkey. She likes it.

(3)   Sheila had a party on Monday. Sam got drunk.

In (2) the pronoun *she* picks up Sheila and *it* the donkey introduced by the first sentence. In the same way the time of Sam's getting drunk in (3) is not some arbitrary time before the utterance time, but picks up the time of the party on Monday.

Similarly, the phenomenon of narrative progression is often, in one way or another, attributed to the anaphoric nature of tense (Partee 13, Hinrichs 6, Kamp and Reyle 8):

(4)   Sheila walked into the room. She sneezed.

Again, the time of Sheila's sneezing is not some arbitary time in the past of the utterance time. Instead, the natural interpretation is that Sheila sneezed after her entrance. One way to obtain this result is to let the first sentence introduce an interval after Sheila's entrance and treat the sneezing time as an anaphor that binds to this interval (cf. Partee 13, Hinrichs 6).

The idea of tense as anaphora is quite naturally captured in the framework of Discourse Representation Theory (Kamp and Reyle 8) with Presupposition-as-Anaphora (van der Sandt 15) (henceforth, DRT+PA).

Let's use (5), with anaphora in the domains of both person and tense, to illustrate this framework:

(5)   Sheila had a party on Monday. She got drunk.

As a dynamic framework, interpretation happens in a context. We'll take the first sentence of (5), represented as in (6), as context:

(6)   Sheila had a party on Monday.

$$\begin{array}{|l|}\hline x\ t\ n \\ \hline \text{sheila}(x) \\ \text{party}(x,t) \\ t<n \\ \text{monday}(t) \\ \hline\end{array}$$

Against this background we can interpret the second sentence. This interpretation starts by assigning a preliminary structure (henceforth PrelDRS) in which presuppositions are marked by dashed boxes:

(7)   She got drunk.

$$\begin{array}{|l|}\hline \\ \hline \text{drunk}(y,t') \\ \overline{\lfloor\ y\ \rfloor}\ \overline{\lfloor\ t'\ \rfloor} \\ |\text{she}(y)|\ |t'<n| \\ \hline\end{array}$$

Next we merge the two and try to find antecedents for the presuppositions. The pronominal presupposition, y, has to bind to a female antecedent, and hence binds to x. The temporal presupposition, t', looks for a past time, t:

(8)   (6) ⊕ (7) =
$$\begin{array}{|l|}\hline x\ t\ n \\ \hline \text{sheila}(x) \\ \text{party}(x,t) \\ t<n \\ \text{monday}(t) \\ \text{drunk}(y,t') \\ \overline{\lfloor\ y\ \rfloor}\ \overline{\lfloor\ t'\ \rfloor} \\ |\text{she}(y)|\ |t'<n| \\ \hline\end{array}$$
⇝
$$\begin{array}{|l|}\hline x\ t\ n \\ \hline \text{sheila}(x) \\ \text{party}(x,t) \\ t<n \\ \text{monday}(t) \\ \text{drunk}(x,t) \\ \hline\end{array}$$

In this way we obtain the desired result: *she* refers back to Sheila and the getting drunk takes place during the party on Monday.

2.2   Temporal *de se* Interpretation

Like the anaphoric feature of tense, its *de se* character is best illustrated in analogy with the domain of person. In the person domain, Perry (14) introduces crazy Heimson who thinks he is Hume, to argue against the standard notion of belief as a propositional attitude. Let's reconstruct this argument first and then transfer it to the temporal domain.

(9)   Heimson thinks he is Hume.

A straightforward DRT+PA analysis of (9), with an intensional, i.e. propositional, belief operator BEL_x would yield (10). The pronoun *he* is bound by *Heimson* and the embedded name *Hume* is resolved globally.

(10)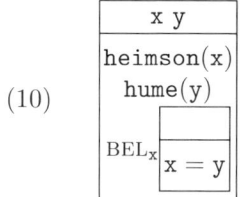

What's left in the belief is an equation between variables, rigidly denoting two different individuals, i.e. a contradiction. Semantically that means that Heimson's belief set is empty and therefore that he believes literally everything. This is clearly incorrect; Heimson is crazy but not that crazy. Such non-propositional beliefs about oneself are called *de se*.

Lewis' (11) solution to this problem of *de se* belief is to reinterpret belief as the self-ascription of a property, like in (11). Here, BEL* is a new belief operator, denoting self-ascription and taking properties as argument. The self-ascribed property, *being Hume*, is constructed through λ-abstraction from the proposition-type embedded DRS. We suggestively use the variable i' to denote the first person within the belief, i.e. the cognitive center that does the believing:

(11)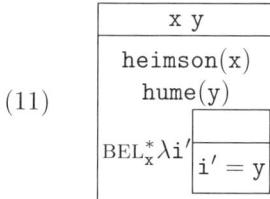

The same observation has been made for the temporal domain. Say Sam is confused about when, rather than who, she is. She thinks it's 10AM when it's actually 11AM. Straightforward interpretation of the present tense as denoting the utterance time **n**, with a propositional belief-operator again gives the wrong result:

(12)   Sam thinks it is 10AM.
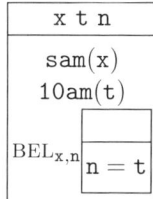

10AM in (12) names a specific time and ends up in the main DRS. The dedicated discourse referent **n** for 'now', representing the present tense in both *thinks* and *is*, denotes 11AM. So, semantically, what Sam is said to believe is the absurd 11AM=10AM

By analogy with the Heimson *de se* problem, we solve this by making the object of belief a property, now of times, rather than a proposition:

(13)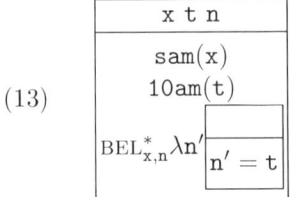

In (13), Sam 'now-ascribes', so to speak, the property of being 10AM, that is, she locates her subjective now n' at 10AM.

A second example to illustrate the need for temporal *de se* representations. Imagine that today is April 3rd and that Sam is confused about the time, thinking it's April 2nd. Then it may be the case that both (14a) and (14b) are true:

(14) a. Sam thinks Sheila is in London.
      b. Sam thinks Sheila is in Paris on April 3.

With belief as propositional attitudes, however, Sam would believe a contradiction, since the beliefs would be represented as (15a) and (15b), respectively:

(15) a. 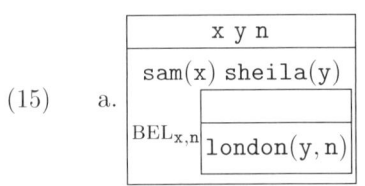 b.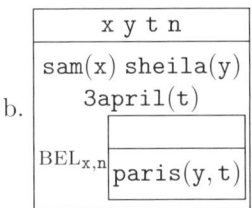

Note that in (15b) we have taken *April 3* from (14b) to be a kind of proper name for a particular time, hence the wide scope representation in the main DRS (as in (10) and (12) above). Since the utterance time is April 3rd, $n = t$, the combination of (15a) and (15b) implies that Sam has the absurd belief about one and the same time, April 3rd, that Sheila is in London and Paris at that time.

With belief as the self-acription of a property, on the other hand, we can represent the difference between temporal *de se*, for (14a), and *de re* for (14b) (on account of the latter's overt mention of a specific time, again represented as a proper name in the main DRS):

(16) a. 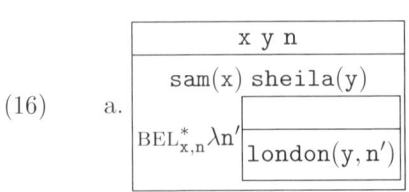 b.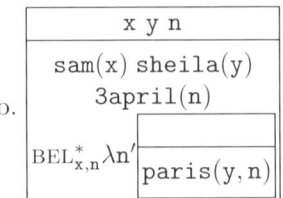

According to (16a) Sam now-ascribes the (temporal) property of Sheila being in London, and in (16b) the belief is really propositional, i.e. equivalent to (15b).[1]

2.3 Backward Shifted Past and Mistaken Time

In the previous subsections, we have indicated two general features of tense interpretation, anaphoricity and *de se* interpretation. Now we turn to past-under-past sentences, sentences with a past tense verb embedded under a past tense attitude verb, like our (1), here repeated for convenience as (17). We show that both features come together in the backward shifted reading of such sentences.

(17)   Sam said that she was in London.

Given the anaphoric nature of tense, let's first see what a simple anaphoric account of tense would do with the interpretation of the embedded past tense in (17). How would the simultaneous and backward shifted reading come about on such account? It would assign to (17) the prelDRS in (18) with the tense presupposition in the dashed box:

(18)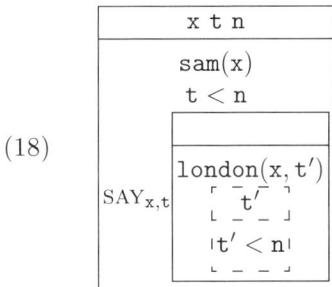

The time of the stay in London t′ looks for a past time and since in (18) t, the time of the saying, is the only time available, it will bind to this time. The output is given in (19).

(19)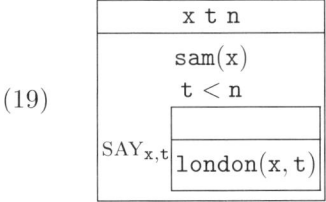

In this way the stay in London ends up simultaneous with the saying, apparently capturing the simultaneous reading.

---

[1] Propositional beliefs can be reformulated in the more powerful property-self-ascription framework: Sam self-ascribes the property of being temporally located at some timepoint in a world in which Sheila is in Paris April on 3rd.

To get the backward shifted reading we must add some context:

(20) Sue asked Sam why she wasn't at the party on Monday.
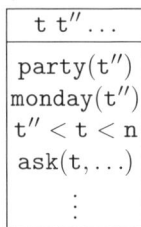

If (20) precedes (17), the natural reading of (17) is a backward shifted one. On an anaphoric account of tense, this is because (20) makes available for t′ a second time to bind to, the time of the party on Monday, t″:

(21) (20) ⊕ (18) =
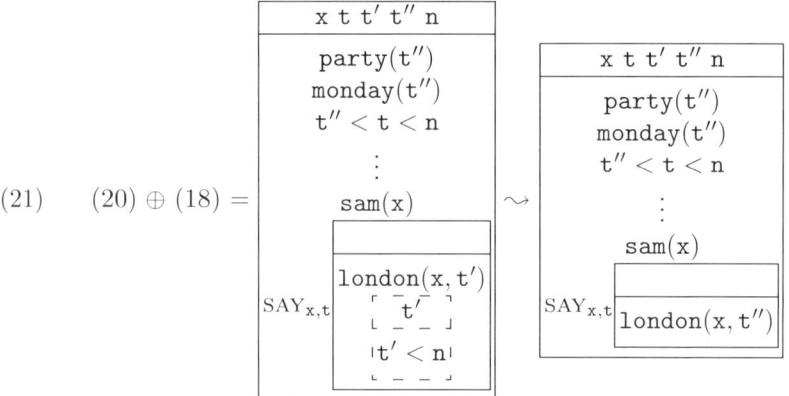

Now let's evaluate this simple anaphoric analysis. First, (19) is not the correct representation of the simultaneous reading of (17), since following the reasoning of section 2.2 with respect to (14a), the present tense equivalent to (17), it follows that the simultaneous reading is really a *de se* reading, as in (22):

(22)
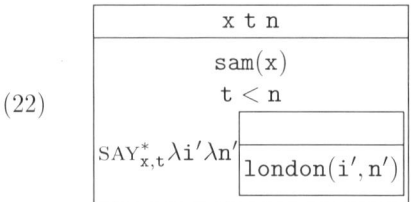

Sam ascribes to her self and now the property of being in London. In other words, she says 'I am now in London'. In order to derive (22), one has to assume a "sequence of tense" rule, since the embedded past tense is not interpreted as a past, but rather as a present, be it a local/narrow one, n′. To obtain this result, one can follow von Stechow (16) in that the binding of tenses by attitude verbs involves a system of morphological feature deletion.

What about the backward shifted reading? In analogy with the simultaneous reading, we expect that it should be represented like the *de se* (23) rather than the *de re* (21):

(23)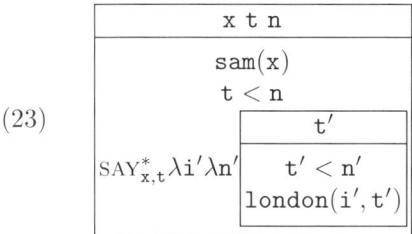

To see the difference between the two representations we must have a mistaken time scenario:

> Sam was invited to Sheila's party in Paris, but she didn't show up. She mistakenly thought the party was on Tuesday, when she happened to be in London, but it was actually on Monday. Sheila asked her on Wednesday why she wasn't at the party.

Schematically:

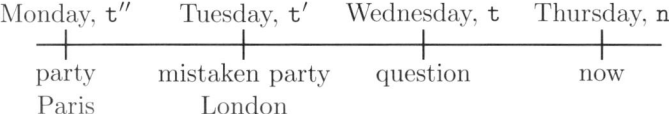

Let's compare (21), the representation provided by the simple anaphoric account, and (23), the *de se* representation, for the interpretation of (17) in this scenario. The purely anaphoric (21) is incorrect, since Sam does not make a statement about the actual time of the party, Monday. That particular time does not play any role in her subjective experience. She would never answer that she was in London at t'' (Monday) because she wasn't—she's not confused about where she was when, only about the time of the party. The *de se* (23), on the other hand, correctly captures this feature by locating the time of the stay in London in the answer, t', in the past of Sam's subjective now n'. The anaphoric element, however, is missing. Sam's utterance is given as an answer to Sheila's question and hence should relate to the party. Therefore the stay in London should not just be located at some arbitrary time in the past of Sam's subjective now, as currently happens in (23).

Intuitively, what we would like to do is to bind t', the time of the stay in London, to the time of the party as represented in Sam's belief worlds. In that way we would capture both the anaphoric and the *de se* feature of the interpretion of the embedded past tense. Even if we would represent Sam's mistaken beliefs about the party in the context DRS, however, this would be impossible in standard DRT. The reason is that the time of the party as represented in her belief worlds would not be accessible to bind to, since it would be embedded under an attitude operator. The next section provides a solution to this problem.

3 Towards a Dynamic Analysis

In the prevous section we have seen that two conflicting features, anaphoricity and *de se* interpretation, come together in the case of the backward shifted interpretation of past-under-past sentences. In this section we propose to account for this observation using an extension of DRT where interpretation consists of updates of the common ground while also keeping track of the changing, complex attitudinal states of the various agents (Kamp 7, 9). The idea is that the content of Sam's answer in (17) is to be evaluated with respect to her contextually given background belief, which contains her (mistaken) idea of a party on Tuesday. On such a view, interpretation is modeled as an update that combines the main DRSs' conditions, but that also merges each of an agent's individual attitude representations. To achieve this we need representations of an agent's total attitudinal state: a 'layered' DRS (Geurts and Maier 4).

In section 3.1 we start with the idea of layered attitudes, followed by the mechanism of embedded updates in section 3.2. Finally, in section 3.3 we show how these two extensions to DRT allow us to deal with the combination of anaphoricity and *de se* binding as found in the backward shifted reading of past-under-past sentences.

3.1 Attitudes in Layers

If we want to have an anaphoric account of tense under attitudes, we must take into account the interaction of different attitudes (we've already encountered two distinct attitudes, believing and saying) and presuppositions. As it happens, belief is rather special among the attitudes in that presuppositions triggered in any attitude report tend to end up in the ascribee's beliefs (Karttunen 10, Heim 5).

Take the hope report in (24), containing the presupposition trigger *her rival*. Note, by the way, that in this subsection and the next we ignore the independent issue of *de se* representation, i.e. for the sake of simplicity, we'll represent attitudes as propositional rather than in terms of the self-ascription of properties):

(24)   Sheila hopes her rival will be hit by a truck.[2]

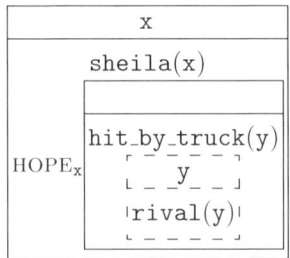

Now, this could in principle be a *de re* report, paraphrasable as: she hopes that that guy (who we know is her rival, perhaps unbeknownst to her) will be hit by a truck. We derive this reading by global resolution of the presupposition:

---

[2] Example from Henk Zeevat.

(25)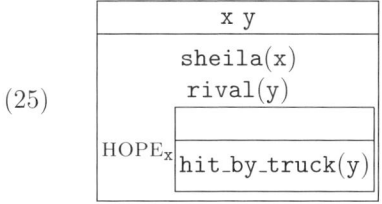

More interesting is the *de dicto* reading, as in 'I hope my rival (whoever it is) will be hit by a truck'. This reading is not so easily represented. We might try a local accommodation of the presupposition:

(26)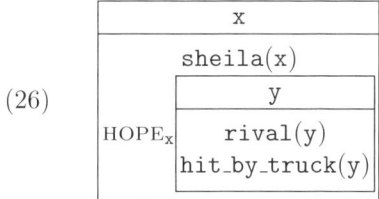

(26) reads as 'Sheila hopes that she has a rival and that he will be hit by a truck'. But of course Sheila doesn't hope that she has a rival. That she has a rival is part of her belief rather than her hope. Her hope is restricted to the condition that this person be hit by a truck. In other words, Sheila hopes of whoever she believes to be her rival that he will be hit by a truck. This dependency of hope and other attitudes on belief (cf. Asher 2) motivates the representation of an agent's total attitudinal state as a complex DRS with different 'compartments' for the different attitudes.

We propose to formalize this using Geurts and Maier's (2003) Layered DRT. This very general framework is meant to represent the interaction of different kinds of content, by splitting a DRS into layers connected by shared discourse referents. The 'kinds of content' here are the different attitudes and the 'interaction' is the observed asymmetric dependency between, for instance, hope and belief. More specifically, in the proposed framework, a complex attitude representation is a Layered DRS (LDRS) consisting of a set of ('narrow') discourse referents common to all attitudes, and conditions making up the various attitudes (belief, hope, assert, ...) about these attitude-internal objects. These conditions are labelled according to the attitude they belong to (*bel, hope, say,* ...). Instead of a belief operator we now need a general 'complex attitude' operator.[3] For our example, this gives:

---

[3] The exact semantics of this operator will have to wait until another occasion. The idea is that a model associates with an individual a set of belief alternative worlds (or rather, contexts), a set of hope alternatives, a set of say alternatives, etc. We then compute the proposition expressed by the LDRS's belief layer as to see if it includes the set of belief alternatives. Next, the belief layer's conditions are used to create an *anchor* against which, finally, the other layers can be evaluated and their propositions can be compared with the corresponding attitude's set of alternatives.

(27)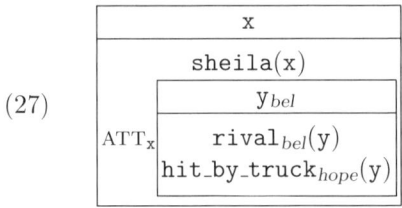

The purely attitude-internal discourse referent y shows that we are dealing with a *de dicto* interpretation. This y, moreover, is shared between the hope and belief layer to capture the fact that Sheila's hope, that he be hit by a truck, is about the same narrow individual that she believes is her rival.

3.2 Embedded Updates

In order to deal with the dynamics of attitude ascriptions we need a further modification of the DRT framework: the update mechanism needs to be extended to cover merges of attitude embedded DRSs.

Let (24) (on the *de dicto* reading) continue as in (28):

(28) [Sheila hopes her rival will be hit by a truck.] But she fears he won't be.

Intuitively, *he* picks up the rival of the first sentence. However, if we were to use the standard DRT+PA common ground update, i.e. merge context and preliminary DRS, we would only get to (29):

(29) (27) ⊕ (28) =

$$
\begin{array}{|l|}
\hline
x \\
\hline
\text{sheila}(x) \\
\text{ATT}_x \left[\begin{array}{l} y_{bel} \\ \text{rival}_{bel}(y) \\ \text{hit\_by\_truck}_{hope}(y) \end{array} \right] \\
\text{ATT}_x \left[\begin{array}{l} \neg \text{hit\_by\_truck}_{fear}(z) \\ \ulcorner z \urcorner \\ \ulcorner \text{he}(z) \urcorner \end{array} \right] \\
\hline
\end{array}
$$

If we were now to resolve the presupposition along its accessibility path, we would be unable to bind it. The intended antecedent y is not accessible because it is embedded under an attitude operator. We would end up with a DRS that ascribes two distinct attitudes to Sheila, missing the fact that she has a fear about the hypothetical rival in her belief worlds.

It is for this reason that we propose to update each agent's attitudinal state along with the common ground, following Asher (1), among others. That is, we merge not only the top-level of the DRS, but also the two attitude representations ascribed to Sheila, before resolving the embedded presupposition:

(30)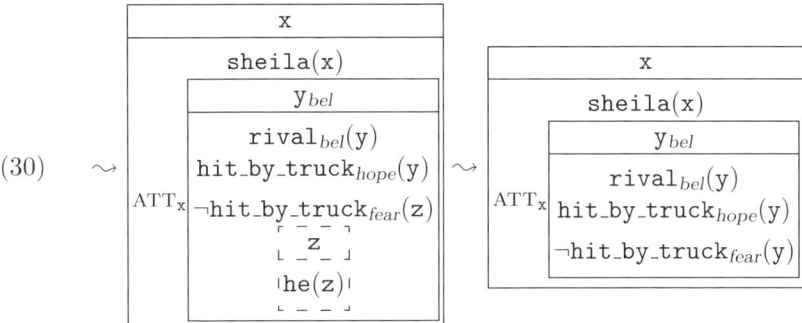

Thus, we can bind z to a local antecedent from the previous sentence, so that Sheila indeed hopes that her rival (whoever he is) is hit by a truck and fears he is not. In the next section we apply this mechanism to reconcile the anaphoricity of tense with the locality of *de se* interpretation.[4]

3.3 Mistaken Past Revisited

We now return to the challenge at hand, the backwards shifted past. Recall from 2.3 that in order to capture both the anaphoric and the *de se* feature of the embedded past tense of (17) we want to bind the time of Sam's stay in London to the time of the party *as represented in her belief worlds* – something that was impossible in standard DRT+PA. The new machinery, layered attitudes and embedded updates, proposed in the previous subsections, however, enable us to do achieve this, as we will show now.

First we represent the context containing the relevant background information from our mistaken identity scenario. Note that at this point we don't (have to) know about the stay in London, as that is what (17) will contribute, but we (i.e. the reporter and her audience – not necessarily including either Sam or Sheila) do know about Sam's mistaken assumption about the day of the party. Also, from here on we take the *de se* character of attitudes with respect to tenses into account again. The relevant context in our enhanced DRT+PA looks like (31):

---

[4] The anaphoric accessibility problem posed by (28) is reminiscent of Geach's (3) Hob-Nob puzzle of intentional identity:

(i) Hob thinks a witch has blighted Bob's mare and Nob wonders whether she killed Cob's sow.

The pronoun *she* in the second conjunct has to pick up the witch narrowly introduced under a belief operator in the first conjunct. The crucial difference between this and (28) is that here an anaphoric dependency is supposed to hold between different attitudes *of different agents*. This more general problem of intentional identity is therefore not solved by our embedded update mechanism which only combines the different attitudes of a single agent to fix anaphoric dependencies within that individual's complex attitudinal state. On the other hand, note that a solution to the general problem of intentional identity could probably be applied for our purposes below. Unfortunately, we are unaware of an elegant and satisfactory solution to the Hob-Nob and related puzzles.

158   C. Bary and E. Maier

(31)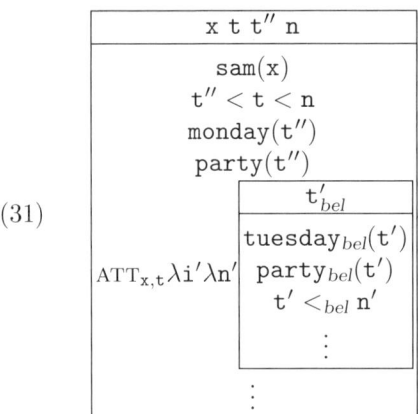

The compositionally derived preliminary representation for the backwards shifted reading of (17) involves a past tense presupposition, more specifically, one that is past with respect to Sheila's local now, n'. Simply adding it to the context in (31), and performing the initial resolutions, gives:

(32)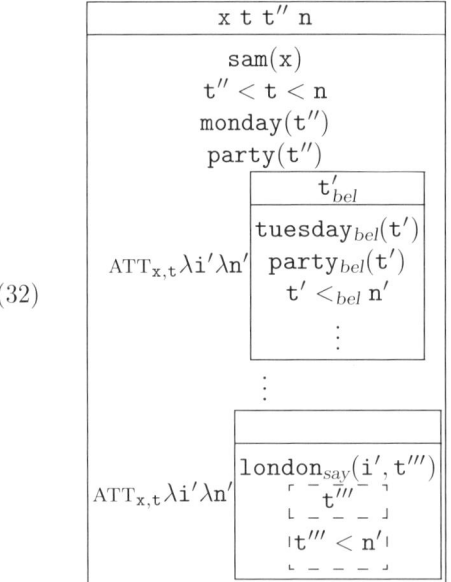

At this point we could bind t''' to t'', the actual time of the party, but this wouldn't give the intended interpretation (see section 2.3). The desired result would be obtained by binding t''' to t', the time of the party according to Sam's belief. That would capture the intuition that t''', the time of the asserted stay in London, coincides with Sam's idea of when the party was, i.e. Tuesday. Currently t' is not accessible for t''' to bind to. But according to the extended merge and update mechanism of 3.2 we can merge the representations of Sam's two attitudes and bind t''' narrowly yet truly anaphorically to t', Sam's internal representation of the time of the party:

(33)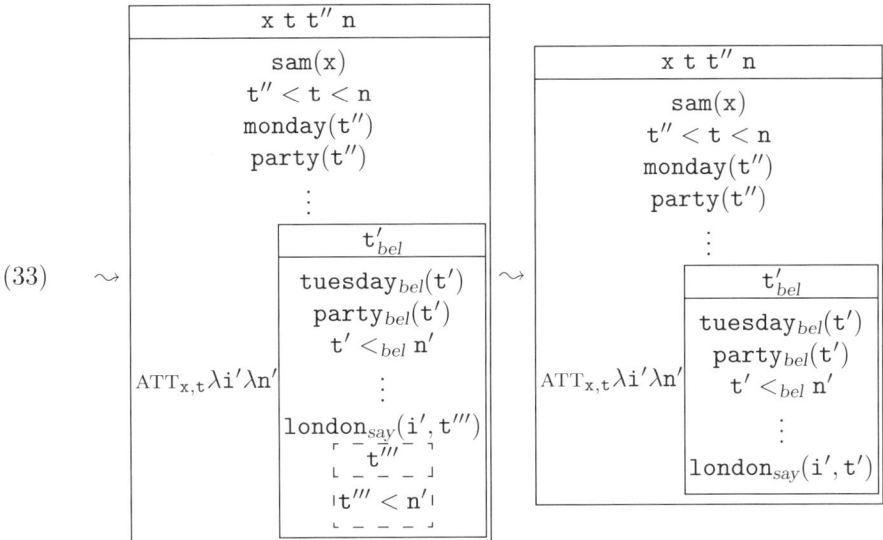

In this final output, Sam's stay in London given as reason for her absence indeed falls on the day she thinks there is a party, t', not the actual day of the party, t''. Through property self-ascription, presupposition-as-anaphora, Layered DRT, complex attitudinal states, and embedded merge we have thus arrived at a correct analysis of the backward shifted past.

4 Conclusion

The tension created by the independently motivated anaphoric and *de se* aspects of tense interpretation is resolved by an extension of DRT in which updates of the common ground are accompanied by updates of each relevant agent's complex attitudinal state. This is necessary in order to deal with the backward shifted reading of the past-under-past. In such constructions the embedded past tense is at the same time anaphoric to a salient past time in the context and *de se*, that is, narrow with respect to the attitude in which it occurs. The extended update mechanism lets the past tense be anaphoric to a narrow, *de se* antecedent in some earlier attitude in the context.

References

Asher, N.: Belief in discourse representation theory. Journal of Philosophical Logic 15(2), 127–189 (1986)

Asher, N.: A typology for attitude verbs and their anaphoric properties. Linguistics and Philosophy 10(2), 125–197 (1987)

Geach, P.: Intentional identity Journal of Philosophy 74, 627–632 (1967)

Geurts, B., Maier, E.: Layered DRT. ms (2003)

Heim, I.: Presupposition projection and the semantics of attitude verbs. Journal of Semantics 9, 183–221 (1992)

Hinrichs, E.: Temporal anaphora and discourses of English. Linguistics and Philosophy 9, 63–82 (1986)

Kamp, H.: Prolegomena to a structural account of belief and other attitudes. In: Anderson, C.A., Owens, J. (eds.) Propositional Attitudes: The Role of Content in Logic, Language, and Mind. Center for the Study of Language and Information, Stanford (1990)

Kamp, H., Reyle, U.: From Discourse to Logic: an Introduction to Modeltheoretic Semantics in Natural Language. In: Formal Logic and Discourse Representation Theory, vol. 1. Kluwer Academic Publishers, Dordrecht (1993)

Kamp, H.: Temporal reference inside and outside propositional attitudes. In: von Heusinger, K., Turner, K. (eds.) Where Semantics Meets Pragmatics. Current Research in the Semantics/Pragmatics Interface, vol. 16, pp. 439–472. Elsevier, Amsterdam (2006)

Karttunen, L.: Presupposition and linguistic context. Theoretical Linguistics, 181–194 (1974)

Lewis, D.: Attitudes de dicto and de se. The Philosophical Review 88, 513–543 (1979)

Partee, B.: Some structural analogies between tenses and pronouns in English. Journal of Philosophy 70, 601–609 (1973)

Partee, B.H.: Nominal and temporal anaphora. Linguistics and Philosophy 7, 243–286 (1984)

Perry, J.: Frege on demonstratives. The Philosophical Review 86(4), 474–497 (1977)

van der Sandt, R.: Presupposition projection as anaphora resolution. Journal of Semantics 9, 333–377 (1992)

von Stechow, A.: On the proper treatment of tense. In: Simons, M., Galloway, T. (eds.) Proceedings from Semantics and Linguistic Theory V, Ithaca, New York, Cornell University, pp. 362–386 (1995)

Argumentative Properties of Pragmatic Inferences

Grégoire Winterstein*

Laboratoire de Linguistique Formelle - Université Paris Diderot-CNRS
gregoire.winterstein@linguist.jussieu.fr

Abstract. In this paper we seek an explanation for the preference to use adversative connectives when reinforcing some implicatures. We begin by examining, and rejecting, an hypothesis according to which the nature of the implicatures can encode their argumentative properties. We then argue that this constraint is not due to the nature of the inferences at hand but rather to distinct argumentative relations between the propositions expressed in the discourse. We provide a solution in an argumentative framework and then extend our observations to cases including an overt restriction rather than implicatures. We conclude by looking at various explanations for the source of the preference we observe.

This paper seeks to provide an explanation for one of the often overlooked discourse constraints that intervene when cancelling or re-asserting the content of some implicatures. Conversational implicatures, as described by Grice (1989), are part of the meaning of a sentence that doesn't belong to what a speaker *said* in Grice's favoured sense. As such, they can supposedly both be freely reasserted and explicitly cancelled since they were never actually uttered and thus never "officially" endorsed by the speaker. As we'll show in this paper, it turns out that the discourse segments reasserting or cancelling implicatures can only be connected to the utterance that gives rise to the implicature by some specific discourse connectives.

In our first section we give the hypothesis we'll assume about the meaning of adversatives and show that implicatures have different argumentative behaviours. In the second section we test the hypothesis of an inference-type based argumentativity. We show how this approach is flawed and in the rest of this work we aim at giving an explanation of these facts in an argumentative perspective based on the works of Anscombre and Ducrot and later proposals by Merin. We show how their argumentative approach to pragmatics provides a straightforward explanation for the licensing of adversatives when reinforcing some implicatures. We also underscore how an *exhaustivity* account (as expounded by van Rooij (2004)), that also includes argumentativity, allows the same kind of predictions. Besides *licensing* it, this opposition seemingly *requires* the presence of contrast. We propose two different views to explain this preference in the fourth section.

---

* I thank Pascal Amsili, Jacques Jayez, Frédéric Laurens, François Mouret and the audiences at *JSM'08*, *FSIM'4* and *LENLS 2008* for their precious help and comments about previous versions of parts of this work.

1 Overview of the Data

1.1 Core-Data

The data presented in (1) is our prime example of study. In (1b), *B*'s answer is interpreted as carrying with it the implicature in (1c)[1]. This is a standard example of *scalar implicature* as presented, among others, in (Horn 1989).

(1) a. *A:* Do you know whether John will come?
    b. *B:* It's possible
    c. +>It's not sure (that John will come)
    d. *B:* It's possible, but it's not sure

The inference (1c) can be reinforced as in (1d). What interests us is that an utterance such as (2), without an adversative discourse marker, sounds degraded compared to (1d) (as an answer to (1a)).

(2) *B:* # It's possible and it's not sure

The preference for (1d) over (2) is somehow unexpected. Since the implicature (1c) is non-controversially conveyed by the utterance of (1b), one has to explain how it can be construed as "opposed to" or as a "denial of expectation of" the utterance that allowed its presence in the first place (as suggested by the adversative *but*). A similar fact is already noted in (Anscombre and Ducrot 1983) about example (3).

(3) Pierre s'imagine que Jacques et moi sommes de vieilles connaissances, mais pourtant on ne s'est jamais rencontrés
Pierre figures that Jacques and I are old-time friends, but we never met

Example (3) illustrates the difference between their notions of argumentation[2] and inference. In the case of (3), although the first part of the utterance allows an inference towards the second part, it is nevertheless argumentatively opposed to it and thus licences a contrast. Horn (1991) shows that, more generally, any kind of content related to an utterance U (by relations of implicature, presupposition, logical entailment...) can be felicitously reasserted as long as it is argumentatively opposed to U. Therefore, as unexpected as the preference for a contrast might be in (1d), the situation appears common.

This prompts us to look at the argumentative properties of the implicatures relative to their mother-utterance. More precisely, what we intend to find is

---

[1] We use the notation $A+>B$ to mean that the utterance of A implicates B.
[2] The notion of *argumentation* is rooted in Anscombre and Ducrot's view on discourse. According to them, a speaker always *talk to a point* and his utterances *argue* for a certain conclusion, quite often the topic of the discourse, which may or may not be explicit. Merin considers that understanding what is this topic is what *"figuring out the speaker's apparent and real intentions"* is about. Anscombre and Ducrot consider that some linguistic items or structures, such as *almost*, bear specific argumentative properties and thus entertain a systematic argumentative opposition or correlation with other propositions.

whether the content of implicatures stands in a systematic argumentative opposition with the content of their mother-utterances (regarding a certain goal). We shall call this the *argumentative relation* between the two propositions. Two configurations are possible:

1. The argumentative relation between implicature and mother-utterance depends on the *nature of the inference*. Different types of implicatures would have different, systematic, argumentative properties, entirely predictible by the mechanisms that gave rise to them. This hypothesis would be desirable because it gives a precise content to the notion of *argumentativity*.
2. The argumentative relation between implicature and mother-utterance is variable and depends on the *context of utterance*. The same inference could entertain one given relation in a context and the opposite in another.

The first option has already been proposed in the litterature and we examine it in Sect.2. We show that this leads to a number of wrong predictions and then go on to explore the second option in Sect.3.

On a last note about the core-data, we wish to mention the case of the scale of quantifiers: ⟨*all*, *some*⟩. Usually, scalar implicatures are exemplified with this latter scale, as in (4).

(4) a. *A:* How is your experiment going?
  b. *B:* I tested some of the subjects.
  c. +>B didn't test all the subjects.
  d. *B:* I tested some of the subjects, but not all.
  e. *B:* # I tested some of the subjects, and not all.

We prefer to rely on (1) because the preference for using an adversative appears stronger in (1d) than in (4d). Neither (2) nor (4e) can be entirely ruled out. Both can be used as *corrections* of a previous statements (in those cases they would probably have specific prosodic patterns). But we also observe that the preference for marking a contrast is less strong for the examples with quantifiers outside of correction cases. Simple Google searches for the french *quelques-uns et pas tous* or english *some and not all* yield several thousands of occurrences, not all of them corrections, whereas a search for *possible and not certain* only provides results of the form **only** *possible and not certain*. The presence of the adverb *only* restricts the meaning of *possible* and these examples aren't conclusive compared to the *some and not all* ones. However, the effect of *only* is an interesting one and we shall return to it below.

1.2 The Meaning of Adversatives

Anscombre and Ducrot (1977) first described the contribution as *but* as in (5)[3].

(5) A sentence *p but q* is felicitous iff. *p* is an argument for a proposition H and *q* is an argument for $\neg H$.

---

[3] We focus on one meaning of *but*, that corresponding to german *aber* or spanish *sino*. For a presentation of the different meanings of *but* see (Anscombre and Ducrot 1977).

We assume this description of the adversative connective throughout this paper. Ducrot doesn't give a precise definition of the notion of argumentativity. One of the aims of this work is to examine the possibility to reduce this notion to that of inference, at least in our cases of interest. We shall however show that the two concepts can not coincide.

About *Contrastive But*: A very frequent use of *but* is often described as *contrastive*. Example (5) shows a contrastive use of *but* which implies a contrast between two sentences, or linguistic elements, rather than between two argumentations.

(6) a. Jean porte un pull rouge, mais Marie porte un pull bleu
John wears a red sweater, but Mary wears a blue sweater

At least in French, possibly in English, we can rely on a substitution test to distinguish between a contrastive and an argumentative use of *but/mais*[4]. If a sentence *"p mais q"* (i.e. *"p but q"*) can be replaced by *"Bien que p, q"* (i.e. *"Although p, q"*) without inducing further assumptions or inferences, then the use of *but* can be said to be argumentative. Whereas, if the resulting sentence is hard to accommodate and requires further assumptions (namely to infer a direct argumentative opposition), the use of *but* in the base utterance is contrastive. We show this test on the french sentence in (7). Interpreting it felicitously would mean that John wearing a red sweater normally entails that Mary doesn't wear a blue one, something that isn't understood in (6).

(7) a. # Bien que Jean ait un pull rouge, Marie a un pull bleu
? Although John wears a red sweater, Mary wears a blue one

Applying the test to our core-data shows that *although/bien que* can be used without inducing a further effect:

(8) a. C'est possible, mais ce n'est pas sûr
It's possible, but it's not sure
b. Bien que cela soit possible, ce n'est pas sûr
Although it's possible, it's not sure

We conclude that the use of *but* in those examples isn't contrastive. Although we won't show the tests everytime, all uses of *but* in this paper will be argumentative.

1.3 Extended Data

Besides our core-example, we observe differences in the argumentative behaviour of implicatures.

Adversary Implicatures: We call *adversary* implicatures those that stand in an argumentative opposition with the utterance that conveys them. To test this opposition we rely on the use of *but* to connect an utterance and its implicature.

---

[4] I thank Jacques Jayez for pointing that out to me.

The case of scalar implicatures, already shown in (1d) belongs to this class. The exemples in (9) show that clausal implicatures in (9a) (as first described by Gazdar (1979)), implicatures based on attitude predicates in (9b), implicatures based on the maxim of Manner in (9c), all appear to be adversary implicatures.

(9) a. Bill is in the kitchen or the living room, ?(but) I don't know which
   b. John thinks that Mary is pregnant, ?(but) she's not
   c. Sam caused Max's death, ?(but) he didn't kill him on purpose

Allied Implicatures: We call *allied* implicatures those that share the same argumentative orientation as the utterance that conveys them. Several examples are given in (10): conjunction buttressing, conditional reinforcement etc.

(10) a. # Gwen took off her socks and jumped into bed, but in that order
   b. # If you finish your thesis by September you'll be eligible for the job, but only in this case
   c. # Billy cut a finger, but it was his
   d. # Sam and Max moved the piano, but together

It should be noted that the sentences in (10) are out only under the assumption that the considered implicatures are present (i.e. those expressed by the second conjuncts). It is easy to imagine contexts for which all these sentences are correct. For example, if sentence (10c) is uttered about some mafia henchman who breaks other people's fingers on a daily basis, the sentence is quite felicitous, but the implicature we're interested in isn't conveyed and nothing can be said about its argumentative orientation.

2 Argumentativity as Inference

In this section we test the hypothesis that the adversary/allied distinction amounts to a distinction between different types of implicatures. To test the hypothesis we use a classical Neo-Gricean framework, and more precisely Horn's distinction between Q-based and R-based implicatures.

2.1 The Q/R Distinction

In (Horn 1989) the derivation of implicatures is reduced to two opposed principles, based on considerations of economy.

- The Q-principle generates implicatures from stronger, more informative, relevant forms the speaker could have uttered but chose not to. This amounts to an economy for the hearer because the speaker *"says as much as possible"* and thus minimizes the effort the hearer needs to produce to interpret the utterance. All implicatures related to Grice's first maxim of quantity and the maxim of manner are *Q-based* implicatures.

– *R-based* implicatures are enrichments of an utterance related to underspecified aspects of the propositional content. This principle means an economy for the speaker because he relies on *stereotypes* to minimize the content of his utterance.

Horn's Q and R principles are quite similar to the Q and I-principle found in (Levinson 2000), except that Horn's Q-principle is broader than Levinson's, and includes Levinson's M-principle.

2.2 Correlation between Q/R and Adversary/Allied Implicatures

Benndorf and Koenig (1998) worked on data related to (1) and (4). They were interested in the dual operation of reinforcement, namely *cancellation*. They observe that the implicatures that can be felicitously cancelled using an adversative connective are exactly the implicatures that were described as *R-based*. We briefly sum up their main observations and conclusions and then show how their proposals aren't satisfactory.

***R-based* Implicatures:** Examples of the cancellation of *R-based* implicatures are presented in (11). An adversative connective is preferred to connect the two discourse segments.

(11) a. Gwen took off her socks and jumped into bed, but not in that order
 b. If you finish your thesis by September you'll be eligible for the job, but not only in this case
 c. Billy cut a finger, but it wasn't his
 d. Sam and Max moved the piano, but not together

These examples are the same as in (10), but with the second conjunct cancelling the implicature.

***Q-based* Implicatures:** All the implicatures presented in (9) are instances of *Q-based* implicatures. Unsurprisingly, these inferences apparently can't be cancelled with an adversative connective; a reformulative connective is preferred:

(12) a. Bill is in the kitchen or the living room, (?but/and in fact) I know which
 b. John thinks that Mary is pregnant, (?but/and in fact) she is indeed expecting a child
 c. Sam caused Max's death, (?but/and in fact) he actually killed him on purpose
 d. It's possible that John will come, (?but/and in fact) it's a sure thing

2.3 Argumentation as an Inference Mechanism

Since *R-based* implicatures are the only implicatures that can be cancelled with an adversative, Benndorf and Koenig identify the *R-based* nature of inferences to that of argumentativity by adapting Ducrot's description of *but* as in (13).

(13) A sentence *p but q* is felicitous iff:
 - *H* is an *R*-implicature or a world inference derived from *p*
 - *q* together with the common ground entails ¬*H*

Their motivation is to provide an inference-based description of the meaning of *but*. If we extend their conclusions, we identify allied implicatures with *R-based* ones, and thus adversary implicatures with *Q-based* ones, as strongly suggested by the data.

2.4 Problems with the Account

The previous generalization isn't satisfactory for two main reasons. First counter-examples can be found, second some *Q*-implicatures do not show the expected argumentative behaviour.

Counter-examples: Should we find a context such that the cancellation of a *Q-based* implicature is marked by an adversative connective the previous generalization would be flawed. We believe (14) is such an example, where *some* in the Father's answer is understood as *not all*, an interpretation that gets cancelled with an adversative.

(14) a. *Mother:* I hope that Kevin has been polite with Granny and has managed to eat some of her terrible cookies.
 b. *Father:* He did eat some of them, but in fact he ate all of them, so Granny said that he was greedy.

One could argue that the implicature from *some* to *not all* in (14b) isn't *Q-based* but *R-based* in this particular case, and therefore still satisfies the criterion for argumentativity. This would mean that, depending on the context, there are two different mechanisms for drawing the same inference. Since the implicature in (14b) appears very similar to the one in (4c), up to the fact that cancelling it demands a reformulative item such as *in fact*, this appears to be a very *ad-hoc* answer. Furthermore, nothing prevents the derivation of the targeted implicature by the *Q*-principle. One then needs to explain the interaction of the two principles when they produce the same inference (a similar point was already made by Carston (1998)).

Another objection to this example would be that the use of *but* is truly argumentative in (14b), whereas it's only contrastive in the previous examples of scalar implicatures such as (1d). However, as we have shown in Sect.1.2 this isn't the case: all the uses of *but* that we consider are argumentative.

Turncoat inferences: Example (15b) is often considered to mean (15c) by the derivation of a *Q*-implicature based on a *contrast set* (for details see for example (Levinson 2000)). This is an intriguing case because the argumentative relations at hand do not behave as other instances of *Q*-implicatures.

(15) a. *A:* Who came to the party?
 b. *B:* Bill and Ted
 c. +>No one else came to the party

The preferences for discourse relations when reinforcing or cancelling these implicatures do not match those in (9), nor are they closer to the ones in (10):

(16) a. *B:* Bill and Ted, (and/but) no one else — (and/but) not George
   b. *B:* Bill and Ted, (and/but) also many other people — (and/but) also George

One needs a specific context to judge whether an adversative or a simple conjunction would be better. The preferences might also be different according to the expression given to the content of the implicature (*No one else came to the party* vs. *George/Kim/etc. didn't came to the party*). We call these inferences *turncoat* because they do not appear to be argumentatively adversary or allied. According to the hypothesis we are evaluating this should not be the case: all implicatures derived from the *Q*-principle should be adversary.

Conclusion: As a conclusion we reject the hypothesis according to which the nature of an inference directly gives its argumentative properties. Not only will it enable us to treat the inferences in (14b) and (4c) in a parallel manner, but it should also provide insight in cases where the presence of an implicature is dubious. As shown by various recent experimental data (Breheny et al. 2005; Noveck and Sperber 2007) implicatures are not generated by default but only on a case-to-case, context-specific, basis. Yet it seems that the preference for a contrast goes beyond these particular cases, including cases for which no implicature seems to be derived as it appears to be in (17).

(17) a. *A:* Is there even a remote possibility that John will come?
   b. *B:* Yes, it's possible, (but) it's not sure

The arguments were given assuming a neo-Gricean treatment of implicatures, but they remain sound for other approaches that do not take argumentativity into account. The roots of our puzzle are in the argumentative relations between propositions rather than between an utterance and its inferences.

This could make the explanation of our core data much simpler. Taking the meaning of *some* as *more than 2 and possibly all*, there is a clear opposition with a *not all* interpretation. Things are however a bit more tricky: as shown by (14b) the argumentative relationship between the *some* and *not all* propositions can vary. Therefore the explanation can not rely on purely semantic opposition either.

3 The Argumentative Approach

In this section, we begin by presenting the basis of an argumentative approach to inferential pragmatics. We base our presentation on the propositions of Ducrot and their later formalization by Merin.

Once these various elements are defined, we see how they fit together to explain the data presented in Sect.1 and extend our observations to cases including an overt restriction.

3.1 Base Mechanisms

Our examples involve two distinct, well-known, concepts. First, these utterances involve the use of an adversative marker such as *but*. Second, their interpretations rely on the derivation of *conversational implicatures*. Argumentative treatments of both these concepts are described below with a side-note on an *exhaustivity*-based approach. A good presentation of all systems is given in (van Rooij 2004) and this will be our main inspiration in this section.

Adversatives: Merin (1999) adopts a probabilistic approach of Ducrot notion of argumentation. He identifies the notion of argumentation with that of *relevance*, as defined by Carnap[5].

Roughly, given a probability P over possible, accessible worlds, a proposition p argues for a proposition q, iff p is positively relevant to q, i.e. iff knowing p increases the probability of q. For Merin, the relevance of a proposition is defined regarding a particular proposition H: the goal of the discourse. In this he differs from Ducrot who considered that a proposition had systematic argumentative properties. For example, a sentence *almost p* always argues in the same way as p although it conveys $\neg p$, as shown in (18).

(18) Mary almost fell but she caught herself.

Our data suggests an interpretation more in line with Merin's proposal.

The description (5) gets the new formulation given in (19) (where $r_H(p)$ stands for the relevance of proposition p to proposition H):

(19) *p but q* is felicitous iff there is a prop. H s.t. $r_H(p) > 0$ and $r_H(q) < 0$

Both Ducrot and Merin consider that the absolute value of the relevance of the second conjunct should be higher than that of the first conjunct. This point has been discussed in (van Rooij 2004) and since it has little bearing on the rest of this work, we ignore this part of the description of the meaning of *but*.

Implicatures: The proper derivation of implicatures has known various refinements in the argumentative perspective. The main argument behind this approach to implicatures is the possibility to give an account of various cases where no logical entailment scale is at play, although there is indeed a preference over propositions. Ducrot, and Merin after him, proposes to replace the ordering of items based on logical relations by a relevance-based order. The ordering of the items is determined by argumentative force relative to the issue at hand. A good illustration, taken from (Hirschberg 1985)), is given in (20). In the context of a job interview, it would be more relevant if Jane spoke Portuguese. Her answer is interpreted as the "next-best" answer, from which we infer that she does not speak Portuguese.

---

[5] This notion of relevance is distinct from the one proposed by Sperber and Wilson (for a recent presentation see (Wilson and Sperber 2005) and for the differences between the two see (Merin 1999)).

(20) a. *Recruiter:* Do you speak Portuguese?
    b. *Applicant Jane:* My husband does.
    c. +>Jane doesn't speak Portuguese.

The apparent ordering of items by informativity in our core-examples (typically assumed in neo-Gricean approaches) is due to the fact that more informative propositions usually have higher argumentative values. In (Ducrot 1980):61 the derivation of an implicature such as (1b) is as follows:

- $\langle sure, possible\rangle_H$ is an *argumentative scale*, i.e. a simple utterance including *sure* has more argumentative power, regarding a certain conclusion H, than one relying on *possible*, and *possible* has a semantic "at least" interpretation
- the utterance of (1b) gets further interpreted by an *exhaustivity law* similar to standard Gricean reasoning that yields the desired meaning: since an argumentatively superior utterance relying on *sure* was not used, one is entitled to infer that the corresponding proposition is false

Merin's approach formalizes this in a slightly different way by postulating that in conversation a speaker S and a hearer H play a game such that they have *opposed* preferences. Roughly, S makes *claims* that the skeptical hearer H will try to *concede* in the less defavourable way possible for him. The content of S's claim, when asserting p, is the set of propositions that are *at least* as relevant to G, the issue at hand, as is p (Merin calls this set the *upward relevance cone* of p). The set of propositions that H is willing to concede is p's *downward relevance cone*: the set of propositions such that they are *at most* as relevant to G as p is. The net meaning of p is the intersection of the two cones which corresponds to the interpreted meaning.

Whatever the version one wishes to adopt, one fact remains true for all argumentative approaches: if p is an utterance from which a conversational implicature q is derived in either of the aforementioned manners, then q is the negation of a proposition $p' = \neg q$ that is argumentatively superior to p. Therefore p and q are *necessarily argumentatively opposed* (since by Ducrot's *law of inversion* $sign(r_H(\neg p)) = -sign(r_H(p))$).

This last fact readily explains why, in the cases where an implicature is indeed derived as such, the argumentative properties of utterance and implicature are compatible with the requirements of an adversative like *but*.

The Case of Exhaustivity: van Rooij (2004) argues against some of the claims of Merin by showing how an exhaustivity-based approach accounts for the same data without running into some of the problems of Merin's approach. To treat all of Merin's examples he proposes a definition of exhaustivity that relies on argumentative properties, represented by *relevance*. We reproduce this definition in (21).

(21) $exh(A, L, h) = \{t \in [A] | \neg \exists t' \in [A] : t' <_h^L t\}$, where
    - A is the sentence to be interpreted
    - L is the set of alternatives induced by the expression
    - h is the conversation's goal

– the ordering of states is defined as:
   $t' <_L^h t$ iff $V(h, \bigcap\{[B]|B \in L, t' \in [B]\}) < V(h, \bigcap\{[B]|B \in L, t \in [B]\})$
– V is a relevance function, possibly the same as Merin's, but not necessarily

An exhaustive interpretation of a sentence A contains all states that verify A and for which no more minimal state exists that also verifies A. The definition used here orders states on argumentative grounds. What changes from Merin's account is the actual mechanism for deriving inferences: intersection of relevance cones for Merin and exhaustification for van Rooij. This actually does not matter much to us. What matters is that all these mechanisms use a relevance function as a representation of the argumentative properties of a proposition and that the resulting implicatures have relevances that are signed differently from their mother-utterances. Thus, the compatibility between the derivation of implicatures and the semantics of adversatives remains a property of the exhaustivity framework.

3.2 On the Explicit Presence of Stronger Terms

We already remarked that items such as the restrictor *only* allowed some discourse forms that would otherwise be odd, namely discourses using the argumentatively neutral connective *and*. An example is given in (22).

(22) It's only possible and not sure.

The properties of *only* conventionally exclude a stronger proposition, as shown by the impossibility of (23).

(23) # It's only possible and in fact sure.

The negation of the stronger proposition is then redundant and its argumentative orientation is similar to the *only*-sentence. According to (Horn 1991), (22) should not be felicitous either because the second conjunct is redundant without being argumentatively opposed to the first. Most speakers feel that (22) comes as a correction of a previous statement (i.e. one that asserts the certainty of the discussed event) and thus the second conjunct would be *echoic*, which would license its presence in (22). Another possibility is to assume that the whole utterance (22) comes as an answer to a question such as *Is it sure?*, and that the second segment is the congruent answer to this question, expressed as a consequence, or result, of the first segment.

In the case of non-entailement based scales the results are the same: (24a) is good and (24b) is not (when placed in the same context as (20)). Here again, the second segment of (24a) can be easily understood as linked by a consequence relation with the first.

(24) a. Only my husband speaks Portuguese, I don't
     b. # Only my husband speaks Portuguese and in fact I also do.

In the presence of an overt restriction, the use of an adversative can not be automatically licensed like in the case of implicatures. We do not claim that it is impossible, but rather that using an adversative connective would convey more than the content of the two conjuncts (whereas in our core-data the contribution of the adversative is less clear, if not completely transparent). The resulting sentences are hard to judge and almost impossible to find with simple searches on corpora. Examples are given in (25). We give french equivalents in (26) for which we have slightly more confident judgements.

(25) a. ? It's only possible, but not sure.
      b. ? Only my husband speaks Portuguese, but I don't.
      c. ? Only some students skipped class, but not all.

(26) a. ? C'est seulement possible, mais pas certain.
      b. # Seul mon mari parle Portugais, mais pas moi.
      c. ? Seuls quelques élèves ont séché les cours, mais pas tous.

Because we can not confidently judge those examples, such data should be further investigated by experiment and deeper corpora-studies. At least in French, the examples including presumptive scalar terms ((26a) and (26c)) are preferred to those relying on purely contextual argumentative scales (as in (26b)). It might be that these particular uses of *but* are accepted out of habit due to the strong tendency to use it in the absence of *only* (as in our core-data). Finally, the differences between examples with an overt restriction and those inducing a scalar implicatures could also prove relevant to the proposition advanced by Chierchia, Fox and Spector (to appear) according to which a restriction operator like *only* yields the same effect as the mechanism of scalar implicature.

Similar considerations can be made about the item *at least*. Instead of restricting the denotation of a proposition, it widens it. The data in (27) (also shown in French in (28)) shows that, even though the usual presumptive implicatures are not derived, the possibility to reinforce their putative content still demands an adversative connective.

(27) a. It's at least possible, but not sure.
      b. ? At least my husband speaks Portuguese, but I don't.
      c. At least some students skipped class, but not all.

(28) a. C'est au moins possible, mais pas certain.
      b. ? Il y au moins mon mari qui parle Portugais, mais pas moi.
      c. Au moins quelques élèves ont séché les cours, mais pas tous.

To be entirely felicitous these examples need a third-party proposition to be construed in the argumentative scale which the two discourse segments belong to. For example, in (27a) the relevant proposition would be along the lines of *It's probable*. If no obvious candidate is available, then the sentences are hard to interpret as in (27b). In that latter case, if no salient person other than Jane and her husband is available then the answer does not make much sense.

3.3 *R-Based* Implicatures

Utterances contrasting the content of an *R-based* implicature with its mother-utterrance are odd (cf. (10)) and interpreting these utterances felicitously implies contexts such that the targeted implicature does not arise in the first place. For these particular inferences, it seems that we can argue for a systematic argumentative orientation regarding their mother-utterance.

Contrary to their *Q-based* counterparts, *R-based* implicatures lack a propositional content of their own (as noted for example in (Levinson 2000)). Expressing them linguistically amounts to explicitly expressing an enriched version of the mother-utterance. Thus, expressing a contrast between an utterance B and the linguistic expression I of an hypothetical R-implicature attached to B means contrasting two identical propositions: if B indeed carries an implicature, its full interpretation is I and B *but* I should be interpreted as I *but* I. The only way to "redeem" the sentence is to reject the implicature I associated with B and interpret B literally or with another implicature. As things stand, we consider that the argumentative behaviour of these inferences is the same as their mother-utterances.

4 The Source of the Preference

We gave arguments to explain why the examples we are interested in systematically license a contrast. We gave no arguments as to why this contrast is *preferred* when overtly marked.

4.1 Maximize Redundancy

A possibility we want to examine is the application of a principle close to Sauerland's *"Maximize Redundancy"*, as stated in (Sauerland 2008). This principle can be roughly paraphrased as urging a speaker to prefer, among a set of alternatives, a sentence that presupposes an already existing proposition over a sentence that presupposes nothing. Thus, a speaker should prefer saying *the father of the victim* rather than *a father of the victim* because the former presupposes a non-controversial proposition. Uttering the latter would suggest that the presupposition does not obtain, contrary to common knowledge. Applied to our case, this means that, given two propositions p and q such that they always are argumentatively opposed, a speaker will prefer to utter p *but* q rather than p *and* q. The second one would suggest that a contrast does not hold between p and q and thus contradict the argumentative configuration, or at least make the speaker sound "dissonant". At this stage we need to further back up this claim on at least two counts:

1. by ensuring that the non-felicitousness of (4e) is related to, and of the same order as, that of utterances such as *"a father of the victim"* usually treated in works about the discussed principle.

2. by ensuring that the predictions made by the Maximization principle apply to the cases we study; the notion of presupposition used by Sauerland is technical and does not necessarily apply to the contrast conveyed by the use of *but* (i.e. what is often called a conventional implicature rather than a presupposition). At the very least, the principle needs to be broadened to different types of content.

4.2 Properties of Contrast

An alternative explanation for the preference for a marked contrast would be to consider this preference as an idiosyncratic property of the relation at hand. This would be in line with the approach of Asher and Lascarides (2003), where it is claimed that the semantics of the relation of *Contrast* (as defined in *SDRT*) are such that the relation requires a specific clue to be used; either an overt cue element such as *but* or intonation alone. Therefore, the preference we observe for adversatives would be a consequence of the particular semantics of the relation of *Contrast*. For example, the first and second segment of (29) are opposed: that John does not like hockey is a default consequence of the first segment; since this relation of opposition is already present, it needs to be overtly marked.

(29) John hates sports, but he likes hockey.

However, the argumentative relations between propositions are not always obvious. An example such as (30) (taken from (Horn 2005)) is a good illustration: if one does not know, among other possible reasons, whether the speaker has a great or small appartment, one can not decide whether it would be a good or a bad thing for the speaker to have all its friend coming to his party.

(30) If some of my friends come to the party, I'll be happy, but if all of them do, I'll be in trouble.

In that case, when the speaker uses an adversative, the quantifiers are reinterpred in the way suggested in (Horn 2005). If it is evident that the speaker can not accommodate all his friends, then the need for reinterpretation is less evident; it is rather the presence of an adversative that is forced to the speaker because of an opposition that is already present. This amounts to say that the presence of an explicit *Contrast* marker has two possible sources: either the speaker wishes to coordinate two propositions that stand in a systematic argumentative opposition (our core data and (29)), or he wishes to convey that a non-obvious opposition holds between the two ((30) and others such as *She's poor but honest*). If the processing of a discourse is seen as an unification process, the exact source for the choice of the adversative does not matter; what matters is that the requirements of the connective match the argumentative properties of the propositions it connects and vice-versa. In the case their relation are not evident, they should be imagined as being under-specified and specified by the adversative.

A last set of fact we wish to take into account is related to other cases of systematic argumentative opposition. We already remarked that an utterance of the form *almost p* is argumentatively opposed to ¬*p*, in the same way our core data implicatures are with their base-utterances. What we observe is that an utterance of the form *almost p, ¬p* is acceptable with and without contrast, as exemplified in (31).

(31) Mary almost fell, (but) she caught herself.

There is a slight difference in interpretation between the *but* and *but-less* versions, pertaining to the discourse relation that connects the two parts of the discourse. While in the former case a contrast is conveyed, in the latter it is an *explanation* (a relation compatible with the null discourse connective). In this case, an argumentative opposition still exists between the two parts (due to the argumentative properties of *almost*) but the speaker seems to favour another relation and uses a connective incompatible with the expression of argumentative opposition. The statistics given on the *RST* website[6] show that the proportions of signaled relations in texts amount to only 30%, meaning that most relations are not explicitely marked in discourse. This could be another argument for the idiosyncratic treatment of the contrast relation and its markers.

5 Conclusion

We observed what seemed to be a constraint on the felicitous reinforcement of some implicatures. The first hypothesis to account for this data meant reducing argumentativity to an argumentativity-independent inference mechanism and was rejected because it proved to be descriptively inadequate. We then took an argumentative approach to discourse and showed that adversatives were legitimated to reinforce some implicatures on the basis of the argumentative properties of the propositions they express. Put more simply, the choice for an adversative is not linked to inferences, but as it happens the content of some implicatures is often argumentatively opposed to the utterance that conveys them, and thus an adversative is licensed for their reinforcement. Finally we studied cases including an overt restriction, but were faced by the difficulty to give definitive judgments about utterances including both a restriction and adversatives.

We still have to give a definitive explanation for the preference for contrast, although a general principle of *mark-if-present* seems to be at work. We gave two possible reasons for it, and we intend to study this in our future research with an experimental approach. The results of these experiments could provide support for the argumentative approach to semantics and pragmatics we presented.

References

[1977] Anscombre, J.-C., Ducrot, O.: Deux mais en français. Lingua 43, 23–40 (1977)
[1983] Anscombre, J.-C., Ducrot, O.: L'argumentation dans la langue. Bruxelles, Pierre Mardaga (1983)

---

[6] http://www.sfu.ca/rst/02analyses/index.html

[2003] Asher, N., Lascarides, A.: Logics of Conversation. Cambridge University Press, Cambridge (2003)
[1998] Benndorf, B., Koenig, J.-P.: Meaning and context: German aber and sondern. In: Koenig, J.-P. (ed.) Discourse and cognition: bridging the gap, pp. 365–386. CSLI Publications, Stanford (1998)
[2005] Breheny, R., Katsos, N., Williams, J.: Are Generalised Scalar Implicatures Generated by Default? An on-line investigation into the role of context in generating pragmatic inferences. Cognition (2005)
[1998] Carston, R.: Informativeness, Relevance and Scalar Implicature. In: Carston, R., Uchida, S. (eds.) Relevance theory: Applications and Implications. John Benjamins, Amsterdam (1998)
[2005] Carston, R.: Relevance Theory and the Saying/Implicating distinction. In: Horn, L., Ward, G. (eds.) The handbook of Pragmatics. Blackwell, Malden (2005)
[to appear] Chierchia, G., Fox, D., Spector, B.: The Grammatical View of Scalar Implicatures and the Relationship between Semantics and Pragmatics. In: Portner, P., Maienborn, C., von Heusinger, K. (eds.) Handbook of Semantics. Mouton de Gruyter, Berlin (to appear)
[1980] Ducrot, O.: Les échelles argumentatives. Les Éditions de Minuit (1980)
[1979] Gazdar, G.: Pragmatics: Implicature, Presupposition and Logical Form. Academic Press, New York (1979)
[1989] Grice, H.P.: Studies in the way of words. Harvard University Press (1989)
[2008] Jayez, J., Tovena, L.: Presque and almost: how argumentation derives from comparative meaning. In: Bonami, O., Cabredo Hofherr, P. (eds.) Empirical Issues in Syntax and Semantics, vol. 7, pp. 1–23 (2008)
[1985] Hirschberg, J.: A theory of scalar implicature. Ph.D. thesis. University of Pennsylvania (1985)
[1989] Horn, L.: A natural history of negation. The University of Chicago Press (1989)
[1991] Horn, L.: Given as new: when redundant information isnt. Journal of Pragmatics 15(4), 313–336 (1991)
[2005] Horn, L.: The border wars: a neo-gricean perspective. In: Turner, et al. (eds.) Where Semantics Meets Pragmatics, pp. 21–48. Elsevier, Amsterdam (2005)
[2000] Levinson, S.C.: Presumptive Meanings: The Theory of Generalized Conversational Implicature. MIT Press, Cambridge (2000)
[1999] Merin, A.: Information, Relevance and Social Decision-Making. In: Moss, L., Ginzburg, J., de Rijke, M. (eds.) Logic, Language, and computation, vol. 2, pp. 179–221. CSLI Publications, Stanford (1999)
[2007] Noveck, I., Sperber, D.: The why and how of experimental pragmatics: The case of 'scalar inferences. In: Burton-Roberts, N. (ed.) Advances in Pragmatics. Palgrave Macmillan, Basingstoke (2007)
[2008] Sauerland, U.: Implicated Presuppositions. In: Steube, A. (ed.) Sentence and Context. Language, Context & Cognition. Mouton de Gruyter, Berlin (to appear)
[2004] van Rooij, R.: Cooperative versus argumentative communication. Philosophia Scientia 2, 195–209 (2004)
[2005] Wilson, D., Sperber, D.: Relevance Theory. In: Horn, L., Ward, G. (eds.) The handbook of pragmatics. Blackwell, Malden (2005)

Prolegomena to Dynamic Epistemic Preference Logic

Satoru Suzuki

Faculty of Arts and Sciences, Komazawa University,
Komazawa 1-23-1, Setagaya-ku, Tokyo, 154-8525, Japan
bxs05253@nifty.com

Abstract. In this paper, we propose a new version of sound and complete dynamic epistemic preference logic (DEPL). Both preference logic and dynamic epistemic logic have gained considerable attention in linguistics, computer science and philosophy. Recently van Benthem and Liu proposed to integrate preference logic with dynamic epistemic logic. They called the resulting logic 'dynamic epistemic upgrade logic (DEUL)'. DEUL cannot deal with the dynamic interactions between knowledge and preferences originating from decisions makings under other circumstances than certainty. On the other hand, DEPL can deal with the dynamic interactions between knowledge and preferences originating from decisions makings under certainty, risk, uncertainty and ignorance. So DEPL has much wider scope of application than DEUL. Providing DEPL with measurement-theoretic semantics enables it to deal with such wide scope of decision problems.

1 Introduction

In this paper, we propose a new version of sound and complete dynamic epistemic preference logic (DEPL).

The notion of preference plays an important role in many disciplines, including philosophy and economics.[1] Some of notable recent developments in ethics make substantial use of preference logic.[2] In computer science, preference logic has become an indispensable device. The founder of preference logic is the founding father of logic itself, Aristotle. Book III of the *Topics* can be regarded as the first treatment of the subject. From the 1950s to the 1960s, the study of preference logic flourished in Scandinavia–particularly by Halldén ([8]) and von Wright ([34]), and in the U.S.A.–particularly by Martin ([21]) and Chisholm and Sosa ([5]). Recently with the help of Boutilier's idea ([3]), van Benthem, Otterloo and Roy reduced preference logic to multi-modal logic ([31]).

On the other hand, epistemic logic gets its start with the recognition that the expressions like 'know that' have systematic properties that are suitable for logical analysis. In addition to its relevance to traditional philosophical problems, epistemic logic has many applications in computer science and economics.

---
[1] [11] gives a comprehensive survey of preference in general.
[2] [10] gives a comprehensive survey of preference logic.

Knowledge has not only static properties but also dynamic ones. 'Dynamic epistemic logic' is an umbrella term for a number of extensions of epistemic logics with dynamic operators that enables us to formalise reasoning information changes.[3] Recently dynamic epistemic logic has gained considerable attention in formal linguistics, computer science and philosophy. The first step toward making epistemic logic dynamic was made by Plaza in 1989 ([23]). Plaza proposed public announcement logic. His results are similar to those by Gerbrandy and Groeneveld in [7]. [7] is seen as a milestone in the update semantics history of public announcement logic. Recently van Benthem and Liu proposed to integrate van Benthem, Otterloo and Roy's preference logic with dynamic epistemic logic ([32]). They called the resulting logic 'dynamic epistemic upgrade logic (DEUL)'. DEUL enables us to reason logically about the dynamic interactions between knowledge and preferences. Decision problems can be classified into the following four types: decision making under (1) certainty, (2) risk, (3) uncertainty, (4) ignorance. DEUL cannot deal with the dynamic interactions between knowledge and preferences originating from decisions makings under other circumstances than certainty. On the other hand, DEPL can deal with the dynamic interactions between knowledge and preferences originating from decisions makings under certainty, risk, uncertainty and ignorance. So DEPL has much wider scope of application than DEUL. Providing DEPL with measurement-theoretic semantics enables it to deal with such wide scope of decision problems.

Measurement theory is one that provides measurement with its mathematical foundation.[4] The mathematical foundation of measurement had not been studied before Hölder developed his axiomatisation for the measurement of mass ([12]). [18], [30] and [20] are seen as milestones in the history of measurement theory. In measurement theory, at least four kinds of measurement have been objects of study: (1) ordinal measurement, (2) extensive measurement, (3) difference measurement, (4) conjoint measurement. On the other hand, there are at least two kinds of decision theory: (1) evidential decision theory,[5] (2) causal decision theory.[6] The former is designed for decision makings that have statistical or evidential connections between actions and outcomes. The latter is designed for decision makings that have causal connections between actions and outcomes. Both theories take the form of subjective expected utility theory. Jeffrey ([15]) is a typical example of the former. Ramsey ([24]) is a typical example of the latter. Ramsey regarded desire as attitude toward outcomes but belief as one toward propositions. Moreover, he regarded preference as attitude toward an ordered pair of gambles, that is, hybrid entities composed of outcomes and propositions. In 1965 Jeffrey ([15]) developed an alternative to Ramsey's theory. He regarded both desire and belief as attitudes toward propositions. Moreover, he regarded preference as attitude toward an ordered pair of propositions. In this sense we call Jeffrey's a mono-set theory. Its initial axiomatisation was provided in terms

---

[3] [33] gives a comprehensive survey of dynamic epistemic logic.
[4] [27] gives a comprehensive survey of measurement theory.
[5] [15] gives a comprehensive survey of evidential decision theory.
[6] [17] gives a comprehensive survey of causal decision theory.

of measurement theory by Bolker ([2]) on the mathematics developed in [1]. Jeffrey ([14]) modified Bolker's axioms to accommodate null propositions. Domotor ([6]) also axiomatised a version of mono-set theory. Mono-set theories are more suitable for the semantics of logic than Ramsey's, for regarding propositions as the semantic values of sentences is simpler than regarding gambles as those when we wish to provide logic with its semantics. Especially, Domotor's theory is the most suitable for the semantics of logic of these three mono-set theories, for constructing the syntactic analogues of the axioms of Domotor's theory is easier than of the other two theories. Like Bolker's and Jeffrey's, Domotor's theory has a conjoint structure. In them, preferences are decomposable into beliefs and desires. From a measurement-theoretic viewpoint of decision theory, there is a tradition to specify or explain an agent's beliefs and desires in terms of his preferences [and vice versa]. This specification takes the form of a representation theorem:

> If [and only if] an agent's preferences satisfy such-and-such conditions, there exist a probability function and a utility function such that he should act as an expected utility maximiser (existence). [In addition, the pair of such probability function and utility function is unique up to a kind of transformation (uniqueness).]

Domotor's representation theorem is the only known one that can furnish conditions of an agent's preferences necessary and sufficient for there existing a probability function and a utility function such that he should act as an expected utility maximiser. So only by virtue of Domotor's representation theorem, an observer can explain ascribing the logical properties to the agent's preferences originating from decision makings under certainty, risk, uncertainty or ignorance in terms of his beliefs and desires via expected utility maximisation.

The structure of this paper is as follows. In Section 2, we prepare the projective-geometric concepts for the measurement-theoretic settings, and define preference space and preference assignment, and state necessary and sufficient conditions for representation: (connectedness) and (projectivity), and prove a Domotor-type representation theorem. In Section 3, we define the language $\mathcal{L}_{\mathsf{EPL}}$ of EPL, and define a multi-agent Domotor-type structured Kripke model $\mathcal{M}$ for knowledge and preference, and provide EPL with a truth definition, and provide EPL with a proof system, and prove the soundness of EPL in the usual way, and prove the completeness of EPL by constructing the canonical model. In Section 4, we define the language $\mathcal{L}_{\mathsf{DEPL}}$ of DEPL, and define the updated multi-agent Domotor-type structured Kripke model $\mathcal{M}_\varphi$ for knowledge and preference, and provide DEPL with a truth definition, and provide DEPL with a proof system, and prove the soundness of DEPL in the usual way, and provide a translation function, and prove the completeness of DEPL by means of it.

2 Measurement-Theoretic Settings

2.1 Projective-Geometric Concepts

We define the preliminaries to the measurement-theoretic settings.

Definition 1 (Preliminaries). **W** *is a nonempty set of possible worlds. Let* $\mathcal{F}$ *denote a Boolean field of subsets of* **W**. *We call* $A \in \mathcal{F}$ *a proposition.*

Because it is impossible to characterise multiplication of probabilities and utilities in terms of union, intersection and preferences, we need a Cartesian product $\times$. A characteristic function is definable also on a Cartesian product of propositions. We define a characteristic function as follows:

Definition 2 (Characteristic Function). *A characteristic function* $\hat{\ } : \mathcal{F} \to \{0,1\}^{\mathbf{W}}$ *is one where for any* $A \in \mathcal{F}$ *we have* $\hat{A} : \mathbf{W} \to \{0,1\}$ *such that*

$$\hat{A}(w) := \begin{cases} 1 & \text{if } w \in A, \\ 0 & \text{otherwise,} \end{cases}$$

for any $w \in \mathbf{W}$. *A Cartesian product of characteristic functions* $\otimes$ *is defined as follows:* $\hat{A} \otimes \hat{B} := \widehat{(A \times B)}$.

By means of $\otimes$ we define an exterior product $\circ$ as follows:

Definition 3 (Exterior Product)
$\hat{A} \circ \hat{B} := \hat{A} \otimes \hat{B} - \hat{B} \otimes \hat{A} = \widehat{(A \times B)} - \widehat{(B \times A)}$.

By means of $\circ$ we define a symmetric product $\odot$ as follows:

Definition 4 (Symmetric Product)

$\odot(\hat{A}, \hat{B}, \hat{C}, \hat{D})$
$:= (\hat{A} \circ \hat{B}) \circ (\hat{C} \circ \hat{D}) + (\hat{C} \circ \hat{D}) \circ (\hat{A} \circ \hat{B}) =$
$\widehat{(A \times B \times C \times D)} + \widehat{(B \times A \times D \times C)} + \widehat{(C \times D \times A \times B)} + \widehat{(D \times C \times B \times A)}$
$- \widehat{(A \times B \times D \times C)} - \widehat{(B \times A \times C \times D)} - \widehat{(C \times D \times B \times A)} - \widehat{(D \times C \times A \times B)}$.

By means of $\odot$ we define a four-fold exterior product $\triangle$ as follows:

Definition 5 (Four-Fold Exterior Product)

$\triangle(\hat{A}, \hat{B}, \hat{C}, \hat{D}) :=$
$\odot(\hat{A}, \hat{B}, \hat{C}, \hat{D}) + \odot(\hat{A}, \hat{C}, \hat{D}, \hat{B}) + \odot(\hat{A}, \hat{D}, \hat{B}, \hat{C}) =$
$\widehat{(A \times B \times C \times D)} + \widehat{(B \times A \times D \times C)} + \widehat{(C \times D \times A \times B)} + \widehat{(D \times C \times B \times A)}$
$- \widehat{(A \times B \times D \times C)} - \widehat{(B \times A \times C \times D)} - \widehat{(C \times D \times B \times A)} - \widehat{(D \times C \times A \times B)}$
$+ \widehat{(A \times C \times D \times B)} + \widehat{(C \times A \times B \times D)} + \widehat{(D \times B \times A \times C)} + \widehat{(B \times D \times C \times A)}$
$- \widehat{(A \times C \times B \times D)} - \widehat{(C \times A \times D \times B)} - \widehat{(D \times B \times C \times A)} - \widehat{(B \times D \times A \times C)}$
$+ \widehat{(A \times D \times B \times C)} + \widehat{(D \times A \times C \times B)} + \widehat{(B \times C \times A \times D)} + \widehat{(C \times B \times D \times A)}$
$- \widehat{(A \times D \times C \times B)} - \widehat{(D \times A \times B \times C)} - \widehat{(B \times C \times D \times A)} - \widehat{(C \times B \times A \times D)}$.

2.2 Preference Space and Preference Assignment

We define preference space and preference assignment as follows:

Definition 6 (Preference Space and Preference Assignment). $W_{a,w} \subseteq \mathbf{W}$ *should be interpreted to mean a set of worlds that* $a \in \mathbf{A}$ *takes into consideration at a time in* $w \in \mathbf{W}$. *Let* $\mathcal{F}_{a,w}$ *denote a Boolean field of subsets of* $W_{a,w}$.

$\preceq_{a,w}$ is a weak preference relation on $\mathcal{F}^2_{a,w}$. $A \preceq_{a,w} B$ should be interpreted to mean that a does not prefer A to B at a time in w. $\sim_{a,w}$ and $\prec_{a,w}$ are defined as follows:

- $A \sim_{a,w} B := A \preceq_{a,w} B$ and $B \preceq_{a,w} A$,
- $A \prec_{a,w} B := A \preceq_{a,w} B$ and $A \not\sim_{a,w} B$.

For any $a \in \mathbf{A}$ and $w \in \mathbf{W}$, $(W_{a,w}, \mathcal{F}_{a,w}, \preceq_{a,w}, \widehat{\ }, \times, +, -)$ is called a preference space. Let $\mathbf{PS}$ denote the set of all preference spaces. $\rho: \mathbf{A} \times \mathbf{W} \to \mathbf{PS}$ is called a preference assignment.

2.3 Conditions for Representation

We state necessary and sufficient conditions for representation as follows:

1. $A \preceq_{a,w} B$ or $B \preceq_{a,w} A$ (**Connectedness**),
2. If ($A_i \preceq_{a,w} B_i$ and $C_i \preceq_{a,w} D_i$ for any $i < n$),
   then (if $A_n \preceq_{a,w} B_n$, then $D_n \preceq_{a,w} C_n$),
   where $\sum_{i \leq n} \odot(\hat{A_i}, \hat{B_i}, \hat{C_i}, \hat{D_i}) = \triangle(\hat{A_n}, \hat{B_n}, \hat{C_n}, \hat{D_n})$ (**Projectivity**).

2.4 Explanation for Projectivity

Under the following representation theorem, (projectivity) essentially says that if

$$\sum_{i=1}^{n} P_{a,w}(A_i)P_{a,w}(B_i)P_{a,w}(C_i)P_{a,w}(D_i)(U_{a,w}(B_i) - U_{a,w}(A_i))(U_{a,w}(D_i) - U_{a,w}(C_i)) = 0$$

and if $U_{a,w}(A_i) \leq U_{a,w}(B_i)$ for $i = 1, \ldots, n$ and $U_{a,w}(C_i) \leq U_{a,w}(D_i)$ for $i = 1, \ldots, n-1$, then $U_{a,w}(D_n) \leq U_{a,w}(C_n)$. Zero on the right hand side comes from the fact that the measure of $\triangle(\hat{A_n}, \hat{B_n}, \hat{C_n}, \hat{D_n})$ happens to be equal to zero:

$P_{a,w}(A_n)P_{a,w}(B_n)P_{a,w}(C_n)P_{a,w}(D_n)((U_{a,w}(B_n) - U_{a,w}(A_n))(U_{a,w}(D_n) - U_{a,w}(C_n))$
$+(U_{a,w}(C_n) - U_{a,w}(A_n))(U_{a,w}(B_n) - U_{a,w}(D_n))$
$+(U_{a,w}(D_n) - U_{a,w}(A_n))(U_{a,w}(C_n) - U_{a,w}(B_n))) = 0.$

Generally, conjoint measurement requires the cancellation axiom as a necessary one. (Projectivity) can be regarded as a generalisation of the cancellation axiom. Domotor's representation theorem follows from Scott's separation theorem ([28]). The latter is based on the general mathematical criterion for the solvability of a finite set of homogeneous linear inequalities.

2.5 Domotor-Type Representation Theorem

We can prove a Domotor-type representation theorem as follows:

Theorem 1 (Representation). *For any* $a \in \mathbf{A}$ *and* $w_1 \in \mathbf{W}$, $(W_{a,w_1}, \mathcal{F}_{a,w_1}, \preceq_{a,w_1}, \widehat{\ }, \times, +, -)$ *satisfies (connectedness) and (projectivity) iff* there are $P_{a,w_1} : \mathcal{F}_{a,w_1} \to \mathbb{R}$ and $U_{a,w_1} : \mathcal{F}_{a,w_1} \setminus \emptyset \to \mathbb{R}$ such that the following conditions hold for any $A, B \in \mathcal{F}_{a,w_1} \setminus \emptyset$:

- $(W_{a,w_1}, \mathcal{F}_{a,w_1}, P_{a,w_1})$ is a finitely additive probability space,
- $A \preceq_{a,w_1} B$ iff $U_{a,w_1}(A) \leq U_{a,w_1}(B)$,
- $U_{a,w_1}(A) = \sum_{w_2 \in A} P_{a,w_1}(\{w_2\}) U_{a,w_1}(\{w_2\})$,
- When $A \in \mathcal{F}_{a,w_1}$, if $P_{a,w_1}(A) = 0$, then $A = \emptyset$.

Proof. Except that the proof is relative to agent and world, it is similar to that of [[6]:184–194].

2.6 Significance of Domotor-Type Representation Theorem and Merit of DEPL

Based upon [[19]: p. 13] with a slight modification, decision problems can be classified into the following four types. We say that an agent is in the realm of decision making under:

1. *Certainty* if each action leads to a specific outcome with the probability of 1 that is known to him,
2. *Risk* if each action leads to one of a set of possible specific outcomes each of which occurs with a probability that is known to him,
3. *Uncertainty* if each action leads to one of a set of possible specific outcomes, some of which occur with a probability that is known to him, but the other of which occur with a probability that is unknown to him,
4. *Ignorance* if each action leads to one of a set of possible specific outcomes each of which occurs with a probability that is unknown to him.

When an observer considers an agent to be a decision maker under certainty, *utility maximisation* is one of the most dominant decision rules. We can prove the following theorem about utility maximisation.

Theorem 2 (Representation, Cantor [4]). *Suppose* $\mathbf{W}$ *is a countable set and* $\preceq^*$ *is a binary relation on* $\mathbf{W}$. *Then* $(\mathbf{W}, \preceq^*)$ *is a weak order iff there is a function* $U^* : \mathbf{W} \to \mathbb{R}$ *satisfying*

$$w_1 \preceq^* w_2 \text{ iff } U^*(w_1) \leq U^*(w_2).$$

Moreover, U^* is unique up to a positive affine transformation.

If an agent's desire state can be represented by a utility function, then by virtue of Theorem 2, an observer can explain ascribing the logical properties to the agent's preferences originating from only decision makings under certainty in terms of his desires via utility maximisation.

On the other hand, when an observer considers an agent to be a decision maker under certainty, risk, uncertainty or ignorance, *expected utility maximisation* is one of the most dominant decision rules. Theorem 1 (Domotor-type representation theorem) is the only known one that can furnish conditions of an agent's preferences necessary and sufficient for there existing a probability function and a utility function such that he should act as an expected utility maximiser. All other representation theorems of expected utility maximisation, such as [2] and [14], can furnish only sufficient conditions for it. So if an agent's belief state can be represented by a probability function and his desire state can be represented by a utility function, then only by virtue of Theorem 1, an observer can explain ascribing the logical properties to the agent's preferences originating from decision makings under certainty, risk, uncertainty and ignorance in terms of his beliefs and desires via expected utility maximisation.

Since the preference spaces in DEUL are weak orders, DEUL cannot deal with the dynamic interactions between knowledge and preferences originating from decisions makings under other circumstances than certainty. On the other hand, we say that $(W_{a,w_1}, \mathcal{F}_{a,w_1}, \preceq_{a,w_1}, \hat{\,}, \times, +, -)$ is a *projective order* if $(W_{a,w_1}, \mathcal{F}_{a,w_1}, \preceq_{a,w_1}, \hat{\,}, \times, +, -)$ satisfies (connectedness) and (projectivity). Since the preference spaces in DEPL are projective orders, DEPL can deal with the dynamic interactions between knowledge and preferences originating from decisions makings under certainty, risk, uncertainty and ignorance. So DEPL has much wider scope of application than DEUL.

3 Epistemic Preference Logic EPL

3.1 Language

The language of EPL $\mathcal{L}_{\mathsf{EPL}}$ is defined as follows:

Definition 7 (Language). *Let* **S** *denote a set of sentential variables,* **A** *a finite set of agents,* $\mathbf{K}_a$ *an epistemic operator,* $\mathbf{WPR}_a$ *a weak preference relation symbol and* **FCP** *a four-fold Cartesian product symbol.* $\mathcal{L}_{\mathsf{EPL}}$ *is given by the following rule:*

$$\varphi ::= s \mid \top \mid \neg\varphi \mid \varphi_1 \wedge \varphi_2 \mid \mathbf{K}_a(\varphi) \mid \mathbf{WPR}_a(\varphi_1, \varphi_2) \mid \mathbf{FCP}(\varphi_1, \varphi_2, \varphi_3, \varphi_4),$$

where $s \in \mathbf{S}$ *and* $a \in \mathbf{A}$. *The set of all well-formed formulae of* $\mathcal{L}_{\mathsf{EPL}}$ *will be denoted by* $\Phi_{\mathcal{L}_{\mathsf{EPL}}}$.

3.2 Semantics

Model By developing the idea of Naumov ([22]) and that of Halpern ([9]), we define a multi-agent Domotor-type structured Kripke model $\mathcal{M}$ for knowledge and preference as follows:

Definition 8 (Model). $\mathcal{M}$ *is a sextuple* $(\mathbf{W}, R, L, V, \rho, \{\approx_a\}_{a \in \mathbf{A}})$, *where* **W** *is a nonempty set of possible worlds,* R *is a relation on* $\mathbf{W}^2$, $(\mathbf{W}, R)$ *is a directed acyclic graph (DAG),* $L : R \to \{\pi_1, \pi_2, \pi_3, \pi_4\}$ *is a function that assigns labels to the edges of the graph, any two edges leaving the same vertex have different labels, any vertex either has* π_1-, π_2-, π_3- *and* π_4-*labeled outgoing edges or none of them, V is a truth assignment to each* $s \in \mathbf{S}$ *for each* $w \in \mathbf{W}$, ρ *is a preference* assignment that assigns to each $a \in \mathbf{A}$ and each $w \in \mathbf{W}$ ($W_{a,w}, \mathcal{F}_{a,w}, \preceq_{a,w}, \hat{\,}, \times, +, -$) that satisfies (connectedness) and (projectivity), $\approx_a$ is an equivalence relation on $\mathbf{W}^2$, and the following conditions hold:

1. For all $a \in \mathbf{A}$ and $w \in \mathbf{W}$, if $\rho(a, w_1) = (W_{a,w_1}, \mathcal{F}_{a,w_1}, \preceq_{a,w_1}, \hat{\,}, \times, +, -)$, then $W_{a,w_1} \subseteq \{w_2 : w_1 \approx_a w_2\}$ **(Consistency)**,
2. For all $a \in \mathbf{A}$ and $w_1, w_2 \in \mathbf{W}$, if $w_2 \in \{w_3 : w_1 \approx_a w_3\}$, then $\rho(a, w_1) = \rho(a, w_2)$ **(World-Dependent Preference)**.

For any $w_1 \in \mathbf{W}$, by $\pi_i(w_1)$ ($i = 1, 2, 3, 4$) we mean the unique $w_2 \in \mathbf{W}$ such that $R(w_1, w_2)$ and $L(w_1, w_2) = \pi_i$ if such world exists.

By virtue of the DAG $(\mathbf{W}, R)$ and the labeling function L, we can provide a fourfold Cartesian product with a truth condition. Some important aspects of the interactions between knowledge and preference can be caught by (consistency) and (world-dependent preference). (Consistency) postulates that an agent assigns preference only to worlds that he considers accessible. (World-dependent preference) postulates that the choice of preference space is the same in all worlds the agent considers accessible.

Truth: We can provide EPL with the following truth definition:

Definition 9 (Truth). *The notion of $\varphi \in \Phi_{\mathcal{L}_{\mathsf{EPL}}}$ being true at $w \in \mathbf{W}$ in $\mathcal{M}$, in symbols $(\mathcal{M}, w) \models_{\mathsf{EPL}} \varphi$, is inductively defined as follows:*

- $(\mathcal{M}, w) \models_{\mathsf{EPL}} s$ iff $V(w)(s) = \mathbf{true}$,
- $(\mathcal{M}, w) \models_{\mathsf{EPL}} \top$,
- $(\mathcal{M}, w) \models_{\mathsf{EPL}} \varphi_1 \wedge \varphi_2$ iff $(\mathcal{M}, w) \models_{\mathsf{EPL}} \varphi_1$ and $(\mathcal{M}, w) \models_{\mathsf{EPL}} \varphi_2$,
- $(\mathcal{M}, w) \models_{\mathsf{EPL}} \neg \varphi$ iff $(\mathcal{M}, w) \not\models_{\mathsf{EPL}} \varphi$,
- $(\mathcal{M}, w_1) \models_{\mathsf{EPL}} \mathbf{K}_a(\varphi)$ iff $(\mathcal{M}, w_2) \models_{\mathsf{EPL}} \varphi$ for all $w_2 \in \{w_3 : w_1 \approx_a w_3\}$,
- $(\mathcal{M}, w) \models_{\mathsf{EPL}} \mathbf{FCP}(\varphi_1, \varphi_2, \varphi_3, \varphi_4)$ iff $(\mathcal{M}, \pi_1(w)) \models_{\mathsf{EPL}} \varphi_1$ and $(\mathcal{M}, \pi_2(w)) \models_{\mathsf{EPL}} \varphi_2$ and $(\mathcal{M}, \pi_3(w)) \models_{\mathsf{EPL}} \varphi_3$ and $(\mathcal{M}, \pi_4(w)) \models_{\mathsf{EPL}} \varphi_4$,
- $(\mathcal{M}, w_1) \models_{\mathsf{EPL}} \mathbf{WPR}_a(\varphi_1, \varphi_2)$ iff $[\![\varphi_1]\!]_{a,w_1} \preceq_{a,w_1} [\![\varphi_2]\!]_{a,w_1}$,

where $[\![\varphi]\!]_{a,w_1} := \{w_2 \in W_{a,w_1} : (\mathcal{M}, w_2) \models_{\mathsf{EPL}} \varphi\}$. If $(\mathcal{M}, w) \models_{\mathsf{EPL}} \varphi$ for all $w \in \mathbf{W}$, we write $\mathcal{M} \models \varphi$ and say that φ is valid in $\mathcal{M}$. If φ is valid in all multi-agent Domotor-type structured Kripke model for knowledge and preference, we write $\models_{\mathsf{EPL}} \varphi$ and say that φ is valid.

3.3 Syntax

Preliminaries: We devise a syntactic analogue of (projectivity). By developing the idea of Segerberg ([29]), we define Γ_i as follows:

Definition 10 (Disjunction of Conjunctions). *For any i ($1 \leq i \leq 4n + 4$), Γ_i is defined as the disjunction of all the following conjunctions:*

$$\bigwedge_{j=1}^{n-1} d_j \mathbf{FCP}(\varphi_j, \psi_j, \chi_j, \tau_j)$$
$$\wedge d_n \mathbf{FCP}(\varphi_n, \chi_n, \psi_n, \tau_n) \wedge d_{n+1}\mathbf{FCP}(\varphi_n, \tau_n, \chi_n, \psi_n)$$
$$\wedge \bigwedge_{j=n+2}^{2n} d_j \mathbf{FCP}(\psi_{j-n-1}, \varphi_{j-n-1}, \tau_{j-n-1}, \chi_{j-n-1})$$
$$\wedge d_{2n+1}\mathbf{FCP}(\chi_n, \varphi_n, \tau_n, \psi_n) \wedge d_{2n+2}\mathbf{FCP}(\tau_n, \varphi_n, \psi_n, \chi_n)$$
$$\wedge \bigwedge_{j=2n+3}^{3n+1} d_j \mathbf{FCP}(\chi_{j-2n-2}, \tau_{j-2n-2}, \varphi_{j-2n-2}, \psi_{j-2n-2})$$
$$\wedge d_{3n+2}\mathbf{FCP}(\tau_n, \psi_n, \chi_n, \varphi_n) \wedge d_{3n+3}\mathbf{FCP}(\psi_n, \chi_n, \tau_n, \varphi_n)$$
$$\wedge \bigwedge_{j=3n+4}^{4n+2} d_j \mathbf{FCP}(\tau_{j-3n-3}, \chi_{j-3n-3}, \psi_{j-3n-3}, \varphi_{j-3n-3})$$
$$\wedge d_{4n+3}\mathbf{FCP}(\psi_n, \tau_n, \varphi_n, \chi_n) \wedge d_{4n+4}\mathbf{FCP}(\chi_n, \psi_n, \varphi_n, \tau_n)$$
$$\wedge \bigwedge_{j=1}^{n-1} e_j \mathbf{FCP}(\varphi_j, \psi_j, \tau_j, \chi_j)$$
$$\wedge e_n \mathbf{FCP}(\varphi_n, \chi_n, \tau_n, \psi_n) \wedge e_{n+1}\mathbf{FCP}(\varphi_n, \tau_n, \psi_n, \chi_n)$$
$$\wedge \bigwedge_{j=n+2}^{2n} e_j \mathbf{FCP}(\psi_{j-n-1}, \varphi_{j-n-1}, \chi_{j-n-1}, \tau_{j-n-1})$$
$$\wedge e_{2n+1}\mathbf{FCP}(\chi_n, \varphi_n, \psi_n, \tau_n) \wedge e_{2n+2}\mathbf{FCP}(\tau_n, \varphi_n, \chi_n, \psi_n)$$
$$\wedge \bigwedge_{j=2n+3}^{3n+1} e_j \mathbf{FCP}(\chi_{j-2n-2}, \tau_{j-2n-2}, \psi_{j-2n-2}, \varphi_{j-2n-2})$$
$$\wedge e_{3n+2}\mathbf{FCP}(\tau_n, \psi_n, \varphi_n, \chi_n) \wedge e_{3n+3}\mathbf{FCP}(\psi_n, \chi_n, \varphi_n, \tau_n)$$
$$\wedge \bigwedge_{j=3n+4}^{4n+2} e_j \mathbf{FCP}(\tau_{j-3n-3}, \chi_{j-3n-3}, \varphi_{j-3n-3}, \psi_{j-3n-3})$$
$$\wedge e_{4n+3}\mathbf{FCP}(\psi_n, \tau_n, \chi_n, \varphi_n) \wedge e_{4n+4}\mathbf{FCP}(\chi_n, \psi_n, \tau_n, \varphi_n)$$

such that exactly i of the d_j's and i of the e_j's are the negation symbols, the rest of them being the empty string of symbols.

By means of Γ_i, we define **DDC** as follows:

Definition 11 (Disjunction of Disjunctions of Conjunctions).

$$\mathbf{DDC}_{i=1}^n(\varphi_i, \psi_i, \chi_i, \tau_i) := \vee_{i=1}^{4n+4} \Gamma_i.$$

Proof System We provide EPL with the following proof system.

Definition 12 (Proof System).

- *Axioms of* EPL

(A1) *All tautologies of classical sentential logic,*

(A2) $\mathbf{WPR}_a(\varphi_1, \varphi_2) \vee \mathbf{WPR}_a(\varphi_2, \varphi_1)$ (***Syntactic Analogue of Connectedness***),

(A3) $\mathbf{DDC}_{i=1}^{n}(\varphi_i, \psi_i, \chi_i, \tau_i) \rightarrow$
$(\wedge_{i=1}^{n}(\mathbf{WPR}_a(\varphi_i, \psi_i) \wedge \mathbf{WPR}_a(\chi_i, \tau_i)) \rightarrow (\mathbf{WPR}_a(\varphi_n, \psi_n) \rightarrow \mathbf{WPR}_a(\tau_n, \chi_n)))$
(Syntactic Analogue of Projectivity),

(A4) $\mathbf{FCP}(\top, \top, \top, \top)$ *(Tautology and Four-Fold Cartesian Product)*,

(A5) $\mathbf{FCP}(\varphi_1 \wedge \varphi_2, \psi_1 \wedge \psi_2, \chi_1 \wedge \chi_2, \tau_1 \wedge \tau_2) \rightarrow (\mathbf{FCP}(\varphi_1, \psi_1, \chi_1, \tau_1) \wedge \mathbf{FCP}(\varphi_2, \psi_2, \chi_2, \tau_2))$
(Conjunction and Four-Fold Cartesian Product 1),

(A6) $(\mathbf{FCP}(\varphi_1, \mu, \nu, \xi) \wedge \mathbf{FCP}(\varphi_2, \mu, \nu, \xi)) \rightarrow \mathbf{FCP}(\varphi_1 \wedge \varphi_2, \mu, \nu, \xi)$
(Conjunction and Four-Fold Cartesian Product 2),

(A7) $(\mathbf{FCP}(\lambda, \psi_1, \nu, \xi) \wedge \mathbf{FCP}(\lambda, \psi_2, \nu, \xi)) \rightarrow \mathbf{FCP}(\lambda, \psi_1 \wedge \psi_2, \nu, \xi)$
(Conjunction and Four-Fold Cartesian Product 3),

(A8) $(\mathbf{FCP}(\lambda, \mu, \chi_1, \xi) \wedge \mathbf{FCP}(\lambda, \mu, \chi_2, \xi)) \rightarrow \mathbf{FCP}(\lambda, \mu, \chi_1 \wedge \chi_2, \xi)$
(Conjunction and Four-Fold Cartesian Product 4),

(A9) $(\mathbf{FCP}(\lambda, \mu, \nu, \tau_1) \wedge \mathbf{FCP}(\lambda, \mu, \nu, \tau_2)) \rightarrow \mathbf{FCP}(\lambda, \mu, \nu, \tau_1 \wedge \tau_2)$
(Conjunction and Four-Fold Cartesian Product 5),

(A10) $\neg \mathbf{FCP}(\varphi, \psi, \chi, \tau)$
$\leftrightarrow (\mathbf{FCP}(\neg\varphi, \psi, \chi, \tau) \vee \mathbf{FCP}(\varphi, \neg\psi, \chi, \tau) \vee \mathbf{FCP}(\varphi, \psi, \neg\chi, \tau) \vee \mathbf{FCP}(\varphi, \psi, \chi, \neg\tau))$
(Negation and Four-Fold Cartesian Product),

(A11) $\mathbf{K}_a(\varphi_1 \rightarrow \varphi_2) \rightarrow (\mathbf{K}_a(\varphi_1) \rightarrow \mathbf{K}_a(\varphi_2))$ *(K)*,

(A12) $\mathbf{K}_a(\varphi) \rightarrow \varphi$ *(T)*,

(A13) $\mathbf{K}_a(\varphi) \rightarrow \mathbf{K}_a \mathbf{K}_a(\varphi)$ *(Positive Introspection)*,

(A14) $\neg \mathbf{K}_a(\varphi) \rightarrow \mathbf{K}_a \neg \mathbf{K}_a(\varphi)$ *(Negative Introspection)*,

(A15) $\mathbf{K}_a(\varphi) \rightarrow \mathbf{IND}_a(\varphi, \top)$ *(Syntactic Analogue of Consistency)*,

(A16) $\mathbf{WPR}_a(\varphi_1, \varphi_2) \rightarrow \mathbf{K}_a(\mathbf{WPR}_a(\varphi_1, \varphi_2))$
(Syntactic Analogue of World-Dependent Preference).

- *Inference Rules of* EPL

(R1) $\dfrac{\varphi_1 \quad \varphi_1 \rightarrow \varphi_2}{\varphi_2}$ *(Modus Ponens)*,

(R2) $\dfrac{\varphi_1 \rightarrow \varphi_2}{\mathbf{WPR}_a(\varphi_2, \varphi_1)}$ *(Weak Preference Necessitation)*,

(R3) $\dfrac{\varphi \wedge \psi \wedge \chi \wedge \tau}{\mathbf{FCP}(\varphi, \psi, \chi, \tau)}$ *(Four-Fold Cartesian Product Necessitation)*,

(R4) $\dfrac{\varphi}{\mathbf{K}_a(\varphi)}$ *(Knowledge Necessitation)*.

A proof of $\varphi \in \Phi_{\mathcal{L}_{\mathsf{EPL}}}$ is a finite sequence of $\mathcal{L}_{\mathsf{EPL}}$-formulae having φ as the last formula such that either each formula is an instance of an axiom, or it can be obtained from formulae that appear earlier in the sequence by applying an inference rule. If there is a proof of φ, we write $\vdash_{\mathsf{EPL}} \varphi$.

3.4 Soundness and Completeness

We can prove the soundness of EPL in the usual way.

Theorem 3 (Soundness). *For every $\varphi \in \Phi_{\mathcal{L}_{\mathsf{EPL}}}$, if $\vdash_{\mathsf{EPL}} \varphi$, then $\models_{\mathsf{EPL}} \varphi$.*

We can prove the completeness of EPL by constructing the canonical model.

Theorem 4 (Completeness). *For every $\varphi \in \Phi_{\mathcal{L}_{\mathsf{EPL}}}$, if $\models_{\mathsf{EPL}} \varphi$, then $\vdash_{\mathsf{EPL}} \varphi$.*

4 Dynamic Epistemic Preference Logic DEPL

4.1 Language

The language of DEPL $\mathcal{L}_{\mathsf{DEPL}}$ is defined as follows:

Definition 13 (Language). *Let $\mathbf{S}$ denote a set of sentential variables, $\mathbf{A}$ a finite set of agents, $\mathbf{K}_a$ an epistemic operator, $\mathbf{WPR}_a$ a weak preference relation symbol, and $[\ ]$ an update operator. $\mathcal{L}_{\mathsf{DEPL}}$ is given by the following rule:*

$$\varphi ::= s \mid \top \mid \neg\varphi \mid \varphi_1 \wedge \varphi_2 \mid \mathbf{K}_a(\varphi) \mid \mathbf{WPR}_a(\varphi_1, \varphi_2) \mid \mathbf{FCP}(\varphi_1, \varphi_2, \varphi_3, \varphi_4) \mid [\varphi_1]\varphi_2,$$

where $s \in \mathbf{S}, a \in \mathbf{A}$. $[\varphi_1]\varphi_2$ should be interpreted to mean that φ_2 is the case after everyone simultaneously and commonly learns that φ_1 is the case. The set of all well-formed formulae of $\mathcal{L}_{\mathsf{DEPL}}$ will be denoted by $\Phi_{\mathcal{L}_{\mathsf{DEPL}}}$.

4.2 Semantics

Updated Expected Utility and Updated Weak Preference Relation:
There are at least two modes of change that cause changes of preference:

1. valuational preference change,
2. doxastic preference change.

The former can be represented by change of the utility $U_{a,w_1}(\{w_2\})$ of $w_2 \in \mathbf{W}$. The latter can be represented by change of the probability function P_{a,w_1}. DEPL is based only on the latter. In DEPL $U_{a,w_1}(\{w_2\})$ is fixed, but according as P_{a,w_1} changes, the expected utility U_{a,w_1} changes. In DEPL the change of probability function is executed by conditionalisation. Conditionalisation is defined as follows:

Definition 14 (Conditionalisation). *Given $a \in \mathbf{A}$ and $w \in \mathbf{W}$, let $\mathcal{P}$ denote the set of all probability functions on $\mathcal{F}_{a,w}$. The function $\oplus : \mathcal{P} \times \mathcal{F}_{a,w} \to \mathcal{P}$ such that for any $A \in \mathcal{F}_{a,w}$,*

$$\oplus(P_{a,w}, A)(B) := \begin{cases} \dfrac{P_{a,w}(A \cap B)}{P_{a,w}(A)} & \text{if } P_{a,w}(A) \neq 0, \\ \text{undefined} & \text{otherwise} \end{cases}$$

is called conditionalisation on A.

The updated expected utility is defined as follows:

Definition 15 (Updated Expected Utility). *Given U_{a,w_1} and $A \in \mathcal{F}_{a,w_1}$, U_{a,w_1} such that for any $B \in \mathcal{F}_{a,w_1}$,*

$$U_{a,w_1,A}(B) := \sum_{w_2 \in B} \oplus(P_{a,w_1}, A)(\{w_2\}) U_{a,w_1}(\{w_2\}) = U_{a,w_1}(A \cap B)$$

is called the updated expected utility on A.

The updated weak preference relation is defined as follows:

Definition 16 (Updated Weak Preference Relation). *When $U_{a,w,A}$ defined by $U_{a,w}$ the existence of which is guaranteed by Theorem 1 is given, $\preceq_{a,w,A}$ such that for any $B, C \in \mathcal{F}_{a,w}$,*

$$B \preceq_{a,w,A} C \text{ iff } U_{a,w,A}(B) \leq U_{a,w,A}(C)$$

is called the updated weak preference relation on A.

From Definition 15, Definition 16 and Theorem 1, the next corollary follows.

Corollary 1 (Original Weak Preference Relation and Updated Weak Preference Relation). *Given $a \in \mathbf{A}$, $w \in \mathbf{W}$ and $A \in \mathcal{F}_{a,w}$, if $(W_{a,w}, \mathcal{F}_{a,w}, \preceq_{a,w}, \times, +, -)$ satisfies (connectedness) and (projectivity), then for any $B, C \in \mathcal{F}_{a,w}$,*

$$B \preceq_{a,w,A} C \text{ iff } A \cap B \preceq_{a,w} A \cap C$$

holds.

Truth: By virtue of Corollary 1, we can provide DEPL with the following truth definition:

Definition 17 (Truth). *When $\mathcal{M} := (\mathbf{W}, R, L, V, \rho, \{\approx_a\}_{a \in \mathbf{A}})$ is given, the notion of $\varphi \in \Phi_{\mathcal{L}_{\mathsf{DEPL}}}$ being true at $w \in \mathbf{W}$ in $\mathcal{M}$, in symbols $(\mathcal{M}, w) \models_{\mathsf{DEPL}} \varphi$, is inductively defined as follows:*

- $(\mathcal{M}, w) \models_{\mathsf{DEPL}} s$ iff $V(w)(s) = \mathbf{true}$,
- $(\mathcal{M}, w) \models_{\mathsf{DEPL}} \top$,
- $(\mathcal{M}, w) \models_{\mathsf{DEPL}} \varphi_1 \wedge \varphi_2$ iff $(\mathcal{M}, w) \models_{\mathsf{DEPL}} \varphi_1$ and $(\mathcal{M}, w) \models_{\mathsf{DEPL}} \varphi_2$,
- $(\mathcal{M}, w) \models_{\mathsf{DEPL}} \neg \varphi$ iff $(\mathcal{M}, w) \not\models_{\mathsf{DEPL}} \varphi$,
- $(\mathcal{M}, w_1) \models_{\mathsf{DEPL}} \mathbf{K}_a(\varphi)$ iff $(\mathcal{M}, w_2) \models_{\mathsf{DEPL}} \varphi$ for all $w_2 \in \{w_3 : w_1 \approx_a w_3\}$,
- $(\mathcal{M}, w_1) \models_{\mathsf{DEPL}} \mathbf{WPR}_a(\varphi_1, \varphi_2)$ iff $[\![\varphi_1]\!]_{a,w_1} \preceq_{a,w_1} [\![\varphi_2]\!]_{a,w_1}$,
- $(\mathcal{M}, w) \models_{\mathsf{DEPL}} [\varphi_1]\varphi_2$ iff $(\mathcal{M}, w) \models_{\mathsf{DEPL}} \varphi_1$ implies $(\mathcal{M}_{\varphi_1}, w) \models_{\mathsf{DEPL}} \varphi_2$,

where $\mathcal{M}_{\varphi_1}$ is the updated multi-agent Domotor-type structured Kripke model for knowledge and preference obtained from replacing each $\approx_a$ with its updated equivalence relation $\approx_{a,\varphi_1} := \{(w_1, w_2) : w_1 \approx_a w_2$ and $(\mathcal{M}, w_2) \models_{\mathsf{DEPL}} \varphi_1\}$ and replacing ρ with the updated preference assignment ρ_{φ_1} such that $\rho_{\varphi_1}(a, w_1) = (W_{a,w_1}, \mathcal{F}_{a,w_1}, \preceq_{a,w_1,[\![\varphi_1]\!]_{a,w_1}}, \widehat{\,\,}, \times, +, -)$, where $[\![\varphi_1]\!]_{a,w_1} := \{w_2 \in W_{a,w_1} : (\mathcal{M}, w_2) \models_{\mathsf{DEPL}} \varphi_1\}$ and, for any $B, C \in \mathcal{F}_{a,w_1}$, $B \preceq_{a,w_1,[\![\varphi_1]\!]_{a,w_1}} C$ iff $[\![\varphi_1]\!]_{a,w_1} \cap B \preceq_{a,w_1} [\![\varphi_1]\!]_{a,w_1} \cap C$.

If $(\mathcal{M}, w) \models_{\mathsf{DEPL}} \varphi$ for all $w \in \mathbf{W}$, we write $\mathcal{M} \models_{\mathsf{DEPL}} \varphi$ and say that φ is valid in $\mathcal{M}$. If φ is valid in all multi-agent Domotor-type structured Kripke model for knowledge and preference, we write $\models_{\mathsf{DEPL}} \varphi$ and say that φ is valid.

It is a nontrivial matter whether or not the updated model satisfies the conditions that the original model satisfied. We must prove that the updated model satisfies such conditions.

Proposition 1 (Original Model and Updated Model). *If $\mathcal{M} := (\mathbf{W}, R, L, V, \rho, \{\approx_a\}_{a \in \mathbf{A}})$ satisfies (consistency) and (world-dependent preference), and $\rho(a, w) := (W_{a,w}, \mathcal{F}_{a,w}, \preceq_{a,w}, \widehat{\,\,}, \times, +, -)$ satisfies (connectedness) and (projectivity), $\mathcal{M}_\varphi := (\mathbf{W}, R, L, V, \rho_\varphi, \{\approx_{a,\varphi}\}_{a \in \mathbf{A}})$ also satisfies (consistency) and (world-dependent preference), and $\rho_\varphi := (W_{a,w}, \mathcal{F}_{a,w}, \preceq_{a,w,[\![\varphi]\!]_{a,w}}, \widehat{\,\,}, \times, +, -)$ also satisfies (connectedness) and (projectivity).*

4.3 Syntax

We provide DEPL with the following proof system.

Definition 18 (Proof System).

- *Axioms of* DEPL

Besides (A1),(A2),(A3),(A4),(A5),(A6),(A7),(A8),(A9),(A10),(A11),(A12),(A13), (A14),(A15) and (A16), the proof system of DEPL *has the following axioms:*

(A17) $[\varphi]s \leftrightarrow (\varphi \to s)$ (***Atomic Permanence***),

(A18) $[\varphi_1]\neg\varphi_2 \leftrightarrow (\varphi_1 \to \neg[\varphi_1]\varphi_2)$ (***Announcement and Negation***),

(A19) $[\varphi_1](\varphi_2 \wedge \varphi_3) \leftrightarrow ([\varphi_1]\varphi_2 \wedge [\varphi_1]\varphi_3)$ (***Announcement and Conjunction***),

(A20) $[\varphi_1]\mathbf{K}_a(\varphi_2) \leftrightarrow (\varphi_1 \to \mathbf{K}_a([\varphi_1]\varphi_2))$ (***Announcement and Knowledge***),

(A21) $[\varphi_1]\mathbf{WPR}_a(\varphi_2, \varphi_3) \leftrightarrow \mathbf{WPR}_a(\varphi_1 \wedge \varphi_2, \varphi_1 \wedge \varphi_3)$
(***Announcement and Weak Preference***),

(A22) $[\varphi_1]\mathbf{FCP}(\varphi_2, \varphi_3, \varphi_4, \varphi_5) \leftrightarrow (\varphi_1 \to \mathbf{FCP}([\varphi_1]\varphi_2, [\varphi_1]\varphi_3, [\varphi_1]\varphi_4, [\varphi_1]\varphi_5))$
(***Announcement and Four-Fold Cartesian Product***),

(A23) $[\varphi_1][\varphi_2]\varphi_3 \leftrightarrow [\varphi_1 \wedge [\varphi_1]\varphi_2]\varphi_3$ (***Announcement and Composition***).

- **Inference Rules of** DEPL

Besides (R1),(R2),(R3) and (R4), the axiom system of DEPL has the following inference rule:

$$(R5) \quad \frac{\varphi_2}{[\varphi_1]\varphi_2} \quad (\textbf{Announcement Necessitation}).$$

A proof of $\varphi \in \Phi_{\mathcal{L}_{\mathsf{DEPL}}}$ is a finite sequence of $\mathcal{L}_{\mathsf{DEPL}}$-formulae having φ as the last formula such that either each formula is an instance of an axiom, or it can be obtained from formulae that appear earlier in the sequence by applying an inference rule. If there is a proof of φ, we write $\vdash_{\mathsf{DEPL}} \varphi$.

4.4 Soundness and Completeness

We can prove the soundness of DEPL in the usual way.

Theorem 5 (Soundness). For every $\varphi \in \Phi_{\mathcal{L}_{\mathsf{DEPL}}}$, if $\vdash_{\mathsf{DEPL}} \varphi$, then $\models_{\mathsf{DEPL}} \varphi$.

In order to prove the completeness of DEPL, we give a translation function $t : \mathcal{L}_{\mathsf{DEPL}} \to \mathcal{L}_{\mathsf{EPL}}$. Because completeness of EPL is proved, it suffices to prove that every well-formed formula is equivalent to its translation in DEPL. This method is usual in the literature of dynamic epistemic logic.[7]

Definition 19 (Translation Function). A translation function $t : \mathcal{L}_{\mathsf{DEPL}} \to \mathcal{L}_{\mathsf{EPL}}$ is defined as follows:

1. $t(s) = s$,
2. $t(\top) = \top$,
3. $t(\neg \varphi) = \neg t(\varphi)$,
4. $t(\varphi_1 \wedge \varphi_1) = t(\varphi_1) \wedge t(\varphi_2)$,
5. $t(\mathbf{K}_a(\varphi)) = \mathbf{K}_a(t(\varphi))$,
6. $t(\mathbf{WPR}_a(\varphi_1, \varphi_2)) = \mathbf{WPR}_a(t(\varphi_1), t(\varphi_2))$,
7. $t([\varphi]s) = t(\varphi \to s)$,
8. $t([\varphi_1]\neg\varphi_2) = t(\varphi_1 \to \neg[\varphi_1]\varphi_2)$,
9. $t([\varphi_1](\varphi_2 \wedge \varphi_2)) = t([\varphi_1]\varphi_2 \wedge [\varphi_1]\varphi_3)$,
10. $t([\varphi_1]\mathbf{K}_a(\varphi_2)) = t(\varphi_1 \to \mathbf{K}_a([\varphi_1]\varphi_2))$,
11. $t([\varphi_1]\mathbf{WPR}_a(\varphi_2, \varphi_3)) = t(\mathbf{WPR}_a(\varphi_1 \wedge \varphi_2, \varphi_1 \wedge \varphi_3))$,
12. $t([\varphi_1]\mathbf{FCP}(\varphi_2, \varphi_3, \varphi_4, \varphi_5)) = t(\varphi_1 \to \mathbf{FCP}([\varphi_1]\varphi_2, [\varphi_1]\varphi_3, [\varphi_1]\varphi_4, [\varphi_1]\varphi_5))$,
13. $t([\varphi_1][\varphi_2]\varphi_3) = t([\varphi_1 \wedge [\varphi_1]\varphi_2]\varphi_3)$.

We can prove the following lemma.

Lemma 1 (Translation). For every $\varphi \in \Phi_{\mathcal{L}_{\mathsf{DEPL}}}$, $\vdash_{\mathsf{DEPL}} t(\varphi) \leftrightarrow \varphi$.

By virtue of Theorem 4 and Lemma 1, we can prove the completeness of DEPL.

Theorem 6 (Completeness). For every $\varphi \in \Phi_{\mathcal{L}_{\mathsf{DEPL}}}$, if $\models_{\mathsf{DEPL}} \varphi$, then $\vdash_{\mathsf{DEPL}} \varphi$.

---

[7] As for this method, refer to [[33]: pp. 186-189].

5 Conclusions

We have proposed a sound and complete epistemic preference logic (EPL) and extended it to dynamic epistemic preference logic (DEPL) that is also sound and complete. Van Benthem and Liu's DEUL cannot deal with the dynamic interactions between knowledge and preferences originating from decisions makings under other circumstances than certainty. On the other hand, DEPL can deal with the dynamic interactions between knowledge and preferences originating from decisions makings under certainty, risk, uncertainty and ignorance. So DEPL has much wider scope of application than DEUL. Providing DEPL with measurement-theoretic semantics has enabled it to deal with such wide scope of decision problems.

References

1. Bolker, E.D.: Functions Resembling Quotients of Measures. Transactions of the American Mathematical Society 124, 292–312 (1966)
2. Bolker, E.D.: A Simultaneous Axiomatisation of Utility and Subjective Probability. Philosophy of Science 34, 333–340 (1967)
3. Boutilier, C.: Toward a Logic for Qualitative Decision Theory. In: Proceedings of the 4th International Conference on Principles of Knowledge Representation and Reasoning (KR 1994), Bonn, pp. 75–86 (1994)
4. Cantor, G.: Beiträge zur Begründung der Transfiniten Mengenlehre I. Mathematische Annalen 46, 481–512 (1895)
5. Chisholm, R.M., Sosa, E.: On the Logic of Intrinsically Better. American Philosophical Quarterly 3, 244–249 (1966)
6. Domotor, Z.: Axiomatisation of Jeffrey Utilities. Synthese 39, 165–210 (1978)
7. Gerbrandy, J.D., Groeneveld, W.: Reasoning about Information Change. Journal of Logic, Language and Information 6, 147–169 (1997)
8. Halldén, S.: On the Logic of 'Better'. CWK Gleerup, Lund (1957)
9. Halpern, J.Y.: Reasoning about Uncertainty. The MIT Press, Cambridge (2003)
10. Hansson, S.O.: Preference Logic. In: Gabbay, D.M., Guenthner, F. (eds.) Handbook of Philosophical Logic, 2nd edn., vol. 4, pp. 319–393 (2001)
11. Hansson, S.O.: Preferences. In: Stanford Encyclopedia of Philosophy (2006)
12. Hölder, O.: Die Axiome der Quantität und die Lehre von Mass. Berichte über die Verhandlungen der Königlich Sächsischen Gesellschaft der Wissenschaften zu Leipzig. Mathematisch-Physikaliche Classe 53, 1–64 (1901)
13. Jeffrey, R.: A Note on the Kinematics of Preference. Erkenntnis 11, 135–141 (1977); rpt. in [16] pp. 238–244
14. Jeffrey, R.: Axiomatising the Logic of Decision. In: Hooker, C.A., et al. (eds.) Foundations and Applications of Decision Theory, vol. 1. Kluwer, Dordrecht (1978); rpt. in [16] pp. 232–237
15. Jeffrey, R.: The Logic of Decision, Corrected Second Edition. University of Chicago Press, Chicago (1990)
16. Jeffrey, R.: Probability and the Art of Judgment. Cambridge UP, Cambridge (1992)
17. Joyce, J.M.: The Foundations of Causal Decision Theory. Cambridge UP, Cambridge (1999)
18. Krantz, D.H., et al.: Foundations of Measurement, vol. 1. Academic Press, New York (1971)

19. Luce, R.D., Raiffa, H.: Games and Decisions. John Wiley & Sons, Inc., New York (1957)
20. Luce, R.D., et al.: Foundations of Measurement, vol. III. Academic Press, San Diego (1990)
21. Martin, R.M.: Intension and Decision. Prentice-Hall, Inc., Englewood Cliffs (1963)
22. Naumov, P.: Logic of Subtyping. Theoretical Computer Science 357, 167–185 (2006)
23. Plaza, J.A.: Logics of Public Communications. In: Emrich, M.L., et al. (eds.) Proceedings of the 4th International Symposium on Methodologies for Intelligent Systems, pp. 201–216 (1989)
24. Ramsey, F.P.: Truth and Probability (1926). In: Mellor, D.H. (ed.) Philosophical Papers, pp. 52–94. Cambridge UP, Cambridge (1990)
25. Rescher, N.: Semantic Foundations of the Logic of Preference. In: Rescher, N. (ed.) The Logic of Decision and Action, pp. 37–62. University of Pittsburgh Press, Pittsburgh (1967)
26. Resnik, M.D.: Choices: An Introduction to Decision Theory. University of Minnesota Press, Minneapolis (1987)
27. Roberts, F.S.: Measurement Theory. Addison-Wesley, Reading (1979)
28. Scott, D.: Measurement Structures and Linear Inequalities. Journal of Mathematical Psychology 1, 233–247 (1964)
29. Segerberg, K.: Qualitative Probability in a Modal Setting. In: Fenstad, J.E. (ed.) Proceedings of the Second Scandinavian Logic Symposium, pp. 341–352. North-Holland, Amsterdam (1971)
30. Suppes, P., et al.: Foundations of Measurement, vol. II. Academic Press, San Diego (1989)
31. Van Benthem, J., et al.: Preference Logic, Conditionals and Solution Concepts in Games. ILLC Prepublication Series PP-2005-28 (2005)
32. Van Benthem, J., Liu, F.: Dynamic Logic of Preference Upgrade. Journal of Applied Non-Classical Logic 17, 157–182 (2007)
33. Van Ditmarsch, H., et al.: Dynamic Epistemic Logic. Springer, Dordrecht (2007)
34. Von Wright, G.H.: The Logic of Preference. Edinburgh UP, Edinburgh (1963)

Monads and Meta-lambda Calculus

Daisuke Bekki

Ochanomizu University
Ootsuka 2-1-1, Bunkyo-ku, Tokyo, Japan

1 Background: Monads in Category Theory, Programming Language, and Natural Language

The notion of monads originates in homological algebra and category theory: a monad in a category $\mathcal{C}$ is a triple $\langle T, \eta, \mu \rangle$ that consists of a functor $T : \mathcal{C} \longrightarrow \mathcal{C}$ and two natural transformations:

$$\eta : Id_{\mathcal{C}} \overset{\cdot}{\longrightarrow} T, \qquad \mu : T^2 \overset{\cdot}{\longrightarrow} T$$

such that the following diagrams commute for any object A in $\mathcal{C}$.

$$\begin{array}{ccc} T^3 A & \overset{T\mu_A}{\longrightarrow} & T^2 A \\ \mu_{TA} \downarrow & & \downarrow \mu_A \\ T^2 A & \underset{\mu_A}{\longrightarrow} & TA \end{array} \qquad \begin{array}{ccccc} TA & \overset{\eta_{TA}}{\longrightarrow} & T^2 A & \overset{T\eta_A}{\longleftarrow} & TA \\ & Id_{\mathcal{C}} \searrow & \downarrow \mu_A & \swarrow Id_{\mathcal{C}} & \\ & & TA & & \end{array}$$

Lambek (1980) established categorical semantics of typed lambda calculi (hereafter TLC), showing that TLC are equivalent to Cartesian closed categories (CCC), in which TLC terms are interpreted as morphisms.

These studies converged to the 'monadic' categorical semantics of TLC in Moggi (1989), where each lambda term is interpreted as a morphism in the Kleisli category generated by a certain monad. This setting is intended to uniformly encapsulate 'impure' aspects of functional programming languages, such as side-effects, exceptions and continuations, within the enhanced data types specified by the monad, and hide them within 'pure' structures of TLC. The method requires, however, some tangled notions such as tensorial strength (Kock (1970)) for the definition of lambda abstraction, evaluation and products.

This complexity motivated Wadler (1992) to propose a simplified model, known as *monad comprehension*, which generalizes the notion of list comprehension. Results from this study were incorporated into the programming language Haskell, and this showed that the monadic analyses can treat a wider range of computational concepts than Moggi (1989) had enumerated, such as state readers, array update, non-determinism, inputs/outputs, and even parsers and interpreters.

Shan (2001) showed that the results of monadic analyses can be imported to the field of natural language semantics, where various semantic/pragmatic/computational aspects such as non-determinism, focus, intensionality, variable binding, continuation and quantification, can be uniformly represented as monads, just as the 'impure' aspects in programming languages.

This enterprise, encapsulation of 'impure' aspects of computation by monads, seems to be an attractive prospect, especially given the lack of standard formal models for the interfaces between semantics/pragmatics or semantics/computation. On the other hand, monadic analyses, as they have drifted among different fields, seem to have become gradually dissociated from the original monad concept.

This paper aims to restore the relation between monadic analyses and categorical monads. In other words, I aim to combine the recent advances in monadic analyses with the categorical semantics of TLC along the lines of Lambek (1980). This is realized through "Meta-Lambda Calculus" (henceforth MLC), an extension of TLC, which is defined in the following way.

2 Meta-lambda Calculus

The syntax of MLC is specified by a quintuple $\langle \mathcal{GT}, \mathcal{C}on, \mathcal{M}con, \Gamma, \Delta \rangle$, which respectively represents a finite collection of ground types, constant symbols, *meta*-constant symbols, variables and *meta*-variables.

Definition 1 (Type and Meta-types). *Given a quintuple, the collections of types (notation $\mathcal{T}yp$) and meta-types (notation $\mathcal{M}typ$) are defined by the following BNF grammar.*

$$\mathcal{T}yp \;:=\; \mathcal{GT} \;|\; \mathcal{T}yp\mathcal{T}yp \;|\; unit \;|\; \mathcal{T}yp \times \cdots \times \mathcal{T}yp$$
$$\mathcal{M}typ \;:=\; \mathcal{T}yp \;|\; \mathcal{M}typ \mapsto \mathcal{M}typ \;|\; munit \;|\; \mathcal{M}typ \otimes \cdots \otimes \mathcal{M}typ$$

Definition 2 (Type Assignment). *The type assignment function Σ maps each variable (a member of Γ) to a member of $\mathcal{T}yp$ and each meta-variable (a member of Δ) to a member of $\mathcal{M}typ$. The sets of constant symbols, meta-constant symbols, variables and meta-variables of type τ are respectively defined as follows.*

$$\mathcal{C}on^\tau \stackrel{def}{\equiv} \{x \in \mathcal{C}on \mid \Sigma(x) = \tau\} \qquad \Gamma^\tau \stackrel{def}{\equiv} \{x \in \Gamma \mid \Sigma(x) = \tau\}$$
$$\mathcal{M}con^\tau \stackrel{def}{\equiv} \{x \in \mathcal{M}con \mid \Sigma(x) = \tau\} \qquad \Delta^\tau \stackrel{def}{\equiv} \{x \in \Delta \mid \Sigma(x) = \tau\}$$

2.1 Interpretation via Covariant Hom-Functor

An *interpretation* of MLC terms is specified by a quadruple $\langle \mathcal{E}, valT, valC, valMC \rangle$ where $\mathcal{E}$ is a Cartesian closed category with small hom-sets, $valT$ is a function that sends each $\tau \in \mathcal{GT}$ to an object in $\mathcal{E}$, $valC$ and $valMC$ are functions that send each $c \in \mathcal{C}on^\tau$ and each $\gamma \in \mathcal{M}con^\tau$ to a global element in $\mathcal{E}$ and $\mathcal{S}et$ respectively. Given a quadruple, *the type interpretation* $\|-\|$ and *meta-type interpretation* $[\![-]\!]$ are defined as follows.

Definition 3 (Interpretation of Types and Meta-types). $\|-\|$ *maps each member of $\mathcal{T}yp$ to an object in $\mathcal{E}$ and $[\![-]\!]$ maps each member of $\mathcal{M}typ$ to an object in $\mathcal{S}et$ via the following rules:*

$$\begin{aligned}
\|\tau \ (\in \mathcal{GT})\| &= valT(\tau) \\
\|\tau_1 \tau_2\| &= \|\tau_2\|^{\|\tau_1\|} \\
\|unit\| &= 1 \\
\|\tau_1 \times \cdots \times \tau_n\| &= \|\tau_1\| \times \cdots \times \|\tau_n\|
\end{aligned} \quad \Big| \quad \begin{aligned}
\lceil \sigma \ (\in \mathcal{T}yp) \rceil &= \mathcal{E}(\|\Gamma\|, \|\sigma\|) \\
\lceil \sigma_1 \mapsto \sigma_2 \rceil &= \lceil \sigma_2 \rceil^{\lceil \sigma_1 \rceil} \\
\lceil munit \rceil &= * \\
\lceil \sigma_1 \otimes \cdots \otimes \sigma_n \rceil &= \lceil \sigma_1 \rceil \times \cdots \times \lceil \sigma_n \rceil
\end{aligned}$$

where 1 is a selected terminal object in $\mathcal{E}$. Let $*$ be any one-point set, which is a terminal object in $\mathcal{S}et$. Suppose that $\Gamma = x_1, \ldots, x_m$ and $\Delta = X_1, \ldots, X_n$, then $\|\Gamma\| = \|\Sigma(x_1)\| \times \cdots \times \|\Sigma(x_m)\|$ and $\lceil \Delta \rceil = \lceil \Sigma(X_1) \rceil \times \cdots \times \lceil \Sigma(X_n) \rceil$.

In contrast to the standard categorical semantics[1] of TLC where an interpretation $[\![-]\!]$ of a lambda term of the type τ is a morphism: $\|\Gamma\| \longrightarrow \|\tau\|$ in $\mathcal{E}$, the categorical semantics of MLC utilizes a *covariant hom-functor*[2] $\mathcal{E}(\|\Gamma\|, -)$: $\mathcal{E} \longrightarrow \mathcal{S}et$, by which a morphism $f : A \longrightarrow B$ in $\mathcal{E}$ is mapped to the morphism $\mathcal{E}(\|\Gamma\|, f) : \mathcal{E}(\|\Gamma\|, A) \longrightarrow \mathcal{E}(\|\Gamma\|, B)$ in $\mathcal{S}et$. $\mathcal{E}(\|\Gamma\|, f)$ is also written as f_* and called "composition with f on the left" or "the map induced by f." $\mathcal{E}(\|\Gamma\|, f)$ maps a morphism $a : \|\Gamma\| \longrightarrow A$ in $\mathcal{E}(\|\Gamma\|, A)$ to $f \circ a : \|\Gamma\| \longrightarrow B$ in $\mathcal{E}(\|\Gamma\|, B)$. The two morphisms $\mathcal{E}(\|\Gamma\|, f)$ and $\mathcal{E}(\|\Gamma\|, g)$ induced by two composable morphisms $f : A \longrightarrow B$ and $g : B \longrightarrow C$ are also composable in $\mathcal{S}et$, as indicated in the following diagram.

$$\begin{array}{c} \|\Gamma\| \\ a \downarrow \\ A \xrightarrow{f} B \xrightarrow{g} C \end{array}$$

Now the following bijection is a natural isomorphism (tp and $\overline{tp}$ are *transposes* of each other).[3]

$$(1) \qquad \mathcal{S}et(*, \mathcal{E}(\|\Gamma\|, -)) \underset{tp}{\overset{\overline{tp}}{\rightleftarrows}} \mathcal{E}(\|\Gamma\|, -)$$

Then, any interpretation of a TLC term M of type τ by the standard categorical semantics, which is also an element of $\mathcal{E}(\|\Gamma\|, \|\tau\|)$, is mapped to the corresponding element in $\mathcal{S}et(*, \mathcal{E}(\|\Gamma\|, \|\tau\|))$, via the (component $tp_{\|\tau\|}$ of) natural transformation tp. tp is specified by the universal arrow which obtains by applying $id_{\|\Gamma\|}$ to tp itself. Namely, $tp([\![M]\!]) = \mathcal{E}(\|\Gamma\|, [\![M]\!]) \circ tp(id_{\|\Gamma\|})$, where $\langle \|\Gamma\|, tp(id_{\|\Gamma\|}) \rangle$ is a universal arrow from $*$ to $\mathcal{E}(\|\Gamma\|, -)$.

$$\begin{array}{ccc}
\|\Gamma\| & \mathcal{E}(\|\Gamma\|, \|\Gamma\|) & \xleftarrow{u = tp(id_{\|\Gamma\|})} * \\
[\![M]\!] \downarrow & \mathcal{E}(\|\Gamma\|, [\![M]\!]) \downarrow & \swarrow tp([\![M]\!]) \\
\|\tau\| & \mathcal{E}(\|\Gamma\|, \|\tau\|) &
\end{array}$$

---

[1] See Lambek (1980), Lambek and Scott (1986) and Crole (1993), among others.
[2] See MacLane (1997), p.34.
[3] Proof of (1) is found in the proof of Proposition 2 in MacLane (1997), p.60. For an element $f \in \mathcal{S}et(*, \mathcal{E}(\|\Gamma\|, -))$, $\overline{tp}(f) = f(*)$.

Let $\mathcal{S}_\mathcal{E}$ be the subcategory of $\mathcal{S}et$, defined by the 'shadow' of the functor $\mathcal{E}(\lfloor\!\lfloor\Gamma\rfloor\!\rfloor, -)$. Then the interpretation of a TLC term of type τ is embedded in $\mathcal{S}_\mathcal{E}$ as morphisms $* \longrightarrow \mathcal{E}(\lfloor\!\lfloor\Gamma\rfloor\!\rfloor, \lfloor\!\lfloor\tau\rfloor\!\rfloor)$.

In general, the interpretation of an MLC term of type τ is a morphism $\lceil\!\lceil\Delta\rceil\!\rceil \longrightarrow \lceil\!\lceil\tau\rceil\!\rceil$. When $\tau \in \mathcal{T}yp$, $\lceil\!\lceil\tau\rceil\!\rceil = \mathcal{E}(\lfloor\!\lfloor\Gamma\rfloor\!\rfloor, \lfloor\!\lfloor\tau\rfloor\!\rfloor)$. Therefore, elements of MLC with no meta-variables (namely, $\Delta = \{\}$ and $\lceil\!\lceil\Delta\rceil\!\rceil = *$) are in one-to-one correspondence with elements of TLC.

2.2 Syntax and Semantics

Given a quintuple $\langle \mathcal{GT}, \mathcal{C}on, \mathcal{M}con, \Gamma, \Delta\rangle$, the set of meta-lambda terms of type $\tau \in \mathcal{M}typ$ in MLC (notation Λ^τ) is recursively defined as follows.

Variables

$$x_i \in \Gamma^\tau$$

$x_i \in \Lambda^\tau$, $[\![x_i]\!] = tp(\pi_i) \circ !_{\lceil\!\lceil\Delta\rceil\!\rceil} : \lceil\!\lceil\Delta\rceil\!\rceil \longrightarrow * \longrightarrow \mathcal{E}(\lfloor\!\lfloor\Gamma\rfloor\!\rfloor, \lfloor\!\lfloor\tau\rfloor\!\rfloor)$

Meta-Variables

$$X_i \in \Delta^\tau$$

$X_i \in \Lambda^\tau$, $[\![X_i]\!] = \pi_i : \lceil\!\lceil\Delta\rceil\!\rceil \longrightarrow \lceil\!\lceil\tau\rceil\!\rceil$

Since a projection π_i in $\mathcal{E}$ is a morphism $\lfloor\!\lfloor\Gamma\rfloor\!\rfloor \longrightarrow \lfloor\!\lfloor\tau_i\rfloor\!\rfloor$, its transpose $tp(\pi_i)$ is a morphism $* \longrightarrow \mathcal{E}(\lfloor\!\lfloor\Gamma\rfloor\!\rfloor, \lfloor\!\lfloor\tau_i\rfloor\!\rfloor)$ in $\mathcal{S}et$. A meta-variable X_i is just interpreted as the projection π_i in $\mathcal{S}_\mathcal{E}$, which selects the i-th member of Δ and returns its value.

Constant Symbols

$$c \in \mathcal{C}on^\tau$$

$c \in \Lambda^\tau$, $[\![c]\!] = tp(valC(c) \circ !_{\lfloor\!\lfloor\Gamma\rfloor\!\rfloor}) \circ !_{\lceil\!\lceil\Delta\rceil\!\rceil} : \lceil\!\lceil\Delta\rceil\!\rceil \longrightarrow * \longrightarrow \mathcal{E}(\lfloor\!\lfloor\Gamma\rfloor\!\rfloor, \lfloor\!\lfloor\tau\rfloor\!\rfloor)$

Meta-Constant Symbols

$$\gamma \in \mathcal{M}con^\tau$$

$\gamma \in \Lambda^\tau$, $[\![\gamma]\!] = valMC(\gamma) \circ !_{\lceil\!\lceil\Delta\rceil\!\rceil} : \lceil\!\lceil\Delta\rceil\!\rceil \longrightarrow * \longrightarrow \lceil\!\lceil\tau\rceil\!\rceil$

Constant and meta-constant symbols are interpreted via $valC$ and $valMC$, which associate them with global elements in $\mathcal{E}$ and $\mathcal{S}_\mathcal{E}$.

Product

$\langle\,\rangle \in \Lambda^{unit}$, $[\![\langle\,\rangle]\!] = tp(!_{\lfloor\!\lfloor\Gamma\rfloor\!\rfloor}) \circ !_{\lceil\!\lceil\Delta\rceil\!\rceil} : \lceil\!\lceil\Delta\rceil\!\rceil \longrightarrow * \longrightarrow \mathcal{E}(\lfloor\!\lfloor\Gamma\rfloor\!\rfloor, \lfloor\!\lfloor unit\rfloor\!\rfloor)$

$$M_1 \in \Lambda^{\tau_1} \quad \cdots \quad M_n \in \Lambda^{\tau_n} \quad \tau_1 \in \mathcal{T}yp \quad \cdots \quad \tau_n \in \mathcal{T}yp$$

$\langle M_1, \ldots, M_n\rangle \in \Lambda^{\tau_1 \times \cdots \times \tau_n}$, $[\![\langle M_1, \ldots, M_n\rangle]\!] = \ltimes \circ \langle [\![M_1]\!], \ldots, [\![M_n]\!]\rangle :$
$\lceil\!\lceil\Delta\rceil\!\rceil \longrightarrow \mathcal{E}(\lfloor\!\lfloor\Gamma\rfloor\!\rfloor, \lfloor\!\lfloor\tau_1\rfloor\!\rfloor) \times \cdots \times \mathcal{E}(\lfloor\!\lfloor\Gamma\rfloor\!\rfloor, \lfloor\!\lfloor\tau_n\rfloor\!\rfloor)$
$\longrightarrow \mathcal{E}(\lfloor\!\lfloor\Gamma\rfloor\!\rfloor, \lfloor\!\lfloor\tau_1\rfloor\!\rfloor \times \cdots \times \lfloor\!\lfloor\tau_n\rfloor\!\rfloor)$

$$P \in \Lambda^{\tau_1 \times \cdots \times \tau_n} \quad \tau_1 \times \cdots \times \tau_n \in \mathcal{T}yp \quad 1 \leq k \leq n$$

$\pi_k(P) \in \Lambda^{\tau_k}$, $[\![\pi_k(P)]\!] = \mathcal{E}(\lfloor\!\lfloor\Gamma\rfloor\!\rfloor, \pi_k) \circ [\![P]\!] : \lceil\!\lceil\Delta\rceil\!\rceil \longrightarrow \mathcal{E}(\lfloor\!\lfloor\Gamma\rfloor\!\rfloor, \lfloor\!\lfloor\tau_k\rfloor\!\rfloor)$

The morphism $\ltimes$, together with its inverse $\rtimes$, is an isomorphism between the following two objects in $\mathcal{S}et$.

$$\mathcal{E}(\lfloor\!\lfloor\Gamma\rfloor\!\rfloor, A) \times \mathcal{E}(\lfloor\!\lfloor\Gamma\rfloor\!\rfloor, B) \cong \mathcal{E}(\lfloor\!\lfloor\Gamma\rfloor\!\rfloor, A \times B)$$

$$\ltimes : f, g, \ldots \mapsto \langle f, g, \ldots \rangle$$
$$\rtimes : \quad f \mapsto \pi_1 \circ f, \pi_2 \circ f, \ldots$$

The pair of $\ltimes$ and $\rtimes$ is a bijection since the hom-functor $\mathcal{E}(\lfloor\!\lfloor\Gamma\rfloor\!\rfloor, -)$ preserves all finite limits.[4]

Meta-Product

$$\langle\!\langle\,\rangle\!\rangle \in \Lambda^{munit}, \quad [\![\langle\!\langle\,\rangle\!\rangle]\!] = !_{[\![\Delta]\!]} : [\![\Delta]\!] \longrightarrow [\![munit]\!]$$

$$\dfrac{M_1 \in \Lambda^{\tau_1} \quad \cdots \quad M_n \in \Lambda^{\tau_n}}{\begin{array}{l}\langle\!\langle M_1, \ldots, M_n\rangle\!\rangle \in \Lambda^{\tau_1 \otimes \cdots \otimes \tau_n}, \\ [\![\langle\!\langle M_1, \ldots, M_n\rangle\!\rangle]\!] = \langle[\![M_1]\!], \ldots, [\![M_n]\!]\rangle : [\![\Delta]\!] \longrightarrow [\![\tau_1]\!] \times \cdots \times [\![\tau_n]\!]\end{array}}$$

$$\dfrac{P \in \Lambda^{\tau_1 \otimes \cdots \otimes \tau_n} \quad 1 \leq k \leq n}{\pi_k(P) \in \Lambda^{\tau_k}, \quad [\![\pi_k(P)]\!] = \pi_k \circ [\![P]\!] : [\![\Delta]\!] \longrightarrow [\![\tau_k]\!]}$$

Meta-products roughly correspond to products in $\mathcal{S}_\mathcal{E}$, whose interpretation is similar to the interpretation of (normal) products in TLC.

Meta-Lambda Abstraction

$$\dfrac{X \in \Delta^\tau \quad M \in \Lambda^\sigma}{\zeta X_i.M \in \Lambda^{\tau \mapsto \sigma}, \quad [\![\zeta X_i.M]\!] = \lambda([\![M]\!]) \circ \pi^\Delta{}_{\Delta \backslash X_i} : [\![\Delta]\!] \longrightarrow [\![\sigma]\!]^{[\![\tau]\!]}}$$

Meta-Functional Application

$$\dfrac{M \in \Lambda^{\tau \mapsto \sigma} \quad N \in \Lambda^\tau}{M\lceil N\rceil \in \Lambda^\sigma, \quad [\![M\lceil N\rceil]\!] = ev \circ \langle[\![M]\!], [\![N]\!]\rangle : [\![\Delta]\!] \longrightarrow [\![\sigma]\!]}$$

Meta-Substitution

$$\dfrac{M \in \Lambda^\sigma \quad N \in \Lambda^\tau \quad X \in \Delta^\tau}{M[N/X_i] \in \Lambda^\sigma, \quad [\![M[N/X_i]]\!] = [\![M]\!] \circ \langle\pi^\Delta{}_{\Delta \backslash X_i}, [\![N]\!]\rangle : [\![\Delta]\!] \longrightarrow [\![\sigma]\!]}$$

The interpretation of meta-lambda abstraction, functional application and substitution in MLC is similar to the interpretation of (normal) elements of TLC.[5] Just as beta conversion is sound in TLC, meta-beta conversion is sound in MLC:

Theorem 4 (Meta-Beta Conversion)

$$(\zeta X.M)\lceil N\rceil = M[N/X]$$

---

[4] See "Theorem 1" and its proof in MacLane (1997), p.116.

[5] The projection $\pi^\Delta{}_{\Delta \backslash X_i}$ is defined as the morphism $\langle \pi_1, \ldots, \pi_{i-1}, \pi_{i+1}, \ldots, \pi_n \rangle$, which maps $\langle X_1, \ldots, X_{i-1}, X_i, X_{i+1}, \ldots, X_n \rangle$ to $\langle X_1, \ldots, X_{i-1}, X_{i+1}, \ldots, X_n \rangle$, namely, the morphism which forget the i-th element. This construction crucially depends on the assumption that Δ is a finite set.

This is proved by a standard triangular identity for a Cartesian closed category.

Proof

$$\begin{aligned}
[\![(\zeta X.M)\lceil N\rceil]\!] &= ev \circ \langle [\![\zeta X.M]\!], [\![N]\!]\rangle \\
&= ev \circ \langle \lambda([\![M]\!]) \circ \pi^{\Delta}{}_{\Delta\backslash X}, [\![N]\!]\rangle \\
&= ev \circ (\lambda([\![M]\!]) \times id) \circ \langle \pi^{\Delta}{}_{\Delta\backslash X}, [\![N]\!]\rangle \\
&= [\![M]\!] \circ \langle \pi^{\Delta}{}_{\Delta\backslash X}, [\![N]\!]\rangle \\
&= [\![M[N/X]]\!]
\end{aligned}$$

$$\mathcal{E}(\|\Gamma\|, \|\sigma\|)^{\mathcal{E}(\|\Gamma\|,\|\tau\|)} \times \mathcal{E}(\|\Gamma\|, \|\tau\|) \xrightarrow{ev} \mathcal{E}(\|\Gamma\|, \|\sigma\|)$$

with $\lambda([\![M]\!]) \times id$ arrow from $\lceil\Delta\rceil = \lceil\Delta\rceil' \times \mathcal{E}(\|\Gamma\|, \|\tau\|)$ and $[\![M]\!]$ diagonal. □

Lambda Abstraction
$x \in \Gamma^{\tau}\quad M \in \Lambda^{\sigma}\quad \sigma, \tau \in \mathcal{T}yp$
$\lambda x.M \in \Lambda^{\tau\sigma},\quad [\![\lambda x.M]\!] = \lambda^{\|\tau\|}{}_{\|\sigma\|} \circ [\![M]\!] : \lceil\Delta\rceil \longrightarrow \mathcal{E}(\|\Gamma\|, \|\sigma\|^{\|\tau\|})$
Functional Application
$M \in \Lambda^{\tau\sigma}\quad N \in \Lambda^{\tau}\quad \sigma, \tau \in \mathcal{T}yp$
$M(N) \in \Lambda^{\sigma},\quad [\![M(N)]\!] = \mathcal{E}(\|\Gamma\|, ev) \circ \ltimes \circ \langle[\![M]\!], [\![N]\!]\rangle :$ $\lceil\Delta\rceil \longrightarrow \mathcal{E}(\|\Gamma\|, \|\sigma\|^{\|\tau\|}) \times \mathcal{E}(\|\Gamma\|, \|\tau\|)$ $\longrightarrow \mathcal{E}(\|\Gamma\|, \|\sigma\|^{\|\tau\|} \times \|\tau\|)$ $\longrightarrow \mathcal{E}(\|\Gamma\|, \|\tau\|)$
Substitution
$M \in \Lambda^{\sigma}\quad N \in \Lambda^{\tau}\quad x \in \Gamma^{\tau}\quad \sigma, \tau \in \mathcal{T}yp$
$M[N/x] \in \Lambda^{\sigma},\quad [\![M[N/x]]\!] = \mathcal{S}ub \circ \langle[\![M]\!], [\![N]\!]\rangle : \lceil\Delta\rceil \longrightarrow \mathcal{E}(\|\Gamma\|, \|\sigma\|)$

For the definition of normal lambda abstractions, functional application and substitutions, some additional notions are required: the morphism λ and $\mathcal{S}ub$.

The substitution rule for meta-variables, which is not described in detail in this paper for the sake of space, is supposed to be immune with respect to the binding of (normal) variables, as the following equation implies.

(2) $\qquad (\zeta X.\lambda x.X)\lceil x\rceil = (\lambda x.X)[x/X] = \lambda x.x$

This means that the following map λ is representable at the level of the object language, which is not the case in TLC.

(3) $\qquad\qquad\qquad \lambda : \phi \mapsto \lambda x.\phi$

Lambda Abstraction Map λ: The *lambda abstraction map* λ^D is a natural transformation: $\mathcal{E}(\|\Gamma\|, -) \xrightarrow{\cdot} \mathcal{E}(\|\Gamma\|, -^D)$, whose component is written as

$\lambda^D{}_A$. The functor $\mathcal{E}(\|\Gamma\|, -^D) : \mathcal{E} \longrightarrow \mathcal{S}et$ maps a morphism $f : A \longrightarrow B$ in $\mathcal{E}$ to a morphism between hom-sets that maps any morphism $a : \|\Gamma\| \longrightarrow A^D \in \mathcal{E}(\|\Gamma\|, A^D)$ to $\lambda(f \circ \overline{a}) : \Gamma \longrightarrow B^D \in \mathcal{E}(\|\Gamma\|, B^D)$.

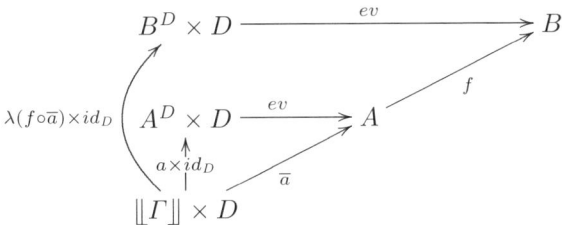

The intuition behind the map $\mathcal{E}(\|\Gamma\|, f^D)$ is illustrated in the following diagram.

$$\begin{array}{c}
B^D \times D \xrightarrow{ev} B \\
\lambda(f\circ\overline{a})\times id_D \Big\uparrow \quad A^D \times D \xrightarrow{ev} A \quad \Big\uparrow f \\
a\times id_D \Big\uparrow \quad \overline{a} \\
\|\Gamma\| \times D
\end{array}$$

Now, by the Yoneda lemma, the following isomorphism exists, and each natural transformation from $(\mathcal{E}(\|\Gamma\|, -)$ to $\mathcal{E}(\|\Gamma\|, -^D)$ is specified by an element of $\mathcal{E}(\|\Gamma\|, \|\Gamma\|^D)$.

$$Nat(\mathcal{E}(\|\Gamma\|, -), \mathcal{E}(\|\Gamma\|, -^D)) \cong \mathcal{E}(\|\Gamma\|, \|\Gamma\|^D)$$

The natural transformation λ^D is thus specified by the morphism $\lambda(id_{\|\Gamma\|}) \circ \pi^\Gamma{}_{\Gamma\setminus D} : \|\Gamma\| \longrightarrow \|\Gamma\|^D$ that makes the following diagram commute.[6]

$$\|\Gamma\| \xrightarrow{\pi^\Gamma{}_{\Gamma\setminus D} \times \pi^\Gamma{}_D} \|\Gamma\|' \times D \xrightarrow{\lambda(id_{\|\Gamma\|}) \times id_D} \|\Gamma\|^D \times D \xrightarrow{ev} \|\Gamma\|$$

(where $\|\Gamma\| = \|\Gamma\|' \times D$)

Then each component $\lambda^D{}_A$ is obtained by applying this morphism to $\mathcal{E}(\|\Gamma\|, f^D)$, which sends a morphism $f : \|\Gamma\| \longrightarrow A$ to the morphism from $\|\Gamma\|$ to B.

$$\lambda^D{}_A : f \mapsto \mathcal{E}(\|\Gamma\|, f^D)(\lambda(id_{\|\Gamma\|}) \circ \pi^\Gamma{}_{\Gamma\setminus D})$$
$$= f \mapsto \lambda(f \circ \overline{\lambda(id_{\|\Gamma\|}) \circ \pi^\Gamma{}_{\Gamma\setminus D}})$$

---

[6] The projection $\pi^\Gamma{}_{\Gamma\setminus A_i}$ is defined as the morphism $\langle \pi_1, \ldots, \pi_{i-1}, \pi_{i+1}, \ldots, \pi_n \rangle$, and $\pi^\Gamma{}_{A_i}$ as π_i, given that $\|\Gamma\| = A_1 \times \cdots \times A_i \times \cdots \times A_n$. As mentioned in fn.5, this depends on the assumption that Γ is a finite set.

Substitution Map $\mathcal{S}ub$: Substitution map $\mathcal{S}ub$ is a morphism from $\mathcal{E}(\|\Gamma\|, A) \times \mathcal{E}(\|\Gamma\|, B)$ to $\mathcal{E}(\|\Gamma\|, A)$ defined as follows, where $m : \|\Gamma\| \longrightarrow A$, $n : \|\Gamma\| \longrightarrow B$ and $\|\Sigma(x)\| = B$.

$$\mathcal{S}ub : m, n \mapsto m \circ \langle \pi^{\Gamma}{}_{\Gamma \setminus x}, n \rangle$$

Theorem 5 (Normal Beta Conversion)

$$(\lambda x.M)(N) = M[N/x]$$

Proof. In the diagram below, the maps $m : \Gamma \longrightarrow \|\sigma\|)$ and $n : \Gamma \longrightarrow \|\tau\|$ are mapped successively to $\langle \lambda(m \circ \overline{\lambda(id)} \circ \pi^{\Gamma}{}_{\Gamma \setminus x}), n \rangle$.

$$\begin{array}{c}
\mathcal{E}(\|\Gamma\|, \|\sigma\|^{\|\tau\|}) \times \mathcal{E}(\|\Gamma\|, \|\tau\|) \xrightarrow{\sim} \mathcal{E}(\|\Gamma\|, \|\sigma\|^{\|\tau\|} \times \|\tau\|) \xrightarrow{\mathcal{E}(\|\Gamma\|, ev)} \mathcal{E}(\|\Gamma\|, \|\sigma\|) \\
\uparrow \lambda^{\|\tau\|}{}_{\|\sigma\|} \times id_{\mathcal{E}(\|\Gamma\|, \|\tau\|)} \\
\mathcal{E}(\|\Gamma\|, \|\sigma\|) \times \mathcal{E}(\|\Gamma\|, \|\tau\|) \\
\uparrow \langle [\![M]\!], [\![N]\!] \rangle \\
[\![\Delta]\!]
\end{array}$$

which is then proved to be equivalent to the substitution map $\mathcal{S}$ as follows.

$$\begin{aligned}
m, n &\mapsto ev \circ \langle \lambda(m \circ \overline{\lambda(id)} \circ \pi^{\Gamma}{}_{\Gamma \setminus x}), n \rangle \\
&= m \circ \overline{\lambda(id_\Gamma)} \circ \pi^{\Gamma}{}_{\Gamma \setminus x} \circ \langle id, n \rangle \\
&= m \circ ev \circ (\lambda(id) \circ \pi^{\Gamma}{}_{\Gamma \setminus x} \times id) \circ \langle id, n \rangle \\
&= m \circ ev \circ \langle \lambda(id) \circ \pi^{\Gamma}{}_{\Gamma \setminus x} \circ id, id \circ n \rangle \\
&= m \circ ev \circ \langle \lambda(id) \circ \pi^{\Gamma}{}_{\Gamma \setminus x}, n \rangle \\
&= m \circ ev \circ (\lambda(id) \times id) \circ (\pi^{\Gamma}{}_{\Gamma \setminus x} \times n) \\
&= m \circ \langle \pi^{\Gamma}{}_{\Gamma \setminus x}, n \rangle
\end{aligned}$$

$\square$

3 Transformation with Internal Monads

3.1 Δ-Indexed Category

In a category $\mathcal{S}_\mathcal{E}$, associate with each object $A \in [\![\Delta]\!]$ a new object A_Δ and to each arrow $f : [\![\Delta]\!] \times A \longrightarrow B$ in $\mathcal{C}$ a new arrow $f_\Delta : A_\Delta \longrightarrow B_\Delta$. These new objects and arrows constitute a category when the composite of f_Δ with $g_\Delta : B_\Delta \longrightarrow C_\Delta$ is defined by:

$$g_\Delta \circ f_\Delta \stackrel{def}{\equiv} g \circ \langle \pi_1, f \rangle$$

Let us call the category constructed as above the Δ-indexed category of $\mathcal{S}_\mathcal{E}$ (notation $\Delta \times \mathcal{S}_\mathcal{E}$).

Theorem 6. *For any MLC terms $M \in \Lambda^{A \mapsto B}$ and $N \in \Lambda^{B \mapsto C}$, the following equation holds for morphisms in a Δ-indexed category.*

$$(\overline{[\![N]\!]})_\Delta \circ (\overline{[\![M]\!]})_\Delta = (\overline{[\![N \circ M]\!]})_\Delta$$

Proof. Equality is proved as follows.

$$\begin{aligned}
(\overline{[\![N]\!]})_\Delta \circ (\overline{[\![M]\!]})_\Delta &= \overline{[\![N]\!]} \circ \langle \pi_1, \overline{[\![M]\!]} \rangle \\
&= ev \circ ([\![N]\!] \times id_B) \circ \langle \pi_1, ev \circ ([\![M]\!] \times id_A) \rangle \\
&= ev \circ \langle [\![N]\!] \circ \pi_1, ev \circ ([\![M]\!] \times id_A) \rangle
\end{aligned}$$

$$\begin{aligned}
(\overline{[\![N \circ M]\!]})_\Delta &= \overline{[\![N \circ M]\!]} \\
&= \overline{[\![\zeta X. N \lceil M \lceil X \rceil \rceil]\!]} \\
&= \overline{\lambda([\![N \lceil M \lceil X \rceil \rceil]\!]) \circ \pi^\Delta_{\Delta \backslash X}} \\
&= \overline{\lambda(ev \circ \langle [\![N]\!], [\![M \lceil X \rceil]\!] \rangle) \circ \pi^\Delta_{\Delta \backslash X}} \\
&= ev \circ (\lambda(ev \circ \langle [\![N]\!], [\![M \lceil X \rceil]\!] \rangle) \circ \pi^\Delta_{\Delta \backslash X} \times id_A) \\
&= ev \circ (\lambda(ev \circ \langle [\![N]\!], [\![M \lceil X \rceil]\!] \rangle) \times id_A) \circ (\pi^\Delta_{\Delta \backslash X} \times id_A) \\
&= ev \circ \langle [\![N]\!], [\![M \lceil X \rceil]\!] \rangle \circ (\pi^\Delta_{\Delta \backslash X} \times id_A) \\
&= ev \circ \langle [\![N]\!], ev \circ \langle [\![M]\!], \pi_A \rangle \rangle \circ \pi_1 \qquad \text{---}(\dagger) \\
&= ev \circ \langle [\![N]\!] \circ \pi_1, ev \circ \langle [\![M]\!], \pi_A \rangle \circ \pi_1 \rangle \\
&= ev \circ \langle [\![N]\!] \circ \pi_1, ev \circ ([\![M]\!] \times id_A) \rangle \qquad \text{---}(\ddagger)
\end{aligned}$$

□

Two remarks should be made concerning this proof. Firstly, the substitution ($\dagger$) is due to the equation $\pi^\Delta_{\Delta \backslash X} \times id_A = \pi_1$, the proof of which is illustrated in the following diagram.

$$\begin{array}{ccc}
 & & [\![\Delta]\!] \times A \\
 & \pi_1 \swarrow & \downarrow \pi^\Delta_{\Delta \backslash X} \times id_A \\
[\![\Delta]\!] & \xleftarrow{\sim} & [\![\Delta]\!]' \times A
\end{array}$$

The second remark concerns the substitution ($\ddagger$), which depends on the equation $\langle [\![M]\!], \pi_A \rangle \circ \pi_1 = ([\![M]\!] \times id_A)$ that holds under the condition that $[\![\Delta]\!] \cong [\![\Delta]\!] \times A$, which in turn depends on our assumption that Δ includes all occurrences of meta-variables. The bijection between $[\![\Delta]\!]$ and $[\![\Delta]\!] \times A$ is illustrated in the following diagram.

$$\begin{array}{ccccc}
[\![\Delta]\!] & \xleftarrow{\pi_1} & [\![\Delta]\!] \times A & \xrightarrow{\pi_2} & A \\
 & \searrow id_{[\![\Delta]\!]} & \uparrow \langle id_{[\![\Delta]\!]}, \pi_A \rangle & \nearrow \pi_A & \\
 & & [\![\Delta]\!] & &
\end{array}$$

Under this assumption, the equation $\langle [\![M]\!], \pi_A\rangle \circ \pi_1 = ([\![M]\!] \times id_A)$ can be shown to hold as follows:

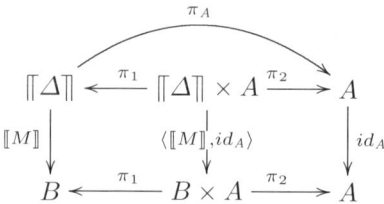

3.2 Internal Monad

Definition 7 (Internal Monad). *An internal monad is a triple $\langle T, \eta, \mu \rangle$ of meta-lambda terms which satisfies the following condition: the triple $\langle \overline{T}, \overline{\eta}, \overline{\mu} \rangle$ constitutes a categorical monad in $\Delta \times S_{\mathcal{E}}$, where $\overline{T}, \overline{\eta}, \overline{\mu}$ are defined as follows:*

$\overline{T} \stackrel{def}{\equiv} f \mapsto \overline{[\![T \ulcorner \zeta X. f \ulcorner X \urcorner \urcorner]\!]}$ *(as the arrow function of the functor $\overline{T}$)*

$\overline{\eta} \stackrel{def}{\equiv} \overline{[\![\eta]\!]}$ *(as a component of a natural transformation)*

$\overline{\mu} \stackrel{def}{\equiv} \overline{[\![\mu]\!]}$ *(as a component of a natural transformation)*

By specifying an internal monad, monadic analyses can be represented by the following interpretation schema.

Definition 8 (Transformation with Internal Monad (call-by-value))

$[\![x]\!]_T = \eta \ulcorner x \urcorner$

$[\![\lambda x.M]\!]_T = T \ulcorner \zeta X. \lambda x.X \urcorner \ulcorner [\![M]\!]_T \urcorner$

$[\![M(N)]\!]_T = \mu(T \ulcorner \zeta X.(T \ulcorner \zeta Y.X(Y) \urcorner \ulcorner [\![N]\!]_T \urcorner) \urcorner \ulcorner [\![M]\!]_T \urcorner)$

$[\![\langle M, N \rangle]\!]_T = \mu(T \ulcorner \zeta Y.(T \ulcorner \zeta X.\langle X, Y \rangle \urcorner \ulcorner [\![M]\!]_T \urcorner) \urcorner \ulcorner [\![N]\!]_T \urcorner)$

Theorem 9. *If a triple $\langle T, \eta, \mu \rangle$ satisfies the following four equations, the corresponding triple $\langle \overline{T}, \overline{\eta}, \overline{\mu} \rangle$ becomes a (categorical) monad; therefore the triple $\langle T, \eta, \mu \rangle$ qualifies as an internal monad:*

T conditions:	$T \ulcorner \zeta X.X \urcorner = \zeta X.X$	$T \ulcorner g \urcorner \circ T \ulcorner f \urcorner = T \ulcorner g \circ f \urcorner$
η and μ conditions:	$T \ulcorner f \urcorner \circ \eta = \eta \circ f$	$T \ulcorner f \urcorner \circ \mu = \mu \circ T \ulcorner T \ulcorner f \urcorner \urcorner$
Square identity:	$\mu \circ T \ulcorner \mu \urcorner = \mu \circ \mu$	
Triangular identity:	$\mu \circ \eta = \zeta X.X$	$\mu \circ T \ulcorner \eta \urcorner = \zeta X.X$

Proof. The following equations show that $\overline{T}$ is an endo-functor in the Δ-indexed category $\Delta \times \mathcal{S}et_{\mathcal{E}}$.

$(\overline{[\![T \ulcorner \zeta X.(g \circ f) \ulcorner X \urcorner \urcorner]\!]})_\Delta = (\overline{[\![T(\zeta X.g \ulcorner X \urcorner \circ \zeta X.f \ulcorner X \urcorner)]\!]})_\Delta$

$= (\overline{[\![T \ulcorner \zeta X.g \ulcorner X \urcorner \urcorner]\!]})_\Delta \circ (\overline{[\![T \ulcorner \zeta X.f \ulcorner X \urcorner \urcorner]\!]})_\Delta$

$$
\begin{aligned}
(\overline{[\![\boldsymbol{T}\lceil\zeta X_i.id\lceil X_i\rceil\rceil]\!]})_\Delta &= (\overline{[\![\boldsymbol{T}\lceil\zeta X_i.X_i\rceil]\!]})_\Delta \\
&= (\overline{[\![\zeta X_i.X_i]\!]})_\Delta \\
&= (\overline{\lambda([\![X_i]\!])\circ\pi^\Delta{}_{\Delta\setminus X_i}})_\Delta \\
&= (\overline{[\![X_i]\!]})_\Delta \\
&= (\pi_i)_\Delta \\
&= id_\Delta
\end{aligned}
$$

The following equations show that $\overline{\eta}: Id_{\Delta\times Set_\mathcal{E}} \xrightarrow{\cdot} \overline{\boldsymbol{T}}$ and $\overline{\mu}: \overline{\boldsymbol{T}}^2 \xrightarrow{\cdot} \overline{\boldsymbol{T}}$ are natural transformations.

$$
\begin{aligned}
&(\overline{\boldsymbol{T}\lceil f\rceil})_\Delta \circ (\overline{\eta})_\Delta & &(\overline{\boldsymbol{T}\lceil f\rceil})_\Delta \circ (\overline{\mu})_\Delta \\
&= (\overline{[\![\boldsymbol{T}\lceil\zeta X.f\lceil X\rceil\rceil]\!]} \circ \overline{[\![\eta]\!]})_\Delta & &= (\overline{[\![\boldsymbol{T}\lceil\zeta X.f\lceil X\rceil\rceil]\!]} \circ \overline{[\![\mu]\!]})_\Delta \\
&= (\overline{[\![\boldsymbol{T}\lceil\zeta X.f\lceil X\rceil\rceil]\!]\circ \eta})_\Delta & &= (\overline{[\![\boldsymbol{T}\lceil\zeta X.f\lceil X\rceil\rceil]\!]\circ \mu})_\Delta \\
&= (\overline{[\![\eta\circ f]\!]})_\Delta & &= (\overline{[\![\mu\circ \boldsymbol{T}\lceil\boldsymbol{T}\lceil f\rceil\rceil]\!]})_\Delta \\
&= (\overline{[\![\eta]\!]})_\Delta \circ (\overline{[\![f]\!]})_\Delta & &= (\overline{[\![\mu]\!]})_\Delta \circ (\overline{[\![\boldsymbol{T}\lceil\boldsymbol{T}\lceil f\rceil\rceil]\!]})_\Delta \\
&= (\overline{\eta})_\Delta \circ f_\Delta & &= (\overline{\mu})_\Delta \circ (\overline{\boldsymbol{T}\lceil\boldsymbol{T}\lceil f\rceil\rceil})_\Delta
\end{aligned}
$$

The square and triangular identities ensure that the triple constitutes a monad in a given category.

$$
\begin{aligned}
(\overline{\mu})_\Delta \circ (\overline{\boldsymbol{T}\lceil\overline{\mu}\rceil})_\Delta &= (\overline{[\![\mu]\!]})_\Delta \circ (\overline{[\![\boldsymbol{T}\lceil\mu\rceil]\!]})_\Delta \\
&= (\overline{[\![\mu\circ \boldsymbol{T}\lceil\mu\rceil]\!]})_\Delta \\
&= (\overline{[\![\mu\circ \mu]\!]})_\Delta \\
&= (\overline{[\![\mu]\!]})_\Delta \circ (\overline{[\![\mu]\!]})_\Delta \\
&= (\overline{\mu})_\Delta \circ (\overline{\mu})_\Delta
\end{aligned}
\qquad
\begin{aligned}
(\overline{\mu})_\Delta \circ (\overline{\eta})_\Delta &= (\overline{[\![\mu]\!]})_\Delta \circ (\overline{[\![\eta]\!]})_\Delta \\
&= (\overline{[\![\mu\circ\eta]\!]})_\Delta \\
&= (\overline{[\![\zeta X.X]\!]})_\Delta \\
\\
(\overline{\mu})_\Delta \circ (\overline{\boldsymbol{T}\lceil\overline{\eta}\rceil})_\Delta &= (\overline{[\![\mu]\!]})_\Delta \circ (\overline{[\![\boldsymbol{T}\lceil\eta\rceil]\!]})_\Delta \\
&= (\overline{[\![\mu\circ \boldsymbol{T}\lceil\eta\rceil]\!]})_\Delta \\
&= (\overline{[\![\zeta X.X]\!]})_\Delta
\end{aligned}
$$

□

4 Examples of Internal Monads

4.1 Non-determinism

The sentence (4) is ambiguous with respect to at least two factors: the antecedent of the pronoun 'he' and the lexical meaning of 'a suit' (clothing or a legal action).

(4) He brought a suit.

Suppose that there are currently two possible antecedents for the subject pronoun, say 'John' and 'Bill'. Then, in the context of standard natural language processing, a parser is expected to spell out the following set of semantic representations for the input sentence (4).

(5) $\{brought'(suit_1)(j'), brought'(suit_2)(j'),$
     $brought'(suit_1)(b'), (brought')(suit_2)(b')\}$

But this kind of 'duplication' of output trees is known to bring about a combinatorial explosion in parsing complexity, which has motivated the pursuit of an 'information packing' strategy. Now, let us consider the following interpretation rules from TLC to TLC.

(6)
$$[\![x]\!]_{nd} = \{x\}$$
$$[\![\lambda x.M]\!]_{nd} = \{\lambda x.[\![M]\!]_{nd}\}$$
$$[\![M(N)]\!]_{nd} = \{mn \mid m \in [\![M]\!]_{nd} \wedge n \in [\![N]\!]_{nd}\}$$
$$[\![\langle M,N\rangle]\!]_{nd} = \{\langle m,n\rangle \mid m \in [\![M]\!]_{nd} \wedge n \in [\![N]\!]_{nd}\}$$

Then, each ambiguity due to the antecedent of 'he' and the lexical ambiguity of 'a suit' can be lexically represented in the following way.

(7)
$$[\![he']\!]_{nd} = \{j', b'\}$$
$$[\![suit']\!]_{nd} = \{suit_1, suit_2\}$$

Using these expressions, the set of representations (5) can be packed into the single representation (8).

(8) $(brought'(suit'))(he')$

The non-deterministic aspects in the sentence (4) are successfully encapsulated and hidden within (8), for the following equations show that the interpretation $[\![-]\!]_{nd}$ of (8) is equivalent to (5).

(9)
$$[\![(brought'(suit'))]\!]_{nd}$$
$$= \{mn \mid m \in [\![brought']\!]_{nd} \wedge n \in [\![suit']\!]_{nd}\}$$
$$= \{mn \mid m \in \{brought'\} \wedge n \in \{suit_1, suit_2\}\}$$
$$= \{brought'(suit_1), brought'(suit_2)\}$$

$$[\![(brought'(suit'))(he')]\!]_{nd}$$
$$= \{mn \mid m \in [\![brought'(suit')]\!]_{nd} \wedge n \in [\![he']\!]_{nd}\}$$
$$= \{mn \mid m \in \{brought'(suit_1), brought'(suit_2)\} \wedge n \in \{j', b'\}\}$$
$$= \{brought'(suit_1)(j'), brought(suit_2)(j'),$$
$$brought'(suit_1)(b'), brought(suit_2)(b')\}$$

Interpretation $[\![-]\!]_{nd}$ in (6) is specified by the internal monad, consisting of the following triple, which gives rise to the definition (6) via the interpretation schema Definition 8.

Definition 10 (Internal Monad of Non-determinism)

$$\boldsymbol{T}_{nd} = \zeta f.\zeta X.\{f\lceil Y\rceil \mid Y \in X\}$$
$$\eta_{nd} = \zeta X.\{X\}$$
$$\mu_{nd} = \zeta X.\bigcup X$$

Theorem 11. $\langle \boldsymbol{T}_{nd}, \eta_{nd}, \mu_{nd}\rangle$ *is an internal monad.*

Proof. **T** conditions:

$$\boldsymbol{T}_{nd} \lceil \zeta X.X \rceil = \zeta X. \{(\zeta X.X) \lceil Y \rceil \mid Y \in X\}$$
$$= \zeta X. \{Y \mid Y \in X\}$$
$$= \zeta X.X$$

$$\boldsymbol{T}_{nd} \lceil g \rceil \circ \boldsymbol{T}_{nd} \lceil f \rceil = \zeta X. \{g \lceil Y \rceil \mid Y \in X\} \circ \zeta X. \{f \lceil Y \rceil \mid Y \in X\}$$
$$= \zeta X. \{g \lceil Y \rceil \mid Y \in \{f \lceil Z \rceil \mid Z \in X\}\}$$
$$= \zeta X. \{(g \circ f) \lceil Y \rceil \mid Y \in X\}$$
$$= \boldsymbol{T}_{nd} \lceil g \circ f \rceil$$

η and μ conditions:

$$\begin{aligned}
&\boldsymbol{T}_{nd} \lceil f \rceil \circ \eta_{nd} \\
&= (\zeta X. \{f \lceil Y \rceil \mid Y \in X\}) \circ (\zeta X. \{X\}) \\
&= \zeta X. \{f \lceil Y \rceil \mid Y \in \{X\}\} \\
&= \zeta X. \{f \lceil X \rceil\} \\
&= \zeta X. \{X\} \circ f \\
&= \eta_{nd} \circ f
\end{aligned}
\qquad
\begin{aligned}
&\boldsymbol{T}_{nd} \lceil f \rceil \circ \mu_{nd} \\
&= (\zeta X. \{f \lceil Y \rceil \mid Y \in X\}) \circ (\zeta X. \bigcup X) \\
&= \zeta X. \{f \lceil Y \rceil \mid Y \in \bigcup X\} \\
&= \zeta X. \bigcup \{f \lceil Y \rceil \mid Y \in \{f \lceil Z \rceil \mid Z \in X\}\} \\
&= \mu_{nd} \circ \boldsymbol{T} \lceil \boldsymbol{T} \lceil f \rceil \rceil
\end{aligned}$$

Square identity:

$$\mu_{nd} \circ \boldsymbol{T}_{nd} \lceil \mu_{nd} \rceil = (\zeta X. \bigcup X) \circ \zeta X. \left\{ (\zeta X. \bigcup X) \lceil Y \rceil \mid Y \in X \right\}$$
$$= (\zeta X. \bigcup X) \circ \zeta X. \left\{ \bigcup Y \mid Y \in X \right\}$$
$$= (\zeta X. \bigcup X) \circ (\zeta X. \bigcup X)$$
$$= \mu_{nd} \circ \mu_{nd}$$

Triangular identity:

$$\begin{aligned}
&\mu_{nd} \circ \eta_{nd} \\
&= \zeta X. \bigcup X \circ \zeta X. \{X\} \\
&= \zeta X. \bigcup \{X\} \\
&= \zeta X.X
\end{aligned}
\qquad
\begin{aligned}
&\mu_{nd} \circ \boldsymbol{T}_{nd} \lceil \eta_{nd} \rceil \\
&= \zeta X. \bigcup X \circ \zeta X. \{(\zeta X. \{X\}) \lceil Y \rceil \mid Y \in X\} \\
&= \zeta x. \bigcup \{\{Y\} \mid Y \in X\} \\
&= \zeta X.X
\end{aligned}$$

□

4.2 Contextual Parameters

Semantic representations sometimes make reference to various kinds of contextual parameters such as speaker/hearer, topic, point of view, for instance. Contextual parameters are often treated as being 'free variables' or 'global variables', but strictly speaking, this is not accurate, since the their values can be overwritten in the middle of the sentences. For example, in the sentence (10), each of the two occurrences of 'you' refers to the hearer at the moment, but its denotation changes by ostention.

(10) (Pointing to John) You passed, (pointing to Mary) and you passed.

Again, if we interpret TLC terms by the following set of rules, contextual parameters can be easily referenced in semantic representations, and can also be changed, even halfway through a single sentence.

(11) $[\![x]\!]_{cp} = \lambda h.\langle x, h\rangle$
$[\![\lambda x.M]\!]_{cp} = \lambda h.\langle \lambda x.[\![M]\!]_{cp}, h\rangle$
$[\![M(N)]\!]_{cp} = \lambda h.\mathrm{let}\ M' = \pi_1[\![M]\!]_{cp}h,\ \mathrm{let}\ h' = \pi_2[\![M]\!]_{cp}h,$
$\quad\quad\quad\quad \mathrm{let}\ N' = \pi_1[\![N]\!]_{cp}h',\ \mathrm{let}\ h'' = \pi_2[\![N]\!]_{cp}h',\ \langle M'(N'), h''\rangle$
$[\![\langle M, N\rangle]\!]_{cp} = \lambda h.\mathrm{let}\ M' = \pi_1[\![M]\!]_{cp}h,\ \mathrm{let}\ h' = \pi_2[\![M]\!]_{cp}h,$
$\quad\quad\quad\quad \mathrm{let}\ N' = \pi_1[\![N]\!]_{cp}h',\ \mathrm{let}\ h'' = \pi_2[\![N]\!]_{cp}h',\ \langle\langle M', N'\rangle, h''\rangle$

The following definitions provide a method to set the current hearer x to the corresponding contextual parameter, and a method to reference it.

(12) $[\![set\_hearer(x)]\!]_{cp} = \lambda h.\langle\top, x\rangle$
$[\![hearer()]\!]_{cp} = \lambda h.\langle h, h\rangle$

Then, the semantic representation of the sentence (10) can be simply stated as follows.

(13) $set\_hearer(j') \wedge passed'(hearer()) \wedge set\_hearer(m') \wedge passed'(hearer())$

When (13) is interpreted by $[\![-]\!]_{cp}$, each occurrence of 'you' successfully refers to the intended individual, although the two representations for 'you passed' in (13) are exactly the same. Suppose that $A \wedge B = \wedge(\langle A, B\rangle)$.

(14) $[\![\wedge]\!]_{cp} = \lambda h.\langle\wedge, h\rangle$
$[\![passed']\!]_{cp} = \lambda h.\langle passed', h\rangle$
$[\![passed'(hearer())]\!]_{cp} = \lambda h.\langle passed'(h), h\rangle$
$[\![\langle set\_hearer(j'), passed'(hearer())\rangle]\!]_{cp} = \lambda h.\langle\langle\top, passed'(j')\rangle, j'\rangle$
$[\![set\_hearer(j') \wedge passed'(hearer())]\!]_{cp} = \lambda h.\langle\wedge(\top, passed'(j')), j'\rangle$
$\quad\quad\quad\quad\quad\quad\quad\quad\quad\quad\quad\quad\quad\quad\quad\quad = \lambda h.\langle passed'(j'), j'\rangle$

Therefore, the following result obtains.

(15) $[\![set\_hearer(j') \wedge passed'(hearer()) \wedge set\_hearer(m') \wedge passed'(hearer())]\!]_{cp}$
$= \lambda h.\langle passed'(j') \wedge passed'(m'), m'\rangle$

The interpretation $[\![-]\!]_{cp}$ in (11) is specified by the following internal monad. Again, this gives rise to the definition (11) via the interpretation schema Definition 8.

Definition 12 (Internal Monad of Contextual Parameters)

$T_{cp} = \zeta f.\zeta X.\lambda h.\langle f\lceil \pi_1(Xh)\rceil, \pi_2(Xh)\rangle$
$\eta_{cp} = \zeta X.\lambda h.\langle X, h\rangle$
$\mu_{cp} = \zeta X.\lambda h.(\pi_1(Xh))(\pi_2(Xh))$

Theorem 13. $\langle \boldsymbol{T}_{cp}, \eta_{cp}, \mu_{cp} \rangle$ *is an internal monad.*

Proof. $\boldsymbol{T}$ conditions:

$$\begin{aligned}
\boldsymbol{T}_{cp} \lceil \zeta X.X \rceil &= \zeta X.\lambda h.\langle (\zeta X.X) \lceil \pi_1(Xh) \rceil, \pi_2(Xh) \rangle \\
&= \zeta X.\lambda h.\langle \pi_1(Xh), \pi_2(Xh) \rangle \\
&= \zeta X.\lambda h.Xh \\
&= \zeta X.X
\end{aligned}$$

$$\begin{aligned}
\boldsymbol{T}_{cp} \lceil g \rceil \circ \boldsymbol{T}_{cp} \lceil f \rceil &= \zeta X.\lambda h.\langle g \lceil \pi_1(Xh) \rceil, \pi_2(Xh) \rangle \circ \zeta X.\lambda h.\langle f \lceil \pi_1(Xh) \rceil, \pi_2(Xh) \rangle \\
&= \zeta X.\lambda h.\langle g \lceil f \lceil \pi_1(Xh) \rceil \rceil, \pi_2(Xh) \rangle \\
&= \boldsymbol{T}_{cp} \lceil g \circ f \rceil
\end{aligned}$$

η and μ conditions:

$$\begin{aligned}
\boldsymbol{T}_{cp} \lceil f \rceil \circ \eta_{cp} &= \zeta X.\lambda h.\langle f \lceil \pi_1(Xh) \rceil, \pi_2(Xh) \rangle \circ \zeta X.\lambda h.\langle X, h \rangle \\
&= \zeta X.\lambda h.\langle fX, h \rangle \\
&= \eta_{cp} \circ f
\end{aligned}$$

$$\begin{aligned}
\boldsymbol{T}_{cp} \lceil f \rceil \circ \mu_{cp} &= \zeta X.\lambda h.\langle f \lceil \pi_1(Xh) \rceil, \pi_2(Xh) \rangle \circ \zeta X.\lambda h.(\pi_1(Xh))(\pi_2(Xh)) \\
&= \zeta X.\lambda h.\langle f \lceil \pi_1((\pi_1(Xh))(\pi_2(Xh))) \rceil, \pi_2((\pi_1(Xh))(\pi_2(Xh))) \rangle \\
&= \zeta X.\lambda h.(\lambda h'.\langle f \lceil \pi_1((\pi_1(Xh))h') \rceil, \pi_2((\pi_1(Xh))h') \rangle)(\pi_2(Xh)) \\
&= \zeta X.\lambda h.(\pi_1(Xh))(\pi_2(Xh)) \\
&\quad \circ \zeta X.\lambda h.\langle \lambda h'.\langle f \lceil \pi_1((\pi_1(Xh))h') \rceil, \pi_2((\pi_1(Xh))h') \rangle, \pi_2(Xh) \rangle \\
&= \mu_{cp} \circ \boldsymbol{T} \lceil \boldsymbol{T} \lceil f \rceil \rceil
\end{aligned}$$

Square identity:

$$\begin{aligned}
\mu_{cp} \circ \boldsymbol{T}_{cp} \lceil \mu_{cp} \rceil &= \zeta X.\lambda h.(\pi_1(Xh))(\pi_2(Xh)) \\
&\quad \circ \zeta X.\lambda h.\langle (\zeta X.\lambda h.(\pi_1(Xh))(\pi_2(Xh)))(\pi_1(Xh)), \pi_2(Xh) \rangle \\
&= \zeta X.\lambda h.(\lambda h'.(\pi_1((\pi_1(Xh))h'))(\pi_2((\pi_1(Xh))h')))(\pi_2(Xh)) \\
&= \zeta X.\lambda h.(\pi_1((\pi_1(Xh))(\pi_2(Xh))))(\pi_2((\pi_1(Xh))(\pi_2(Xh)))) \\
&= \zeta X.\lambda h.(\pi_1(Xh))(\pi_2(Xh)) \circ \zeta X.\lambda h.(\pi_1(Xh))(\pi_2(Xh)) \\
&= \mu_{cp} \circ \mu_{cp}
\end{aligned}$$

Triangular identity:

$$\begin{aligned}
\mu_{cp} \circ \eta_{cp} &= \zeta X.\lambda h.(\pi_1(Xh))(\pi_2(Xh)) \circ \zeta X.\lambda h.\langle X, h \rangle \\
&= \zeta X.\lambda h.Xh \\
&= \zeta X.X
\end{aligned}$$

$$\begin{aligned}
\mu_{cp} \circ T_{cp} \lceil \eta_{cp} \rceil &= \zeta X.\lambda h.(\pi_1(Xh))(\pi_2(Xh)) \\
&\quad \circ \zeta X.\lambda h.\langle(\zeta X.\lambda h.\langle X, h\rangle)(\pi_1(Xh)), \pi_2(Xh)\rangle \\
&= \zeta X.\lambda h.(\pi_1(Xh))(\pi_2(Xh)) \circ \zeta X.\lambda h.\langle \lambda h.\langle \pi_1(Xh), h\rangle, \pi_2(Xh)\rangle \\
&= \zeta X.\lambda h.(\lambda h.\langle \pi_1(Xh), h\rangle)(\pi_2(Xh)) \\
&= \zeta X.\lambda h.\langle \pi_1(Xh), \pi_2(Xh)\rangle \\
&= \zeta X.\lambda h.Xh \\
&= \zeta X.X \qquad \qquad \square
\end{aligned}$$

5 Conclusion

Meta-Lambda Calculus (MLC) is an extended TLC with meta-constructions, whose categorical semantics is defined by means of a hom-functor from a Cartesian closed category to $\mathcal{S}et$. In this setting, TLC is naturally regarded as a special case of MLC, namely, MLC with no meta-variables. I also proved that both normal and meta- beta conversions are sound in this categorical semantics.

Each computational monad in "monadic analyses" is specified by an "internal monad", which is a triple of MLC terms, that serves as a parameter in the transformation rules. I proved that if a triple satisfies the set of conditions (T conditions, η and μ conditions, square identity, triangular identity), there exists a categorical monad in "Δ-indexed category" which exactly corresponds to that triple.

As examples of such computational monads, I presented two internal monads for non-determinism and contextual parameters, and proved that they indeed satisfy the conditions for internal monads.

References

[Crole (1993)] Crole, R.L.: Categories for Types. Cambridge University Press, Cambridge (1993)
[Kock (1970)] Kock, A.: Strong functors and monoidal monads, Various Publications Series 11. Aarhus Universitet (August 1970)
[Lambek (1980)] Lambek, J.: From λ-calculus to cartesian closed categories. In: Seldin, J.P., Hindley, J.R. (eds.) To H.B. Curry: Essays on Combinatory Logic, Lambda Calculus and Formalism. Academic Press, London (1980)
[Lambek and Scott (1986)] Lambek, J., Scott, P.J.: Introduction to higher order categorical logic. Cambridge University Press, Cambridge (1986)
[MacLane (1997)] MacLane, S.: Categories for the Working Mathematician, 2nd edn. Graduate Texts in Mathematics. Springer, Heidelberg (1997)
[Moggi (1989)] Moggi, E.: Computational lambda-calculus and monads. In: Proceedings of Fourth Annual IEEE Symposium on Logic in Computer Science, pp. 14–23 (1989)
[Shan (2001)] Shan, C.-c.: Monads for natural language semantics. In: Striegnitz, K. (ed.) The ESSLLI-2001 student session (13th European summer school in logic, language and information, 2001), pp. 285–298 (2001)
[Wadler (1992)] Wadler, P.: Comprehending Monads. In: Mathematical Structure in Computer Science, vol. 2, pp. 461–493. Cambridge University Press, Cambridge (1992)

Part III
Juris-Informatics

Overview of JURISIN 2008

Katsumi Nitta, Ken Satoh, and Satoshi Tojo

International Workshop on Juris-Informatics (*i.e.*: JURISIN workshop) was organized to study legal issues from the perspective of informatics. The main purpose of the JURISIN workshop is to discuss both the fundamental and practical issues in jurisinformatics among people from various backgrounds such as law, social science, information and intelligent technology, logic and philosophy, including the conventional "AI and law" area.

The first JURISIN workshop was held at Miyazaki in conjunction with the 21st annual conference of the Japanese Society for Artificial Intelligence (JSAI) last year. Each submitted paper was reviewed by three PC members, and eight papers were accepted in total. After the workshop, four papers were selected and piblished as Lecture Notes in Artificial Intelligence 4914. As the first workshop was successful, we held the second JURISIN workshop in conjunction with the 22nd annual conference of JSAI. In this workshop, ten papers were accepted. They cover various topics such as legal reasoning, argumentation theory, computer-aided law education, text processing of legal documents, use of informatics and AI in law, and so on. After the workshop, we asked authors to rewrite their papers according to the discussion during the workshop. PC members reviewed these rewritten papers again, and following four papers are selected.

Masato Hagiwara, Yasuhiro Ogawa and Katsuhiko Toyama proposed an algorithm which automatically extracts dictionary term candidates from unsegmented legal text. The Japanese government released the standard Japanese- English bilingual dictionary of legal terms. However, the translation from Japanese statute law to English is still difficult because Japanese is unsegmented language. The proposed algorithm supports legal experts to make the final decision and select Japanese dictionary term candidates.

Yusuka Kimura, Masato Nakamura and Akira Shimazu developed a system which translates legal documents into logical formulae. Legal sentences often include itemized expressions and references, which make tanslating documents difficult. They proposed a method to rewrite such legal sentences into independent, plain sentences.

Hiroyuki Kido and Masahito Kurihara formalized dialectical thought as a reasoning method based on specialization and generalization. They showed that by using this formalization, the negotiation process of resolving a conflict by drawing an alternative solution is described clearly.

Toshiko Wakaki and Katsumi Nitta proposed a method for Dung's argumentation semantics along with semi-stable semantics in Answer Set Programming. In their approach, a given argumentation framework is translated into a single normal logic program. They showed the soundness and completeness of the translation.

Finally, we would like to thank all the PC members for reviewing the submitted papers.

Katsumi Nitta
Ken Satoh
Satoshi Tojo

Workshop Chairs

Katsumi Nitta, Tokyo Institute of Technology, Japan Ken Satoh, National Institute of Informatics and Sokendai, Japan Satoshi Tojo, Japan Advanced Institute of Science and Technology, Japan

Program Committee

Kevin Ashley, University of Pittsburgh, USA Aditya Ghose, University of Wollongong, Australia Guido Governatori, University of Queensland, Australia Tokuyasu Kakuta, Nagoya University, Japan Henry Prakken, University of Utrecht & Groningen, The Netherlands Seiichiro Sakurai, Meiji Gakuin University, Japan Giovanni Sartor, European University Institute, Italy Hajime Sawamura, Niigata University, Japan Akira Shimazu, Japan Advanced Institute of Science and Technology, Japan Katsuhiko Toyama, Nagoya University, Japan Takahira Yamaguchi, Keio University, Japan John Zeleznikow, Victoria University, Australia

Bootstrapping-Based Extraction of Dictionary Terms from Unsegmented Legal Text

Masato Hagiwara, Yasuhiro Ogawa, and Katsuhiko Toyama

Graduate School of Information Science, Nagoya University
Furo-cho, Chikusa-ku, Nagoya 464-8603, Japan
{hagiwara,yasuhiro,toyama}@kl.i.is.nagoya-u.ac.jp
http://www.kl.i.is.nagoya-u.ac.jp/

Abstract. Recent demands for translating Japanese statutes into foreign languages necessitate the compilation of standard bilingual dictionaries. To support this costly task, we propose a bootstrapping-based lexical knowledge extraction algorithm *Monaka*, to automatically extract dictionary term candidates from unsegmented Japanese legal text. The algorithm is based on the *Tchai* algorithm and extracts reliable patterns and instances in an iterative manner, but instead uses character n-grams as contextual patterns, and introduces a special constraint to ensure proper segmentation of the extracted terms. The experimental results show that this algorithm can extract correctly segmented and important dictionary terms with higher accuracy compared to conventional methods.

Keywords: bootstrapping, lexical knowledge acquisition, dictionary terms, unsegmented legal text, dictionary compilation.

1 Introduction

There has been recent increase of social demand for translation of Japanese statute laws such as acts, cabinet orders, and ministry ordinances, into foreign languages, especially into English [13]. This demand has been further driven by social and economic globalization, including promotion of international transactions and investment towards Japan, and technical assistance to legal reform in developing countries and former socialist countries. For this reason legal information about Japan should be available in readable languages to anyone in the world.

In response to these demands, in March 2006, the Japanese government decided to establish an infrastructure for promoting translation of Japanese statutes into foreign languages [9]. At the same time, the government released the first version of *the standard Japanese-English bilingual dictionary of legal terms* (SBD) [10] containing 3,315 Japanese terms that often appear in statutes[1], and English translations of Japanese statues that comply with it. The governmental

---

[1] The dictionary was revised in March 2007 and it now includes 3,466 Japanese terms.

plan includes translating more than 250 major statutes into English by 2009, and 120 of them have been already released so far[2].

Since SBD is useful in keeping word choices consistent within and across translations and preventing misunderstanding, its use has been strongly recommended to translators and lawyers when they translate legal text. However, since the compilation of such a dictionary would be very expensive, it should be technically supported, although the final decisions in editing dictionary lexicons are made by legal experts. Toyama et al. [13] proposed a method to support the dictionary compilation with the natural language processing (NLP) technologies, namely, the word alignment technique [5], which automatically extracts bilingual lexicons from parallel corpora. Although this method greatly reduces the compilation cost, Japanese term candidates are extracted based on simple character n-grams and appropriate dictionary terms still need to be selected by legal experts.

The aim of this paper is, therefore, to support legal experts when making the final decision and selecting Japanese dictionary terms, by automatically and accurately extracting dictionary term candidates from unsegmented legal text. Here we need to make it clear what kind of terms should be selected and included as dictionary term candidates. While SBD entries are, in general, important and frequently appear in statutes, the final selection is largely dependent on subjective human judgment, making them difficult to define. A partial solution to this problem can be found in *definition sentences* described at the beginning of a statute, where precise meanings of important terms are defined to be used throughout the statute. These *defined terms*, largely consisting of nouns, compound nouns, and noun phrases, are obviously important and should therefore be included as dictionary terms. The definition sentences follow strict convention in Japanese legislation as shown in the following examples:

Ex. 1 この法律において「商品取引所」とは、会員商品取引所及び株式会社商品取引所をいう。
(The term "Commodity Exchange" as used in this Act shall mean a Member Commodity Exchange and an Incorporated Commodity Exchange.)
(Act No. 239, 1950)

Ex. 2 この法律において、次の各号に掲げる用語の意義は、当該各号に定めるところによる。
　一　著作物　思想又は感情を創作的に表現したものであつて、文芸、学術、美術又は音楽の範囲に属するものをいう。
　二　著作者　著作物を創作する者をいう。
(In this Act, the meanings of the terms listed in the following items shall be as prescribed respectively in those items:
(i) "work" means a production in which thoughts or sentiments are expressed in a creative way and which falls within the literary, scientific, artistic or musical domain;

---

[2] http://www.cas.go.jp/jp/seisaku/hourei/data1.html

(ii) "author" means a person who creates the work;)

(Act No. 48, 1970)

The first type defines one term per paragraph, while the second type is used when two or more terms are defined in a single paragraph. In both cases, such definition sentences are written in a highly fixed manner, suggesting that the defined terms can be easily extracted from these definition sentences by simple template-based string matching.

However, how to extract important terms besides these defined terms still remains a major problem. To detect other important terms, we paid attention to the *contextual patterns* in which the terms appear, assuming that other important words should appear in similar context to that of the defined terms. Here the word *contextual pattern*, or simply *pattern*, means a fixed sequence of language units (e.g., words, phrases, or even characters) which appears close to (or next to) the target term. Pattern-based lexical knowledge acquisition has been well studied so far [1, 3] with a considerable success. Assuming that such terms appear in fixed patterns as the defined terms do, other important terms can be easily discovered using such fixed patterns as clues and newly discovered terms can be used to induce more effective patterns to find more important terms. There have been a certain number of studies regarding such iterative extraction, or *bootstrapping*, aimed at lexical knowledge acquisition [2, 6, 8, 12]. Among them, we focus on the *Espresso* [6] and *Tchai* [2] algorithms, which are both the state-of-the-art, minimally supervised bootstrapping methods. Given a small number of seeds, they automatically extract instances of lexical relations or terms related to the seeds in an iterative manner based on contextual patterns.

Although their algorithms showed relatively high performances in extracting lexical knowledge, *Espresso* is essentially designed for extracting binary relations from explicitly segmented English text, and *Tchai* is designed for extracting semantic categories of words from short Japanese web search query sentences. However, Japanese legal sentences pose additional challenges here — they are unsegmented, i.e., written without any whitespaces in between, generally long, and they often have complex dependency structure and many out-of-vocabulary words. This makes it difficult to apply existing tools such as morphological analyzers and parsers because segmentation errors cause noises and prevent the accurate extraction. We can use conventional NLP tools by tailoring them especially for legal text, but this process may require additional cost. Thus we have to find a way to directly process unsegmented plain text, especially in legal domain.

Therefore, in this paper we propose a new algorithm called *Monaka*, which automatically discovers the related words to the seeds without depending on explicit segmentation. We use this algorithm to find important terms, i.e., dictionary term candidates from Japanese legal texts. The algorithm is largely based on the previously-introduced *Tchai* algorithm, although we made some modifications, namely, character n-gram based instance/pattern induction, and the bidirectional adjacency constraint (BAC), so that it can be reliably applied to unsegmented text. We conduct experiments to show that the proposed method is

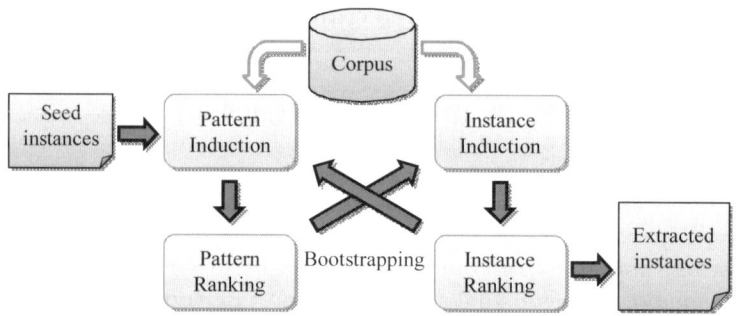

Fig. 1. Overview of Bootstrapping-based lexical knowledge acquisition

effective for automatically extracting important dictionary terms from Japanese legal text.

The rest of this paper is organized as follows: in Section 2 we introduce the related works: *Espresso* and *Tchai*, and describe how they work for lexical knowledge extraction. The following Section 3 describes our algorithm *Monaka*. Section 4 is experimental, where the performance evaluation is conducted and the result is shown. Finally, Section 5 concludes this paper.

2 Related Works

In this section, we describe the *Espresso* and *Tchai* algorithms in some detail, which our algorithm proposed in this paper is based on.

2.1 The *Espresso* Algorithm

Espresso is a general purpose, bootstrapping-based algorithm designed for harvesting binary relationships, such as *is-a* and *part-of* relationships. It takes a few seed instances and iterates between the following four phases: pattern induction, pattern ranking/selection, instance inducion, and instance ranking/selection. The overview of the bootstrapping algorithm is illustrated in Fig. 1.

In the first step, pattern induction, the algorithm extracts contextual patterns co-occurring with input instances from corpora. Given the set of all instances I, *Espresso* finds all the occurrences of terms x and y of an instance $i = \{x, y\} \in I$ from a corpus, and collects all substrings linking x and y to create a set of extracted patterns P.

The next step, pattern ranking/selection, ranks all patterns in P and selects *reliable patterns*, where the reliability of a pattern is calculated assuming that patterns that are highly associated with many reliable input instances should also be reliable. Here the degree of association between an instance i and a pattern p is given by pointwise mutual information (PMI):

$$pmi(i,p) = \log \frac{P(i,p)}{P(i)P(p)} = \log \frac{|x,p,y|}{|x,*,y||*,p,*|}, \quad (1)$$

where $|x,p,y|$ denotes the frequency of pattern p instantiated with terms x and y, and the asterisks represent wildcards, i.e. $|x,*,y| = \sum_p |x,p,y|$ and $|*,p,*| = \sum_{x,y} |x,p,y|$. Based on PMI and the instance reliability r_ι, the reliability of the pattern p is defined as:

$$r_\pi(p) = \frac{1}{|I|} \sum_{i \in I} \frac{pmi(i,p)}{\max_{pmi}} \cdot r_\iota(i), \quad (2)$$

where $\max_{pmi}$ is the maximum PMI between all patterns and instances. Since it is widely known that PMI is biased towards infrequent events, we multiplied PMI with the following discounting factor $w(i,p)$ [7], as done in [6]:

$$w(i,p) = \left(\frac{|x,p,y|}{|x,p,y|+1} \cdot \frac{\min(|x,*,y|,|*,p,*|)}{\min(|x,*,y|,|*,p,*|)+1} \right) \quad (3)$$

$$pmi(i,p) = w(i,p) \cdot \log \frac{|x,p,y|}{|x,*,y||*,p,*|}. \quad (4)$$

After the ranking, the most reliable k patterns are chosen, where k is set $k = 5$ for the first iteration and it is incremented by one per iteration.

The third step, instance induction, extracts instances that match the previously induced reliable patterns.

Finally, the fourth step ranks and selects the *reliable instances* based on the instance reliability r_ι, which is defined analogously to the pattern reliability r_π:

$$r_\iota(i) = \frac{1}{|P|} \sum_{p \in P} \frac{pmi(i,p)}{\max_{pmi}} \cdot r_\pi(p). \quad (5)$$

Again, the underlying assumption is that reliable instances are instantiated with many reliable patterns, meaning that the pattern and instance reliabilities are recursively defined. The reliability of the manually supplied seed instances are fixed as $r_\iota(i) = 1$. In *Espresso*, instances are cumulatively learned (i.e, once acquired, the instances continue to be used in the subsequent iterations), but patterns are discarded at the end of each iteration.

We note here that, although *Espresso* also introduces another confidence metric to filter out ambiguous instances that induce too many patterns with low precision, we take a different approach to detect such ambiguous instances and patterns as *Tchai* does. The detail of ambiguous instance/pattern detection is described later in Section 3.3.

2.2 The *Tchai* Algorithm

The *Tchai* algorithm works in almost the same manner as *Espresso*, except that the former aims at extracting semantic categories of words, i.e., unary relations, from Japanese web query logs. It also differs from *Espresso* in these three aspects:

pattern induction, local PMI max, and ambiguous instance/pattern filtering, which we describe in detail below.

Pattern induction: Since *Tchai* does not deal with binary relations but unary relations, it uses everything but the instance string in a query as the pattern. For example, when the seed word is "JAL", the query "JAL+flight_schedule" yields the pattern "#+flight_schedule"[3]. Accordingly, the PMI value is calculated as the degree of association between an instance word i and a pattern p as:

$$pmi(i,p) = \log \frac{P(i,p)}{P(i)P(p)} = \log \frac{N|i,p|}{|i,*||*,p|}, \qquad (6)$$

where N is the total number of all co-occurrences, i.e., $N = \sum_{i,p} |i,p|$.

Local PMI max: Because absolute value of PMI varies greatly across instances and patterns when computing $r_\pi(p)$, *Tchai* utilizes local maximum of PMI instead of global one. Specifically, it uses $\max_{\text{pmi}}(p) = \max_{i'} pmi(i',p)$ instead for Equation (2) and $\max_{\text{pmi}}(i) = \max_{p'} pmi(i,p')$ for Equation (5), respectively. Komachi and Suzuki [2] reported that this modification had a positive impact on the effectiveness of the algorithm.

Ambiguous instance/pattern filtering: Because Komachi and Suzuki [2] could not confirm the effectiveness of the confidence metric proposed by Pantel and Pennacchiotti [6] to filter out ambiguous instances, instead they defined ambiguous instance as one that induces more than 1.5 times the number of patterns of previously accepted reliable instances. They also removed every ambiguous pattern, which was defined as one that extracts more than twice the number of previously extracted reliable instances.

3 The *Monaka* Algorithm

In this section we propose *Monaka*, the modified version of the bootstrapping-based lexicon extraction algorithm. The following sections give the specifics.

3.1 n-Gram based Pattern and Instance Induction

While *Espresso* targets at segmented English text, and *Tchai* targets at Japanese short query logs, the *Monaka* algorithm is especially designed to directly process unsegmented Japanese text. This is made possible by dealing with character n-grams instead of words. In *Monaka*, patterns are character n-grams which precede or succeed the instance in the text. For example, when the input instance "商品取引所" ("Commodity Exchange") is matched against the example sentence **Ex. 1**, all the preceding and succeeding character n-grams within a given range are extracted as patterns:

---

[3] '+' denotes a white space, and '#' indicates where the instance is found in a context pattern.

"「#",
"て「#",
"いて「#",
...,
"#」",
"#」と",
"#」とは",
...,

and so forth, where "#" represents the instance slot. Similarly, at the instance induction step, all the character n-grams that match the slot within a given range are instantiated. For example, when a pattern "いて「#" is given as the input, the above example sentence yields

"商",
"商品",
"商品取",
...,

and so forth, as instances. We set the range of n to $2 \leq n \leq 6$ for pattern induction, and $2 \leq n \leq 10$ for instance induction. If the matched pattern or instance is located too close to the beginning or the end of a sentence to extract sufficient length of n-grams, unigrams are extracted instead.

3.2 Bidirectional Adjacency Constraint (BAC)

The pattern and instance induction described in the previous section do not depend on word segmentation or even character classes such as *hiragana* and *kanji*. While it greatly helps to keep the generality and robustness of this algorithm to other languages, it tends to yield a huge number of incorrectly segmented instances, which are largely substrings or superstrings of other correct instances. To prevent this algorithm from generating low-quality instances and hindering the efficient selection of dictionary terms, we introduce the following constraint to the instance induction, that is, highly reliable instances must be located between reliable preceding *and* succeeding patterns. This is the reason why this algorithm is named after a sandwich-like Japanese sweet *Monaka*.

Specifically, we divide the extracted patterns into two classes: *preceding patterns* and *succeeding patterns*, and calculate instance reliability by using them separately. Preceding patterns are the ones which come *before* instances, such as "「#", "て「#", and "いて「#", and succeeding patterns come *after* instances, such as "#」", "#」と", and "#」とは". Letting P_p as the set of reliable preceding patterns, the preceding instance reliability r_p is calculated by Equation (5) using P_p instead of P, i.e.,

$$r_p(i) = \frac{1}{|P_p|} \sum_{p \in P_p} \frac{pmi(i,p)}{\max_{pmi}} \cdot r_\pi(p), \qquad (7)$$

The succeeding instance reliability r_s is defined similarly, by using P_s, the set of reliable succeeding patterns, instead of P. Finally, these two reliability values are combined using the generalized mean:

$$r_\iota(i) = \sqrt[m]{\frac{1}{2}\left(r_p^m(i) + r_s^m(i)\right)}, \qquad (8)$$

where the parameter m can be adjusted to flexibly control the strength of this constraint — when $m = 1$, the mean equals arithmetic mean, and r_ι will be large if *either* of r_p or r_s is large, which is essentially the same as the normal instance reliability without this constraint. On the other hand, when $m \to 0$ it approximates geometric mean, and r_ι will be large only if *both* of r_p and r_s are large, making the "sandwich" constraint acute. In the experiment, we set $m = 0.1$, and the result shows this constraint greatly helps to assume the precise term boundaries as well as to improve the extracted instance quality.

3.3 Ambiguous Patterns and Instances

Because of the character n-gram based modeling of this algorithm, the negative effect of generic or ambiguous patterns is even more serious. Although the former two algorithms define ambiguous patterns based on the relative number of instances which the pattern induces, in *Monaka* the number of induced instance is even more unpredictable and a clear threshold is difficult to set. Therefore, we adopted a simpler strategy instead and simply discarded 10 most ambiguous patterns after the pattern selection step. The ambiguity of a pattern is defined as the number of instance types co-occurring with the pattern. We confirmed by a preliminary experiment that this ambiguous pattern elimination increases the precision of the extracted instances, especially at the early stages of bootstrapping.

We took a different approach to ambiguous instance filtering as well, based on the assumption that ambiguous instances are generic and expected to appear in many statutes. Since our corpus consists of 228 statutes as described in Section 4.1, by considering each statute as a document we can define the instance ambiguity as the document frequency (DF) value of that instance. We simply discarded instances which appear more than 70% of the 228 statutes after the instance extraction step. In doing this, we take the risk of increasing false negatives, i.e, deleting frequent but important dictionary term candidates, but such frequent terms can be easily found, even without using this algorithm, and thus they can be safely disregarded. Furthermore, only 3 instances which occur more that 70% of the 228 statutes are found in the answer set of the 1,225 defined terms. This suggests that the risk of false negatives is marginal.

4 Experiments

Now we describe the experimental settings and the results of automatic dictionary term extraction in this section.

4.1 Experimental Settings

Corpus and preprocessing: We used 228 Japanese acts[4] which are included in the governmental translation project described in Section 1 as the corpus. Article, paragraph, and item numbers at the beginning of every line, as well as their trailing whitespaces, were removed and replaced with a special marker which signifies the beginning of a line. On the other hand, parentheses were left intact, because they turned out to be important clues to detect dictionary term candidates.

Seed instances: We firstly extracted defined terms which appeared in the corpus and used them as the answer set. To extract defined terms, we made use of the patterns shown in **Ex. 1** and **2**, and the paragraphs which matched regular expression patterns:

/この法律において、?「.*」とは/

and

/この法律で、?「.*」とは/,

as well as the paragraphs which define multiple terms by the statement

"この法律において、次の各号に掲げる用語の意義は..."
("In this Act, the meanings of the terms listed in the following items...")

were collected. The defined terms in these paragraphs and items were then extracted by using regular expressions, and this process yielded a total of 1,225 unique terms, from which 100 seed instances were randomly chosen. At every iteration of bootstrapping, 100 new instances were cumulatively acquired, and these newly acquired ones were combined with the input instances of the current iteration and passed to the next one.

Other parameters: The number of patterns extracted is initially set to 100, and the number is incremented by 10 per each iteration.

4.2 Evaluation

Since defining "importance" of words is not a simple matter and completely subjective evaluation of extracted instances is also too costly, we conducted two tasks which use two separate answer sets, or *gold standard* sets, to evaluate the effectiveness of the current algorithm. The first one is the closed, *defined term reproducibility test*, where the defined terms collected as described in the previous section were used as the gold standard set, and how the algorithm can reproduce the whole answer set was evaluated based on the precision/recall measures. The second one is the open, *SBD coverage test*, where all the dictionary entries of SBD which appeared at least once in the corpus were used as the answer set. The number of such SBD entries was 3,510. Note that this number is larger

---

[4] http://www.cas.go.jp/jp/seisaku/hourei/070323gojuu.pdf

Table 1. Result of the defined term reproducibility test

Iter.	Monaka–BAC		Monaka+BAC	
	Num. of instances (correct / total)	Precision / Recall	Num. of instances (correct / total)	Precision / Recall
0	100 / 100	100.0% / 8.2%	100 / 100	100.0% / 8.2%
1	118 / 200	59.0% / 9.6%	136 / 200	68.0% / 11.1%
2	138 / 300	46.0% / 11.3%	165 / 300	55.0% / 13.5%
3	161 / 400	40.3% / 13.1%	198 / 400	49.5% / 16.2%
4	178 / 500	35.6% / 14.5%	216 / 500	43.2% / 17.6%
5	202 / 600	33.7% / 16.5%	236 / 600	39.3% / 19.3%
6	211 / 700	30.1% / 17.2%	250 / 700	35.7% / 20.4%
7	225 / 800	28.1% / 18.4%	268 / 800	33.5% / 21.9%
8	236 / 900	26.2% / 19.3%	284 / 900	31.6% / 23.2%
9	248 / 1,000	24.8% / 20.2%	305 / 1,000	30.5% / 24.9%
10	260 / 1,100	23.6% / 21.2%	321 / 1,100	29.2% / 26.2%

than the number of total entries, i.e., 3,315, contained in the SBD mentioned in Section 1. This is because in this experiment we used a modified version of SBD — a computer-friendly version[5] where single entries are expanded so that the dictionary contains variations such as verb forms of nouns as different entries. As such, the upper bound of the recall in the SBD coverage test is lower than 100%, because it is impossible for this algorithm to extract the expanded verb forms and some other variations contained in this modified dictionary.

In matching terms between the extract set and the answer set, we simply ignored the suffix "等" ("etc.") to avoid unwanted mismatches. In both tasks, we removed the definition sentences from which defined words were extracted — if not, such patterns as **Ex. 1** and **2** would be immediately detected as reliable patterns and the defined terms would be easily reproduced, which might lead to unrealistic and trivial experimental results.

4.3 Results

Starting from 100 seeds, we iterated the algorithm 10 times, and extracted a total of 1,100 instances. Table 1 shows the result of the defined term reproducibility test, comparing the performance of the algorithm without using the bidirectional adjacency constraint (*Monaka*–BAC) and with using BAC (*Monaka*+BAC). The former setting is essentially the same as the conventional methods introduced in Section 1. The result shows that, after the 10th iteration, *Monaka*+BAC extracted almost one fourth of the defined terms with the precision of 29.2%.

While the precision of extracted terms seems quite low at first glance, the actually extracted instances, which are listed in Table 2, look quite promising. We notice that most of the newly found non-defined terms (without check marks

---

[5] http://www.kl.i.is.nagoya-u.ac.jp/told/

Table 2. Examples of the extracted instances

Monaka−BAC	DT	SBD	Monaka+BAC	DT	SBD
銀行等 (bank etc.)	✓		銀行等 (bank etc.)	✓	
*証券会 (securities company)			特定目的信託 (special purpose trust)	✓	
設立事業所 ((fund-) established place of business)			登記 (registration)		✓
石油 (oil)			紛争 (dispute)		✓
同項第二号 (item (ii) of the same paragraph)			地域 (area)		✓
*再生債務者の (rehabilitation debtor)			破産手続 (bankruptcy proceedings)	✓	
*処分に (deposition)			都市 (city)		
販売 (sale)		✓	外国 (foreign state)		✓
再生計画 (rehabilitation plan)	✓		道路 (road)	✓	✓
廃業 (disposal)		✓	港務局 (port bureau)		
*製造時等 (manufacturing (inspection))			労働者 (worker)	✓	✓
*不動 (real (estate))			建設業 (construction industry)	✓	✓
建設 (construction)		✓	条例 (ordinance)		✓
第一種 (Type I)			証券 (securities)		✓
行う業務 (business)			清算人 (liquidator)		✓
*高年 (middle-aged)			株式等 (shares of stock, etc.)	✓	✓
*株式交換完全子 (wholly-owned subsidiary through share exchange)			介護老人保健施設 (long-term care health facility for the elderly)	✓	
協会 (association)			商品市場 (commodity market)	✓	
*地域密 (community-based)			信託契約 (trust contract)		
土地売買等の契約 (contract on land sales, etc.)			請求人 (demandant)		✓

DT: defined term, SBD: SBD term, * incorrectly segmented term

Table 3. Result of the SBD coverage test

Iter.	Monaka−BAC		Monaka+BAC	
	Num. of instances (correct / total)	Precision / Coverage	Num. of instances (correct / total)	Precision / Coverage
0	19 / 100	19.0% / 0.5%	19 / 100	19.0% / 0.5%
1	51 / 200	25.5% / 1.5%	71 / 200	35.5% / 2.0%
2	87 / 300	29.0% / 2.5%	120 / 300	40.0% / 3.4%
3	128 / 400	32.0% / 3.6%	171 / 400	42.8% / 4.9%
4	148 / 500	29.6% / 4.2%	211 / 500	42.2% / 6.0%
5	180 / 600	30.0% / 5.1%	234 / 600	39.0% / 6.7%
6	198 / 700	28.3% / 5.6%	278 / 700	39.7% / 7.9%
7	220 / 800	27.5% / 6.3%	321 / 800	40.1% / 9.1%
8	242 / 900	26.9% / 6.9%	351 / 900	39.0% / 10.0%
9	272 / 1,000	27.2% / 7.7%	384 / 1,000	38.4% / 10.9%
10	294 / 1,100	26.7% / 8.4%	415 / 1,100	37.7% / 11.8%

in the DT row) can be considered important enough to be included in the dictionary. They include some general words, e.g., bank, area, and city, but these words can be given special meanings in legal text and it is therefore desirable to extract such words as dictionary term candidates as well.

Furthermore, although this algorithm relies only on character n-grams, all the listed instances are properly segmented. This is because the "sandwich" effect of BAC ensured that for incorrectly segmented words, at least one of the preceding instance reliability r_p or the succeeding instance reliability r_s was low, and it prevented incorrectly segmented terms from being ranked higher. Although we did not investigate the effect of m used for the generalized mean of BAC, it is expected that if we used a lower value for m, it would increase the number of incorrectly segmented words appearing in the results.

Table 3 shows the similar result for the SBD coverage test. It suggests that almost a quarter of the defined terms and about 10% of the SBD terms were reproduced without depending on the definition sentences (recall that they were removed from the corpus beforehand). The precision and recall/coverage values may look quite low, but these gold standard sets do not include general but important words as described above, and the actual performance of this algorithm is higher than the evaluation metrics suggest. This result strongly supports the effectiveness of our algorithm.

In contrast, the performance of *Monaka*−BAC quickly decreased as the iterations proceeded, and the final precision and recall shown in Table 1 were lower than that of *Monaka*+BAC by approx. 5%. There can be seen many incorrectly segmented instances in the list of Table 2, which we suppose are disastrous in this task. Once we have such incorrectly segmented instances at early stages of iteration, they naturally induce more unreliable and incorrect patterns and would aggravate the quality of subsequently extracted instances in a spiral matter.

Some examples of reliable patterns extracted after the pattern selection step are shown in Table 4, and a large portion of other reliable patterns were their

Table 4. Examples of the extracted reliable patterns

Preceding patterns	Succeeding patterns
(以下「# ((hereinafter referred to as #)	#（以下 (# (hereinafter))
(...) 規定により# (# pursuant to ...)	#及び (# and)
その他の# (other #)	#その他の (# and other)
当該# (the #, that #)	#」という。 (referred to as #)
(...) において、# (in ..., #)	#に係る (concerning #)
における# (with respect to #)	#に関する (concerning #)
に係る# (# concerning)	#については、 (with regard to #)
に規定する# (# provided for in)	#又は (# or)
(...) による# (# by ...)	#若しくは (# or)
若しくは# (or #)	#をいう。 (means #)

variations, i.e, substrings and superstrings. Notice that many of these patterns are quite generic by themselves, and a single pattern may induce too many incorrect instances when applied alone. In other words, two or more of these patterns have to be applied at the same time, along with an appropriate constraint, to ensure proper segmentation. This result, along with the comparison experiment results, shows that the reliability measure introduced in Section 2.1 was considerably effective to rank reliable patterns/instances and the bidirectional adjacency constraint proposed in this paper is almost essential for automatically extracting terms from unsegmented text.

5 Conclusion

In this paper, we proposed a bootstrapping-based lexical knowledge acquisition algorithm *Monaka* to automatically extract dictionary term candidates from unsegmented Japanese legal text. The algorithm adopted simple character n-gram based instance/pattern induction and introduced the bidirectional adjacency constraint to accurately estimate the segmentation boundaries. Although comprehensive evaluation based on human judgment is required as the future work, the experimental results based on the defined term reproducibility and the SBD coverage showed that this algorithm was able to extract many correctly segmented and important dictionary terms. We believe that the algorithm can work for lexical knowledge acquisition from any unsegmented text in other domains and languages, although its behavior, especially the effect of topic drift, is yet to be examined in the future.

There have been several other methods proposed for important term extraction or named entity recognition, which do not rely on bootstrapping [4, 11, 14]. Comparison of the proposed method in this paper and these methods is necessary as a future task.

The contribution of this study is that, it paved the way for lexical knowledge acquisition from unsegmented languages such as Chinese and Japanese. It is also effective for the languages for which language resources and/or tools are still scarce. The countries where such languages are mainly used express high demands to translate their own statutes into English, where English bilingual dictionaries are essential. While advanced NLP tools such as morphological analyzers and parsers are still unavailable for some of these languages, the proposed algorithm can still work quite favorably and support the task.

We attribute the success of this algorithm to the characteristics of Japanese statutes, where legal sentences are written in highly fixed, conventional expressions in a consistent manner, and this makes the pattern-based lexical acquisition algorithm suitable for the task. This characteristics implies that other statistical NLP techniques may also be effective for legal information processing, and their successful results are anticipated in the future.

References

1. Hearst, M.A.: Automatic Acquisition of Hyponyms from Large Text Corpora. In: Proc. of COLING 1992, pp. 539–545 (1992)
2. Komachi, M., Suzuki, H.: Minimally Supervised Learning of Semantic Knowledge from Query Logs. In: Proc. of IJCNLP 2008, pp. 358–365 (2008)
3. Lin, D., Zhao, S., Qin, L., Zhou, M.: Identifying Synonyms among Distributionally Similar Words. In: Proc. of IJCAI 2003, pp. 1492–1493 (2003)
4. Nakano, K., Hirai, U.: Japanese Named Entity Extraction with Bunsetsu Features. Transactions of Information Processing Society of Japan 45(3), 934–941 (2004)
5. Och, F.J., Ney, H.: Improved Statistical Alignment Models. In: Proc. of ACL 2000, pp. 440–447 (2000)
6. Pantel, P., Pennacchiotti, M.: Espresso: Leveraging Generic Patterns for Automatically Harvesting Semantic Relations. In: Proc. of ACL 2006, pp. 113–120 (2006)
7. Pantel, P., Ravichandran, D.: Automatically labeling semantic classes. In: Proc. of HLT/NAACL 2004, pp. 321–328 (2004)
8. Riloff, E., Jones, R.: Learning Dictionaries for Information Extraction by Multi-Level Bootstrapping. In: Proc. of AAAI 1999, pp. 474–479 (1999)

9. Study Council for Promoting Translation of Japanese Laws and Regulations into Foreign Languages: Final Report (2006), http://www.cas.go.jp/jp/seisaku/hourei/report.pdf
10. Study Council for Promoting Translation of Japanese Laws and Regulations into Foreign Languages: Standard Bilingual Dictionary (2006), http://www.cas.go.jp/jp/seisaku/hourei/dictionary.pdf
11. Takeda, Y., Umemura, K.: Selecting Indexing Strings Using Adaptation. In: Proceedings of ACM SIGIR 2002, pp. 427–428 (2002)
12. Thelen, M., Riloff, E.: A Bootstrapping Method for Learning Semantic Lexicons using Extraction Pattern Contexts. In: Proceedings of EMNLP 2002, pp. 214–221 (2002)
13. Toyama, K., Ogawa, Y., Imai, K., Matsuura, Y.: Application of Word Alignment for Supporting Translation of Japanese Statutes into English. In: Legal Knowledge and Information Systems, JURIX 2006: The 19th Annual Conference, pp. 141–150. IOS Press, Amsterdam (2006)
14. Yumoto, H., Mori, T., Nakagawa, H.: Term Extraction Based on Occurrence and Concatenation Frequency. In: IPSJ SIG Notes, 2001-NL-145, pp. 111–118 (2001)

Computational Dialectics Based on Specialization and Generalization – A New Reasoning Method for Conflict Resolution

Hiroyuki Kido and Masahito Kurihara

Graduate School of Information and Science, Hokkaido University

Abstract. The purpose of this paper is two-fold. Firstly, to formalize one aspect of dialectical thought, i.e., our way of thinking about conflict resolution. Secondly, to show that this way of thinking allows agents to resolve a conflict by argumentation. To this end, we propose a dialectical reasoning method by means of specialization and generalization defined by a logical implication. This method has three features. First, it does not limit its premises to logical contradictions in accordance with philosophical knowledge that an antithesis is not adequately expressed as logical negation of a thesis. Second, it embraces our actual and familiar thoughts exemplified in this paper. Third, it has the ability to draw conclusions that are not just logical deductions from its premises. Further, by applying it to argumentation, we show that it allows agents to resolve a conflict by drawing an alternative solution not deduced from any consistent subset of the union of all agents' knowledge base. In other words, it allows agents to develop argumentation dialogically in terms of producing an alternative solution that is not obtained at the beginning of argumentation.

1 Introduction

Argumentation has its roots in nonmonotonic reasonings of computer science. However, these types of argument, e.g., deduction, induction, abduction, and analogy, and the role of nonmonotonicity in reasonings are different in the case of many other nonmonotonic reasonings and argumentation. The default reasoning which is the most typical approach to realize nonmonotonic reasoning deals only with deductive arguments. Further, it attempts to maintain a consistent source of information by using exceptional rules, i.e., the role of nonmonotonicity in reasoning is conflict avoidance. On the other hand, argumentation deals not only with deductive arguments but also inductive, analogical, and abductive reasonings. Further, it attempts to resolve any conflicts caused by reasoning from subjective, inconsistent, uncertain, imperfect, decentralized, and open sources of information, i.e., the role of nonmonotonicity in reasoning is conflict resolution. Therefore, unlike many other nonmonotonic reasoning approaches, methods to resolve the inevitable contradictions and conflicts are essential requirements of argumentation. In particular, when the purpose of argumentation is to achieve social decision making or consensus building, not only competition, but also collaboration, concession, compromise, etc., are essential factors. Hence, in computer science, dialectics has become the focus of attention as guidelines in recent times. This led to the study of computational dialectics, which attempts to analyze dialectics computationally, in computer science [1,2,3].

In the past, Routley and Meyer formalized dialectical logic DL and DM aiming to transform dialectics into a formal logic [5]. Mitroff and Mason constructed a model of dialectical reasoning based on a plausibility measure and Toulmin's model of an argument [2]. Recently, from the view of computer science, Sawamura realized concession and compromise on dialectical logics DL and DM by introducing seven dialectical inference rules [1]. We think, however, these existing studies have three issues with respect to dialectics. First, in [1,2,5], the proposed reasoning methods limit their premises to logical contradictions owing to implicitly, assuming that an antithesis is adequately expressed as a logical negation of a thesis. However, there is a philosophical opinion opposed to the interpretation of the antithesis [3]. Second, in [2,5], the authors showed no concrete example of thought they tried to model. Third, in [1], the dialectical inference rules 1- 6 discussed later are weak in the sense that they do not have the ability to draw new propositions not appearing in the original premise.

In consideration of these issues, we formalize one aspect of dialectical thought as a reasoning method by means of specialization and generalization defined by a logical implication. It has three features. First, it does not limit its premises to logical contradictions in accordance with philosophical knowledge that dialectical negation is an antithesis (counterplan), i.e., an alternative solution not adequately expressed as a logical negation of a thesis. Second, it embraces our actual and familiar thoughts exemplified in this paper. Third, it has the ability to draw conclusions that are not just logical deductions from its premise. Further, by applying it to argumentation, we show that it allows agents to resolve a conflict through drawing an alternative solution not deduced from any consistent subset of the union of all agents' knowledge base. In other words, it allows agents to develop argumentation dialogically in terms of producing an alternative solution that is not obtained at the beginning of argumentation.

Section 2 briefly discusses dialectics and the existing studies of computational dialectics. In section 3, we give the algorithm for dialectical reasoning and its strategies. In section 4, we define collaboration, concession, and compromise. In section 5, we introduce an argumentation model basically defined in [9]. In section 6, we provide an application of conflict resolution by applying dialectical reasoning in argumentation. In section 7, we contrast the proposed method with existing computational dialectics. In section 8, the conclusion is given.

2 Dialectics

2.1 What Is Dialectics?

Etymologically speaking, dialectics means 'dialogue', 'skills of dialogue', etc. Psychologist Richard interpreted dialectics as having the meaning of focusing on contradictions and how to resolve them, to transcend them, or to find the truth in both. Furthermore, in his studies, he contrasted a logical approach with the dialectical approach for conflicting propositions: The logical approach would seem to require rejecting one of the propositions in favor of the other in order to avoid possible contradiction. The dialectical approach would favor finding some truth in both, in a search for the Middle Way [4]. From this standpoint, we think our thought called collaboration, concession, and compromise are one of the dialectical approaches for this conflict. At the risk of doing damage to the spirit of dialecticism, we generally call these dialectical thoughts. In addition, from this standpoint we provide a typical examples of dialectical thinking from every day life.

Example 1 (purchase of a camera)

- A_1: I want to buy a compact and light camera 'a.'
- A_2: We can not buy it, because it is out of stock.
- A_2: I want to buy a high-resolution camera 'b' with a long battery life.
- A_1: No, I do not want to buy it, because it is beyond my budget.
- A_1: Then let us buy a user-friendly camera 'c' with a long battery life.

This is because A_1 knows it is user-friendly if it is compact and light.

Example 2 (menu decision)

- A_1: I want to eat a curry rice 'a.'
- A_2: No, I do not want to eat it.
- A_2: I want to eat Chinese noodles 'b.'
- A_1: No, I do not want to eat it.
- A_1: Then let us eat curry noodles 'c.'

This is because A_1 knows curry rice is a curry, Chinese noodles are noodles, and curry noodles are a curry and noodles.

2.2 Existing Studies on Computational Dialectics

Routley and Meyer formalized dialectical logic DL and DM with the aim to transform dialectics into formal logic [5]. Mitroff and Mason constructed a model of dialectical reasoning based on a plausibility measure and Toulmin's developed a model of an argument [2]. It computes all maximal consistent subsets of an inconsistent set of formulae constituting the argument, and applies it based on the dialectical plausibility measure assigned to each. Recently, from the view of computer science, Sawamura identified dialectics as a new object of study that is different from other studies of reasoning such as deduction, induction, abduction, and analogy. He realized concession and compromise on DL and DM[1] as formal logic by introducing the dialectical inference rules as follows. They rationally enable to draw a satisfiable conclusion from inconsistent premises.

---
[1] Refer to [5] for detailed definitions of DL and DM.

1. $A, \neg A \Rightarrow A$
2. $A, \neg A \Rightarrow \neg A$
3. $A \wedge B, \neg B \Rightarrow A$
4. $A \wedge B, \neg B \Rightarrow B$
5. $A \wedge B, \neg B \Rightarrow A \wedge \neg B$
6. $A \wedge \neg B, \neg A \wedge B \Rightarrow A \wedge B$
7. $A(a), \neg A(a) \Rightarrow A(a) \wedge \neg A(b)$

However, it is thought that these existing studies have three issues with respect to dialectics. First, in [1,2,5], the proposed reasoning methods limit their premises to logical contradiction owing to implicitly assuming that an antithesis is logical negation as a thesis. However, there is a philosophical opinion opposed to the interpretation of an antithesis as a logical negation as a thesis: This is severely hampered by the interpretation of the antithesis (counterplan) as logical negation of a thesis, because this prevents a full positive statement of the antithesis and provides no place for the rationale of the antithesis [3]. Second, in [2,5], the authors showed no concrete example of thought they tried to model. Third, in [1], the dialectical inference rules 1- 6 are weak in the sense that they do not have the ability to draw new propositions not appearing in the original premise.

In consideration of these issues, we formalize one aspect of dialectical thought as a reasoning method by means of specialization and generalization defined by a logical implication. It has three features. First, it does not limit its premises to logical contradiction in accordance with philosophical knowledge that a dialectical negation is an antithesis (counterplan), i.e., an alternative solution is not adequately expressed as logical negation as a thesis. Second, it embraces our actual and familiar thoughts exemplified in this paper. Third, it has the ability to draw conclusions that are not just logical deductions from its premise. Further, by applying it to argumentation, we show that it allows agents to resolve conflicts through drawing alternative solutions not deduced from any consistent subset of the union of all agents' knowledge base. In other words, it allows agents to develop argumentation dialogically in terms of producing alternative solutions that are not obtained at the beginning of argumentation.

3 Reasoning Method

3.1 Algorithm for Dialectics

In this section, we formalize one aspect of dialectical thought by capturing our thought on conflict resolution. First, we show typical examples representing our thought process in conflict resolution.

Example 3 (process of drink decision)

- A_1 : I want to drink a cup of black tea. ($p_1 = drink(a) \wedge blackTea(a)$)
- A_2 : I want to drink a cup of green tea. ($p_2 = drink(b) \wedge greenTea(b)$)
- A_1 : I intend to stand my ground. ($p_3 = p_1$)

- A_2 : Okay, either will be fine. ($p_4 = p_1 \vee p_2$)
- A_1 : Thanks! ($p_5 = p_1$)

Example 4 (process of menu decision)
- A_1 : If it is curry rice then I will eat it. ($p_1 = \forall x.eat(x) \leftarrow curriedRice(x)$)
- A_2 : If it is Chinese noodles then I will eat it. ($p_2 = \forall x.eat(x) \leftarrow chineseNoodle(x)$)
- A_1 : It might be a good idea to eat it if it is a noodles. ($p_3 = p_1 \vee \forall x.eat(x) \leftarrow noodle(x)$)
- A_2 : It also might be a good idea to eat it if it is curry. ($p_4 = p_2 \vee \forall x.eat(x) \leftarrow curry(x)$)
- A_1 : Then let us eat it if it is noodles and curry. ($p_5 = \forall x.eat(x) \leftarrow noodle(x) \wedge curry(x)$)

In example 3 and 4, it should be noted that p_3, p_4 and p_5 are fully implemented only by specialization and generalization defined by a 'logical implication' relation. In addition, the process of calculation fits into our thought process on conflict. Actually, in example 3, p_3 is a specialization of p_1, i.e., $p_1 \models p_3$, p_4 is a specialization of p_2, i.e., $p_2 \models p_4$, and p_5 is generalization of p_3 and p_4, i.e., $p_5 \models p_3$ and $p_5 \models p_4$. In example 4, $p_1 \models p_3$, $p_2 \models p_4$, $\{p_5\} \cup \Delta \models p_3$, and $\{p_5\} \cup \Delta \models p_4$ hold under background knowledge $\Delta = \{curry(x) \leftarrow curryRice(x), noodles(x) \leftarrow chineseNoodles(x)\}$.

Example 3 and 4 do not explain why A_1 and A_2 yield in such a manner. In this paper, we initially focus on only the logical aspect of the process of conflict resolution that is normally influenced by various factors, e.g., emotion of the main parties. We think that the reason and the degree of yielding depend strongly on such factors. Therefore, they are not reflected in the following algorithm. In the next subsection, however, we define reasoning strategies based on the two reasonable assumptions related to these factors to restrict the reasoning. First, we give a reasoning algorithm for dialectics from a logical point of view. The inputs of the algorithm are contingent first-order formulae A and B, and the set of first-order formulae Γ such that both $\{A\} \cup \Gamma$ and $\{B\} \cup \Gamma$ are consistent. The output is a set by first-order formulae C. Algorithm 1 consists of specialization at line 4-5 and generalization at line 9.

Figure 1 represents the logical relation between formulae appearing in the algorithm. The nodes represent the formulae and edges represent logical relation between them. The dialectics follows the arrows.

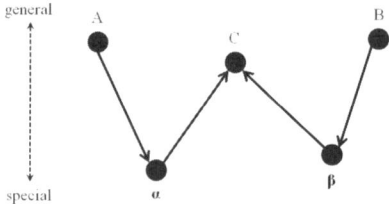

Fig. 1. dialectical reasoning

Algorithm 1. Dialectical Reasoning

1: $\mathcal{C} := \emptyset$
2: $\alpha := null$
3: $\beta := null$
4: computes $\mathcal{A} \subseteq \{\alpha \mid \text{not } \Gamma \models \alpha, \{A\} \cup \Gamma \models \alpha\}$
5: computes $\mathcal{B} \subseteq \{\beta \mid \text{not } \Gamma \models \beta, \{B\} \cup \Gamma \models \beta\}$
6: **for all** (α, β) in $\mathcal{A} \times \mathcal{B}$ **do**
7:    $\mathcal{C}_i := \emptyset$
8:    $C := null$
9:    computes $\mathcal{C}_i \subseteq \{C \mid \{C\} \cup \Gamma \models \alpha, \{C\} \cup \Gamma \models \beta\}$
10:   $\mathcal{C} := \mathcal{C} \cup \mathcal{C}_i$
11: **end for**
12: return $\mathcal{C}$

3.2 Reasoning Strategies

We introduce some strategies of the reasoning defined in the previous subsection. When we face a conflict, we usually try to search for a solution that takes into account our intentions as much as possible and does not take into account unintentional considerations. Further, if agents show willingness to compromise, they meet each other halfway toward each other. We capture these points computationally from the view of the degree and the direction of specialization and generalization.

Specialization. At line 4 and 5 in algorithm 1, agents compute α and β such that $A \models \alpha, \{\alpha\} \cup \Gamma \models \gamma, B \models \beta$, and $\{\beta\} \cup \Gamma \models \gamma$, where γ is the first-order formula representing the greatest lower bound of set $\{A, B\}$. It is $A \vee B$ in the case of first-order logic. These conditions are related to the direction of the specialization. On the other hand, for the degree of specialization, agents compute the specialization of A and B, i.e., α and β, by using downward refinement operator defined in the next subsection that enables the calculation of specialization step by step.

Generalization. At line 9 in algorithm 1, agents compute least upper bound of the set $\{\alpha, \beta\}$. It is $A \wedge B$ in the case of first-order logic. However, it is not necessarily in the case of clausal logic. This condition is related to both the direction and the degree of generalization.

Example 5. In example 3 and 4, every p_3, p_4, and p_5 complies with the strategies in specialization and generalization.

3.3 Algorithms for Specialization and Generalization

Subsequently, in this section, by limiting the target of computing to definite program clauses, we are going to show some concrete algorithms to compute specialization and generalization based on the quasi-order on clauses with background knowledge, i.e., Buntine's generalized subsumption [8], respectively. We are going to build the above strategies into the algorithms based on the results of inductive logic programming.

Let A and α be definite program clauses and Δ be a definite program. Then it is noted that α is a specialization of A relative to Δ under generalized subsumption (denoted by $A \geq_\Delta \alpha$) iff there exists an SLD-deduction of α, with A as top clause and members of Δ as input clauses [8]. Based on this, we provide concrete algorithm computing specialization under generalized subsumption. The inputs of the algorithm are the definite program clause A and the definite program Δ. The output is the definite program $\mathcal{A} \subseteq \{\alpha \mid A \geq_\Delta \alpha\}$.

Algorithm 2. Downward refinement operator

1: $\mathcal{A} := \rho_L(A)$
2: **for all** (A, δ) in $\{A\} \times \Delta$ **do**
3:    computes binary resolvent α of A and δ
4:    **if** α is computable **then**
5:       $\mathcal{A} := \mathcal{A} \cup \{\alpha\}$
6:    **end if**
7: **end for**
8: **return** $\mathcal{A}$

Algorithm 2 is a downward refinement operator for $<\mathcal{C}, \geq_\Delta>$, where $\mathcal{C}$ is a clausal language, such that $\rho(A, \Delta) \subseteq \{\alpha \mid A \geq_\Delta \alpha\}$ for every $A \in \mathcal{C}$. The set of one-step refinements, n-step refinements, and refinements of some A are respective:

- $\rho^1(A, \Delta) = \rho(A, \Delta)$
- $\rho^n(A, \Delta) = \{\alpha \mid \text{there is an } \beta \in \rho^{n-1}(A, \Delta) \text{ such that } \alpha \in \rho(\beta, \Delta)\}, n \geq 2$
- $\rho^*(A, \Delta) = \rho^1(A, \Delta) \cup \rho^2(A, \Delta) \cup \cdots$

ρ_L at line 1 in the above algorithm is also a downward refinement operator for $<\mathcal{C}, \succeq>$, where $\succeq$ is a subsumption relation, that computes the specialization of the clause by applying several different kinds of substitutions or adding new literal to the clause [8]. For every combination $(A, \delta) \in \{A\} \times \Delta$, ρ attempts to compute the binary resolvent α of A and δ, and adds it to the set $\mathcal{A}$ if it is computable. Next, we give the concrete algorithm combining the strategies for specialization. The inputs to the algorithm are definite program clauses A and B, the definite program Δ, and a number of refinements steps n. The output is a definite program $\mathcal{A} \subseteq \{\alpha \mid A \geq_\Delta \alpha\}$. Algorithm 3 uses algorithm 2 along with a number of refinements steps n to restrict the degree of specialization. The algorithm accumulates the program clauses satisfying the strategies in the specialization.

Next we give the concrete algorithm to compute generalization of the set of the specialized program clauses. We compute the least generalization under generalized subsumption (denoted by LGGS) of the set of definite program clauses in accordance with the strategy of generalization. It should be noted that the generalized subsumption can be translated to ordinary subsumption, and the

Algorithm 3. Specialization

1: $\mathcal{A} := \emptyset$
2: **for** $i := 1$ to n **do**
3:   **for all** α in $\rho^i(A, \Delta)$ **do**
4:     **if** $\{\alpha\} \cup \Delta \models A \vee B$ **then**
5:       $\mathcal{A} := \mathcal{A} \cup \{\alpha\}$
6:     **end if**
7:   **end for**
8: **end for**
9: **return** $\mathcal{A}$

LGGS can be computed by constructing a least generalization under the subsumption (denoted by LGS) [8]. In the following algorithm, it is particularity helpful to denote that the positive literal of the clause D by D^+, the set of negative literals of the clause D by D^-, and the set of negations of the formulae in the set M by $\overline{M}$. The inputs of the algorithm are definite program clauses D_1 and D_2 such that they have the same predicate symbol as their head, and the definite program $\mathcal{B}$. The output is the LGGS of $\{D_1, D_2\}$.

Algorithm 4. Generalization

1: computes the skolem substitutions $\sigma_i (i = 1, 2)$ for D_i with respect to $\mathcal{B} \cup \{D_1, D_2\}$
2: computes the least Herbrand models $M_i (i = 1, 2)$ of $\mathcal{B} \cup D_i^- \sigma_i$
3: computes the LGS C of $\{\{D_1^+ \sigma_1\} \cup \overline{M_1}, \{D_2^+ \sigma_2\} \cup \overline{M_2}\}$
4: **return** C

For each $D_i (i = 1, 2)$, algorithm 4 computes the skolem substitution σ_i and the Herbrand model M_i to treat generalized subsumption as subsumption. The algorithm indirectly computes the LGGS of $\{D_1, D_2\}$ based on the LGS of $\{\{D_1^+ \sigma_1\} \cup \overline{M_1}, \{D_2^+ \sigma_2\} \cup \overline{M_2}\}$.

Next example shows the calculation process of algorithm 1 combined with the above algorithms 3 and 4.

Example 6 (dialectical reasoning). Consider the following two clauses C_1 and C_2, and background knowledge $\mathcal{B}$.

$C_1 = buy(x) \vee \neg camera(x) \vee \neg compact(x) \vee \neg light(x)$
$C_2 = buy(x) \vee \neg camera(x) \vee \neg resolution(x, high) \vee \neg battery(x, long)$
$\mathcal{B} = \{userFriendly(x) \leftarrow compact(x) \wedge light(x)\}$

Following D_1 and D_2 are the outputs of algorithm 3 whose inputs are C_1, C_2, $\mathcal{B}$, and 3, for D_1, and C_2, C_1, $\mathcal{B}$, and 2, for D_2, respectively.

$$D_1 = buy(x) \vee \neg camera(x) \vee \neg compact(x) \vee \neg light(x) \vee \neg battery(x, long)$$
$$D_2 = buy(x) \vee \neg camera(x) \vee \neg resolution(x, high) \vee \neg battery(x, long)$$
$$\vee \neg userFriendly(x)$$

D_1 is derived from C_1 by adding the literal $\neg battery(y, z)$ and applying the substitutions $\{y/x\}$ and $\{z/long\}$ to C_1 in accordance with ρ_L.[2] D_2 is derived from C_2 by adding the literal $\neg userFriendly(y)$ and applying the substitution $\{y/x\}$ to C_2. Let us assume $\sigma_1 = \{x/a\}$ and $\sigma_2 = \{x/b\}$ to be Skolem substitutions for D_1 and D_2, respectively. Then

$$M_1 = \{camera(a), compact(a), light(a), battery(a, long), userFriendly(a)\}$$
$$M_2 = \{camera(b), resolution(b, high), battery(b, long), userFriendly(b)\}$$

Following E is an LGS of $\{(\{D_1^+\sigma_1\} \cup \overline{M_1}), (\{D_2^+\sigma_2\} \cup \overline{M_2})\}$, and hence also an LGGS of $\{D_1, D_2\}$. This means E is the output of algorithm 4 whose inputs are D_1, D_2, and $\mathcal{B}$.

$$E = buy(x) \vee \neg camera(x) \vee \neg battery(x, long) \vee \neg userFriendly(x)$$

It is noteworthy that $\{C_1, C_2\} \cup \mathcal{B} \models E$ does not hold true, i.e., algorithm 1 can produce formulae not logically deduced from premise.

4 Semantics

4.1 Collaboration, Concession, and Compromise

The results of the negotiation studies showed relationships among collaboration, concession, compromise, and avoidance or postponement as shown in Figure 2. Each axis represents the degree of consideration of the result. Value 100 means that the result was taken into full account, while a value 0 means that it was not taken into account at all. Based on Figure 2, we define collaboration, concession, and compromise as follows.

Definition 1. *(collaboration, concession, and compromise). Let C be a output of algorithm 1 whose inputs are contingent formulae A and B, and a set of formulae Δ such that both $\{A\} \cup \Delta$ and $\{B\} \cup \Delta$ are consistent.*

- *C is collaboration between A and B iff $\{C\} \cup \Delta \models A$ and $\{C\} \cup \Delta \models B$.*
- *C is concession between A and B (or B and A) iff $\{C\} \cup \Delta \models A$ and not $\{C\} \cup \Delta \models B$.*
- *C is compromise between A and B iff neither $\{C\} \cup \Delta \models A$ nor $\{C\} \cup \Delta \models B$.*

Example 7. In example 3, p_5 is a concession between p_1 and p_2, and, in example 4, p_5 is a compromise between p_1 and p_2. Further, in example 6, E is a compromise between C_1 and C_2.

---

[2] We can not show the detailed definitions of ρ_L due to limitations of space. Refer to [8] for details.

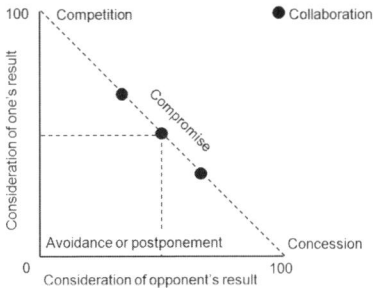

Fig. 2. Competition, collaboration, concession, compromise, and avoidance or postponement [6,7]

5 Argumentation Model

We basically use Prakken and Sartor's argumentation framework [9]. A defeasible rule, or simply rule, is an expression of the form '$r : L_1 \wedge \cdots \wedge L_j \wedge \sim L_{j+1} \wedge \cdots \wedge \sim L_{n-1} \Rightarrow L_n$', where every $L_i (1 \leq i \leq n)$ is an atomic first-order formula or its classical negation [9]. For each $\sim L_i (j+1 \leq i \leq n-1)$ in r, it reads as 'there is no evidence that L' and $\neg L_i$ is called an assumption of r. When no assumption exists in the rule we call it a strict rule and use '$\rightarrow$' for the expression. Further, the conjunction at the left of the arrow is called an antecedent of the rule and the literal at the right of the arrow is called a consequent of the rule. When no antecedent exists in the rule we call it a fact and omit the arrow.

Definition 2. *An argument is a finite sequence $A = [r_1, \cdots, r_n]$ of ground instances of rules such that:*

1. *For every $i (1 \leq i \leq n)$, for every strong literal L_j in the antecedent of r_i there is a $k < i$ such that L_j is the consequent of r_k.*
2. *For every $i (1 \leq i \leq n-1)$, there is a $i < k$ such that the consequent of r_i is the strong literal in the antecedent of r_k.*
3. *No two distinct rules in the sequence have the same consequent.*

The key difference between above definition and Prakken and Sartor's is the addition of condition 2. It ensures that argument is a sequence of the minimum number of rules for deducing consequent of r_n. For any argument $A = [r_1, \cdots, r_n]$, $Conc(A)$ and $Ass(A)$ denote the set of the consequents of rules in A and a set of the assumptions of rules in A, and thus we call them a conclusion of A and an assumption of A, respectively. Further, we call r_n a warrant of A.

Rebutting is a symmetrical relation and undercutting is an unsymmetrical relation on the set of arguments.

Definition 3. *Let A_1 and A_2 be arguments.*

- *A_1 rebuts A_2 iff $L \in Conc(A_1)$ and $\neg L \in Conc(A_2)$*
- *A_1 undercuts A_2 iff $L \in Conc(A_1)$ and $\neg L \in Ass(A_2)$*

If an argument rebuts or undercuts itself we call it incoherent. Based on the rebutting and undercutting, defeat is defined as a relation on the set of arguments.

Definition 4. [9] *Let A_1 and A_2 be two arguments. Then A_1 defeats A_2 iff A_1 is empty and A_2 is incoherent, or else if*

- *A_1 undercuts A_2; or*
- *A_1 rebuts A_2 and A_2 does not undercut A_1.*

We say that A_1 strictly defeats A_2 iff A_1 defeats A_2 and A_2 does not defeat A_1.

Example 8. Let $Arg_1 = [p(a), p(a) \wedge \sim q(a) \Rightarrow r(a)]$ and $Arg_2 = [q(a), q(a) \rightarrow \neg r(a)]$. Then Arg_1 and Arg_2 are arguments and Arg_2 strictly defeats Arg_1.

Definition 5. *Let A be an argument.*

- *A is justified if no argument defeats A or if every argument which defeats A is also strictly defeated.*
- *A is overruled if A is defeated by the justified argument.*
- *A is defensible if A is neither justified nor overruled.*

6 Application in Argumentation-Based Negotiation

We can find solutions related to the issues in argumentation by increasing our understanding of them through discussing opposing viewpoints in the course of argumentation. Such argumentation involves change, revision, or a leap of thinking about our opinions associated with deepening of understanding. The argumentation model in the previous section focuses on not how our opinions can be changed, but what opinions are justified through interaction of the opposing viewpoints. Our dialectical reasoning focuses on the latter and, therefore, can provide guidelines for developing argumentation. In this section, we apply it to conflict resolution as shown in Example 1. We assume following settings for argumentation.

- Every arguing agent i has theory S_i, where it contains only strict rules. The theory is unchanged during argumentation.
- There is an agenda 'Issue' of argumentation at the start of the argumentation. It is represented as the conjunction of literals and is unchanged during argumentation.
- Argumentation terminates when there is no main argument that is not presented before or some main argument is justified.

Argumentation consists of two phases. In phase 1, agents make their main arguments whose conclusions have the ground instance of the issue. In phase 2, they make arguments defeating opponent's arguments. In each phase, they make arguments from their own theory. In phase 1, if agents can make no argument not yet presented, then they create new strict rules by applying the proposed reasoning method and make new main arguments based on it. In the following example, agents apply the proposed reasoning method to the warrants of the mutually defeating arguments. In phase 2, tenability of the main argument is evaluated. This is shown as follows where Arg_i^j denotes argument i made by agent j.

$$Issue = buy(x) \land camera(x)$$
$$S_1 = \{camera(a), camera(c), compact(a), light(a), battery(c, long),$$
$$userFriendly(c), overTheBudget(b),$$
$$compact(x) \land light(x) \land camera(x) \to buy(x),$$
$$overTheBudget(x) \to \neg buy(x),$$
$$compact(x) \land light(x) \to userFriendly(x)\}$$
$$S_2 = \{camera(b), outOfStock(a), battery(b, long), resolution(b, high),$$
$$resolution(x, high) \land battery(x, long) \land camera(x) \to buy(x),$$
$$outOfStock(x) \to \neg buy(x)\}$$

First, agent 1 tries to make a main argument and agent 2 tries to defeat it.

Phase 1: $Arg_1^1 = [compact(a), light(a), camera(a), compact(a) \land light(a) \land camera(a) \to buy(a)]$ (I want to buy 'a.' Since it is a compact and light camera.)

Phase 2: $Arg_2^2 = [outOfStock(a), outOfStock(a) \to \neg buy(a)]$ (It is out of stock.)

Agent 1 can not make the argument defeating Arg_2^2. Next, agent 2 tries to make a main argument and agent 1 tries to defeat it.

Phase 1: $Arg_3^2 = [resolution(b, high), battery(b, long), camera(b), resolution(b, high) \land battery(b, long) \land camera(b) \to buy(b)]$ (Would you like 'b?' Because it is a high-resolution camera with a long battery life.)

Phase 2: $Arg_4^1 = [overTheBudget(b), overTheBudget(b) \to \neg buy(b)]$ (It exceeds the budget.)

Main arguments Arg_1^1 and Arg_3^2 are not justified. Furthermore, both agents can not make another main argument. Then agent 1 can make main argument Arg_5^1 whose warrant is a compromise between the warrants of Arg_1^1 and Arg_3^2.

Phase 1: $Arg_5^1 = [userFriendly(c), battery(c, long), camera(c), userFriendly(c) \land battery(c, long) \land camera(c) \to buy(c)]$ (I will then buy 'c.' Since this is a user-friendly camera with a long battery life.)

Agent 2 can not make the argument defeating Arg_5^1. Therefore, it is justified. Note that any argument from $S_1 \cup S_2$ can not have $buy(c)$ in its conclusion. In other words agents can develop argumentation dialogically by producing an alternative solution that is not drawn at the beginning of the argumentation.

7 Discussion

In this section, we contrast the proposed reasoning method with existing computational dialectics. The dialectical reasonings proposed in [1,2] adopted logical contradiction as the premises of the reasoning. In contrast, our method does not limit its premises to logical contradiction. Therefore, not only logical contradiction, but also conflicts or differences caused by the existence of alternative solutions can be the object of computing. Further, algorithm 1 has the ability to draw propositions derived by applying dialectical inference rules 1-7 in [1]. In addition, our method can draw conclusions which are not derived from them. Example 6 is one such example.

In section 4, we define concession, compromise, and cooperation. Our definitions are contrast to the following definition.

Definition 6. [1] *(Compromise/Aufheben). Given two conflicting propositions, A and B, a proposition C is said to be a higher-order agreement (Aufheben) lifted up from A and B or simply a compromise if (i) neither $\vdash A \rightarrow C$ nor $\vdash B \rightarrow C$, and (ii) C shares some atomic propositions with A or B.*

Definition 7. [1] *(Concession/weaker Aufheben). Given two conflicting propositions, A and B, a proposition C is said to be a higher-order agreement (weaker Aufheben) lifted up from A and B or simply a concession if (i) it is not the case $\vdash A \rightarrow C$ and it is the case that $\vdash B \rightarrow C$, or it is the case that $\vdash A \rightarrow C$ and it is not the case that $\vdash B \rightarrow C$, and (ii) C shares some atomic propositions with A or B.*

The condition (i) in definition 6 means that compromise C is not logically deduced from either A and B, and semantically, it means that compromise is not logically of less value than its premise. On the other hand, definition 1 means that compromise C does not imply both A and B with respect to background knowledge Δ, i.e., means that compromise is not logically of greater value than its premise. This difference is due to the alignment of Figure 2 and, similarly, it can be seen in the definition of concession.

8 Conclusion

We formalized one aspect of dialectical thought as a reasoning method based on specialization and generalization defined by a logical implication. It has three features: First, it does not limit its premise to logical contradiction. It targets any contingent formulae based on the understanding that an antithesis encompasses conflicts and differences not adequately expressed as a logical negation. Second, it embraces our actual and familiar thoughts exemplified in this paper. We showed concrete thought seen in electronic commerce. Third, it has the ability to draw conclusions that are not just logical deduction from its premise. Further, by applying this reasoning method to argumentation, we show that it allows agents to resolve a conflict through drawing an alternative solution not deduced from any consistent subset of the union of all agents' knowledge base. In other words, it allows agents to develop argumentation dialogically in terms of producing an alternative solution that are not obtained at the beginning of argumentation.

References

1. Sawamura, H., Yamashita, M., Umeda, Y.: Applying dialectic agents to argumentation in e-commerce. Electronic Commerce Research 3(3-4), 297–313 (2003)
2. Mitroff, I.I., Mason, R.O.: On the structure of dialectical reasoning in the social and policy sciences. Theory and Decision 14(4), 331–350 (1982)
3. Sabre, R.M.: An alternative logical framework for dialectical reasoning in the social and policy sciences. Theory and Decision 30(3), 187–211 (1991)
4. Nisbett, R.E.: The Geography of thought: How Asians and Westerners Think Differently..and Why. Free Press (2003)
5. Routley, R., Meyer, R.K.: Dialectical logic, classical logic, and the consistency of the world. Studies in East European Thought 16(1-2), 1–25 (1976)
6. Dean, G.P., Jeffrey, Z.R.: Social Conflict: Escalation, Stalemate and Settlement. Random House (1986)
7. Nozawa, S.: Negotiation study for conflict resolution. PHP Laboratory (2004) (in Japanese)
8. Nienhuys-Cheng, S.H., de Wolf, R.: Foundation of Inductive Logic Programming. Springer, Heidelberg (1997)
9. Prakken, H., Sartor, G.: Argument-based extended logic programming with defeasible priorities. Applied Non-Classical Logics 7(1), 25–75 (1997)

Treatment of Legal Sentences Including Itemized and Referential Expressions – Towards Translation into Logical Forms

Yusuke Kimura, Makoto Nakamura, and Akira Shimazu

School of Information Science
Japan Advanced Institute of Science and Technology
1-1, Asahidai, Nomi, Ishikawa, 923-1292, Japan
{mnakamur,shimazu}@jaist.ac.jp

Abstract. This paper proposes a framework for analyzing legal sentences including itemized or referential expressions. Thus far, we have developed a system for translating legal documents into logical formulae. Although our system basically converts words and phrases in a target sentence into predicates in a logical formula, it generates some useless predicates for itemized and referential expressions. We propose a front end system which substitutes corresponding referent phrases for these expressions. Thus, the proposed system generates a meaningful text with high readability, which can be input into our translation system. We examine our system with actual data of legal documents. As a result, the system was 73.1% accurate in terms of removing itemized expressions in a closed test, and 51.4% accurate in an open test.

1 Introduction

A new research field called *Legal Engineering* was proposed in the 21st Century COE Program, Verifiable and Evolvable e-Society [1,2,3]. Legal Engineering serves for computer-aided examination and verification of whether a law has been established appropriately according to its purpose, whether there are logical contradictions or problems in the document per se, whether the law is consistent with related laws, and whether its revisions have been modified, added, and deleted consistently. One approach to verifying law sentences is to convert law sentences into logical or formal expressions and to verify them based on inference [4].

This paper reports our ongoing research effort to build up a system for automatically converting legal documents into logical forms. The system analyzes law sentences, determines logical structures, and then generates logical expressions. Thus far, we have shown our system provides high accuracy in terms of generating logical predicates corresponding to words and their semantic relations [5]. However, some predicates generated concerned with itemization and reference were meaningless, because predicates converted from words and phrases, such as "the items below," "Article 5," and so on are not intrinsic to a logical representation of the sentence. These words should be replaced with appropriate phrases before the process of translation. Accordingly, our purpose in this paper is to propose a method to rewrite legal sentences including itemization or reference into an independent, plain sentence. We consider that this system is useful not only for the front end processor of our main system for translating legal sentences into logical forms, but also for assistance for reading legal documents.

In this paper, we introduce our current system and its problems in Section 2. In Section 3 we show analysis of law sentences including itemization or reference, and we propose a method to rewrite the law sentences into plain sentences in Section 4. We also examine our new method and report its results in Section 5. Finally, we conclude and describe our future work in Section 6.

2 The Current System and Problems

In this section, we describe our current system for translating legal documents into logical forms, and its problems. We call our system WILDCATS[1].

2.1 Work Related to Wildcats

Acquisition of knowledge bases by automatically reading natural language texts has widely been studied. Because the definition of semantic representation differs depending on what the language processing systems deal with, a few systems try to generate logical formulae based on first order predicate logic [6]. A study of knowledge acquisition by Mulkar et al. [7,8] is one of those systems. They extracted well-defined logical formulae from textbooks of biology and chemistry. As a result, their model succeeded in solving some high school AP exam questions. Legal documents are different from the textbooks in that they are described with characteristic expressions in order to avoid ambiguous description. Therefore, we take into account analysis of the expressions based on the linguistic investigation.

In most cases, a law sentence in Japanese Law consists of a law requisite part and a law effectuation part, which designate its legal logical structure [9,10]. Structure of a sentence in terms of these parts is shown in Fig. 1. The law requisite part is further divided into a subject part and a condition part, and the law effectuation part is divided into an object, content, and provision part.

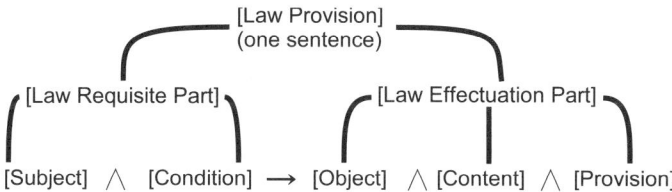

Fig. 1. Structure of requisition and effectuation [9]

---

[1] WILDCATS is an abbreviation of " 'Wildcats' Is a Legal Domain Controller As a Translation System."

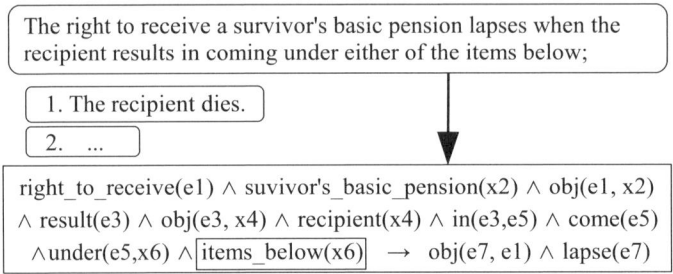

Fig. 2. Converting a law sentence including a reference phrase

Dividing a sentence into these two parts in the pre-processing stage makes the main procedure more efficient and accurate. Nagai et al. [10] proposed an acquisition model for this structure from Japanese law sentences. Dealing with strict linguistic constraints of law sentences, their model succeeded in acquiring the structures at fairly high accuracy using a simple method, which specifies the surface forms of law sentences. Our approach is different from theirs in that we consider some semantic analyses in order to represent logical formulae.

2.2 Wildcats

Here, we explain an outline of our current system. The following list is the procedure for one sentence. We repeat it when we process a set of sentences.

1. Analyzing morphology by JUMAN [11] and parsing a target sentence by KNP [12].
2. Splitting the sentence based on the characteristic structure of a law sentence.
3. Assignment of modal operators with the cue of auxiliary verbs.
4. Making one paraphrase of multiple similar expressions for unified expression.
5. Analyzing clauses and noun phrases using a case frame dictionary.
6. Assigning variables and logical predicates. We assign verb phrases and *sahen*-nouns[2] to a logical predicate and an event variable, e_i, and other content words to x_j, which represents an argument of a logical predicate.
7. Building a logical formula based on fragments of logical connectives, modal operators, and predicates.

The procedure is roughly divided into two parts. One is to make the outside frame of the logical form (Step 1 to 3 and 7), which corresponds to the legal logical structure shown in Fig. 1. The other (Step 4 to 6) is for the inside frame. We assign noun phrases to bound variables and predicates using a case frame dictionary. We show an example of input and output in Fig. 2.

2.3 Problems of Wildcats

When our system converts a law sentence including referential phrases, they are not interpreted correctly. For example, in Fig. 2, the enclosed predicate

---
[2] A *sahen*-noun is a noun which can become a verb with the suffix *-suru*.

"items_below(x6)" is useless. This is because the generated predicates lack information which must be referred. These phrases should be replaced with appropriate phrases in the items before the process of translation into logical forms. Therefore, substituting corresponding referent phrases for these expressions appropriately, our proposed system in this paper generates a meaningful text with high readability, and then the generated text can be input to the translation system. For example, the system should process the following instead of the input sentences in Fig. 2; "The right to receive a survivor's basic pension lapses when the recipient dies."

We have found other kinds of related problems such as treatment of tables in National Pension Law. However, the scope of the study in this paper is restricted to itemized and referential expressions. Therefore, in the following sections we show analysis of law sentences and explain our methodology, which is based on the previous study by Ogawa et al. [13], who proposed a method for rewriting texts using regular expressions in order to consolidate legal sentences and amendment sentences.

3 Analysis of Law Sentences

In this section, we analyze sentences in National Pension Law, which is often picked up in the field of Legal Engineering as one of laws in which law enforcement information systems have been developed, such as Income Tax Law, Road Traffic Law, and so on.

3.1 Analysis of Reference in Law Sentences

There are reference phrases in law sentences, for example "X -ni kitei-suru Y (Y which is prescribed in X)." In National Pension Law, typical reference phrases are shown in Table 1.

In these phrases, X acts as a pointer to another law sentence. We show some examples of reference phrases found in National Pension Law, as follows:

- Item a, Paragraph b, Article c (absolute pointer)
- the previous paragraph (relative pointer)

Table 1. Typical reference phrases in National Pension Law

Reference phrases		Frequency
X-*ni kitei-suru* Y$_{noun}$ Y$_{noun}$ which is prescribed in X	(X に規定する Y(名詞))	103
X-*no kitei-niyoru* Y$_{noun}$ Y$_{noun}$ which is prescribed in X	(X の規定による Y(名詞))	71
X-*no kitei-niyori* Y$_{verb}$ Y$_{verb}$ as prescribed in X	(X の規定により Y(動詞))	109

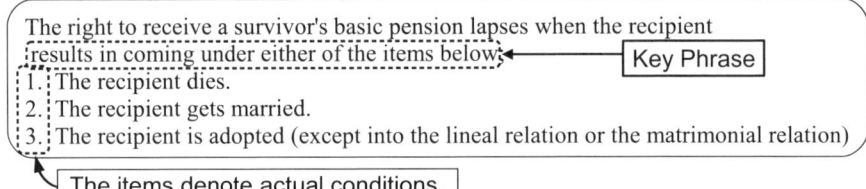

Fig. 3. Itemization of conditions in the law requisite part

- Paragraph *b* in the previous article (combination)
- the same article
- the previous *n* articles
- a proviso in the previous article
- this law (self-reference)

We also examined frequency in the use of the noun Y in the sentence indicated by a pointer X, because we consider that the noun Y is explained in detail in the sentence indicated by X. For example, a phrase "the postponement of issuance which is prescribed in Paragraph 1, Article 28" implies that we can find a more detailed phrase "postponement of issuance of the old age basic pension" in Paragraph 1, Article 28. Therefore, we regarded the sentence indicated by X as an explanation of the noun Y.

We targeted the phrase "X-*ni kitei-suru* Y (Y which is prescribed in X)," as it appears most frequently among reference phrases where Y is a noun phrase in National Pension Law (see Table 1). A pointer X indicates another law document in 21 cases out of 103, and we examined the remaining 82 cases. As a result, in 49 cases the noun Y appears only once in the sentence indicated by X, and twice or more in 24 cases, while the sentence indicated by X does not contain the noun Y in only 9 cases. Therefore, it is easy to find the part of the explanation, which is located near the noun Y. With this idea, we consider a method to extract an explanation from a sentence indicated by X in Section 4.1.

3.2 Analysis of Itemization in Law Sentences

Some law sentences include itemization of conditions in the law requisite part, an example of which is shown in Fig. 3. The enclosed phrase should be replaced with one of the items denoting actual conditions. When one or more conditions are satisfied, the description in the law effectuation part becomes effective. We found 34 sentences of such a style in National Pension Law. Therefore, we considered a method to embed itemized conditions instead of cue phrases of itemization.

We defined *Key Phrases*, which always appear in sentences before itemization[3]. As we analyzed sentences from all 215 articles of the National Pension Law, the set of Key Phrases can be expressed as a regular expression, the diagram of which is shown in Fig. 4. For example, the phrase *"Tsugi no kaku gou*

---

[3] There may be a proviso between the sentence and itemization

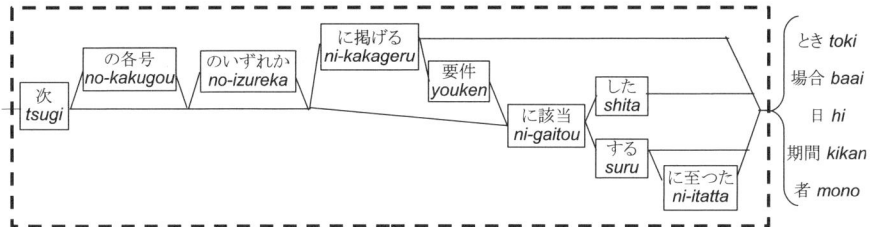

Fig. 4. Key phrases for itemization

Table 2. Frequency of Key Phrases

(**KP**: Key Phrase)	
Format of KPs / Frequency	
KP + *toki* (とき)	9
KP + *baai* (場合)	9
KP + *mono* (者)	6
KP + *hi* (日)	3
KP + *kikan* (期間)	1
KP + *youken* (要件)	1
KP + a noun	5
Total	34

Table 3. Frequency of Condition Items

CI: Condition Items	
Format of CIs / Frequency	
CI + *toki* (とき)	106
CI + *koto* (こと)	4
CI + *mono* (もの)	3
CI + *mono* (者)	2
CI + a noun	9
Total	124

ni gaitou suru ni itatta," meaning "to result in coming under either of the items below[4]," which is derived from the generative rule in Fig. 4, is regarded as a Key Phrase.

Itemized condition sentences appear next to sentences which contain Key Phrases. The last words of these sentences are "*Toki* (time)," "*Mono* (person)," and so on. In this paper, we call these sentences excluding the last words *Condition Items*. Key Phrases and Condition Items appearing in National Pension Law are shown in Table 2 and Table 3, respectively.

We will describe a method to remove itemization using Key Phrases and Condition Items in Section 4.2.

4 Method for Substituting Referent Phrases

4.1 Extracting an Explanation from Referent

As was mentioned in Section 3.1, we show a method to extract a detailed explanation of a reference phrase, such as "X-*ni kitei-suru* Y (Y which is prescribed in X)," from a referent sentence. The procedure is shown as follows;

---

[4] If we do not care about word-to-word translation for the Japanese law sentence, the following phrase is more appropriate; "to be included in one of the following cases."

1. Identifying a reference expression
2. Searching for the same words in the reference expression and the referent sentence
3. Syntactic analysis of the referent sentence and extraction of supplements

In the first step, if the sentence includes one of the phrases in Table 1, the system recognizes the phrase as a reference expression. We show an example of a reference expression in Fig. 5-A. The phrase "which is prescribed in" is the reference phrase, and the referent sentence is shown in Paragraph 1, Article 28.

In the next step, the system searches for a phrase in the referent sentence, which is matched with the noun phrase corresponding to Y described in the reference sentence. A difficult thing is to determine the region of words as an identified phrase. The system recognizes the longest matched words as the noun phrase Y. In Fig. 5, the system extracted a phrase corresponding to Y as "apply for postponement of issuance."[5]

Finally, the system analyzes the referent sentence with the Japanese morphological analyzer, JUMAN, and Japanese dependency analyzer, KNP. We regard elements which modify Y in the dependency tree as supplements for the word Y. Then, we replace the phrase "X-*ni kitei-suru*" with the supplements for the word Y. In this example shown in Fig. 6, "which is prescribed in Paragraph 1, Article 28" is replaced with "of the old age basic pension."

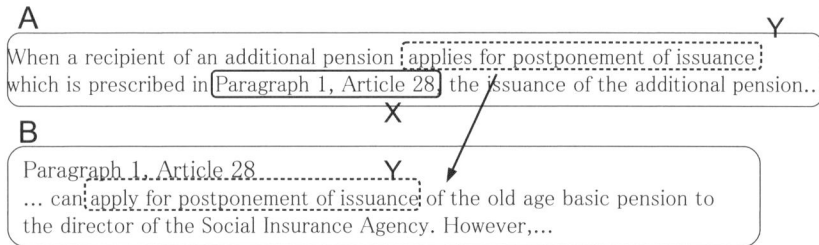

Fig. 5. (A) a reference expression, and (B) a referent sentence

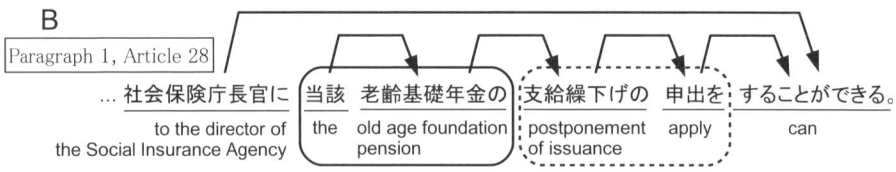

Fig. 6. The dependency tree of the referent sentence

4.2 Removing Itemization

In Section 3.2, we defined Key Phrases as cue phrases that always appear with itemization, like "*tsugi-no kaku gou no izureka ni gaitou-suru* ((something) to

---

[5] In Japanese, the verb 'apply' is expressed as a *sahen*-noun.

```
... -ni oite Key mono-ga, ... -toki, ...-suru.         ・・・において キー 者が、・・・とき、・・・する。
(For ..., a person who Key is ... then ...)            一 条件1 こと。
  1. Condition-1 -koto.                                二 条件2 こと。
  2. Condition-2 -koto.                                三 条件3 こと。
  3. Condition-3 -koto.
```

↓

```
... -ni oite Condition-1 -mono-ga, ...-toki, ...-suru.   ・・・において 条件1 者が、・・・とき、・・・する。
... -ni oite Condition-2 -mono-ga, ...-toki, ...-suru.   ・・・において 条件2 者が、・・・とき、・・・する。
... -ni oite Condition-3 -mono-ga, ...-toki, ...-suru.   ・・・において 条件3 者が、・・・とき、・・・する。
(For ..., a person who Condition is ... then ...)
```

Fig. 7. Removing itemization

(a) Input

```
The right to receive a survivor's basic pension lapses
when the recipient results in coming under either of the items below;
  1. The recipient dies.
  2. The recipient gets married.
```

(b) Output

```
- The right to receive a survivor's basic pension lapses when the recipient dies.
- The right to receive a survivor's basic pension lapses when the recipient gets married.
```

Fig. 8. An example of removing itemization

which either of the following items is applicable)," and we search for itemization with it. If a Key Phrase is found, we regard the following items as Condition Items, and replace the Key Phrase with one of the Condition Items for each. Then we have sentences which are understandable separately[6], as shown in Fig. 7. We show an example of the pair of input and output in Fig. 8.

5 Experiments and Results

5.1 Reference Expressions in National Pension Law

We tested our system on reference phrases "X-*ni kitei-suru* Y (Y which is prescribed in X)" in National Pension Law. The result is shown in Table 4. The system derived correct information from 41.5 percent of reference phrases in National Pension Law. For 20.8 percent of reference expressions, generated sentences were ungrammatical or not enough, since some necessary words or phrases were not expressed in output sentences. For example, some referent sentences contain a number of reference expressions. An example is shown in Fig. 9. In

---

[6] Even though the converted logical formulae are repetitive, there is no problem as long as the system gives the same logical predicates and variables to the repetitive phrases.

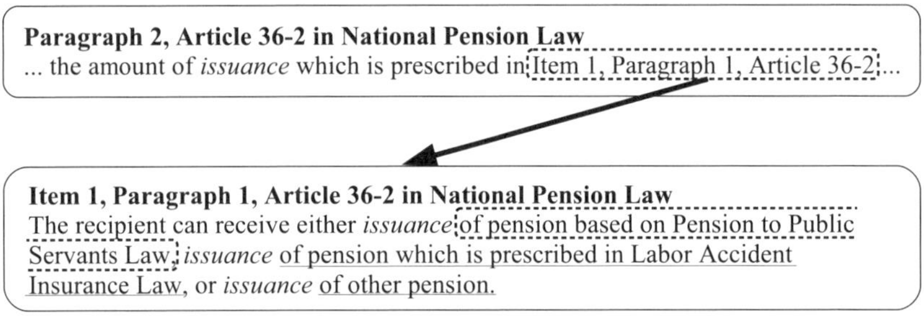

250   Y. Kimura, M. Nakamura, and A. Shimazu

> **Paragraph 2, Article 36-2 in National Pension Law**
> ... the amount of *issuance* which is prescribed in Item 1, Paragraph 1, Article 36-2 ...

> **Item 1, Paragraph 1, Article 36-2 in National Pension Law**
> The recipient can receive either *issuance* of pension based on Pension to Public Servants Law, *issuance* of pension which is prescribed in Labor Accident Insurance Law, or *issuance* of other pension.

Fig. 9. An example of partially extracted reference expressions

Table 4. Result for the reference expression "X-*ni kitei-suru* Y"

	Sentence	%
Extracted correctly	22	41.5%
Extracted partially	11	20.8%
Extracted nothing	20	37.7%
Total	53	100%

Table 5. Result for identifying itemization

Identifying	Itemization Frequency	Conditions
Succeeded	33	119
Failed	1	5
Total	34	124
Misidentify	1	2

Paragraph 2, Article 36-2 in National Pension Law, there exists a phrase referring to Item 1, Paragraph 1, Article 36-2, in which three phrases should be referred such as (1) issuance of pension based on Pension to Public Servants Law, (2) issuance of pension which is prescribed in Labor Accident Insurance Law, and (3) issuance of other pension. Even though all of them are an explanation of the reference expression, the system extracts only the one of them which appears first in the sentence, and ignores the rest of expressions. Therefore, the generated phrase became "the amount of issuance of pension based on Pension to Public Servants Law." We judged the result to be partially extracted.

5.2 Experiment for Itemization

We tested our system on itemization in National Pension Law. From the point of view of identifying itemization, our system found most itemization structures, shown in Table 5. The result of removing itemization is shown on the left hand side of Table 6.

All of the errors are items which denote a combination of a Condition Item and an object part in the law effectuation part, which are separated by space. In other words, the objects of these sentences change depending on the Condition Items. An example is shown in Fig. 10. This article determines the revision of the rate after the base year about the national pension. An important thing here is that each item consists of a condition part and its result. That is, the first Key Phrase denoting "In the case of the following items," enclosed corresponds to the first phrase of each item, while the second Key Phrase denoting "on the

Table 6. Result for removing itemization

	National Pension Law		Income Tax Law	
	conditions	%	conditions	%
Succeeded	87	73.1%	219	51.4%
Wrong sentence	21	17.7%	123	28.9%
Error	11	9.2%	84	19.7%
Total	119	100%	426	100%

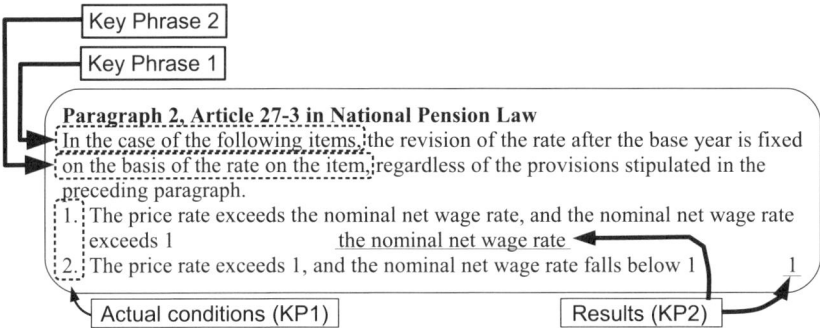

Fig. 10. An example of wrong sentence

basis of the rate on the item" corresponds to the second phrases underlined of each item. Therefore, the first item should be interpreted as follows: "When the price rate exceeds the nominal net wage rate, and the nominal net wage rate exceeds 1, the revision of the rate after the base year is fixed to the nominal net wage rate." Our system did not deal with this type of itemization.

We also inspected the system with Income Tax Law as an open test, shown on the right hand side of Table 6. The system was 51.4% accurate in terms of removing itemized expressions, while it was 73.1% accurate in the closed test. There seems to be some difference in notation between National Pension Law and Income Tax Law. Particularly, we found the increase of itemization consisting of a combination of a Condition Item and an object part as mentioned in Fig. 10. Results will be improved after an analysis of the mistakes.

6 Discussion

Our purpose is to transform law sentences into logical forms which are able to be provided for advanced inference in Legal Engineering. We can think of alternative ways to solve the problem which was dealt with in this paper. Thus, it could be a method that the expansion of itemized expressions is done on the logical forms instead of on natural language sentences as this paper. That is, as a first step, each referent sentence such as "The recipient dies." is transformed into a logical form, then the predicate transformed from an itemized expression such as "items_below(x6)" is replaced with the transformed referents. The expansion in this method might be easier because the reference and referent expressions are normalized as logical forms before the expansion process. A conceivable problem would occur in terms of how to associate variables of referent logical predicates with reference ones.

Let us consider advantages of both this alternative way and our proposed method. Advantages of our method are as follows:

1. We can independently develop our method from the main system 'Wildcats.'
2. Our system can generate a natural language text with high readability. It could be a spin-off dealing with other problems like a text-to-speech system.

In fact, the first item was the most important reason because our main system, 'Wildcats,' has been under development.

Meanwhile, the alternative method could have the following advantages:

1. The system need not care about grammar of Japanese unlike our method which sometimes generated ungrammatical sentences.
2. Generated logical forms could be more accurate than the current system, because the system need not analyze generated long sentences with dependency parser.

The best way would be to merge these two approaches. Anyway, it is effective to extract reference phrases by the pattern-match with a regular expression.

7 Conclusion

In this paper we proposed a method to rewrite legal sentences including itemization or reference into independent, plain sentences. In the experiments, we showed that the system successfully extracted itemized expressions with some exceptions. For referential expressions, focusing on a referential phrase "X-*ni kitei-suru* Y" in National Pension Law, we showed the system worked well for extracting reference expressions. We consider that the system is useful not only for the front end of our main system, Wildcats, but also for assistance in reading legal documents.

Some tasks still remain in our future work: (1) As was shown in Section 5, our system failed for some sentences. We can deal with some of the failures easily. (2) We can improve this system by introducing a method for measuring readability of the output sentences. (3) We will test our main system, Wildcats, using the proposed model as the front end system.

Acknowledgment. This research was partly supported by the 21st Century COE Program 'Verifiable and Evolvable e-Society' and Grant-in-Aid for Scientific Research (19650028). We would like to give special thanks to Yoko Shibata, Yoshiko Oyama, and Akiko Hayashi, who analyzed law sentences and their logical representations. We also thank the anonymous three referees for their valuable comments that greatly improved the quality of this paper.

References

1. Katayama, T.: The current status of the art of the 21st COE programs in the information sciences field (2): Verifiable and evolvable e-society - realization of trustworthy e-society by computer science - (in Japanese). IPSJ (Information Processing Society of Japan) Journal 46(5), 515–521 (2005)
2. Katayama, T.: Legal engineering – an engineering approach to laws in e-society age. In: Proc. of the 1st Intl. Workshop on JURISIN (2007)
3. Katayama, T., Shimazu, A., Tojo, S., Futatsugi, K., Ochimizu, K.: e-Society and legal engineering (in Japanese). Journal of the Japanese Society for Artificial Intelligence 23(4), 529–536 (2008)
4. Hagiwara, S., Tojo, S.: Stable legal knowledge with regard to contradictory arguments. In: AIA 2006: Proceedings of the 24th IASTED international conference on Artificial intelligence and applications, Anaheim, CA, USA, pp. 323–328. ACTA Press (2006)
5. Nakamura, M., Nobuoka, S., Shimazu, A.: Towards Translation of Legal Sentences into Logical Forms. In: Satoh, K., Inokuchi, A., Nagao, K., Kawamura, T. (eds.) JSAI 2007. LNCS, vol. 4914, pp. 349–362. Springer, Heidelberg (2008)
6. Hobbs, J.R., Stickel, M., Martin, P., Edwards, D.: Interpretation as abduction. In: Proceedings of the 26th annual meeting on Association for Computational Linguistics, Morristown, NJ, USA. Association for Computational Linguistics, pp. 95–103 (1988)
7. Mulkar, R., Hobbs, J.R., Hovy, E.: Learning from reading syntactically complex biology texts. In: Proceedings of the 8th International Symposium on Logical Formalizations of Commonsense Reasoning. Part of the AAAI Spring Symposium Series (2007)
8. Mulkar, R., Hobbs, J.R., Hovy, E., Chalupsky, H., Lin, C.Y.: Learning by reading: Two experiments. In: Proceedings of IJCAI 2007 workshop on Knowledge and Reasoning for Answering Questions (2007)
9. Tanaka, K., Kawazoe, I., Narita, H.: Standard structure of legal provisions - for the legal knowledge processing by natural language - (in Japanese). In: IPSJ Research Report on Natural Language Processing, pp. 79–86 (1993)
10. Nagai, H., Nakamura, T., Nomura, H.: Skeleton structure acquisition of Japanese law sentences based on linguistic characteristics. In: Proc. of NLPRS 1995, vol. 1, pp. 143–148 (1995)
11. Kurohashi, S., Nakamura, T., Matsumoto, Y., Nagao, M.: Improvements of Japanese morphological analyzer JUMAN. In: Proceedings of the Workshop on Sharable Natural Language Resources, pp. 22–28 (1994)
12. Kurohashi, S., Nagao, M.: KN parser: Japanese dependency/case structure analyzer. In: Proceedings of the Workshop on Sharable Natural Language Resources, pp. 48–55 (1994)
13. Ogawa, Y., Inagaki, S., Toyama, K.: Automatic Consolidation of Japanese Statutes Based on Formalization of Amendment Sentences. In: Satoh, K., Inokuchi, A., Nagao, K., Kawamura, T. (eds.) JSAI 2007. LNCS, vol. 4914, pp. 349–362. Springer, Heidelberg (2008)

Computing Argumentation Semantics in Answer Set Programming

Toshiko Wakaki[1] and Katsumi Nitta[2]

[1] Shibaura Institute of Technology, 307 Fukasaku, Minuma-ku, Saitama, Japan
twakaki@sic.shibaura-it.ac.jp
[2] Tokyo Institute of Technology, 4259 Nagatsuta, Midori-ku, Yokohama, Japan
nitta@dis.titech.ac.jp

Abstract. We propose a *simple* and *generic* method for computing Dung's standard argumentation semantics along with semi-stable semantics in Answer Set Programming (ASP). The different semantics captured by argumentation frameworks are all uniformly represented in our ASP setting. It is based on Caminada's reinstatement labellings for argumentation frameworks as well as our method of computing circumscription in ASP. In our approach, a given argumentation framework is translated into a *single* normal logic program w.r.t. the chosen semantics whose answer set (if exists) yields an argument-based extension expressed by means of a reinstatement labelling for the semantics. We show *soundness* and *completeness* theorems for our translation, which allow us not only to compute argument-based extensions but also to decide whether an argument is *sceptically* or *credulously* accepted w.r.t. the chosen semantics. Based on our theorems, the prototype argumentation system was implemented using the ASP solver, DLV, whose evaluation results verified correctness of our approach.

1 Introduction

In the last two decades, *Answer Set Programming* based on stable model semantics [11,12] has been recognized as a fruitful paradigm for solving many NP-complete problems in a very concise way. At present, many efficient ASP solvers such as smodels [15], DLV [8] and so on are available, which contribute to apply Answer Set Programming (or ASP, for short) to many class NP, or co-NP problems in the research field of nonmonotonic reasoning. In fact, we have succeeded in computing not only preferred answer sets of Prioritized Logic Programs (PLPs) [18] but also models of prioritized circumscription [13,14] in ASP settings [19,20,21].

In this study, we explore another interesting ASP application, which enables us to compute not only Dung's various argumentation semantics but also to decide whether an argument is *sceptically* or *credulously* accepted w.r.t. the chosen semantics in a uniform way.

According to Dung's theory of abstract argumentation [5], four argumentation semantics such as *preferred, grounded, stable* and *complete semantics* are given in terms of the respective *extensions* under a given argumentation framework. In the last decade, based on the notion of the *acceptability* of arguments, considerable efforts have been invested in proof procedures (e.g.[6,4,17]) to compute extensions as well as to have a test for extension membership of individual arguments w.r.t. various argumentation semantics.

On the other hand, quite recently, Caminada presented the method of reinstatement labellings [2] to capture such argumentation semantics. Moreover, he found another new semantics called *semi-stable semantics* [3] having a place between preferred semantics and stable one, which coincides with reinstatement labellings with minimal undec (i.e. undecided). That is, a semi-stable extension may have the minimal defensible arguments which are neither credulously justified nor credulously overruled (i.e. neither labelled in nor out)) though a stable extension allows none of them.

It is obvious that human argumentation is crucially nonmonotonic. However, to the best of our knowledge, so far there exist few studies to apply Answer Set Programming for computing Dung's argumentation semantics as well as to decide whether a specific argument is in at least one extension (i.e. *credulously justified*), or if it is in all extensions (i.e. *sceptically justified*) under particular semantics [4,2].

Under such circumstances, we propose a *simple* and *generic* method for computing Dung's four argumentation semantics along with semi-stable semantics in ASP. The different semantics captured by argumentation frameworks are all uniformly represented in our ASP setting based on the technique of Caminada's reinstatement labellings. The basic idea of our approach is to transform a given argumentation framework into a *single* normal logic program w.r.t. the chosen argumentation semantics whose answer set (if exists) yields the reinstatement labelling expressing an argument-based extension for the semantics. Especially for computing preferred (resp. grounded, semi-stable) semantics, our method to compute circumscription in ASP whose performance is shown to be efficient [21], is applied to find answer sets expressing Caminada's reinstatement labellings with maximal in (resp. minimal in, minimal undec). We show *soundness* and *completeness* theorems for our translation, which allow us not only to compute argument-based extensions but also to decide whether an argument is *sceptically* or *credulously* accepted w.r.t. the chosen semantics. Based on our theorems, we implemented the prototype argumentation system using the ASP solver, DLV [8], whose evaluation results verified correctness of our approach.

This paper is organized as follows. In Section 2, we provide preliminaries. In Section 3, we present our translated logic programs to compute Dung's argumentation semantics and soundness and completeness theorems for them. In Section 4, comparison between our approach and related work is given. Finally, we conclude and give some direction for future research in Section 5.

2 Preliminaries

We briefly review the basic notions used throughout this paper.

2.1 Dung's Standard Semantics

Dung's theory of abstract argumentation [5] is defined as follows.

Definition 1. *(Argumentation Framework).* *An argumentation framework is a pair (Ar, def) where Ar is a set of arguments and def is a binary relation over Ar, i.e. def $\subseteq$ Ar $\times$ Ar. $(a,b) \in def$, or equivalently a def b, means that a attacks b. A set S of arguments attacks an argument a if a is attacked by an argument of S.*

Definition 2. *(Acceptable / Conflict-free).* *A set $S \subseteq Ar$ is conflict-free iff there are no arguments a and b in S such that a attacks b. An argument $a \in Ar$ is acceptable w.r.t. a set $S \subseteq Ar$ iff for any $b \in Ar$ such that $(b,a) \in def$, there exists $c \in S$ such that $(c,b) \in def$.*

Definition 3. *(Acceptability Semantics)*
Let $Args \subseteq Ar$ be a conflict-free set of arguments and $F : 2^{Ar} \to 2^{Ar}$ be a function with $F(Args) = \{a \mid a$ is acceptable w.r.t. $Args\}$.

Acceptability Semantics is defined as follows. Args is admissible iff $Args \subseteq F(Args)$. Args is a complete extension iff $Args = F(Args)$. Args is a grounded extension iff Args is a minimal (w.r.t. set-inclusion) complete extension. Args is a preferred extension iff Args is a maximal (w.r.t. set-inclusion) complete extension. Args is a stable extension iff Args is a preferred extension that attacks every argument in $Ar \setminus Args$.

2.2 Reinstatement Labellings Versus Argument-Based Semantics

Caminada's method of Reinstatement Labellings [2] is shown as follows.

Definition 4. *Let (Ar, def) be a Dung-style argumentation framework. An* AF-labelling *is a (total) function $\mathcal{L} : Ar \to \{\text{in}, \text{out}, \text{undec}\}$. We define* in*($\mathcal{L}$) as $\{ a \in Ar \mid \mathcal{L}(a) = \text{in}\}$,* out*($\mathcal{L}$) as $\{ a \in Ar \mid \mathcal{L}(a) = \text{out}\}$ and* undec*($\mathcal{L}$) as $\{ a \in Ar \mid \mathcal{L}(a) = \text{undec}\}$.*

Definition 5. *(Reinstatement Labellings) Let $\mathcal{L}$ be an AF-labelling. We say that $\mathcal{L}$ is a reinstatement labelling iff it satisfies the following conditions:*

- $\forall a \in Ar : (\mathcal{L}(a) = \text{out} \equiv \exists b \in Ar : (b \text{ def } a \land \mathcal{L}(b) = \text{in}))$ and
- $\forall a \in Ar : (\mathcal{L}(a) = \text{in} \equiv \forall b \in Ar : (b \text{ def } a \supset \mathcal{L}(b) = \text{out}))$.

Results 1 (Caminada, 2006) [2]
- The following concepts are equivalent: (a) complete extensions; (b) reinstatement labellings .
- The following concepts are equivalent: (a) grounded extensions; (b) reinstatement labellings with minimal in; (c) reinstatement labellings with minimal out; (d) reinstatement labellings with maximal undec.
- The following concepts are equivalent: (a) preferred extensions; (b) reinstatement labellings with maximal in; (c) reinstatement labellings with maximal out.
- The following concepts are equivalent: (a) stable extensions; (b) reinstatement labellings with empty undec.

- The following concepts are equivalent: (a) semi-stable extensions; (b) reinstatement labellings with minimal undec.

With respect to decision problems about extension membership of an argument, there are the *sceptical* and the *credulous* approaches under particular argument-based semantics, which is defined in terms of reinstatement labellings as follows.

Definition 6. (Sceptical / Credulous Query-Answering) *[2,17]*
Given an argumentation framework (Ar, def) and an argument $a \in Ar$, the following holds for each argument-based semantics:

- *a is sceptically (resp. credulously) justified iff it is labelled* in *in every (resp. at least one) reasonable position (=reinstatement labelling).*
- *a is sceptically (resp. credulously) overruled iff it is labelled* out *in every (resp. at least one) reasonable position.*
- *Otherwise, a is sceptically (resp. credulously) defensible.*

2.3 Logic Programs and Answer Set Semantics

Logic programs we consider in this paper are normal logic programs as follows.

Definition 7. *A normal logic program (NLP) [11] is a set of rules of the forms as follows:*

$$H \leftarrow B_1, \ldots, B_m, not B_{m+1}, \ldots, not B_n \qquad (1)$$
$$\leftarrow B_1, \ldots, B_m, not B_{m+1}, \ldots, not B_n \qquad (2)$$

where $n \geq m \geq 0$, each of H and B_i ($1 \leq i \leq n$) is an atom, and "not" means negation as failure. Each rule with variables stands for the set of its ground instances as usual. The left-hand (right-hand) side of $\leftarrow$ is called the head (body) of the rule. Each rule of the form (2) is called an integrity constraint. For a rule with an empty body, we may write H instead of $H \leftarrow$.

The semantics of NLP is given by *answer sets* (i.e. *stable models*) defined as follows.

Definition 8. *(Answer Set Semantics) [11,12] Let $\mathcal{B}_P$ be the Herbrand base for the language of a NLP P. First, let P be a not-free NLP (i.e. $m = n$) and $S \subseteq \mathcal{B}_P$. Then, S is an answer set (i.e. a stable model) of P if S is a minimal set (called the least model of P) satisfying the following two conditions:*

(i) For each ground instance of a rule: $H \leftarrow B_1, \ldots, B_m$ in P,
  $\{B_1, \ldots, B_m\} \subseteq S$ implies $H \in S$;
(ii) In particular, for each ground integrity constraint: $\leftarrow B_1, \ldots, B_m$ in P,
  $\{B_1, \ldots, B_m\} \not\subseteq S$ holds;

Secondly, let P be a NLP and $S \subseteq \mathcal{B}_P$. The reduct P^S of P by S is a not-free NLP defined as follows: A rule $H \leftarrow B_1, \ldots, B_m$ (resp. $\leftarrow B_1, \ldots, B_m$) is in P^S iff there is a ground rule $H \leftarrow B_1, \ldots, B_m, not B_{m+1}, \ldots, not B_n$ (resp. $\leftarrow B_1, \ldots, B_m, not B_{m+1}, \ldots, not B_n$) from P such that $\{B_{m+1}, \ldots, B_n\} \cap S = \emptyset$. Then, S is an answer set (i.e. a stable model) of P if S is an answer set of P^S.

We say that a NLP is consistent if it has a stable model (namely a consistent answer set); otherwise, it is inconsistent.

3 Computing Argumentation Semantics in ASP

We show that Caminada's Reinstatement Labelling method enables us not only to compute extensions for Dung's any argumentation semantics but also to decide the extension membership of a given argument under particular semantics in Answer Set Programming.

3.1 Computing Argument-Based Extensions

The basic idea of our approach is to translate a given argumentation framework into the logic program for the respective semantics whose answer set (if exists), say S, embeds a reinstatement labelling $\mathcal{L}$ such that an atom $in(a)$ is in S if and only if the argument a is labelled in by $\mathcal{L}$, (that is, $in(a) \in S$ iff $a \in \text{in}(\mathcal{L})$) where $\mathcal{L}$ satisfies the conditions for the respective semantics (e.g. minimal $\text{in}(\mathcal{L})$, maximal $\text{in}(\mathcal{L})$).

First of all, we show NLP Π as follows, which faithfully describes the conditions of reinstatement labellings given in Definition 5 by means of ASP.

Definition 9. *Given an argumentation framework (Ar, def), NLP Π is defined as $\Pi_{AF} \cup \Pi_{Lab}$, where Π_{AF} is the set of domain-dependent rules as follows:*

1. $ag(a) \leftarrow,$ *for any argument $a \in Ar$,*
2. $def(a,b) \leftarrow,$ *for any pair $(a,b) \in def$,*

and Π_{Lab} is the set of domain-independent rules as follows,

3. $in(X) \leftarrow ag(X), not\ ng(X),$
   $ng(X) \leftarrow in(Y), def(Y,X),$
   $ng(X) \leftarrow undec(Y), def(Y,X),$
4. $out(X) \leftarrow in(Y), def(Y,X),$
5. $undec(X) \leftarrow ag(X), not\ in(X), not\ out(X).$

where a, b are individual constants, X, Y are individual variables and ag, def, in, out, $undec$, ng are predicate symbols. For an argument a, $in(a)$ (resp. $out(a)$, $undec(a)$) means that a is labelled in (resp. out, undec). Hereafter, we denotes the Herbrand base of Π by $\mathcal{B}_\Pi$.

Translated logic programs for complete and stable semantics are defined as follows. Especially w.r.t. stable semantics, the integrity constraint, $\leftarrow undec(X)$ is included in the program to express reinstatement labellings with empty undec.

Definition 10. *Let (Ar, def) be an argumentation framework. Then for complete semantics and stable semantics, (Ar, def) is translated into the respective NLPs defined as follows:*

$tr[Ar, def;\ \texttt{complete}] \stackrel{def}{=} \Pi,$
$tr[Ar, def;\ \texttt{stable}] \stackrel{def}{=} \Pi \cup \{\leftarrow undec(X)\}.$

It should be noted that a normal logic program Π (resp. $\Pi \cup \{\leftarrow undec(X)\}$) yields answer sets expressing complete (resp. stable) extensions based on *soundness and completeness theorems* shown as follows.

Definition 11. *For an answer set S and a set X, we write*
$$S|_X \stackrel{def}{=} S \cap X,$$
which we call X-projection of S.

Definition 12. *Given an argumentation framework (Ar, def), $\mathcal{I}$, $\mathcal{O}$ and $\mathcal{U}$ are sets of ground atoms defined as follows:*
$$\mathcal{I} = \{in(a) \mid a \in Ar\}, \quad \mathcal{O} = \{out(a) \mid a \in Ar\}, \quad \mathcal{U} = \{undec(a) \mid a \in Ar\}$$

Lemma 1. *Let (Ar, def) be an argumentation framework. If M is an answer set of $tr[Ar, def;$ complete$]$ (resp. $tr[Ar, def;$ stable$]$), there is the reinstatement labelling $\mathcal{L}$ (resp. $\mathcal{L}$ with undec$(\mathcal{L}) = \emptyset$) such that $in(\mathcal{L}) = \{a \mid in(a) \in M|_{\mathcal{I}}\}$, out$(\mathcal{L}) = \{a \mid out(a) \in M|_{\mathcal{O}}\}$ and undec$(\mathcal{L}) = \{a \mid undec(a) \in M|_{\mathcal{U}}\}$.*

Conversely, if $\mathcal{L}$ is a reinstatement labelling (resp. a reinstatement labelling with undec$(\mathcal{L}) = \emptyset$), there is the answer set M of $tr[Ar, def;$ complete$]$ (resp. $tr[Ar, def;$ stable$]$) such that $M|_{\mathcal{I}} = \{in(a) \mid a \in in(\mathcal{L})\}$, $M|_{\mathcal{O}} = \{out(a) \mid a \in out(\mathcal{L})\}$ and $M|_{\mathcal{U}} = \{undec(a) \mid a \in undec(\mathcal{L})\}$.

Proof: See Appendix.

Theorem 1. (Soundness and Completeness Theorems)
Let (Ar, def) be an argumentation framework and $Sname$ be anyone of complete *and* stable. *Then there is the extension E of $Sname$ semantics for (Ar, def) such that $E = \{a \mid in(a) \in M|_{\mathcal{I}}\}$ if M is an answer set of $tr[Ar, def; Sname]$. Conversely, there is the answer set M of $tr[Ar, def; Sname]$ such that $M|_{\mathcal{I}} = \{in(a) \mid a \in E\}$ if E is an extension of $Sname$ semantics for (Ar, def).*

Proof: This is immediately proved based on both Results 1 and Lemma 1 with respect to complete and stable semantics.

Example 1. Let us consider the argument framework (Ar, def) [1] as follows:
$$Ar = \{a, b, c, d, e\} \quad def = \{(a,b), (c,b), (c,d), (d,c), (d,e), (e,e)\},$$
where $\mathcal{I} = \{in(a), in(b), in(c), in(d), in(e)\}$, $\mathcal{O} = \{out(a), out(b), out(c), out(d), out(e)\}$, and $\mathcal{U} = \{undec(a), undec(b), undec(c), undec(d), undec(e)\}$.

Since NLP Π_{AF} for this (Ar, def) is constructed as follows:
$\Pi_{AF} = \{ag(a), ag(b), ag(c), ag(d), ag(e),$
$\qquad def(a,b), def(c,b), def(c,d), def(d,c), def(d,e), def(e,e)\}.$
$tr[Ar, def;$ complete$] = \Pi = \Pi_{AF} \cup \Pi_{lab}$ has 3 answer sets N_1, N_2, N_3 s.t.
$\quad N_1|_{\mathcal{I} \cup \mathcal{O} \cup \mathcal{U}} = \{in(a), out(b), in(c), out(d), undec(e)\},$
$\quad N_2|_{\mathcal{I} \cup \mathcal{O} \cup \mathcal{U}} = \{in(a), out(b), out(c), in(d), out(e)\},$
$\quad N_3|_{\mathcal{I} \cup \mathcal{O} \cup \mathcal{U}} = \{in(a), out(b), undec(c), undec(d), undec(e)\},$
whereas $tr[Ar, def;$ stable$] = \Pi \cup \{\leftarrow undec(X)\}$ has only one answer set, N_2 which does not include any atom from $\mathcal{U}$. Hence, we obtain the results that there

---

[1] This is given in Example 1 of P. Besnard and S. Doutre's paper [1].

exist three complete extensions $\{a, c\}$, $\{a, d\}$, $\{a\}$ corresponding to N_1, N_2, N_3 respectively and only one stable extension, $\{a, d\}$ corresponding to N_2 based on Theorem 1.

Next, we will explain the idea to construct translated logic programs for preferred (resp. grounded, semi-stable) semantics as follows.

According to Caminada's Results 1 shown in section 2, for any reinstatement labelling $\mathcal{L}$ of an argumentation framework $AF = (Ar, def)$, in$(\mathcal{L})$ is a complete extension of AF, whereas such in$(\mathcal{L})$ becomes a preferred (resp. grounded, semi-stable) extension of AF if and only if such $\mathcal{L}$ satisfies the condition such as maximal in (resp. minimal in, minimal undec). Thus, any complete extension of AF can be regarded as a candidate of preferred (resp. grounded, semi-stable) extension. So, in a similar way to our method of computing circumscription by *integration of guess and check program* [21,9], we make the translated logic program for preferred (resp. grounded, semi-stable) semantics consist of the guess program Π and the respective check program, say Π_{check} such that a complete extension of AF as a candidate is generated as the answer set S of Π, whereas Π_{check} tests if the candidate expressed by the answer set S satisfies the respective conditions of the specified semantics given by Result 1. Hence, it is required that such $\Pi \cup \Pi_{check}$ for preferred (resp. grounded) semantics yields an answer set M which embeds some answer set S of Π expressing the reinstatement labelling $\mathcal{L}$ such that in$(\mathcal{L}) = \{a \mid in(a) \in S \subseteq M\}$ is a preferred (resp. grounded) extension if and only if there is no answer set S' of Π expressing the reinstatement labelling $\mathcal{L}'$ such that in$(\mathcal{L}') = \{a \mid in(a) \in S'\}$ satisfies in$(\mathcal{L}) \subset$ in$(\mathcal{L}')$ (resp. in$(\mathcal{L}') \subset$ in$(\mathcal{L})$). Similarly, undec$(\mathcal{L})$ should be used to construct $\Pi \cup \Pi_{check}$ for semi-stable semantics. To explain how to construct such Π_{check}, we prepare some definitions as follows.

Definition 13. *Given an argumentation framework (Ar, def), let AS be a set of answer sets of NLP Π, and ξ be the cardinality of AS, i.e. $|AS|$. Then there is a bijective function $\psi : AS \to \{1, 2, \ldots, \xi\}$ such that for each $S \in AS$, there is an integer j $(1 \leq j \leq \xi)$ such that $\psi(S) = j$, which we call such j a cardinal number of S.*

In order to realize our idea mentioned above, we use the techniques of *meta-programming* as well as integrity constraints as follows.

First, we provide the set $\mathcal{C}$ of newly introduced constants L_ts expressing atoms in $\mathcal{I} \cup \mathcal{U}$ as follows.

$$\mathcal{C} \stackrel{def}{=} \{L_t \mid L_t \text{ is the term denoting an atom } L \in \mathcal{I} \cup \mathcal{U}\}.$$

along with unary and binary predicate symbols, m_1 and m_2, whose meanings are given as follows. For the following constant L_t denoting an atom $L \in \mathcal{I} \cup \mathcal{U}$ and an answer set M of $\Pi \cup \Pi_{check}$,

- $m_1(L_t) \in M$ means $L \in M|_{\mathcal{I} \cup \mathcal{U}} = S|_{\mathcal{I} \cup \mathcal{U}}$ for an answer set $S = M \cap \mathcal{B}_\Pi$ of Π which expresses the candidate reinstatement labelling to be checked; and
- $m_2(L_t, j) \in M$ means $L \in S'|_{\mathcal{I} \cup \mathcal{U}}$ for an answer set S' of Π such that $\psi(S') = j$ $(1 \leq j \leq \xi)$.

In other words, w.r.t. S and S' mentioned above, it holds that,
$in(a) \in S|_\mathcal{I}$ iff $m_1(ia) \in M$, $undec(b) \in S|_\mathcal{U}$ iff $m_1(ub) \in M$
$in(a) \in S'|_\mathcal{I}$ iff $m_2(ia,j) \in M$, $undec(b) \in S'|_\mathcal{U}$ iff $m_2(ub,j) \in M$
for $in(a) \in \mathcal{I}, undec(b) \in \mathcal{U}$ and $ia, ub \in \mathcal{C}$ denoting $in(a), undec(b)$ respectively.

Second, integrity constraints are included in Π_{check}, which play a role that $\Pi \cup \Pi_{check}$ yields an answer set M unless the reinstatement labelling $\mathcal{L}$ expressed by the answer set $S = M \cap \mathcal{B}_\Pi$ of Π violates the the condition such that it has maximal $\texttt{in}(\mathcal{L})$ (resp. minimal $\texttt{in}(\mathcal{L})$, minimal $\texttt{undec}(\mathcal{L})$) for preferred semantics (resp. grounded semantics, semi-stable semantics), in other words, the condition such that there is no answer set S' of Π satisfying $S|_\mathcal{I} \subset S'|_\mathcal{I}$ (resp. $S'|_\mathcal{I} \subset S|_\mathcal{I}$, $S'|_\mathcal{U} \subset S|_\mathcal{U}$).

Now, we are ready to show the respective translated logic programs for preferred, grounded and semi-stable semantics as follows.

Definition 14. *Let (Ar, def) be an argumentation framework and Π be the NLP constructed from (Ar, def). Then for preferred, grounded and semi-stable semantics, (Ar, def) is translated into the respective NLPs defined as follows:*

$$tr[Ar, def; \texttt{preferred}] \stackrel{def}{=} \Pi \cup \Gamma \cup \Xi_{pr},$$
$$tr[Ar, def; \texttt{grounded}] \stackrel{def}{=} \Pi \cup \Gamma \cup \Xi_{gr},$$
$$tr[Ar, def; \texttt{semistable}] \stackrel{def}{=} \Pi \cup \Gamma \cup \Xi_{semi}.$$

where Γ is the set of domain dependent rules as follows:

1. $m_1(L_t) \leftarrow L,$ for any $L \in \mathcal{I} \cup \mathcal{U}$
   where $L_t \in \mathcal{C}$ is the term expressing the atom L.
2. $m_2(L_t, j) \leftarrow,$ $cno(j) \leftarrow,$ $(1 \leq j \leq \xi)$
   for any answer set S' of Π such that $\psi(S') = j$, where $L_t \in \mathcal{C}$ is the term expressing an atom $L \in S'|_{\mathcal{I} \cup \mathcal{U}}$.
3.1 $i(L_t) \leftarrow,$ for any $L \in \mathcal{I}$,
    where $L_t \in \mathcal{C}$ is the term expressing the atom L.
3.2 $u(L_t) \leftarrow,$ for any $L \in \mathcal{U}$,
    where $L_t \in \mathcal{C}$ is a term expressing the atom L.

and Ξ_{pr}, Ξ_{gr} and Ξ_{semi} are sets of domain-independent rules instantiated over constants in $\mathcal{C}$ and j $(1 \leq j \leq \xi)$ such that Ξ_{pr} has rules of no. 4 and no. 6, Ξ_{gr} has rules of no. 4 and no. 7 and Ξ_{semi} has rules of no. 5 and no. 7 as follows:

4. $c(Y) \leftarrow cno(Y), m_1(X), i(X), not\ m_2(X,Y),$
   $d(Y) \leftarrow m_2(X,Y), i(X), not\ m_1(X),$
5. $c(Y) \leftarrow cno(Y), m_1(X), u(X), not\ m_2(X,Y),$
   $d(Y) \leftarrow m_2(X,Y), u(X), not\ m_1(X),$
6. $\leftarrow d(Y), not\ c(Y),$
7. $\leftarrow c(Y), not\ d(Y).$

where X, Y denote individual variables, and i, o, u, cno, c, d are predicate symbols.

Let us explain $tr[Ar, def; \texttt{preferred}] = \Pi \cup \Gamma \cup \Xi_{pr}$ for preferred semantics as follows. Let M be an answer set of $tr[Ar, def; \texttt{preferred}]$. It is obvious that $S = M \cap \mathcal{B}_\Pi$ embedded in M is the answer set of Π expressing the reinstatement labelling $\mathcal{L}$ whose $\texttt{in}(\mathcal{L}) = \{a \mid in(a) \in S|_\mathcal{I}\}$ is the candidate complete extension of (Ar, def) to be tested if it is preferred one. Now, suppose that $e_t \in \mathcal{C}$ denotes the term (i.e. constant) corresponding to an atom $e \in \mathcal{I} \cup \mathcal{U}$.

Then due to rule no. 1, $m_1(e_t) \in M$ iff $e \in M|_{\mathcal{I} \cup \mathcal{U}} = S|_{\mathcal{I} \cup \mathcal{U}}$. This means that for any atom $in(a) \in S|_\mathcal{I} \subseteq M$, there is the atom $m_1(ia)$ in M, where $ia \in \mathcal{C}$ is the newly introduced individual constant denoting the atom $in(a) \in \mathcal{I}$. Note that due to rule no. 1, $S|_\mathcal{I}$ are embedded in M by means of the set of atoms having the predicate symbol m_1 (e.g. $m_1(ia)$).

On the other hand, due to rule no. 2, $m_2(e_t, j) \in M$ iff $e \in S'|_{\mathcal{I} \cup \mathcal{U}}$ for an answer set S' of Π s.t. $\psi(S')=j$, where each S' expresses the complete extension $\texttt{in}(\mathcal{L}') = \{a \mid in(a) \in S'|_\mathcal{I}\}$ for the respective reinstatement labelling $\mathcal{L}'$ according to Theorem 1. This means that if an atom $L \in \mathcal{I}$, say $in(b)$, is contained in an answer set S' of Π (i.e. $in(b) \in S'|_\mathcal{I}$) whose cardinal number is j $(1 \leq j \leq \xi)$, then there is the atom $m_2(L_t, j)$, say $m_2(ib, j)$, in M, where $ib \in \mathcal{C}$ is the newly introduced constant denoting the atom $in(b) \in \mathcal{I}$. Note that due to rule no. 2, $S'|_\mathcal{I}$ s.t. $\psi(S')=j$ are also embedded in M as the tester by means of the set of atoms having the predicate symbol m_2 (e.g. $m_2(ib, j)$).

Rule no. 3.1 denotes that $i(e_t) \in M$ iff $e \in \mathcal{I}$, as used for preferred and grounded semantics, and rule no. 3.2 denotes that $u(e_t) \in M$ iff $e \in \mathcal{U}$, as used for semi-stable semantics. In other words, with respect to atoms $in(a) \in \mathcal{I}$ (resp. $undec(a) \in \mathcal{U}$) for any argument $a \in Ar$, there are atoms $i(ia)$ (resp. $u(ua)$) in M in order to express that the constant $ia \in \mathcal{C}$ (resp. $ua \in \mathcal{C}$) denotes the atom $in(a) \in \mathcal{I}$ (resp. $undec(a) \in \mathcal{U}$).

Rules no. 4 means that, $c(Y)$ becomes true if $(S|_\mathcal{I} \setminus S'|_\mathcal{I}) \neq \emptyset$ and $d(Y)$ becomes true if $(S'|_\mathcal{I} \setminus S|_\mathcal{I}) \neq \emptyset$ for an answer set S' of Π s.t. $\psi(S')=Y$ $(1 \leq Y \leq \xi)$, which are decided via atoms having predicate symbols m_1 and m_2.

Finally Rule no. 6 means that, $tr[Ar, def; \texttt{preferred}]$ has an answer set M unless there exists some Y $(1 \leq Y \leq \xi)$ such that $d(Y)$ is true and $c(Y)$ is not true, that is, unless there is some S' satisfying $S|_\mathcal{I} \subset S'|_\mathcal{I}$ where $S = M \cap \mathcal{B}_\Pi$.

We show *soundness and complete theorems* with respect to translated logic programs for preferred, grounded and semi-stable semantics as follows.

Lemma 2. *Let (Ar, def) be an argumentation framework. If M is an answer set of $tr[Ar, def; \texttt{preferred}]$ (resp. $tr[Ar, def; \texttt{grounded}]$, $tr[Ar, def; \texttt{semistable}]$), there is the reinstatement labelling $\mathcal{L}$ with maximal $\texttt{in}(\mathcal{L})$ (resp. minimal $\texttt{in}(\mathcal{L})$, minimal $\texttt{undec}(\mathcal{L})$) such that $\texttt{in}(\mathcal{L}) = \{a \mid in(a) \in M|_\mathcal{I}\}$, $\texttt{out}(\mathcal{L}) = \{a \mid out(a) \in M|_\mathcal{O}\}$ and $\texttt{undec}(\mathcal{L}) = \{a \mid undec(a) \in M|_\mathcal{U}\}$.*

Conversely, if $\mathcal{L}$ is a reinstatement labelling with maximal $\texttt{in}(\mathcal{L})$ (resp. minimal $\texttt{in}(\mathcal{L})$, minimal $\texttt{undec}(\mathcal{L})$), there is the answer set M of $tr[Ar, def; \texttt{preferred}]$ (resp. $tr[Ar, def; \texttt{grounded}]$, $tr[Ar, def; \texttt{semistable}]$) such that $M|_\mathcal{I} = \{in(a) | a \in \texttt{in}(\mathcal{L})\}$, $M|_\mathcal{O} = \{out(a) \mid a \in \texttt{out}(\mathcal{L})\}$ and $M|_\mathcal{U} = \{undec(a) \mid a \in \texttt{undec}(\mathcal{L})\}$.

Proof: See Appendix.

Theorem 2. (Soundness and Completeness Theorems)
Let (Ar, def) be an argumentation framework and Sname be anyone of preferred, grounded and semistable. Then there is the extension E of Sname semantics for (Ar, def) such that $E = \{ a \mid in(a) \in M|_\mathcal{I}\}$ if M is an answer set of $tr[Ar, def; \text{Sname}]$. Conversely, there is the answer set M of $tr[Ar, def; \text{Sname}]$ such that $M|_\mathcal{I} = \{in(a) \mid a \in E\}$ if E is an extension of Sname semantics for (Ar, def).

Proof: This is immediately proved based on both Results 1 and Lemma 2 with respect to preferred, grounded and semi-stable semantics.

Example 2. Let us consider the argument framework given in Example 1. Corresponding to $\mathcal{I} \cup \mathcal{U} = \{in(a), in(b), in(c), in(d), in(e), undec(a), undec(b),$
$undec(c), undec(d), undec(e)\}$,
we provide the set $\mathcal{C}$ of the newly introduced constants as follows:
$$\mathcal{C} = \{ia, ib, ic, id, ie, ua, ub, uc, ud, ue\}.$$
Then using $\mathcal{I} \cup \mathcal{U}$, $\mathcal{C}$ and answer sets N_1, N_2, N_3 of Π obtained in Example 1, Γ is constructed as follows:
$\Gamma = \{m_1(ia) \leftarrow in(a), \quad m_1(ib) \leftarrow in(b), \quad m_1(ic) \leftarrow in(c), \quad m_1(id) \leftarrow in(d),$
$\quad m_1(ie) \leftarrow in(e), \quad m_1(ua) \leftarrow undec(a), \quad m_1(ub) \leftarrow undec(b),$
$\quad m_1(uc) \leftarrow undec(c), \quad m_1(ud) \leftarrow undec(d), \quad m_1(ue) \leftarrow undec(e),$
$\quad m_2(ia, 1), m_2(ic, 1), m_2(ue, 1), cno(1), m_2(ia, 2), m_2(id, 2), cno(2),$
$\quad m_2(ia, 3), m_2(uc, 3), m_2(ud, 3), m_2(ue, 3), cno(3),$
$\quad i(ia), i(ib), i(ic), i(id), i(ie), u(ua), u(ub), u(uc), u(ud), u(ue)\}.$
Thus $tr[Ar, def; \text{preferred}] = \Pi \cup \Gamma \cup \Xi_{pr}$ has two answer sets, M_1, M_2 s.t.
$$M_1|_{\mathcal{I} \cup \mathcal{O} \cup \mathcal{U}} = \{in(a), out(b), in(c), out(d), undec(e)\},$$
$$M_2|_{\mathcal{I} \cup \mathcal{O} \cup \mathcal{U}} = \{in(a), out(b), out(c), in(d), out(e)\},$$
while $tr[Ar, def; \text{grounded}] = \Pi \cup \Gamma \cup \Xi_{gr}$ has the answer set, M_3 such that
$$M_3|_{\mathcal{I} \cup \mathcal{O} \cup \mathcal{U}} = \{in(a), out(b), undec(c), undec(d), undec(e)\},$$
and $tr[Ar, def; \text{semistable}] = \Pi \cup \Gamma \cup \Xi_{semi}$ has the answer set, M_4 such that
$$M_4|_{\mathcal{I} \cup \mathcal{O} \cup \mathcal{U}} = \{in(a), out(b), out(c), in(d), out(e)\}.$$
As a result, we obtain the results that there exist two preferred extensions, $\{a, c\}$, $\{a, d\}$ corresponding to M_1, M_2 respectively, only one grounded extension, $\{a\}$ corresponding to M_3 and only one semi-stable extension, $\{a, d\}$ corresponding to M_4 based on Theorem 2.

3.2 Sceptical/Credulous Query-Answering

The sceptical (resp. credulous) query-answering problem is also uniformly handled for any argumentation semantics in our ASP setting based on Theorem 1 as well as Theorem 2.

Theorem 3. (Sceptical Query-Answering) *Let (Ar, def) be an argumentation framework and Sname be anyone of* complete, stable, preferred, grounded *and* semistable. *Then for an argument $a \in Ar$,*

- *a is sceptically justified under Sname semantics iff $tr[Ar, def; \text{Sname}] \cup \{\leftarrow in(a)\}$ is inconsistent;*

- a is sceptically overruled under $Sname$ semantics iff $tr[Ar, def; Sname] \cup \{\leftarrow out(a)\}$ is inconsistent;
- otherwise, a is sceptically defensible under $Sname$ semantics,

where we especially suppose that $tr[Ar, def;$ stable$]$ is consistent.

Theorem 4. (Credulous Query-Answering) *Let (Ar, def) be an argumentation framework and $Sname$ be anyone of* complete, stable, preferred, grounded *and* semistable. *Then for an argument $a \in Ar$,*
- a is credulously justified under $Sname$ semantics iff $tr[Ar, def; Sname] \cup \{\leftarrow not\ in(a)\}$ is consistent;
- a is credulously overruled under $Sname$ semantics iff $tr[Ar, def; Sname] \cup \{\leftarrow not\ out(a)\}$ is consistent;
- otherwise, a is credulously defensible under $Sname$ semantics,

where we especially suppose that $tr[Ar, def;$ stable$]$ is consistent.

Note that the sceptical query-answering coincides with the credulous query-answering for grounded semantics because its extension is unique.

Example 3. Consider the argument framework (Ar, def) given in Example 2. Let us use Theorem 3 and Theorem 4 in which $Sname$ is replaced with preferred. Then a is sceptically *justified* under preferred semantics since $tr[Ar, def;$ preferred$] \cup \{\leftarrow in(a)\}$ is inconsistent due to the results obtained in Example 2. On the other hand, c is credulously *justified* as well as credulously *overruled* under preferred semantics since both $tr[Ar, def;$ preferred$] \cup \{\leftarrow not\ in(c)\}$ and $tr[Ar, def;$ preferred$] \cup \{\leftarrow not\ out(c)\}$ are consistent.

Based on our theorems, we have developed the prototype argumentation system using the ASP solver, DLV and C language, whose binary is available at our Web site, http://www.ailab.se.shibaura-it.ac.jp/compARG.html.

The execution result of our system for Examples 2 and 3 is shown as follows, where not only preferred extensions are computed but also the query, a (resp. c) is sceptically (resp. credulously) evaluated under the specified preferred semantics.

```
$ Comp_Arg_in sample.txt -preferred -sq a -cq c
**********Preferred Extensions**********
{a, d}
{a, c}
<< Sceptical Query Evaluation >>
[a] is sceptically justified.
<< Credulous Query Evaluation >>
[c] is credulously justified.
[c] is credulously overruled.
```

4 Related Work

To the best of our knowledge, Nieves et al. [16] are the first to apply ASP to compute preferred extension. However, their method is different from ours since it is based on not Caminada's reinstatement labellings but Besnard and Doutre's propositional formulas expressing the conditions for a set of arguments to be extensions of the respective argumentation semantics [1]. Their method is applicable only for preferred semantics, and they do not show how to compute extensions for argumentation semantics such as complete, stable and semi-stable semantics in ASP, whereas our approach allows us to compute extensions of Dung's every standard semantics along with semi-stable semantics in ASP,

On the other hand, though Egly *et al.* [10] showed a generic approach to implement Dung's four argumentation semantics, their method is different from ours since it is represented in terms of QBFs (Quantified Boolean Formulas) instead of ASP, which coincides with the encodings to propositional logic given by Besnard and Doutre [1]. However, it is not shown the way how to compute extensions for semi-stable semantics in their QBF setting.

5 Conclusion

We present a method for computing Dung's four argumentation semantics along with semi-stable semantics in ASP based on Caminada's reinstatement labelling. So far, we have succeeded in computing minimal models of parallel/ prioritized circumscription [21,20] as well as computing preferred answer sets of Prioritized Logic Programs [19] in ASP. Both are based on the same idea (or the similar techniques) to construct the translated logic programs, which is applied again to our approach to compute argumentation semantics presented in this paper.

With respect to complexity, the sceptical reasoning problem for preferred semantics (resp. stable semantics) was shown to be Π_2^p-complete (resp. co-NP-complete) [7]. It is obvious that our encoding for stable semantics match this complexity, whereas our encoding for preferred semantics is as efficient as our encoding to compute circumscription whose performance is shown to be efficient due to its performance evaluation results shown in [21], since the former is based on the latter for problem having the same complexity. [2]

Though the method presented in this paper is about how to compute deductive argumentation, *abductive argumentation* addressed in [17] is crucially required for arguing multi-agents in various application domains. For example, when dispute should be proceeded under some hypotheses due to lack of evidence in the court, each arguing agent tries to derive argumentation to be the safe situation for him/her using hypothesis, that is, tries to find hypotheses so that arguments satisfying his/her desire (goal) may be always contained in a preferred extension. Thus, our future work is to extend our method to compute deductive argumentation in ASP presented in this paper, and explore a method to compute such abductive argumentation in ASP setting by making use of *abductive logic programming* based on answer set semantics [11,12].

Acknowledgments. The authors thank Kouta Itoh at Shibaura Institute of Technology for his assistance of implementing the argumentation system. This

---
[2] it should be noted that literal entailment from circumscription is also Π_2^p-complete.

research is partially supported by Grant-in-Aid for Scientific Research from JSPS, No. 20500141.

References

1. Besnard, P., Doutre, S.: Checking the acceptability of a set of arguments. In: Proceedings of the 10th International Workshop on Non-Monotonic Reasoning (NMR 2004), pp. 59–64 (2004)
2. Caminada, M.: On the issue of reinstatement in argumentation. In: Fisher, M., van der Hoek, W., Konev, B., Lisitsa, A. (eds.) JELIA 2006. LNCS (LNAI), vol. 4160, pp. 111–123. Springer, Heidelberg (2006)
3. Caminada, M.: Semi-stable semantics. In: Proceedings of the first International Conference on Computational Models of Argument (COMMA 2006), pp. 121–130. IOS Press, Amsterdam (2006)
4. Cayrol, C., Doutre, S., Mengin, J.: On decision problems related to the preferred semantics for argumentation frameworks. Journal of Logic and Computation 13(3), 377–403 (2003)
5. Dung, P.M.: On the acceptability of arguments and its fundamental role in non-monotonic reasoning, logic programming, and n-person games. Artificial Intelligence 77, 321–357 (1995)
6. Dung, P.M., Kowalski, R.A., Toni, F.: Dialectic proof procedures for assumption-based, admissible argumentation. Artificial Intelligence 170(2), 114–159 (2006)
7. Dunne, P.E., Bench-Capon, T.J.M.: Coherence in finite argument systems. Artificial Intelligence 141, 187–203 (2002)
8. Eiter, T., Leone, N., Mateis, C., Pfeifer, G., Scarcello, F.: A deductive system for nonmonotonic reasoning. In: Fuhrbach, U., Dix, J., Nerode, A. (eds.) LPNMR 1997. LNCS (LNAI), vol. 1265, pp. 364–375. Springer, Heidelberg (1997), http://www.dbai.tuwien.ac.at/proj/dlv/
9. Eiter, T., Polleres, A.: Towards automated integration of guess and check programs in answer set programming. In: Lifschitz, V., Niemelä, I. (eds.) LPNMR 2004. LNCS, vol. 2923, pp. 100–113. Springer, Heidelberg (2004)
10. Egly, U., Woltran, S.: Reasoning in argumentation frameworks using quantified boolean formulas. In: Proceedings of the first International Conference on Computational Models of Argument (COMMA 2006), pp. 133–144. IOS Press, Amsterdam (2006)
11. Gelfond, M., Lifschitz, V.: The stable model semantics for logic programming. In: Proceedings of the fifth International Conference and Symposium on Logic Programming (ICLP/SLP 1988), pp. 1070–1080. MIT Press, Cambridge (1988)
12. Gelfond, M., Lifschitz, V.: Classical negation in logic programs and disjunctive databases. New Generation Computing 9, 365–385 (1991)
13. Lifschitz, V.: Computing circumscription. In: Proceedings of the Ninth International Joint Conference on Artificial Intelligence (IJCAI 1985), pp. 121–127 (1985)
14. McCarthy, J.: Applications of circumscription to formalizing commonsense knowledge. Artificial Intelligence 28, 89–116 (1986)
15. Niemelä, I., Simons, P.: Smodels: An implementation of the stable model and well-founded semantics for normal logic programs. In: Fuhrbach, U., Dix, J., Nerode, A. (eds.) LPNMR 1997. LNCS, vol. 1265, pp. 421–430. Springer, Heidelberg (1997), http://www.tcs.hut.fi/Software/smodels/

16. Nieves, J.C., Cortes, U., Osorio, M.: Preferred extensions as stable models. Theory and Practice of Logic Programming 8(4), 527–543 (2008)
17. Prakken, H., Vreeswijk, G.A.W.: Logics for defeasible argumentation. In: Gabbay, D.M., Guenthner, F. (eds.) Handbook of Philosophical Logic, 2nd edn., vol. 4, pp. 218–319. Kluwer, Dordecht (2001)
18. Sakama, C., Inoue, K.: Prioritized logic programming and its application to commonsense reasoning. Artificial Intelligence 123, 185–222 (2000)
19. Wakaki, T., Inoue, K., Sakama, C., Nitta, K.: Computing preferred answer sets in answer set programming. In: Y. Vardi, M., Voronkov, A. (eds.) LPAR 2003. LNCS (LNAI), vol. 2850, pp. 259–273. Springer, Heidelberg (2003)
20. Wakaki, T., Inoue, K.: Compiling prioritized circumscription into answer set programming. In: Demoen, B., Lifschitz, V. (eds.) ICLP 2004. LNCS, vol. 3132, pp. 356–370. Springer, Heidelberg (2004)
21. Wakaki, T., Tomita, T.: Circumscriptive theorem prover based on integration of guess and check program. Transactions of the Japanese Society for Artificial Intelligence, pp. 472–481 (2006); also the revised version is, Wakaki, T., Tomita, T.: Circumscriptive theorem prover based on integration of guess and check program. Transactions of the Japanese Society for Artificial Intelligence 22(5), 472–481 (2007) (in Japanese)

Appendix: Proofs of Theorems

Proof of Lemma 1
(1) Proof for $tr[Ar, def; \texttt{complete}]$:
($\Longrightarrow$) Let M be an answer set of $tr[Ar, def; \texttt{complete}]$, that is, Π, and U be the Herbrand universe of Π, which is equivalent to Ar. Since M is an unique least model of the reduct Π^M, the following holds w.r.t. Definition 9.

1. According to rules of no. 1 and no. 2 of Π, it holds that, for M,
 $ag(a) \in M$ iff $a \in U = Ar$, $\quad def(a,b) \in M$ iff $(a,b) \in def$.
2. According to rules no. 3 of Π, $in(a) \in M$ denotes $ng(a) \notin M$ such that $ag(a) \in M$ (i.e. $a \in Ar$), which means that
 (i) $def(b,a) \notin M$ for any $b \in U = Ar$;
 (ii) otherwise, if there is $b \in U = Ar$ such that $def(b,a) \in M$, it holds that, both $in(b) \notin M$ and $undec(b) \notin M$, which leads to $out(b) \in M$ due to rule no.5 from Π;
3. According to rule no. 4, if $out(a) \in M$, there exists $b \in U = Ar$ such that $in(b) \in M$ as well as $def(b,a) \in M$.
4. According to rule no. 5, if $undec(a) \in M$, it holds that $in(a) \notin M$ as well as $out(a) \notin M$, where $ag(a) \in M$, i.e. $a \in Ar$.

Now let us define the labelling $\mathcal{L}'$ for the answer set M such that, $\texttt{in}(\mathcal{L}') = \{a|\ in(a) \in M\}$, $\texttt{out}(\mathcal{L}') = \{a|\ out(a) \in M\}$ and $\texttt{undec}(\mathcal{L}') = \{a|\ undec(a) \in M\}$. Then according to Definition 5, it is obvious that the above items 2, 3 and 4 express that $\mathcal{L}'$ is the reinstatement labelling for the argumentation framework (Ar, def) constructed from M based on the item 1.

($\Longleftarrow$) Suppose $\mathcal{L}$ is a reinstatement labelling for (Ar, def). Let M be a Herbrand interpretation of Π constructed by $\mathcal{L}$ as follows:

$$M \stackrel{def}{=} \{ag(a) \mid a \in Ar\} \cup \{def(a,b) \mid (a,b) \in def\}$$
$$\cup \{in(a) \mid a \in \mathtt{in}(\mathcal{L})\} \cup \{out(a) \mid a \in \mathtt{out}(\mathcal{L})\} \cup \{undec(a) \mid a \in \mathtt{undec}(\mathcal{L})\}$$
$$\cup \{ng(a) \mid (b,a) \in def \text{ for } b \in \mathtt{in}(\mathcal{L}) \cup \mathtt{undec}(\mathcal{L})\ \}$$

It is easily shown that M is a least model of the reduct Π^M. Thus M is an answer set of Π, i.e. an answer set of $tr[Ar, def; \mathtt{complete}]$ such that $M|_{\mathcal{I}} = \{in(a) \mid a \in \mathtt{in}(\mathcal{L})\}$, $M|_{\mathcal{O}} = \{out(a) \mid a \in \mathtt{out}(\mathcal{L})\}$ and $M|_{\mathcal{U}} = \{undec(a) \mid a \in \mathtt{undec}(\mathcal{L})\}$.□

(2) Proof for $tr[Ar, def; \mathtt{stable}]$:
($\Longrightarrow$) Let M be an answer set of $tr[Ar, def; \mathtt{stable}]$, that is, an answer set of $\Pi \cup \{\leftarrow undec(X)\}$. Since it is obvious that M is also an answer set of Π, items 1 $\sim$ 4 mentioned above also holds for this M. However, since M satisfies the integrity constraint, $\leftarrow undec(X)$, there is no $undec(a) \in M$ for any $a \in U = Ar$, i.e. $\qquad\qquad\qquad undec(a) \notin M \qquad\qquad for\ \forall a \in Ar \qquad\qquad (3)$
Now, let $\mathcal{L}''$ be a reinstatement labelling which is constructed from the answer set M of $tr[Ar, def; \mathtt{stable}]$ such that, $\mathtt{in}(\mathcal{L}'') = \{a \mid in(a) \in M\}$, $\mathtt{out}(\mathcal{L}'') = \{a \mid out(a) \in M\}$ and $\mathtt{undec}(\mathcal{L}'') = \{a \mid undec(a) \in M\}$. Then $\mathtt{undec}(\mathcal{L}'')$ should be empty due to (3). As a result, it follows that such $\mathcal{L}''$ obtained from the answer set M of $tr[Ar, def; \mathtt{stable}]$ is the reinstatement labelling with $\mathtt{undec}(\mathcal{L}'') = \emptyset$ for the argumentation framework (Ar, def) embedded in M.

($\Longleftarrow$) The converse is easily proved in a similar way.

□

Proof of Lemma 2

In the following, the proof of the lemma is given only for the translated logic program for preferred semantics, i.e. $tr[Ar, def; \mathtt{preferred}]$. The proofs of lemma 2 w.r.t. translated logic programs for grounded and semi-stable semantics are omitted since they are proved in a similar way to that for preferred semantics.

Let M be an answer set of $tr[Ar, def; \mathtt{preferred}]$ and $\mathcal{B}_\Pi$ be the Herbrand base of Π. Then it is obviously concluded that M is also an answer set of the following NLP: $tr[Ar, def; \mathtt{preferred}] \setminus \{\leftarrow d(Y), not\ c(Y)\}$.

Since $\Gamma \cup \Xi_{pr} \setminus \{\leftarrow d(Y), not\ c(Y)\}$ is a stratified logic program whose each rule has the ground head atom not occurring in $\mathcal{B}_\Pi$, M is an augmented answer set of Π which not only includes some answer set of Π but also has ground head atoms of the rules in $\Gamma \cup \Xi_{pr} \setminus \{\leftarrow d(Y), not\ c(Y)\}$. Thus $S = M \cap \mathcal{B}_\Pi$ should be an answer set of Π.

Then, according to rule no. 1 in Definition 14, it is obvious that
$$m_1(e_t) \in M \quad \text{iff} \quad e \in M|_{\mathcal{I} \cup \mathcal{U}} = S|_{\mathcal{I} \cup \mathcal{U}}$$
where $e_t \in \mathcal{C}$ is the term (i.e. constant) expressing an atom $e \in \mathcal{I} \cup \mathcal{U}$. According to rule no. 2, for each answer set S' of Π such that $\psi(S')=j$ $(1 \leq j \leq \xi)$,
$$m_2(g_t, j) \in M \quad \text{iff} \quad g \in S' \cap (\mathcal{I} \cup \mathcal{U}) \text{ s.t. } \psi(S')=j,$$
where $g_t \in \mathcal{C}$ is the term expressing an atom $g \in \mathcal{I} \cup \mathcal{U}$.

Thus, according to rules in Definition 14, it follows that,

M is an answer set of $tr[Ar, def; \mathtt{preferred}]$
iff there is no integer Y $(1 \leq Y \leq \xi)$ satisfying that $d(Y) \in M$ and $c(Y) \notin M$,
iff there is no integer Y $(1 \leq Y \leq \xi)$ satisfying that
 ($\exists e_t \in \mathcal{C}$ s.t. $m_2(e_t, Y) \in M \wedge i(e_t) \in M \wedge m_1(e_t) \notin M$)

$\wedge \neg (\exists g_t \in \mathcal{C}$ s.t. $m_1(g_t) \in M \wedge i(g_t) \in M\ m_2(g_t, Y) \notin M)$,
iff there is no integer Y ($1 \le Y \le \xi$) satisfying that
$(\exists e \in \mathcal{I}$ s.t. $e \in S'|_\mathcal{I} \setminus S|_\mathcal{I}) \wedge \neg (\exists g \in \mathcal{I}$ s.t. $g \in S|_\mathcal{I} \setminus S'|_\mathcal{I})$,
where $S = M \cap \mathcal{B}_\Pi$ and S' is an answer set of Π such that $\psi(S')=Y$,
iff there is no answer set S' of Π such that $S|_\mathcal{I} \subset S'|_\mathcal{I}$ where $S = M \cap \mathcal{B}_\Pi$,
iff there is no reinstatement labeling $\mathcal{L}'$ such that $\mathtt{in}(\mathcal{L}) \subset \mathtt{in}(\mathcal{L}')$ where
$\mathtt{in}(\mathcal{L}) = \{a \mid in(a) \in S|_\mathcal{I}\}$ and $\mathtt{in}(\mathcal{L}') = \{a \mid in(a) \in S'|_\mathcal{I}\}$
for $S = M \cap \mathcal{B}_\Pi$ and any answer set S' of Π.
iff there is the reinstatement labelling $\mathcal{L}$ such that $\mathtt{in}(\mathcal{L})$ is maximal where
$\mathtt{in}(\mathcal{L}) = \{a \mid in(a) \in M|_\mathcal{I}\}$, $\mathtt{out}(\mathcal{L}) = \{a \mid out(a) \in M|_\mathcal{O}\}$,
$\mathtt{undec}(\mathcal{L}) = \{a \mid undec(a) \in M|_\mathcal{U}\}$
since $M|_{\mathcal{I} \cup \mathcal{O} \cup \mathcal{U}} = S|_{\mathcal{I} \cup \mathcal{O} \cup \mathcal{U}}$ for $S = M \cap \mathcal{B}_\Pi$. □

In the following, Theorem 3 and Theorem 4 are proved only for preferred semantics. Proofs for complete, grounded and semi-stable semantics are omitted since they are proved in a similar way to those for preferred semantics.

Proof of Theorem 3
According to Definition 6 and Results 1, it holds that, for an argument $a \in Ar$,
   a is sceptically *justified* (resp. *overruled*) under preferred semantics iff a is labelled $\mathtt{in}$ (resp. $\mathtt{out}$) in every reinstatement labelling $\mathcal{L}$ with maximal $\mathtt{in}$.

Now, due to Lemma 2, it holds that, for an argument $a \in Ar$,
a is labelled $\mathtt{in}$ (resp. $\mathtt{out}$) in every reinstatement labelling $\mathcal{L}$ with maximal $\mathtt{in}$
iff there is $in(a) \in M$ (resp. $out(a) \in M$) in every answer set M of
$tr[Ar, def; \mathtt{preferred}]$,
iff $tr[Ar, def; \mathtt{preferred}] \cup \{\leftarrow in(a)\}$ (resp. $\{\leftarrow out(a)\}$) is inconsistent.   □

Proof of Theorem 4
According to Definition 6 and Results 1, it holds that, for an argument $a \in Ar$,
   a is credulously *justified* (resp. *overruled*) under preferred semantics
   iff a is labelled $\mathtt{in}$ (resp. $\mathtt{out}$) in at least one reinstatement labelling $\mathcal{L}$ with maximal $\mathtt{in}$.

Now, due to Lemma 2, it holds that, for an argument $a \in Ar$,
   a is labelled $\mathtt{in}$ (resp. $\mathtt{out}$) in at least one reinstatement labelling $\mathcal{L}$ with maximal $\mathtt{in}$
iff there is $in(a) \in M$ (resp. $out(a) \in M$) in at least one answer set M of
$tr[Ar, def; \mathtt{preferred}]$,
iff $tr[Ar, def; \mathtt{preferred}] \cup \{\leftarrow not\ in(a)\}$ (resp. $\{\leftarrow not\ out(a)\}$) is consistent.
□

Part IV

Laughter in Interaction and Body Movement

LIBM 2008 - First International Workshop on Laughter in Interaction and Body Movement

Hitoshi Iida[1], Masashi Okamoto[1], and Katsuya Takanashi[2]

[1] Tokyo University of Technology
1404-1 Katakuramachi, Hachioji City, Tokyo 192-0982 Japan
okamotoma@media.teu.ac.jp
[2] Kyoto University
Yoshida-Honmachi, Sakyo-ku, Kyoto 606-8501 Japan
takanasi@ar.media.kyoto-u.ac.jp

Laughter takes a great role in leading a social life for humans. It not only comes out as just a physiological phenomenon, but is ingeniously designed and created as a resource for constructing a social relationship or bringing about smooth communication. Social laughter cannot be created by a single person but by a collaborative activity among participants in a conversation. Furthermore, configuration and body movements of the participants also comprise the essential factors of laughter besides linguistic ones.

Such an emotive factor as laughter thus cannot be overlooked when we establish a smooth social relationship with computers. However, though human-computer interaction (HCI) has recently become familiar in everyday life, it is on rather limited occasions that HCI makes positive use of laughter.

This workshop focuses attention on the phenomenon of laughter in interactions and body movements of participants. In particular, it focuses on what physical/cognitive factors and conditions socially enact laughing situations or moments, and on how laughter is perceived and utilized as a resource for social interaction by participants. Therefore, this workshop does not treat the laughter itself, but rather aims at clarifying the structure of the social or communicative environment surrounding laughter, which would become the basis for constructing socially smooth and natural HCI.

According to the scope of this workshop above, topics of interest include but are not limited to:

- Laughter and smile in conversation
- Realizing body movements of a natural and emotive robot/agent
- Pragmatic meaning and effects of laughter
- Organization of laughter in interaction and communication
- Laughter recognition for emotive computing
- Humor recognition/realization in multi-modal communication
- Laughter-synchronizing in multi-party conversation
- Stand-up comedy as 'open communication'
- Creating/utilizing humor in human-computer interaction

- Body movements of laughmakers or comedians
- Humorous interaction in stand-up comedy/team comedy
- What to become a trigger of waves of laughter in audiences

The workshop was held at Asahikawa Convention Bureau, Hokkaido, Japan, June 10, 2008, and consisted of two invited talks and eight presentations. This section has selected one invited talk and four general presentations to present them as revised papers, locally edited by Hitoshi Iida and Masashi Okamoto, Tokyo University of Technology, and Katsuya Takanashi, Kyoto University, who are workshop chair and program co-chairs, respectively.

We'd like to express our deepest thanks to the other program committee, Mayumi Bono (UCLA/JSPS), Yasuharu Den (Chiba University), Mika Enomoto (Tokyo University of Technology), Hiromichi Hosoma (The University of Shiga Prefecture), Masato Ohba (Tokyo University of Technology), and Mamiko Sakata (Doshisha University). Thanks also to the guest reviewers, Yosuke Matsusaka (AIST) and Takanori Komatsu (Shinshu University).

Last but not least, the editors are grateful to the authors of the papers, as well as to the other presenters who have not contributed to this volume for various reasons. As a result of their hard work the achievement of this workshop will serve as a timely and comprehensive reference for researchers and practitioners in all the related disciplines.

A final note. In connection with the preparation of this workshop, LIBM website was created at http://www.teu.ac.jp/iap/LIBM08/ as a permanent reference and portal for those interested in the workshop series.

November 2008

Hitoshi Iida
Masashi Okamoto
Katsuya Takanashi

Laughter around the End of Storytelling in Multi-party Interaction

Mika Enomoto, Masashi Okamoto, Masato Ohba, and Hitoshi Iida

Tokyo University of Technology
1404-1 Katakura-cho, Hachiouji-shi, Tokyo, 192-0982, Japan
http://www.teu.ac.jp/iap/

Abstract. This research argues that the sequence organization around the end of a storytelling is affected by which of the hearers inserts a laughter to which position in the sequence. Laughters before the beginning point of possible completion of storytelling never affect on the sequence organization, while those which occur within a transition space change who is to speak first after the storytelling. Though an oriented recipient (OR) is a default candidate who can speak first after the storytelling, laughs within a transition space let the OR pass his/her own occasion for speech to another participant.

Keywords: storytelling, laughter, sequence organization, oriented recipient, non-oriented recipient.

1 Introduction

In this paper, we examine several examples of acoustic laughter which occurs around the end of a storytelling in the sequential organization of multi-party interaction. And we show you that laughter has power to change the sequential organization around the ending part of storytelling, depending on where laughter is inserted. Once a storytelling has been begun by one speaker, he/she should proceed to tell the story to its completion. The other participants thus can only respond to it with back-channels as hearer within the course of the storytelling. If hearers want to talk within it, they might be forced to do their talking interruptively (Sacks[8]). In contrast, however, the completion point of the storytelling is the place where the turn-taking organization restarts, and then hearers can take a turn again. Meanwhile, since the ending part of every funny story usually delivers a punchline, hearers are encouraged to laugh there. Then, how are hearers' laughs and their turns to re-engage turn-by-turn talk designed? How are they arranged in the course of the ending sequence of storytelling?

As laughing is a prime exception to the 'no more than one at a time' speaker turn-taking rule for conversation, laughs can overlap (Sacks[8]). Laughter can also penetrate into another turn. Primitively speaking, hearers will laugh in chorus at the exact moment when the turn reaches the punchline before the story completion point, and then one of them will begin the next turn. However, it is obvious at a glance that laughs spread out all over the sequence around the end of a storytelling. Moreover, it is natural that some hearers laugh and others don't at the same point of the sequence.

This paper focuses on laughter around the end of storytelling, sketching out a systematic design of insertion of laughs into the course of the story ending sequence in which a turn-by-turn talk is re-organized.

2 A Sequence Organization around the End of Storytelling

Before describing our analysis of the design of laughter, let us start with drawing a sequence organization around the end of a storytelling.

2.1 Re-engagement in the Turn-Taking Organization

Jefferson[5] has analyzed how stories occur within common turn-by-turn talk situations. According to her, stories emerge from turn-by-turn talk, and, upon their completion, re-engage turn-by-turn talk. Enomoto & Den[2] illustrate that the following sequence organization can be seen around the end of storytelling:

- **T1** Presentment of a possible completion point of storytelling
- **R2** Brief acknowledgement of the ongoing story (Avoidance of re-engagement)
- **T3** Extension of storytelling + Re-presentment of a possible completion point
- **R4** Re-engagement into turn-by-turn talk

T1 is the first possible completion point, where a hearer is expected to respond. The hearer's response, then, becomes either R2 or R4. R2 and R4 are not always carried out by the same participant (actually, B and A in the example below takes on R2 and R4 respectively). Furthermore, the sequence from R2 to T3 sometimes drops out or repeats itself.

The following is an example of this type of sequence organization. C is telling a story that waitresses in Hakone inns rarely put their noses into guests. The example below shows the ending part of the storytelling. C presents a possible completion point at 03 (T1), which can be certified by the follow-on pause of about 0.5 seconds (04). If A or B had begun an utterance to take her own turn, then she would have been re-engaged in turn-by-turn talk. However, B just gives a brief acknowledgement ("Hmm") at 05 and avoids the re-engagement (R2). C also utters "Hmm" at 06 and puts a long pause of 1.8 seconds (07), waiting for B to make a response. During that moment, C is continuously looking at B. Since B does not make any responses, C restarts her storytelling with "So,", and extends the storytelling at 09 and re-presents a possible completion point (T3). Then, A makes a substantial utterance at 12, "Ah, they are those who dislike to be asked!", which leads all the participants to be re-engaged in turn-by-turn talk.

```
(1) 0632:486.4320-503.3775
01 C: 箱根は:(0.294)そっち聞かれれば:答えるけど:
      As for Hakone (inns),(a waitress) makes a reply only when asked,but
```

```
02 A: [ふーーーん          ]
      Hmmmm
03 C: [特に自分からは何も言わ]ず:T1
      never speaks willingly,
04    (0.451)
05 B: ふ[ーん]:R2
      Hmm
06 C:   [ふー]ん
         Hmm
07    (1.795)
08 C: うん
      So,
09 C: なんだから不倫が多[いのかな]:T3
      that is why many guests in amorous liaisons stay there
10 B:                  [うわ  ]
                        Wow
12 A: あ(0.121)色々聞かれちゃ困る[ひ]とだ:R4
      Ah, they are those who dislike to be asked!
```

This is a typical sequence pattern around the end of storytelling.

2.2 Turn-Taking Priority in Accordance with the Hearer's Status

In addition, Enomoto & Den[2] argue that which hearer should take a turn at which point depends upon the hearer's status in a storytelling sequence. They point out that the hearer who takes the first turn around the end of storytelling is the one who has been frequently looked at by a speaker, that is, an 'oriented recipient (OR)'. And then, another hearer that is not looked at by the speaker, that is, a 'non-oriented recipient (NOR)', is able to speak after OR has made an utterance. In other words, which hearer should take a turn at R2 or R4 is determined by his/her status of OR or NOR. OR has a right to take the first turn around the end of storytelling. NOR is allowed to speak after OR has made an utterance. If OR takes a turn at R2 or R4, NOR thereafter can take a turn. If OR speaks at R2, NOR can speak at R4. If OR speaks at R4, NOR will take a turn after a turn-taking restarting. This is summarized as below.

(Pattern 1)
    T1
    R2 OR takes a turn
    T3
    R4 NOR can take a turn
(Pattern 2)
    T1
    R4 OR take a turn
    —————————————————
              ↓ turn-taking restarts
    NOR can take a turn

In the example (1), since C keeps looking at B in her storytelling, B is the OR. When T1 (a possible completion point) appears at 03, B (as OR) gives R2 (a brief acknowledgement) back to C at 05. And then C extends her storytelling (T3) at 09, and its possible completion point allows A (as NOR) to utter R4 at 12, so that all the participants can be re-engaged in turn-by-turn talk. Anyway, the turn-taking priority around the end of storytelling is OR, followed by NOR.

```
(2) 1232:93.9730-105.1630
21 B: それをすっごい怒って:(0.257)あいつがー=
     That made her very angry, (and then) she
22 A: =えっ
     Holy cow!
23 A: [んだって]
     What?
23 B: [ありえ ]ないありえない(0.259)言って
     said, "That's impossible!"
24 C: うん
     yeah
25 B: オッマエ(0.126)じゃ[フォ]ローこいよ:ってゆう:T1
     so I wanted to say, "YOU should come and help me!"
26 A:           [え ]
                Oh,
27 A: 面と向って言うの:R4
     (Did she say so) to your face?
28 B: 面と向ってゆう
     To my face.
29 A: まじで?
     Really?
30 B: うん
     Yeah
31 C: へえ:
     Wow!
```

(2) is an example of Pattern 2. Since B keeps looking at A in her storytelling, A is the OR. When T1 (a possible completion point) appears at 25, A (as OR) gives R4 (re-engagement into turn-by-turn talk) back to C at 27. It makes all the participants re-engaged in turn-by-turn talk. C finally takes a turn at line 31.

Then, how and where are laughs inserted into this ending part of storytelling?

3 Laughter Positions in a Storytelling Sequence

As for the organization of laughter in the end part of a storytelling sequence, we found that there are the following four positions where laughter is located:

    T1/T3   [**L1**] Laughter before a possible completion point
    (R2/R4) [**L2**] Laughter within a transition space

[L1] is a position for laughter located before the first/second possible completion point of a storytelling within T1/T3. If T1 or T3 includes the punchline of a story, a laughter is expected to occur at that point.

It is pointed out by Glenn[3] that laughs routinely appear at an earlier recognition point at which the laughable nature of the utterance-in-progress becomes evident. This is because, according to Sacks[8], a laugh should make it clear which of the utterances it is intended to respond to. If a laugh should be delayed, what is its target talk will be misled. Thus, [L1] is a position where a laugh can be adequately understood to respond to a specific target talk without being confused with another target.

[L2] is a position for laughter where the first/second possible completion has just started and a hearer can take a turn. This position is noted by Jefferson[6] as the transition space which entails a slight incursion into the T1 utterance in progress. If a hearer produces R2 to bypass the re-engagement into turn-by-turn talk, a current speaker extends the storytelling using T3 recursively. T3 then has a next possible completion point and provides the second possible position of laughter as [L1]. If a laugh occurrs within the transition space from T3 to R4, then the laugh is that of [L2].

However, if hearers choose to laugh, they cannot speak at the same time . That is why the start of R2/R4 will be delayed. If a storyteller produces T3 while a hearer is laughing, the hearer has to postpone a chance for utterance. The same goes for a position after T3.

Then, how is that 'laughter vs. speech' competition utilized by hearers? And, as a result, how is the ending sequence of storytelling affected by the insertion of laughs? They are our research questions, so we focus on laughter around the end of storytelling sketching out a systematic design of the laughter insertion.

In the following sections we pick up several cases with each of the laughter positions and show how hearers tactically use their laughter in accordance with their hearer's status.

4 Data: Multimodal Three-Party Conversations

The data and the transcription and annotation methods we used in this research are as follows:

4.1 Participants

Twelve triads, consisting of 36 different individuals, participated in the recording. They were all native speakers of Japanese, and they ranged in age from 18 to 33 years. The participants of each triad were friends on campus and of the same gender. A half of triads were male groups and the other half female ones.

4.2 Topics of Conversation

Each triad produced three conversations, each of which lasted approximately 10 minutes. The initial topic of each conversation was determined by throwing a

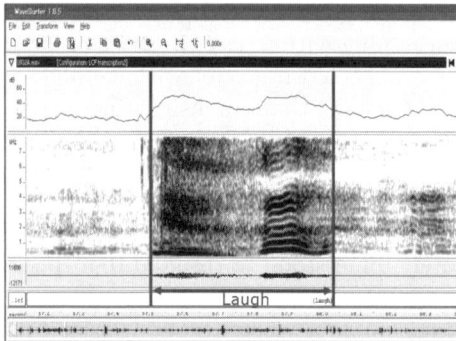

Fig. 1. The audio spectrogram of Laugher

dice whose faces showed six different topics, such as embarrassing, surprising, and exasperating experiences. We instructed the participants not to feel restricted to the initial topic, and the actual topics brought into the conversations became diverse.

4.3 Transcription and Annotation

We transcribed all the audio data in standard Japanese orthography. We segmented the utterances in terms of turn-constructional units (TCUs)[9]. A TCU is a minimal unit by which a turn in conversation can be constructed. At the end of a TCU, a speaker change may, but need not, occur. A TCU may be a sentence, a clause, a phrase, or even a single word depending on the context. As for backchannels, we transcribed them in distinction from TCU's.

Regarding laughters in those conversations, we transcribed each start and end time of them based on the audio spectrogram(Figure 1) generated by Wavesurfer 1.8.5.

As an annotation of nonverbal behavior, we marked every occurrence of eye gaze at participants. Each of the eye gaze actions was identified by evaluating the bust shot of each participant on a frame-by-frame basis. In order to precisely locate these actions, we used the video annotation tool Anvil (Kipp[7]). Eye gaze was marked with the name of the participant whom the participant being labeled is gazing at. When a gaze starts shifting away from the current participant to the other participant or some other place, the current gaze ends. A new gaze starts when the participant being labeled starts shifting her/his gaze toward on a participant. Gazes at a place or an object other than the conversation participants was not marked.

5 Method

For acquiring the target data in this study, we extracted the completion points of storytelling. Since turn-taking system is suspended by storytelling, we extract storytelling completion points from calculating the duration while two participants keep silent for over 22.9 seconds except for producing backchannels. It is

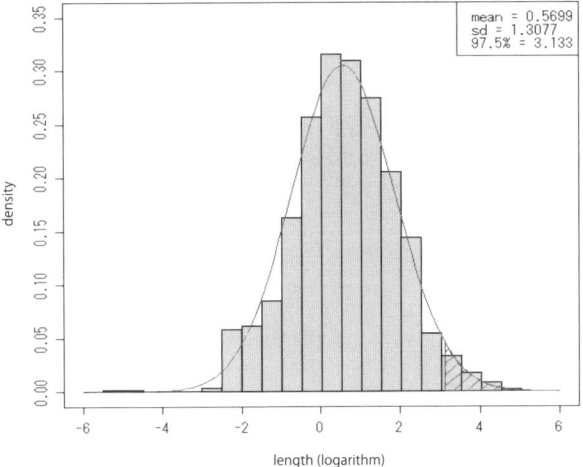

Fig. 2. Lengths of listening time

because the upper 2.5 % of the occurrence of length of listening time is 22.9 seconds. Figure 2 shows the the histogram of the lengths of listening time after a logarithmic transformation. The shaded portion is the upper 2.5 %.

We select 29 cases which contain the ending parts of storytelling, from 83 cases which belong to the upper 2.5 %. They are our target data in this study.

6 Analysis 1: Laughter at L1 - No Affect on Sequence Organization

First we examine the [L1] type of laughter, which occurs before a possible completion point of T1/T3. Case 1 (Fig. 3) below is an example of [L1].

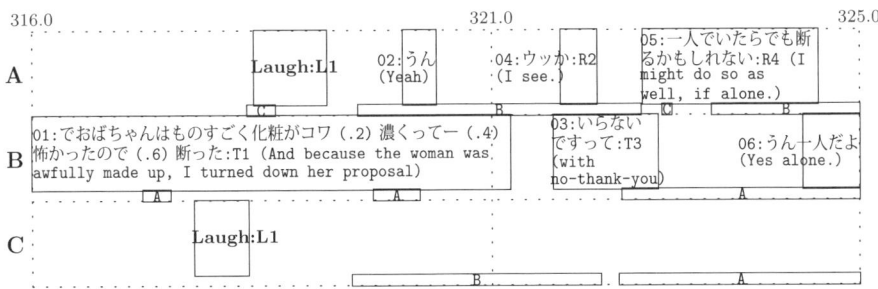

Fig. 3. Case 1. Each box in the figure shows transcripts (upper) and eye-direction (lower). The number of the top line shows an elapsed time from the start point of the conversation. Numbers within single parenthesis in the transcripts mark silence in seconds.

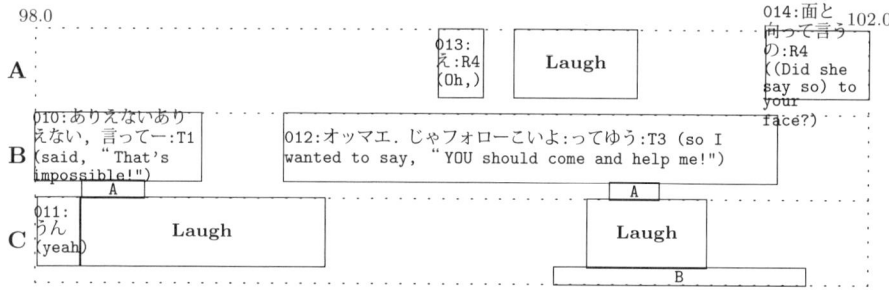

Fig. 4. Case 2

The conversation in this case mainly illustrates that B is telling a story that she encountered a woman who wanted to share her lunch with B in a Shinkansen. The utterance #01 in the figure is T1, which includes a possible completion point of the storytelling. As B has been looking only at A during her storytelling, A becomes OR while C is NOR. Both A and C are laughing at the punchline of B's story, i.e. the woman's dreadful make-up, when their laughs occur far before the completion of #01 to be regarded as [L1]. More precisely speaking, both of their laughs occur within a prolonged syllable duration of a TCU, that is, "化粧が濃くって— keshou ga koku tte:"('was awfully made up'). The [L1] type of laughter has no effect on the sequence organization for re-engagement around the ending part of storytelling shown in Case 1.

When T1 (#01) reaches its possible completion point, A avoids the re-engagement just giving a brief acknowledgement, "ウッカ" ('I see') at #04. And then B extends her story with T3; "いらないですって" ('with no-thank-you'), which causes A (as OR) to follow it with R4 (#05). The turn-by-turn talk has now been revived.

The same goes for laughter at T3. Case 2, which is the same example as (2) in 2.2, illustrates the [L1] type of laughter which occurred during T3 as the ending part of B's storytelling. In this example, A is OR and C is NOR. Though A (as OR) and C (as NOR) was laughing in the course of B's T3, A produced R4 at the possible completion point of T3 according to the sequence organization rule.

In short, laughs before a possible completion point never affect on the default sequence organization around the ending of a storytelling as described in Section 3. Though both OR and NOR happened to laugh at the same time in this example, there are many other cases where one laughs while the others don't. In any cases of [L1], whichever participant laughs doesn't matter to the follow-up sequential organization.

7 Analysis 2: Laughter at L2 - Avoidance of Taking a Turn

Second, we present several examples of [L2] type laughter. What will happen when OR laughs at L2 position? Case 3 (Fig.5) below is one of its examples.

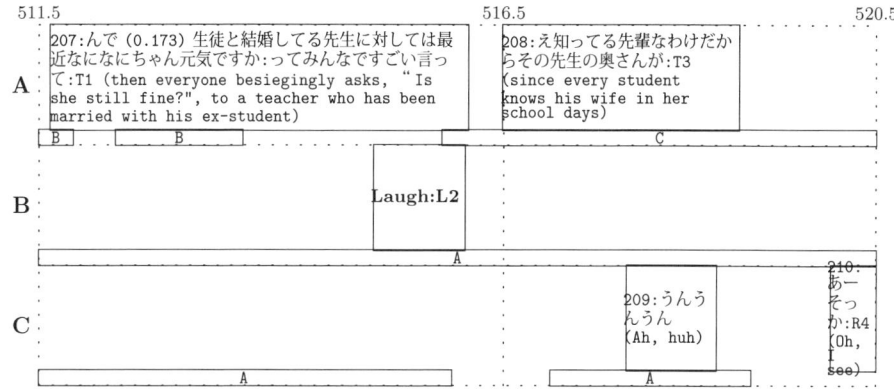

Fig. 5. Case 3

In this case the storyteller is A. A is talking about her high school days. Her main topic is that there were many fresh teachers who had been married with their students and, because of that, they were frequently bantered. The first OR in this conversation is B, who was being looked at by A and kept chiming in with A. That is why the NOR is the other hearer, C. C kept silent for over 20 seconds.

At the possible completion point of A's utterance #207 (i.e. T1), B (as OR) laughs without making an utterance such as R2 and R4. This is a [L2] type of laughter. Let us focus on the A's gaze at the moment. After the B's laughter, A turns his gaze at C. Then C, who used to be NOR, begins producing backchannels (#209) and makes an utterance as R4 at a possible completion point of T3. C hereupon begins her own experience in her school days.

What is happening in this example? The answer is that OR loses its own status when OR starts laughing. Since B laughs instead of producing R2/R4, A terminates T1 turning her gaze toward C and initiates T3. In other words, A's gaze toward C has changed the status as OR of her storytelling from B to C when A found that B does not try to re-engage into turn-by-turn talk. That enables C to start backchannels toward the storyteller and to hereupon produce R2/R4.

The same goes for the following Case 4 (Fig.6).

In this case, the storyteller is A while the OR is C (being looked at by A) and the NOR is B. #30 is T1 of this storytelling. At the possible completion point of #30, C as OR laughs, without making an utterance such as R2 and R4[1]. Then, A expands her storytelling by means of #33, while B as NOR tries to produce R4 at #32. Since both utterances of A and B happened to overlap, B suspends her utterance, but restarts it and takes a turn at #34 just after T3. What matters here is that C's laughter at L2 allowed B to take a turn at R4.

This is how OR's laughter within the transition space around T1 lets him/her pass his/her own occasion for speech to another participant, NOR.

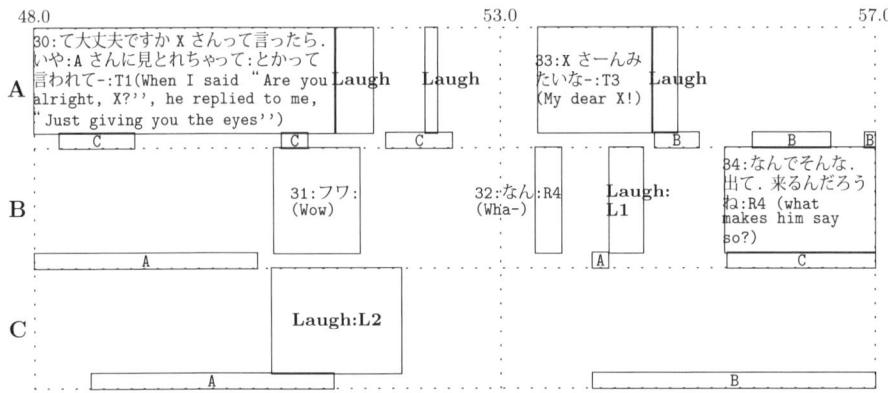

Fig. 6. Case 4

Case 5 (Fig. 7) below is an example in which OR does not have willingness to produce R2/R4. C is talking about her experience of not having her egg soft-boiled by her mother. As C is talking with her eyes toward B, B is OR while A is NOR. C utters #45 to B as T1, but B produces no utterances other than laughter at the possible completion point of T1. Instead, B turns her gaze toward A. Though we have no idea what A actually wants to say, A initiates some utterance with "Zan-". However, its timing was overlapped by the starting point of T3 produced by C, which prevented A from continuing that utterance. A seems to have chosen to laugh instead. C takes a glance at A because of A's laughter, but closes her story toward B again in due course. During and after that moment B is watching A with laughter, and then A (NOR) finally starts R4 and also acquires C's gaze.

This example illustrates a case where OR declines his/her own right to take a turn. It would appear that OR yields up a chance for taking a turn to NOR by combining or repeating such acts like producing laughter instead of speech and gazing at another hearer.

These cases in this section suggest that OR's laughter located at L2 functions as avoidance of taking a turn. We found out that when OR, who should be involved in the completion of storytelling, chooses laughter instead of speech, the storyteller or another hearer as NOR changes the sequential organization around (or after) the end of storytelling.

However, in order for NOR to be given a chance for speech by OR, NOR should not inadvertently laugh at L2. If both OR and NOR happen to laugh at L2, that would just bring the delay in the beginning of R2/R4. Case 6 (Fig.8) instantiates this phenomenon.

In this example, C is talking about crossing the path of a girl he knows. According to him, he passed by her without a word because she was walking

---

[1] #31 by B is not considered to be R2 because it is inserted as a kind of backchannels.

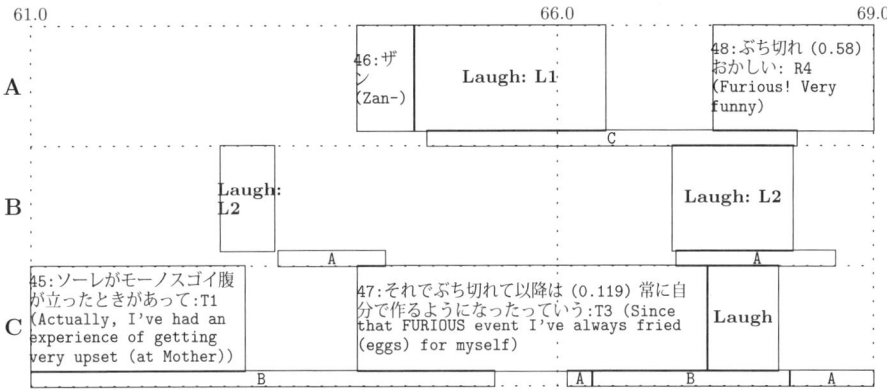

Fig. 7. Case 5

together with unknown men. C is talking with his eyes on A, so A is OR while B is NOR. C's utterance #373 could be possibly completed at "付いちゃうじゃん" ('would get such an impression of me'), where, in fact, A and B burst into laughter simultaneously. However, A stops laughing because he has noticed that the C's utterance still continues. After that, A begins to laugh again where the C's utterance meets the second possible completion point. On the contrary, B as NOR keeps laughing during that time. Then A stops laughing and takes a turn at R4 (#375).

As shown above the occurrence of laughter at L2 does not always delegate a turn-taking right to NOR when the laughter is produced by both OR and NOR. Actually OR takes the next turn in this case. NOR's laughter does not succeed in making C (storyteller) turn his gaze toward NOR. As a result, the laughter at L2 brings a slight delay of R2/R4 or gets another T3 produced by the same storyteller.

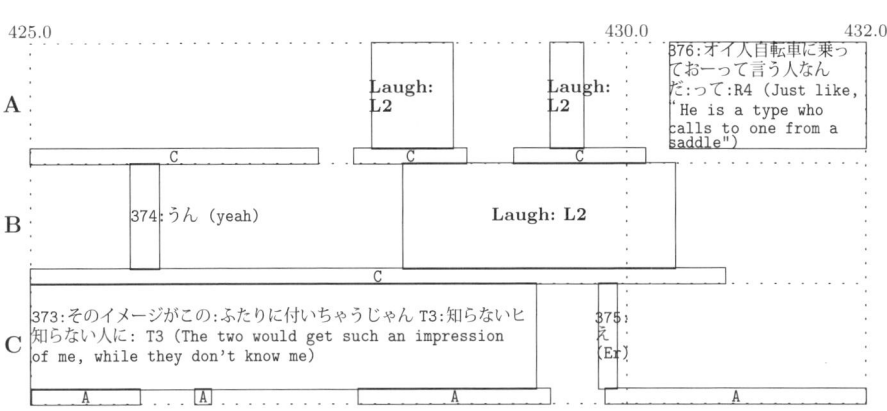

Fig. 8. Case 6

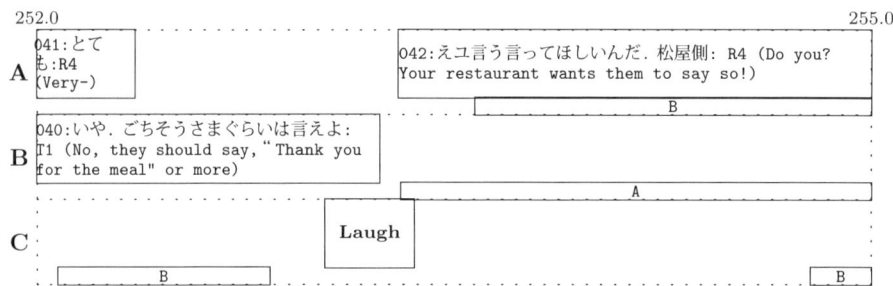

Fig. 9. Case 7

By the way when NOR alone laughs at the same position, the following sequential organization around the end of storytelling is never affected. In Case 7 (Fig. 9) the storyteller is B, who is talking with his eyes on A, so A is OR while C is NOR. A's utterance (#041) happens to be inserted because A has wrongly found a possible completion point of B's storytelling. The possible completion point which B has intended is, in fact, the end part of #040. At the same position, C as NOR alone laughs and A as OR inadvertently begins R4.

8 Discussion

In this paper we have examined how laughter is exquisitely embedded in the sequence organization around the end of storytelling. The functions of laughter vary according to the hearer's status (OR/NOR) and the occurrence position (L1/L2). Laughs within a storyteller's turn (L1), regardless of the hearer's status, never affect on the follow-up sequence organization. Also, laughs of NOR at a transition space (L2) don't affect on the follow-up sequence organization. Meanwhile, when only OR laughs at a transition space (L2), NOR gets a chance to produce R2 or R4 instead of OR. the case when OR and NOR laughs at the same time has an effect of delay in initiating R2 or R4. We can conclude that the laughs at L2 change the interaction on the following sequence design.

In particular, it is a curious result that OR's behavior at a possible completion point of storytelling affects the following design of the conversation. If OR laughs there without taking a turn, a storyteller shifts gaze from OR to NOR, which causes NOR to become OR. Our another research (Den & Enomoto[1]) investigates turn-by-turn talk in the same data and reveals that a non-next-speaking hearer (who doesn't take a next turn) frequently shifts gaze from a speaker to a next-speaking hearer at a possible completion point of a turn. The results in this paper suggest that the gaze-shift of a non-next-speaking hearer is to inspect whether or not a next-speaking hearer is willing to take a turn at that moment. We should verify that our results are also applicable to turn-by-turn talk in general.

Furthermore, though we dealt only with distinct cases with clear-cut hearer's status in this paper, there remains many other cases where both hearers are considered to be OR in that a storyteller looks at each hearer one after the other. In those cases, two hearers often start their talk simultaneously. But, even if both of the hearers are looked at by turns, the portion of the gaze duration and the position in the sequence where the gaze occurs might affect on the hearers' status. How will the design around the end of storytelling be changed according to the difference? These are our future tasks, too.

References

1. Den, Y., Enomoto, M.: A scientific approach to conversational informatics: Description, analysis, and modeling of human conversation. In: Nishida, T. (ed.) Conversational informatics: An engineering approach, pp. 307–330. Wiley and Sons Inc., Chichester (2007)
2. Enomoto, M., Den, Y.: How can hearers take a turn after a long interval. In: Proceedings of the 20th Conference on the Japanese Association of Sociolinguistic Science, pp. 58–61 (2007) (in Japanese)
3. Glenn, P.: Conversation analysis and the study of laughter. In: Laughter in Interaction, pp. 35–52. Cambridge University Press, Cambridge (2003)
4. Goffman, E.: Forms of Talk. University of Pennsylvania Press (1981)
5. Jefferson, G.: Sequential aspects of storytelling in conversation. In: Schenkein, J. (ed.) Studies in the Organization of Conversational Interaction, pp. 219–248. Academic Press, New York (1978)
6. Jefferson, G.: Notes on some orderlinesses of overlap onset. In: D'Urso, V., Leojardi, P. (eds.) Discorse analysis and natural rhetorics, pp. 11–38. CLEUP (1984)
7. Kipp, M.: Gesture Generation by Imitation: From Human Behavior to Computer Character Animation. Dissertation.com, Boca Raton, FL (2004), http://www.dfki.de/kipp/anvil/
8. Sacks, H.: Analysis of the course of a joke's telling in conversation. In: Bauman, R., Scherzer, J. (eds.) Explorations in the Ethnography of Speaking, pp. 337–353. Cambridge University Press, Cambridge (1974)
9. Sacks, H., Schegloff, E.A., Jefferson, G.: A simplest systematics for the organization of turn-taking for conversation. Language 50, 696–735 (1974)

Preliminary Notes on the Sequential Organization of Smile and Laughter

Hiromichi Hosoma*

University of Shiga Prefecture
2500 Hassaka, Hikone, Shiga, Japan 522-8533
http://www.shc.usp.ac.jp/hosoma/index-e.html

Abstract. Sequence analysis of smiling revealed that participants control the timing of smiling in different ways than they do the timing of laughter. Though the sequence of smiling often follows a format of invitation, met by either acceptance or declination, the invitation is not required as with laughter. A smile can occur without an accompanying utterance or recognition point, and may signal the opening of a new topic. While laughter is often terminated quickly when the other speaks, a smile can be maintained while the other speaks or until the other's gaze elicits a different response. In multi-party interaction, laughter is broadcasted while smiles and gaze can be addressed to an individual party and thus play a different role in the interaction.

Keywords: Conversation analysis, gaze, facial expression.

1 Introduction

Smiling and laughter are often categorized as the same thing. In modern Japanese, the word warau means both smiling and laughing. Indeed, beyond Japan, a smile is often understood as a precursor to or weaker version of laughter[1]. However, van Hooff [1] conducted a comparative study of facial expressions among various primates and concluded that the two expressions have different origins. The smile has evolved from fearful screaming, while laughter has evolved from ritualized gnawing or biting with accompanying vocalizations, such as coughing sounds or our burst of laughter. Recently, Kawakami et al. [4] found a discrepancy between smiling and laughter in the development of laterality, which suggests that a spontaneous smile and a spontaneous laugh might be different behaviors from the beginning.

If smiling and laughter are qualitatively different, then the two expressions should be organized differently in the sequence of conversations. Sequence analysis of conversation is the first step toward examining the process of laughter and smile production. In the field of laughter research, Jefferson [2] has examined the detailed process of laughter production in conversational sequence. She pointed out several features of laughter in conversations: 1. A speaker's utterance has a recognition point, a legitimate and expectable place for the recipient

---

* University of Shiga Prefecture.

to respond in the course of an ongoing utterance; 2. There is an invitation to laughter and acceptance sequence, in which the speaker indicates, by laughing him/herself, that laughter is appropriate and the recipient thereupon laughs; 3. When a recipient declines the invitation to laugh, the recipient begins speaking immediately after the previous speaker has recognizably started to laugh; and 4. In multi-party conversation, the first-responding recipient behaves like the current speaker, issuing minimal or equivocal invitations.

While the sequence analysis of laughter has progressed, most researches focusing on smiling have concentrated on examining the functions of smiling by counting the frequency of smiles under different conditions (see LaFrance and Hecht [5]), without considering their sequential organization in interactions.

In this paper, I examine whether Jefferson's finding about laughter can be applied to smiling to examine how smiling can be organized in conversational sequence. To examine smiling in the context of conversation, I have used a collection of video data that capture some of the details of smiling.

2 Transcription of Smile and Gaze

In a transcript format, a smile is marked by a dotted line beneath the utterance that it accompanied. A capital letter at the beginning of the line shows the place in the conversation where the smile is observed by the other person.

In the diagram shown in Fig. 1, a capital letter indicates a party in the conversation. A circle around the letter indicates a smile (*1). An arrow from the letter shows the direction of that party's gaze (*2). A small circle in front of a letter shows that the party is not looking at the other person, but is looking down, up, or at objects on the table (*3). A small dot in front of the character shows that the gaze of the party is in transition (*4).

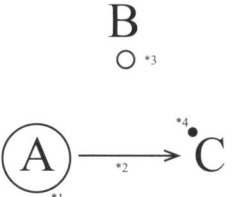

Fig. 1. transcription of diagram

3 Invitation of Smile without an Utterance

If a smile is a weak form of laughter and has the same function as laughter, we can assume that a sequence of utterances that includes a smile will have the same format as when such a sequence includes laughter. In the latter case, the speaker invites a recipient to laugh and the recipient accepts that invitation [2]. Fragment (a1) is a good example of such an invitation/acceptance sequence (Fig. 2) .

```
C:    _ _ _ _ _ _ _ _ _ _ _ _ _ _ _
A: (0.4)   Atashi  to   Celica  meccha   tabeteru  _ kedo
           I       and  Celica  much     eating      but
           "I      and  Celica  are eating a lot,    but"
```

Fig. 2. Transcript of fragment (a1). The second line of the transcript is the word-by-word glosses. The third line is the approximate English translation. The left bracket bridging multi-lines indicates a point of overlap onset, and the right bracket indicates the offset.

Though smiling may show the invitation/acceptance format, we found a very different configuration in the sequence. While laughter tends to occur just after a recognition point, when the speaker has completed an utterance [2], in this situation, Celica smiles first when no utterance has occurred and without a recognition point. Moreover, while laughter following an utterance tends to be a response to a prior recognition point [3], Azusa's smile following an utterance accompanies the opening of a new topic. Both a smile without invitation and a smile that follows an utterance and opens a new topic can be observed in fragment (b) (Fig. 3).

Azusa answers the phone and continues to listen to the caller even as she begins to smile at Celica (line5). Celica asks, A tutor? and initiates her smile in the middle of her utterance. Azusa's smile in line 5 might be a reaction to the sound of Celica's gulping, but Celica does not mention the sound and opens a new topic, guessing who the caller is.

There is another difference between smiling and laughter in invitation/acceptance sequence: tolerance for overlap. Jefferson [3] found that laughter is produced carefully to avoid overlap with the core of an utterance; if overlap

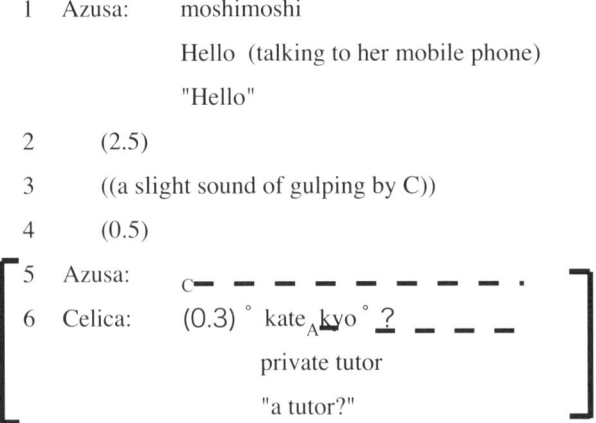

Fig. 3. Transcript of fragment (b)

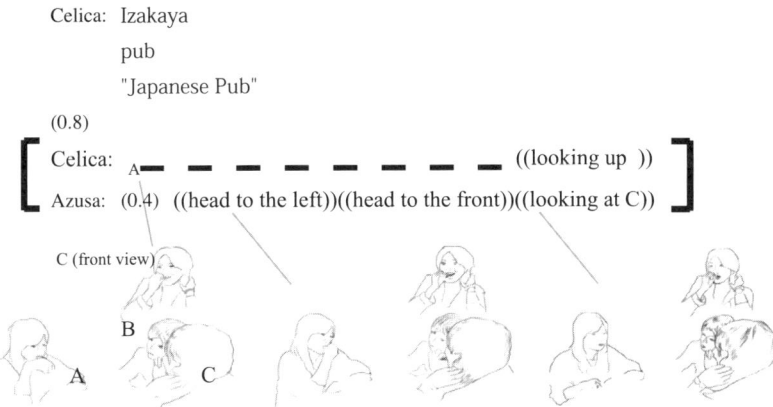

Fig. 4. Transcript of fragment (c)

occurs, a repair sequence follows. In contrast, the smiling in fragment (a) and (b) reveal no such control of timing; the smile persists until the utterance of the next speaker ends. While laughter produces sounds, smiles produce no sounds and, therefore, carry no risk of masking other utterances. This difference in communication channel might underlie this difference in tolerance for overlapping other's utterances. We will see the significance of this difference later in a multiparty conversation.

4 Invitation/Declination Sequence of Smile

Recipients of a smile do not always smile in return. Some smiles intended as invitations evoke negative expressions rather than smiling (Fig. 4).

In fragment (c), Azusa asks Beniko and Celica whether they know of any good part-time jobs for her. Celica replies, (Working at) Japanese pub, but Azusa does not respond for 0.8 seconds. Celica begins to smile, and rejecting her invitation, Azusa keeps silent for 0.4 seconds, does not smile, and lowers her head. When Azusa raises her head again and looks at Celica, Celica dramatically stops smiling and looks up to avoid Azusa's gaze. This sequence of obvious declination has several features: The initial smile remains even when the recipient responds negatively (by lowering her head), while the laughter stops immediately at the point when the recipient begins to speak without laughing (Jefferson [2]). The party who smiles first awaits the gaze of the recipient to show the recipient that the smile has terminated.

5 Smile and Gaze in Multi-party Interaction

When we observe multi-party interaction, we find another feature of smiling, namely its role in visual communication. The following transcript of fragment (a) (Fig. 5) containing the diagram of gaze reveals this feature.

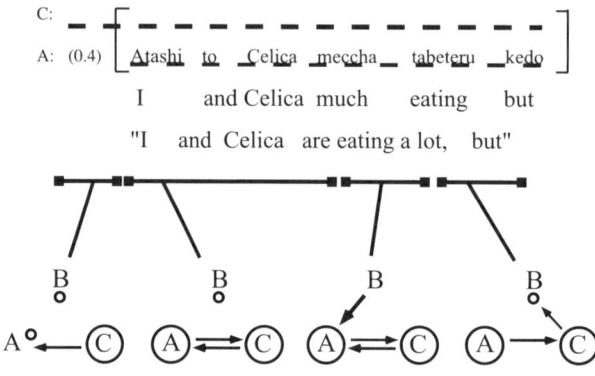

Fig. 5. Gaze and smile transition in fragment (a1)

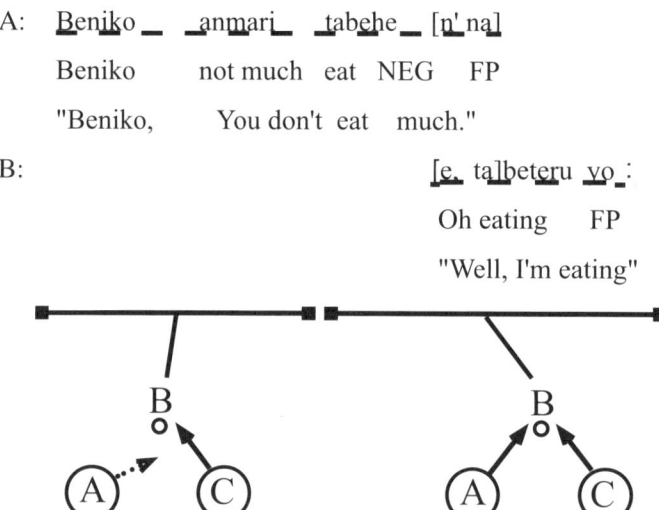

Fig. 6. Gaze and smile transition in fragment (a2). In the second line of the transcript, NEG is the abbreviation of "Negative" and FP is that of "Final Particle".

The focal phrase, I and Celica does not include the name of Beniko, who is excluded from the mutual gaze and smiles between Azusa and Celica. The absence of Beniko's name projects the subsequent division between the two parties and Beniko. Beniko may notice this projection just after the phrase, as she turns her gaze to Azusa, observes her smile to Celica, and looks down again without a smile (Fig. 5). At the same time, Celica dramatically turns her gaze and smile to Beniko, and Azusa begins to talk about Beniko in the subsequent sequence (Fig. 6).

In fragment (a2), Azusa calls Beniko's name and turns her smile to Beniko. When Beniko replies, Well I'm eating, Azusa and Celica both smile at Beniko; Beniko keeps looking down without a smile, and the mutual gaze is not achieved.

Here we can see another feature of smiling as visual communication. In acoustic communication, an expression can be broadcasted and delivered immediately to others and we cannot close our ears. The message can only be avoided if another expression masks it. In visual communication, however, we have to secure the gaze of others to communicate the expression; thus, recipients can refuse an expression by looking away, even if they are aware of the expression through indirect observation. In other words, the direction of the gaze is crucial in visual communication to indicate to whom the expression is addressed. These features prolong the invitation of a smile until the recipient sees the smile, revealing the division of participants into two categories: those who return the gaze and smile and those who do not return the gaze and do not smile.

6 Conclusion

This analysis has focused on the features of smiling in the sequential organization of conversation. We found that, while smiles have the interactive format of invitation followed by acceptance or declination, the manner of the organization is different from that seen with laughter. Laughter occurs at an identifiable recognition point that signals an invitation to laugh, and we tend to see laughter as the response to that signal. In contrast, smiling does not always involve a response to an obvious recognition point; rather, it can start without an utterance inviting the recipient to smile and talk. In the examples offered in this paper, smiling seems to be a precursor to a new topic rather than a precursor to laughter.

Some types of smiles do accompany laughter, and these are organized differently in multi-party interaction (Hosoma, in preparation). Our future work will focus on comparing different types of smiles and rethinking the biological difference between smiling and laughter.

References

1. van Hooff, J.A.R.A.M., Preuschoft, S.: Laughter and smiling:The intertwining of nature and culture. In: de Waal, F.B.M., Tyack, P.L. (eds.) Animal social complexity: Intelligence, culture, and individualized societies, pp. 260–287. Harvard University Press, Cambridge (2003)
2. Jefferson, G.: A technique for inviting laughter and its subsequent acceptance/declination. In: Psathas, G. (ed.) Everyday language: Studies in ethnomethodology, pp. 79–96. Irvington Publishers, New York (1979)
3. Jefferson, G., Sacks, H., Schegloff, E.A.: Notes on Laughter in the Pursuit of Intimacy. In: Button, G., Lee, J.R.E. (eds.) Talk and Social Organization, pp. 152–205. Multilingual Matters, Clevedon (1987)
4. Kawakami, K., Takai-Kawakami, K., Tomonaga, M., Suzuki, J., Kusaka, T., Okai, T.: Origins of smile and laughter: A preliminary study. Early Human Development 82, 61–66 (2006)
5. LaFrance, M., Hecht, M.A.: Option or Obligation to Smile: The effects of power and gender on facial expression. In: Philippot, P., Feldman, R.S., Coats, E.J. (eds.) The social context of nonverbal behavior, pp. 45–70. Cambridge University Press, Cambridge (1999)

Laughter for Defusing Tension: Examples from Business Meetings in Japanese and in English

Kazuyo Murata

Ryukoku University
67, Fukakusa-Tsukamoto-cho, Fushimi-ku, Kyoto, 612-8577, Japan
murata@law.ryukoku.ac.jp

Abstract. The present study addresses one function of laughter in workplace meetings, namely laughter which does not reflect amusement and which occurs where there is tension between speakers and hearers. In this study, this laughter is illustrated with examples from authentic business meeting data in Japanese and in English, recorded in Japan and New Zealand respectively. Based on analysis of meeting data, the following differences were found: (1) laughter alone (not associated with humor) serves to defuse tension in the Japanese data; (2) laughter associated with humor and funniness serves the same function in the English data.

Keywords: Laughter1, Laughter2, defusing tension.

1 Introduction

It is often heard that non native speakers of Japanese cannot understand why the Japanese laugh meaninglessly at non-humorous situations. In my experience, one such example is in TV news. In a recent Japanese newscast, for example, a reporter interviewed local residents just after a big earthquake. One local resident talked about how awful things were during the earthquake with accompanying laughter. Another example is at a faculty meeting. In a serious discussion, a professor disagreed with another professor, raised an objection and finished it with laughter.

It is generally agreed that people laugh in various situations, but are there any differences between the manifestation and function of laughter in Japanese and in English in non-humorous or serious situations? In English interaction, there are also cases where laughter occurs in situations of discomfort, embarrassment, and anxiety. Emerson [5], Ragan [22], and Mallet & A'Hern [16] examine laughter in medical situations such as conversations between patients and medical staff. In contrast to the Japanese laughter illustrated above, the patients talk in a humorous tone and the laughter is associated with humor.

In the present study, laughter which occurs in situations of tension will be analyzed from a relational, or politeness, framework. The data is from naturally-occurring business meetings in a Japanese and a New Zealand company. The data set comprises video and audio recordings totaling approximately 200 minutes recorded in the Japanese workplace and 220 minutes recorded in the NZ workplace.

2 Study on Laughter from a Relational Perspective

Laughter has received attention from various disciplines such as physiology and psychology, and in most studies it has been addressed as a physical phenomenon (Glenn [7]; Hayakawa [8]). However, the question, "why people laugh", has traditionally been explored from philosophical perspectives. Three major theories of humor provide possible answers to this question: firstly superiority theory deriving from the work of the philosophers Plato and Aristotle, and more recently Hobbes; secondly, incongruity theory deriving from the work of Kant and Schopenhauer; and thirdly relief theory associated with Freud (Morreall [17]).

These major theories of humor are mainly concerned with the causes of laughter; they treat laughter as a passive phenomenon, a response to a stimulus. However, as Osborne & Chapman [20] and Brown, Brown, & Ramos [1] contend, laughter occurs more often when people are together, and it is most fruitfully studied in terms of its functions in interaction.

From a discourse analysis point of view, conversation analysts (e.g., Jefferson [14]; Jefferson, Sacks, & Schegloff [15]) study laughter through detailed observation and description of conversations and focus mainly on its sequence organization in interaction. For example, Jefferson [14] regards sequence-involved laughter as comprising an invitation and acceptance/declining, pointing out that "laughter can be managed as a sequence in which speaker of an utterance invites recipient to laugh and accepts that invitation" ([14]: 93).

However, laughter is not only a constituent of a conversational sequence but also a component of conversants' communicative behaviors, serving particular discourse functions in interaction. It is thus reasonable to study laughter from a relational point of view in order to shed light on its functions and motivations.

There is some previous research which examines laughter by focusing on its social role, from a sociological perspective (e.g., Hertzler [9]) or ethological perspective (e.g., Provine [21]). It is generally agreed that laughter serves an affiliative function. Among the research on laughter from a relational perspective, the most recent comprehensive sociolinguistic studies are Glenn [7] and Hayakawa [8]. Glenn [7] focuses on the production and interpretation of laughter in English interactions, while Hayakawa [8] examines laughter in Japanese interactions.

Glenn [7] uses a CA framework to analyze laughter in English natural conversational data. He approaches laughter as "intentional social action" ([7]: 32) and his focus is "on what people display to each other and accomplish in and through their laughter" ([7]: 33). He identifies two categories of laughter: The major kind of laughter is called shared laughter, or *laughing with*, which proves important socially as a means of showing affiliation with others. The second kind of laughter is called *laughing at*, which may not be shared among the conversants. He suggests that *laughing at* may be used to indicate disaffiliation. It is marked by four characteristics: (1) a laughable referent that designates someone co-present as butt of the humor; (2) first laugh by someone else; (3) second laugh by someone else or not-occurring; and (4) continued talk on topic ([7]: 165). Showing that the shift from *laughing with* to *laughing at* and vice versa often occurs dynamically in interaction, he emphasizes that it is important to analyze laughter discursively.

Hayakawa [8] analyzes laughter in Japanese natural conversational data, and suggests that laughter displays speakers' cooperative orientations towards the conversation-in-progress and contributes to its smooth development. She categorizes laughter into the following three kinds:

(A) Joyful laughter indicating identification with the in-group (laughter for promoting conversation)

This kind of laughter occurs among intimates and indicates that the speaker and the hearer are members of the same in-group. The speaker expects hearers to share what he or she thinks is funny and enjoyable. The atmosphere among the participants reflects enjoyment, even if the speakers do not necessarily say anything funny. The ensuing laughter promotes conversations.

(B) Balancing laughter for easing tension

This kind of laughter "is used to keep a balance in one's mind when what one is about to say or do is likely to take the conversation in a direction which will impact negatively on the sense of cooperation between the participants" (Hayakawa [8]: 328). This laughter occurs "when one reveals something in one's field that one does not want to be seen clearly, such as embarrassment or shame" ([8]: 229). It also occurs when "one gets into the listener's field and asks something, or requests something" ([8]: 229).

(C) Laughter as a cover-up

This kind of laughter is used by a speaker to maintain his or her turn in order to make the conversation more cooperative. It is used as an avoidance mechanism when speakers don't want to answer or reveal their opinions.

Though there are different functions in each category of laughter, Hayakawa concludes that "in all cases the goal is to strengthen the unity within a group of participants" ([8]: 327).

Glenn [7] and Hayakawa [8] agree that laughter plays an important role in the creation and maintenance of interpersonal relationships. However, differences are apparent in the interpretation of the social meaning of the laughter in the English data analyzed by Glenn [7] and the Japanese data analyzed by Hayakawa [8]. Glenn's [7] main focus is laughter which is associated with things which are laughable or funny, while Hayakawa's [8] main focus is laughter which does not indicate amusement or humor.

3 What Characterizes Japanese Laughter?

In Murata [18], I analyzed intercultural conversations conducted in English between American and Japanese participants on their first encounter. I also analyzed the follow-up interviews with the participants. The results indicated interesting differences between the participants.

While the Americans laughed only at comments which were obviously intended to be funny, the Japanese not only laughed at humorous comments but also at more general and neutral comments. The Americans did not seem to know how to interpret the Japanese laughter where it did not reflect amusement, and this caused misunderstanding between the Americans and the Japanese (see Murata [18] for further discussion).

From the results of this analysis, it appears that Japanese laughter, like American laughter, may reflect amusement or enjoyment: however, it is equally evident that, unlike American laughter, Japanese laughter does not always necessarily reflect amusement.

Taking these results into consideration, I analyzed laughter in Japanese business meetings (see Murata [19] for further details). The study categorized laughter into (1) laughter which indicates enjoyment (Laughter1); and (2) laughter for reasons other than indicating enjoyment (Laughter2).

In the data, Laughter2 was observed in the following situations: (a) making requests; (b) showing reluctance to accept requesting or advice; (c) disagreeing; (d) criticizing; (e) being unwilling to express something which is not good for the business goal; (f) performing greetings (when meeting for the first time in a while). It can be generalized that all these situations are those in which there is the potential for heightened tension between speakers and hearers.

4 Framework of the Analysis

The theory I adopt for focusing on the interpersonal aspect of communication derives from politeness theory. It is generally agreed that Brown & Levinson's [2] politeness theory, which is based on *face*, is still the most comprehensive framework in this area. In Brown & Levinson's politeness theory, face refers to basic and universal human desires as they pertain to social interaction. Face consists of two specific kinds of desires: the desire not to be imposed on and to have freedom of action (negative face), and the desire to be accepted, liked, and understood by others (positive face) ([2]: 13).They contend that the motivation behind speakers' employing politeness strategies is to redress face threat.

Holmes & Stubbe [13] explored how the relational aspect of communication plays a role in the workplace discourse. Drawing on data from Language in the Workplace Project (see section 5), Holmes & Stubbe ([13]: 5) found that "most workplace interactions provide evidence of mutual respect and concern for the feeling or face needs of others, that is, of politeness", though, in the workplace discourse, transactional efficiency is also required in order to achieve a task.

Building on this work, Holmes & Marra [11] and Holmes & Schnurr [12] examined the issue of what it means to be polite in workplace discourse and found that *relational practice* (hereafter RP), which derives from Fletcher's [6] work, is a useful term for discussing politeness in the workplace. These authors emphasize the value of RP in analyzing workplace interaction, incorporating Brown & Levinson's [2] notion of face, and delineate the following three crucial components of RP:

(1) RP is oriented to the (positive and negative) face need of others.
(2) RP serves to advance the primary objectives of the workplace.
(3) RP practices at work are regarded as dispensable, irrelevant, or peripheral.
                       (Holmes & Marra [11]: 378; Holmes & Schnurr [12]: 125)

RP is manifested as discursive strategies negotiated among interactants and emphasizes the dynamic nature of interaction. Analyzing RP thus requires detailed linguistic analysis taking the ongoing process of interaction into consideration.

RP has been selected as an appropriate framework for the present study for the following two reasons: (1) the data of the present study comprises business meetings which are workplace interactions; (2) the data will be analyzed from an interpersonal point of view.

5 Data and Methods

The data analyzed in this paper is from naturally-occurring business meetings in a Japanese and a New Zealand company. The data set comprises video and audio recordings totally approximately 200 minutes recorded in the Japanese workplace and 220 minutes recorded in the NZ workplace.

The Japanese meetings took place in an IT (Information Technology) company. In analyzing the Japanese data, follow-up interviews which clarified participants' reasons for laughing were taken into consideration.

The New Zealand data conducted in English is drawn from the Language in the Workplace Corpus. Language in the Workplace Project (hereafter LWP) started in 1996 under the direction of Professor Janet Holmes, Victoria University of Wellington. The team has collected approximately 1,500 interactions, involving a total of 500 people. A total of 220 minutes' video and audio recordings of NZ business meetings were selected for this research from the corpus. The meetings took place in a production company. In analyzing the New Zealand data, follow-up interviews with researchers of LWP were conducted. I asked them about the company's background information, the human relationships among the meeting participants, and situations where laughter occurs. Information gathered in interviews with the workplace participants were taken into consideration.

6 Laughter2: Laughter in Tension

In this section, I will illustrate some examples of Laughter2 in the Japanese business meetings. Then, from the New Zealand business meetings, Laughter2, which occurs in situations of tension, will be shown.

6.1 Examples from the Japanese Data

In example (1), from a meeting of 16 participants, N, the salesperson in an IT company, is talking about his client company which is interested in employing environmental accounting. The consultant T is asking N to let him know more about those aspects of environmental accounting that the client wants to incorporate into their company before selling the company's product (utterance 1). The salesperson N is not familiar with accounting and is asking T, the business consultant, for his advice about the client. When making a request to T, N adds laughter in the middle of his utterance (utterance 6). Then, T responds with laughter in his utterance (utterance 7).

(1)
1 T: (　)を含めての対応だとは思うんですけれども。ま、それで、逆に、あのお手伝いていうか、何をしたいんかということと、その環境会計のどの部分をおりこんでくれ、ていう話を聞かせていただければ
　　I think that we should address it including (　). I was wondering if you could let me know what the client wants and what aspect of environment accounting they employ
2 N: (2.0) [メモを取っている]　はい
　　(2.0) [taking memo] Yes
3 T: 少し、あの、考えることも可能かと思います
　　I think I would be able to think about advice for your client
4 N: はい。そこをポイントに次回アポイントをとれたらヒアリングを//やりたい\と思います
　　OK. I'll ask my client about those points when I make an appointment with them.
5 T: /はい\\
　　/Yes\\
6 N: えっと、またご相談させて頂くと思いますんで// [笑] よろしくお願いいたします。
　　Well, I think I will ask you about it // [**laughs**] \ If it is alright with you
7 T: / [笑]\\ はい。ちょっとお時間ください。これは即答なかなか
　　/ [**laughs**]\\ Well, give me time, please. I'm afraid I can't answer quickly
(KAI02-3, 4:43)

Requesting is a face threatening act and it is clear that there is tension between speakers and hearers when making a request. N is employing hedges like "*etto* (well)" and "*omoimasunde* (I think)" to mitigate the effect of his face threatening utterance when asking T for his advice. It is reasonable to think that adding laughter also serves to ease the tension. T expresses his hesitation to accept N's request by saying "*kore wa sokutou nakanaka* (I'm afraid I can't answer quickly)". Not accepting a request would be uncomfortable for hearers and the tension would occur between speakers and hearers. T shows consideration toward N by responding with laughter in his utterance and laughter here seems to function to mitigate the tension. It can be argued that the motivation behind mitigating the tension between speakers and hearers is to maintain or enhance good relationships between them. Thus, in this example, laughter discursively serves as a relational role, or RP.

In example (2), again from a meeting of 16 participants, the salesperson K is reporting his sales results. K's client company has a deficit problem and cannot afford to buy the company's product. In this situation, he is reporting that the client will not buy the company's product even if he strongly advises him to do so, and adds laughter. Following the speaker's laughter, a second participant responds with laughter.

(2)
  1 K: もう今後、赤字（　　）部門だったオンライン事業は撤退というところで、プラスの見込める、えー、コミュニティーサイトの運営企画と、あとは受託開発というところに絞って、やっていくというところなので、まあ、今期なんとかプラスに持ち直したいというような状況の会社で，えー、であります [笑]

They will give up online business which is affected by the deficit and focus on planning and managing the community website and on developing products on commission. Well, this company is in a situation where they do hope that the management condition will improve in this term [**laughs**]

  2 S: [笑]
       [**laughter**]

(KAI02-2, 28:20)

Reporting bad sales results stands in contrast to business objectives and it makes the reporter feel uncomfortable at the supposed failure. The reporter employs hedges such as "*ee/maa* (well)" to soften his admission. The speaker's laughter here serves the same function as the hearer's laughter which expresses sympathy to the speaker. Both cooperatively reduce the tension occurring among the meeting members in talks against business objectives, and laughter in this example also serves a relational role, or RP.

Example (3) is a scene from a business meeting of 5 participants. Just before starting the interaction, the CEO was talking about how to promote the sale of the company's product, but there was misunderstanding of the way of promoting it in his talk. Following his turn, the consultant T and the outside director M start to talk.

(3)
  1 T: いや、もうそれはよくわかるんですけど。
       Well, I understand that well…
  2 M: えーっとですね、えーっと、どう言えばいいんですかね//[笑]\Tさん
       Well, actually, I was wondering how I could say, //[**laughs**]\ Mr. T
  3 T: /えっ?\\
       /What?\\
  4 M: 多分思っていることは一緒だと思うんですけど。
       Probably, what I am thinking would be the same as what you are saying.
  5 T: うーん。
       Well, yes.
  6 M: ということをデモでやられてるんですよね、普段。まだそこまでやってないんですかね。
       You usually indicate such things during demonstrations of the product. Or you haven't done that so far, have you?
  7 H: いや、そういうことを説明しているんですよ。
       No, we only explain such things there.

(BEF05, 13:30)

The consultant T and the outside director M would like to point out and correct the CEO's misunderstanding, but out of respect they cannot. Correcting your interlocutor is also considered a face threatening act by Brown and Levinson [2], especially problematic here where the CEO is of higher status and when they are outside consultants at this company. These factors prevent them from explicitly pointing out and correcting the CEO's misunderstanding. On the other hand, their role is to give advice to the company and they should make the correction in order to achieve their transactional objectives. This discrepancy results in tension for both M and T. M's laughter in this example serves to mitigate the tension.

The common characteristic among the three examples illustrated above is that laughter serves as RP to mitigate tension and maintain good relationships among the meeting members, and that it does not accompany humor[1] but instead follows utterances unmarked for humor.

6.2 Examples from the English Data

Example (4) is a scene from a business meeting between S and J in a production company. S, the marketing manager, and J, the general manager, are explaining a client's needs based on the sudden death of a key member of the client's company. They do not have any procedure for dealing with this kind of matter and did not know what to do with the products related to the client.

(4)
1   S: but this morning I had a woman ring me from um <project name> and someone has died + someone who's a quite significant figure within the what's the word
2   J: (   )
3   S: that's it
4   J: I knew it was one of them //[**laughs**]\
5   S: /yeah\\ and um + her name is mentioned in a lot of a lot of their products cos she has a lot to do with the <project name> and also her photograph appears in the products and so everything with her name on it or where her photograph appears has to be destroyed and reprinted
6   J: cool
7   S: yeah that's what I thought //but I didn't say it to her + (   ) [**laughs**]\
8   J: /[**laughs**] sorry oh that how sad [**laughs**]\\
9   S: yeah //um\
10 J: /okay\\ yeah

(A01P1-10/7-8)

It could be argued that talking about serious matters makes these interactants feel uncomfortable. To overcome their unease at their good fortune (i.e., extra funds to replace the products with the new staff member), the members talk in a humorous

---

[1] I employ Holmes's [10] definition of humor regarding what counts as humorous: "Instances of humour included in this analysis are utterances which are identified by the analyst, on the basis of paralinguistic, prosodic and discoursal clues, as intended by the speaker(s) to be amusing and perceived to be amusing by at least some participants "(Holmes [10]: 163).

tone cooperatively, and laughter takes place throughout the discussion. This indicates that laughter accompanying humor in this example functions as RP.

In example (5), from a meeting of 11 participants, the topic is the result of a customer survey conducted by the company. While J is talking, R disagrees by negating J's utterance. This causes amusement for the group because this R's utterance might be what J thinks though J claimed he was not criticizing the "guys".

(5)
1   J: I think I think the other thing too to note is that we're actually not even already judging these //guys\
2   S: /no\\
3   J: we don't we're not saying that they're doing it wrong we're saying that they're really that's they're doing the best they can //+ but it's not that no but we no we said hear me out we're saying they're\ doing the best they can but that's not gonna be good enough when <retail shops in the same industry> comes along because we're gonna be able to offer such a better system such a better service
4   R: /oh no i'm saying they're doing it wrong [**laughs**]\\
5   S: they just don't know any better do they
6   J: they just don't any better //it's guys it's guys\ he is running the press he is answering the phones he is doing the quoting
7   R: /but the the the serv-\\

(AMMVM-02/67)

In the example above, in contrast to the Japanese business meeting data, disagreeing, a face threatening act, is conducted in a humorous tone (utterance 4), and laughter accompanying humor here serves as RP by mitigating the tension among the meeting members.

In example (6), from a meeting of 11 participants, the meeting participants are discussing their company's re-branding. They are discussing renaming the business and changing to bright colors.

(6)
1   B: so there's gonna be no more <company's old name>
2   W: //no\
3   J: /correct\\
4   B: no
5   H: oh
6   J: gone
7   W: gone
8   H: ok, so we're back to plain brown
9   W: //no\\
10 E: /[**laughs**]\\
11 B: /[**laughs**]\\
12 J: /let's not (think this)\\
13 B: there'll be no mistaking them
14 W: they'll be //orange and green now\

15 B: that was the whole idea + of having all of our cartons
    [laughter]
                                                    (AMMVM-042/67)

Re-branding is a serious matter for a company. Whether the company is going to succeed or not depends on the decision of the meeting. It seems reasonable to assume that some anxiety and tension may be generated by this topic. It can be argued that talking in a humorous tone cooperatively and discursively following laughter serves to mitigate this tension and that the humor functions as RP in this discourse.

The common characteristic among the three examples illustrated above is that laughter associated with humor and funniness is observed, and it serves a relational role by mitigating the tension to maintain good relationships among the meeting participants. As opposed to the Japanese data, in each of these examples the laughter accompanies humorous talk about a sensitive or a serious topic where tension could occur.

7 Conclusion

In sum, the Japanese participants in the data use laughter alone (not associated with humor) when communication becomes tense, while the New Zealand participants in the data use humor, and associated laughter, to alleviate tension in their meetings.

This difference suggests a contrast in the role and the function of humor between English speaking societies and Japan. Humor serves an essential role from a relational perspective (e.g. Holmes & Marra [11]; Holmes & Schnurr [12]), and can also contribute to productivity in the workplace (e.g. Consalvo [4]; Caudron [3]). The research literature indicates that humor is particularly important in the workplace in English speaking societies. Takekuro [23] conducted a contrastive study on humor in Japanese and in English by analyzing movies, TV dramas, and authentic conversations. She showed that there were no occurrences of humor in Japanese formal business settings while there were many occurrences of humor in similar settings in English. These findings suggest that humor may simply not be appropriate in Japanese workplace settings.

This study is based on a limited amount of data and it is impossible to generalize the results. More and more empirical research on laughter in tension in Japanese and English interaction clearly needs to be conducted in order to shed light on cultural differences in laughter. Nonetheless, the results are interesting and suggestive.

The analysis indicates that laughter is linked to RP both in Japanese and NZ business meetings: in both datasets, the meeting participants laugh cooperatively in stretches of discourse related to the defusing of tension. On the other hand, the manifestation of laughter is different between the Japanese and NZ business meetings. In the NZ business meetings laughter is a response to humor, while this is not the case in the Japanese business meetings. This difference might appear trivial, but because of its relational function, it could well be the seed of misunderstanding in intercultural communication. The present research is a good starting point for exploring potential cultural differences in the functions of laughter from a relational perspective.

Acknowledgments

I thank those who allowed their business meetings to be recorded and members of Language in the Workplace who allowed me to analyze their valuable data. I would also like to thank Janet Holmes, Meredith Marra, and Rebecca Adams who read drafts of this article and provided helpful comments and advice.

References

1. Brown, G.E., Brown, D., Ramos, J.: Effects of a Laughing versus a Nonlaughing Model on Humor Responses in College Students. Psychological Reports 48, 35–40 (1981)
2. Brown, P., Levinson, S.: Politeness: Some Universals in Language Usage. Cambridge University Press, Cambridge (1987)
3. Caudron, S.: Humor is Healthy in the Workplace. Personnel Journal 71(6), 63–66 (1992)
4. Consalvo, C.M.: Humor in Management: No Laughing Matter. Humor 2(3), 285–297 (1989)
5. Emerson, J.: Negotiating the Serious Import of Humor. Sociometry 32, 169–181 (1969)
6. Fletcher, J.K.: Disappearing Acts: Gender, Power, and Relational Practice at Work. The MIT Press, Cambridge (1999)
7. Glenn, P.: Laughter in Interaction. Cambridge University Press, Cambridge (2003)
8. Hayakawa, H.: The Meaningless Laughter: Laughter in Japanese Communication. Unpublished PhD Thesis, University of Sydney, Australia (2003)
9. Hertzler, J.O.: Laughter: A Socio-Scientific Analysis. Exposition Press, New York (1970)
10. Holmes, J.: Politeness, Power and Provocation: How Humour Functions in the Workplace. Discourse Studies 2(2), 159–185 (2000)
11. Holmes, J., Marra, M.: Relational Practice in the Workplace: Women's Talk or Gendered Discourse? Language in Society 33, 377–398 (2004)
12. Holmes, J., Schnurr, S.: Politeness, Humor and Gender in the Workplace: Negotiating Norms and Identifying Contestation. Journal of Politeness Research 1, 121–149 (2005)
13. Holmes, J., Stubbe, M.: Power and Politeness in the Workplace. A Sociolinguistic Analysis of Talk at Work. Longman, London (2003)
14. Jefferson, G.: A Technique for Inviting Laughter and Its Subsequent Acceptance Declination. In: Psathas, G. (ed.) Everyday Language: Studies in Ethnomethodology, pp. 79–96. Harvard University Press, New York (1979)
15. Jefferson, G., Sacks, H., Schegloff, E.: Notes on Laughter in the Pursuit of Intimacy. In: Button, G., Lee, J.R.E. (eds.) Talk and Social Organisation, pp. 152–205. Multilingual Matters, Clevedon (1987)
16. Mallett, J., A'hern, R.: Comparative Distribution and Use of Humour within Nurse-Patient Communication. International Journal of Nursing Studies 33(5), 530–550 (1996)
17. Morreall, J.: Taking Laughter Seriously. State University of New York Press, Albany (1983)
18. Murata, K.: Ibogowasha gurupu kaiwa ni mirareru "warai" no bunseki: poraitonesu no kanten kara [Laughter in Intercultural Conversations from a Politeness Perspective]. In: The JASS (Japanese Association of Sociolinguistic Sciences) 15th Conference, pp. 120–123 (2005)
19. Murata, K.: Nihongo bijinesu mithingu ni mirareru warai: taijinkankei kinoumen kara no bunseki [Laughter in Japanese Business Meetings from a Relational Perspective]. In: The JASS (Japanese Association of Sociolinguistic Sciences) 21st Conference, pp. 56–59 (2008)

20. Osborne, K.A., Chapman, A.J.: Suppression of Adult Laughter: An Experimental Approach. In: Chapman, A.J., Foot, H.C. (eds.) It's a Funny Thing, Humour, pp. 429–432. Pergamon, New York (1977)
21. Provine, R.R.: Laughter: A Scientific Investigation. Viking, New York (2000)
22. Ragan, S.L.: Verbal Play and Multiple Goals in the Gynaecological Exam Interaction. Journal of Language and Social Psychology 9, 67–84 (1990)
23. Takekuro, M.: Conversational Jokes in Japanese and English. In: Davis, J.M. (ed.) Understanding Humor in Japan, pp. 85–98. Wayne State University Press, Detroit (2006)

Appendix: Transcription Conventions

[laughs]	Paralinguistic features, descriptive information
<company name, product name>	
(3.0)	Pause of special number of seconds
+	Pause of up to one second
....// ...... \...	Simultaneous speech, interrupted (overlapped) speech
.../ .... \\	interrupting (overlapping) speech
(hello)	Transcriber's best guess at an unclear utterance
( )	Indecipherable speech
serv-	Incomplete or cutoff utterance

Robots Make Things Funnier

Jonas Sjöbergh and Kenji Araki

Graduate School of Information Science and Technology
Hokkaido University
{js,araki}@media.eng.hokudai.ac.jp

Abstract. We evaluate the influence robots can have on the perceived funniness of jokes. We let people grade how funny simple word play jokes are, and vary the presentation method. The jokes are presented as text only or said by a small robot. The same joke is rated significantly higher when presented by the robot. We also let one robot tell a joke and have one more robot either laugh, boo, or do nothing. Laughing and booing is significantly funnier than no reaction, though there was no significant difference between laughing and booing.

1 Introduction

While humans use humor very often in daily interactions, computer systems are still far from able to use humor freely. Research on humor has been done in many different research areas, for instance psychology, philosophy, sociology and linguistics. When it comes to computer processing of humor in various ways, a good overview of the recent research can be found in [1]. Two main areas of computer implementations exist, humor recognition and humor generation. For humor generation, systems generating quite simple forms of jokes, e.g. word play jokes, have been constructed [2,3,4,5,6]. Recognition systems that try to recognize whether a text is a joke or not have also been constructed [7,8,9].

Our paper is mainly relevant for generation systems. What is considered amusing varies a lot from person to person. Many things have an influence on how funny something is perceived to be, such as the general mood at the time or who is delivering the joke. This makes evaluating and comparing jokes and joke generating systems complicated. We evaluate the effects of different ways of delivering simple jokes to evaluators. Our hypothesis was that jokes would be perceived as funnier when presented by a small robot than when presented in text form. We also hypothesised that the same joke would be perceived as funnier if another robot for instance laughs at the joke than with no reaction.

We evaluate the effects of different ways of delivering simple jokes to evaluators by showing simple word play jokes to volunteer evaluators. Some jokes were told by a small robot, while some were presented only as text. We also evaluated the effects of feedback on the jokes, in the form of another robot laughing, booing, or showing no reaction after the first robot told a joke. Despite some problems with for instance the voice of the robot being hard to hear and understand, both hypotheses were confirmed.

2   Evaluation Method

We have collected a large set of simple word play jokes in Japanese. These were collected by searching the Internet for a few seed jokes. Any page containing at least two of the seed jokes was then automatically processed to find the largest common left and right contexts of instances of the two jokes in the page. If the common contexts were at least four characters each, anything appearing with such a left and right context in the same page was saved as a new joke. For instance, if two seed jokes occur in an HTML-list, all list items in the list would be saved. This method has been used earlier to expand sets of named entities [10].

It is of course possible to run the method repeatedly, using the newly found jokes as seeds for the next run, to find more jokes. Sometimes things that are not jokes are also downloaded, for instance when two posters in a web forum us two different seed jokes as their signatures. This generally leads to grabbing all the signatures on the page, not all of which are necessarily jokes. We have run our program a few times, and also done some manual clean up to remove things that are obviously not jokes. This has resulted in a collection of 2,780 jokes. Many of these are small variations of other jokes in the collection though, so there are not 2,780 unique jokes.

For our experiments in this paper we selected 22 jokes from this collection. The main criteria when selecting jokes were that the jokes should be very short (since the robot model we use has a very limited amount of memory for voice samples) and be understandable in spoken form (some jokes in the collection are only understandable in writing).

Two robots were used, both of the same model: Robovie-i[1], a fairly small robot that can move its legs and lean the body sideways, see Figure 1. It also has a small speaker, though the sound volume is quite low and the sound quality is poor. The main features of the Robovie-i are that it is cute, easily programmable, and fairly cheap. One of the robots used is gold colored and one is blue. Whenever a robot was about to speak, it first moved its body from side to side a little, and then slightly leaned backwards, looking up at and pointing the speaker (mounted on the stomach) towards the evaluator. Other than that, the robots did not move.

The robot voice was generated automatically using a text-to-speech tool for Japanese, AquesTalk[2]. The robots use different synthetic voices, so it is possible to distinguish which robot is talking only by listening. The text-to-speech conversion works fairly well, though the produced speech is sometimes difficult to understand. It is flat, lacking rhythm, intonation, joke timing etc. The voice is somewhat childlike, and sounds "machine like", like most cheap text-to-speech.

For the first experiment, ten jokes were divided into two sets, set 1 and set 2, of five jokes each. Jokes in set 1 were always presented first and then the jokes in set 2. To half of the evaluators (group A) the jokes in set 1 were presented using one of the robots and to the other half (group B) these jokes were presented only in text form. The same was done for the jokes in set 2 too, but if an evaluator

---

[1] http://www.vstone.co.jp/top/products/robot/Robovie-i.html
[2] http://www.a-quest.com/aquestal/

Fig. 1. The robots used

had set 1 presented using the robot then the same evaluator would have set 2 presented using text and vice versa. Any one evaluator was only shown the same joke once, all jokes were shown to all evaluators, and all the jokes were always presented in the same order. Evaluators were assigned to group A or B based on the order they arrived in, e.g. the first ten to arrive ended up in group A, the next ten in group B, etc. This means that all jokes were evaluated an equal number of times using the robot and using text.

For the second experiment twelve jokes were divided into three sets of four jokes each. These were then presented by having one robot tell the joke and the other robot either laugh a little and say "*umai*" ("good one"), say "*samui*" ("cold", as in "not funny"), or do nothing. As in the first experiment, the jokes were presented to all evaluators in the same order, and all evaluators were presented with each joke exactly one time. Set 1 was made up of jokes 0, 3, 4, and 8; set 2 of jokes 1, 2, 5, and 9; and set 3 of jokes 6, 7, 10, and 11. Evaluators were assigned to either group C, D, or E. All groups had different reactions for each set of jokes, so the second robot would laugh at four jokes each time, boo at four jokes, and make no reaction at four jokes, but different jokes for different groups. Which group had which reaction to which set of jokes is shown in Table 3. All jokes were presented with each reaction to the same number of evaluators.

Evaluators were found by going to a table in a student cafeteria and setting up the robots and a sign saying that in exchange for participating in a short robot experiment volunteers would get some chocolate. Only native speakers of Japanese could participate. The evaluations were done one person at a time, so if many arrived at the same time some would have to wait their turn. Evaluators were asked to grade all jokes on a scale from 1 (boring) to 5 (funny).

As the cafeteria background was fairly noisy, compounded by the poor speaker, it was sometimes hard to hear what the robot was saying. In such cases the joke was repeated until the evaluator heard what was said. A more quiet background

Table 1. Mean evaluation scores for the three sets of jokes using different presentation methods. Which group evaluated which set using which method is given in parenthesis.

Set	Robot	Text
1	2.5 (A)	2.2 (B)
2	3.0 (B)	2.4 (A)
All	2.8	2.3

would have been better but finding a large number of evaluators prepared to go to a different experiment place would have been very difficult. We have since then managed to find better speakers, though they were not available in time for the experiment.

3 Results

In general, the evaluators were happy to participate, though most people passing by ignored the evaluation. In total, 60 evaluators, 17 women and 43 men, participated in the experiment. The scores of the jokes vary wildly from person to person. The lowest mean score for all jokes for one person was 1.3 and the highest 3.9 for the first experiment and 1.3 and 3.8 for the second experiment.

3.1 Robot vs. Text

The results of the first experiment are presented in Tables 1 and 2. Table 1 shows the mean scores of the different sets of jokes using the robot and text, and Table 2 shows the scores of each joke. These are of course also influenced by how interested each evaluator was in this type of jokes in general.

The total average scores in Table 1 is perhaps the most interesting result to focus on. It gives a good comparison between the two methods. Any specific evaluator is giving a score to the same number of jokes for both methods, and every joke is present an equal number of times for both methods. As hypothesized, the robot presentation method gets a higher mean score than text, 2.8 compared to 2.3. Though the standard deviation in the scores is quite high, 1.2 for both methods, the difference is significant ($\alpha = 0.01$ level, Student's t-test).

Looking at the individual jokes in Table 2, nine of the ten jokes were perceived as funnier when presented by the robot than by text, though in many cases the difference was small. Accounting for the multiple number of comparisons, only two jokes (jokes 5 and 7) were significantly funnier at the $\alpha = 0.05$ level using the robot.

The Pearson correlation between the jokes in text form and the same jokes presented by the robot is 0.73, indicating a fairly high correlation. This indicates that the robot improves the impression of the jokes, and not that the robot is simply funny in itself (which would make all jokes told by the robot be about as funny). Some jokes are improved more than others, which could depend on

Table 2. Mean evaluation scores using different presentation methods

Joke	Total	Robot	Text
0	2.2	**2.5**	2.0
1	1.9	**2.0**	1.9
2	2.8	**3.0**	2.5
3	3.0	**3.2**	2.9
4	1.8	**2.0**	1.5
5	2.5	**3.1**	1.9
6	2.3	**2.7**	2.0
7	2.8	**3.2**	2.4
8	2.7	**2.8**	2.6
9	3.1	3.1	**3.2**
Average	2.5	2.8	2.3
# Highest Score		9	1

many things. Some factors are the quality of the robot voice for the words in question, if the joke is new or old, if the joke is a joke on the person telling the joke etc. Joke 1 (scored similarly in text and using the robot) is for instance a very well known Japanese joke that most people no longer find interesting while joke 5 (scored a lot higher using the robot than using text) is a joke that has a repeated sound that sounds funny, but does not come through quite as well in text it seems.

3.2 Laughter, Booing, or No Reaction

The results of the second experiment evaluating the influence of a second robot either laughing, booing, or giving no reaction at all to the telling of a joke, are presented in Tables 3 and 4. Table 3 shows the mean scores of the different sets of jokes having different reactions, and Table 4 shows each individual joke.

As before, the total average score for each presentation method in Table 3 is perhaps the most interesting result to focus on, since any specific evaluator is giving a score to the same number of jokes for every reaction type, and every joke is present an equal number of times with each reaction. As hypothesized, the mean scores are higher with some form of reaction than with no reaction,

Table 3. Mean evaluation scores for the three sets of jokes using different presentation methods. Which group evaluated which set using which method is given in parenthesis.

Set	Jokes	No reaction	Laughter	Booing
1	{0, 3, 4, 8}	1.9 (E)	3.1 (D)	2.9 (C)
2	{1, 2, 5, 9}	2.0 (C)	2.2 (E)	2.5 (D)
3	{6, 7, 10, 11}	2.7 (D)	3.1 (C)	2.4 (E)
All		2.2	2.8	2.6

Table 4. Mean evaluation scores using different presentation methods

Joke	Total	No Reaction	Laughter	Booing
0	2.6	1.6	3.0	**3.0**
1	2.5	2.3	2.5	**2.8**
2	2.0	1.9	**2.1**	**2.1**
3	3.0	2.5	**3.3**	3.1
4	2.7	1.7	**3.2**	3.1
5	2.3	1.9	2.1	**2.8**
6	2.5	2.2	**3.2**	2.2
7	2.7	2.5	**3.0**	2.5
8	2.4	1.9	**2.9**	2.5
9	2.0	1.8	1.8	**2.4**
10	3.0	**3.4**	3.1	2.5
11	2.6	2.6	**2.9**	2.2
Average	2.5	2.2	2.8	2.6
# Highest Score		1	7	5

averaging 2.8 for laughter and 2.6 for booing, compared to 2.2 for no reaction. Again, the standard deviation in the scores is quite high, 1.0 for laughter and no reaction, and 1.1 for booing. The differences between laughter and no reaction and between booing and no reaction are significant on the $\alpha = 0.01$ level (Student's t-test, α adjusted for multiple comparisons), while the difference between laughter and booing is not significant.

Looking at the individual jokes in Table 4, only for one joke out of twelve was the no reaction presentation better than the other methods.

3.3 Discussion

In total, despite some problems with hearing and understanding what the robots said, the robots did make things funnier. The difference in mean scores of 0.5 between text and robot is rather large on a scale from 1 to 5, especially considering that the average score was only 2.5. The same is true for the difference between no reaction and laughter (or booing), 0.6 (0.4) for an average score of 2.5.

Evaluations of the impressions of robots performing *manzai* (Japanese stand-up comedy) have shown similar results to ours, i.e. that robots telling jokes give a funny impression. The overall impression of the robots was rated higher than viewing amateur comedians perform the same routine on TV [11].

Some general problems with the evaluations were: the noise in the cafeteria, the low quality robot speakers, the text-to-speech results sometimes being hard to understand, and the fact that simple word play jokes are not very funny without context. Some of these (speaker and text-to-speech) are pretty straightforward to improve, while the others might be more difficult.

The robots worked quite well in telling jokes and evaluators seemed to relate to them. Many evaluators commented on the robot's reactions with things like "Yes, I agree, that was not very funny" (when booing) or "Ha ha, for sure it is lying now!" (when laughing at a joke the evaluator obviously did not think was very funny), despite the robots being obviously just machines. Jokes mentioning the speaker (such as "I am so out of shape I get tired just by pushing my luck") also tended to get a better reaction when embodied by the robot than when just read in text form.

4 Conclusions

We evaluated the impact of different presentation methods for evaluating how funny jokes are. We found that the same joke was perceived as significantly funnier when told by a robot than when presented only using text. The average scores were 2.8 (robot) and 2.3 (text), which is a quite large difference on the scale from 1 to 5 used. This means that it can be difficult to compare the evaluations of different joke generating systems (or other sources of humor) evaluated at different times, since even the presentation method used has a very large impact on the results. There are likely many other factors that influence the evaluation results too, making it difficult to compare different systems.

We also evaluated the impact of having another robot laugh, boo, or do nothing when a joke was told. This too made a significant difference to the perceived funniness of a joke, with an averages of 2.8 (laugh), 2.6 (boo), and 2.2 (no reaction). The robot always laughed and booed in the exact same way. A more varied set of reactions would probably be even funnier.

In future experiments we want to examine the effect of speech only (is the voice or the robot funny?), and include a small training evaluation to remove any effect of a joke being funny because it is the first appearance of the robot. We already have better speakers for the robots, and would like to have better text-to-speech quality. We also want to evaluate automatically generated jokes, and have already used the robots for this in some other work [6].

Acknowledgments

This work has been funded by The Japanese Society for the Promotion of Science (JSPS). We also thank the anonymous reviewers for insightful comments.

References

1. Binsted, K., Bergen, B., Coulson, S., Nijholt, A., Stock, O., Strapparava, C., Ritchie, G., Manurung, R., Pain, H., Waller, A., O'Mara, D.: Computational humor. IEEE Intelligent Systems 21(2), 59–69 (2006)
2. Binsted, K.: Machine Humour: An Implemented Model of Puns. PhD thesis, University of Edinburgh, Edinburgh, United Kingdom (1996)
3. Binsted, K., Takizawa, O.: BOKE: A Japanese punning riddle generator. Journal of the Japanese Society for Artificial Intelligence 13(6), 920–927 (1998)
4. Yokogawa, T.: Generation of Japanese puns based on similarity of articulation. In: Proceedings of IFSA/NAFIPS 2001, Vancouver, Canada (2001)

5. Stark, J., Binsted, K., Bergen, B.: Disjunctor selection for one-line jokes. In: Proceedings of INTETAIN, Madonna di Campiglio, Italy, pp. 174–182 (2005)
6. Sjöbergh, J., Araki, K.: A complete and modestly funny system for generating and performing Japanese stand-up comedy. In: Coling 2008: Companion volume: Posters and Demonstrations, Manchester, UK, pp. 109–112 (2008)
7. Taylor, J., Mazlack, L.: Toward computational recognition of humorous intent. In: Proceedings of Cognitive Science Conference 2005 (CogSci 2005), Stresa, Italy, pp. 2166–2171 (2005)
8. Mihalcea, R., Strapparava, C.: Making computers laugh: Investigations in automatic humor recognition. In: Proceedings of HLT/EMNLP, Vancouver, Canada (2005)
9. Sjöbergh, J., Araki, K.: Recognizing humor without recognizing meaning. In: Masulli, F., Mitra, S., Pasi, G. (eds.) WILF 2007. LNCS, vol. 4578, pp. 469–476. Springer, Heidelberg (2007)
10. Wang, R., Cohen, W.: Language-independent set expansion of named entities using the web. In: Perner, P. (ed.) ICDM 2007. LNCS, vol. 4597, pp. 342–350. Springer, Heidelberg (2007)
11. Hayashi, K., Kanda, T., Miyashita, T., Ishiguro, H., Hagita, N.: Robot manzai - robots' conversation as a passive social medium. In: IEEE International Conference on Humanoid Robots (Humanoids 2005), Tsukuba, Japan, pp. 456–462 (2005)

Laughter: Its Basic Nature and Its Background of Equivocal Impression

Yutaka Tani

Professor Emeritus, Kyoto University, Japan
yu-tani@orion.ocn.ne.jp

Abstract. When we look at laughters uttered in conversation, we can easily realize that the traditional incongruity theory has not a general validity. Moreover, laughter is often uttered in a situation where there is no playful tone. Analyzing not only speakers' but also recipients' laughter, I will point out that any laugher laughs when he is not what he is presenting or has presented as self x and is leaking a minimum hint for the others to negatively qualify his ongoing self in such a manner, i.e. he is non (x). Therefore I would define laughter as a collaborative meta-communication to avoid mutual misunderstandg about the participation stance of self. Nevertheless the message <now he is not x> does not specify <what he is now>. The equivocality of laughter derives from the basic nature of its message, the surrounding context and the availability of relevant informations.

1 Several Questions on Laughter

Laughter is one of the pan-human expressive acts. It can be described by the following facial and vocal expressions simultaneously produced; 1: showing the teeth partially bared by opening the mouth and 2: repetition of the glottalstop aspirated h often accompanied with a vowel("hahahaha" or "hihihihi" etc.). This basic characteristic form doesn't vary across different cultures and individuals.

On the other hand, in spite of a general unifomity of its basic physical form, we know that there are various expressions that qualify each actual laughter: for example, sarcastic, embarrassed, hilarious, bitter, sardonic, flattering and so on. Sometimes, a recipient of laughter asks "Why did you laugh?" or interprets it as despising even if the laugher hasn't any intention of despising. The laugher often finds it difficult to give a proper answer to such questioning or criticism. As a matter of fact, laughter shows a chameleon nature and defies a univocal qualification. Moreover, sarcasm and embarassment are oppositional in orientation. Hilarious and satanic are oppositional in their impression. Why can these two oppositional impressions be produced by fundamentally the same physical form of laughter?

There is a similar phenomenon in the linguistic expression. For example, the word <stupid> has its own linguistic denotation: <foolishness to commit unexpected failure> independently from a contextual situation where it is uttered. However, the utterance "stupid !" can be read as sarcasm when it is said in front of somebody else's failure, while it is interpreted as embarassment in front of one's own failure. The connotative differentiation between sarcasm and embarassment derives from different contexts. In the same way, can these oppositional impressions of laughter be seen as connotative secondary products depending on external contexts surrounding it? Does laughter itself carry its own denotative referent, independent from the surrounding contexts? I must confess that it is not easy to find such a denotative referent in laughter which is just a combination of facial and vocal displays. What kind of communicational message does laughter convey?

In comparison to laughter, let's first examine weeping. A weeper's eyes are focused on an internal sentiment such as sadness or regret and weeping can be interpreted as a self-referential expression of such a sentiment. Weeping can last well beyond the moment <here and now> in the conversational context that rapidly shifts from one thing to the next one, probably because such a sentiment lasts for a certain time.

On the contrary, each laughter usually doesn't last long, even if it sometimes happens that a person's laugh follows after another's, and after several seconds of duration, it leaves off. A retarded laughter is considered out of focus. Laughter seems to aim at an acute intervention into a special <here and now> event in the interactional flow. And, as seen above in the possibility of laughter to espress either sarcasm or embarassment, the laugher's eyes can be focused on an event occurred to others as well as to himself / herself.

Let me remind you that the voice of laughter can be described as a repetition of glottal aspirated h accompanied by a vowel. We realise that one of these units corresponds to the voice of surprise or astonishment: <ha>, <ho> etc. Surprise is a cognitive experience. Independently from whether the surprising event has occurred on others or oneself, one is surprised as far as the event is unexpected to him. And it is probably because the unexpected event becomes already known after the moment of astonishment that the voice of surprise doesn't repeat and immediately leaves off after its occurence: in fact a vocal intervention of surprise is acute and doesn't last long.

In the above mentioned modes of laughter, we can find the same kind of occurence mode as in the surprise voice. Of course, laughter is not surprise. But the fact that both of them share the same occurence mode suggests that laughter is produced in relation not to some emotional but to some cognitive state of the laugher. Moreover we know that the presence of others increases the occurence degree of laughter. This fact suggests that a laugher not only self-referentially represents that he is in some cognitive state, but also he is intervening into ongoing social interaction. If so, what kind of interactional function does laughter have?

I have raised several questions beginning by asking why and how various impressions of laughter are produced in the same physical form. In order to give an answer to this first question, I must previously answer the last question concerning the basic nature and function of laughter. So I will discuss it first analyzing various examples that I have collected in ordinary conversational situations.

2 Critical Comment to Previous Approaches

Before tackling conversational situations of laughter, I will make a brief critical comment to previous traditionalistic approaches based on analysis of humor.

Many philosophers, psychologists and scholars of literature have discussed the nature of laughter by analysing humor, parody, wit, puns and comical plays which are regarded to have a special mechanism that provokes laughter. Most of these scholars thought that laughter is an automatic response to a humorous stimulous. Leaving aside the tension reduction theory which was based on a modern mechanical idea of man, the so-called incongruity theorists tried to identify a laugh provoking stimulous in humour. J. Lock found that there is a rapid shift of the cognitive state, W. Hatzlitt laid attention on incongruity, C. Melinand found the possibility of double reading in the ridiculous, J. Beatty pointed out the ambivalence between congruity and incongruity. And finally A. Koestler paid attention to the unexpected bisociation of two independent domains of ideas. All of them notify some kind of ambivalent incongruity found in humorous discourses and take it as the trigger of laughter[1].

As far as we think of the following examples of humor, they seem to have touched a vital point.

Example 1:

One day, after a dinner party, Napoleon was dancing with an Italian lady. Pointing at many dancing Italians, he said to her; "Italians are bad at dancing." She immediately replied to him, "Non tutti, ma BUONA PARTE si' (Not all of them, but most do)."

In Italian, <buona parte> means <most>, but with this word the lady hints also at Napoleon Buonaparte. So, her reply can be an agreement to Napoleon's judgement with a reservation, but, at the same time, can be in opposition to Napoleon with an implicit suggestion of despise. In her reply, we can find a double meaning producing mechanism which is intentionally fabbricated. Responding in this way, she succeeded in avoiding possible blaming both by Napoleon and by Italians. After this kind of witty story telling, we are likely to laugh.

We can show the same kind of laughter occurrence in an actual conversational situation.

Example 2: Yes, we did, but in Japanese

In the committee meeting of a museum, external committee members and several inner administrators of the museum are talking about a recently prepared videotek. After talking of monthly statistical data of the users' number, one external committee member K asks a staff administrator of the museum S about the access guide push botton for foreigners with the caption "FOR FOREIGNERS" on it, as follows;

---

[1] On incongruity theory, see [1].

1-K: *Tokorode, gaikokujinyoo no akusesugaido, pusshu botan F to iunodeshita ne?*
By the way, the access guide push botton "F" was meant for foreigners, wasn't it?

2-S: *Hai soudesu*
Yes, it was.

3-K: *Are, arewa chanto shite aru no desu ne?*
That one. It is set as we decided, isn't it ?

4-S: *Hai, shite arimasu (pause) tadashi nihongo de*
Yes, as decided, (pause) but written in Japanese

5-*: *HAHHAHHAHhahhaa.*   *: Most of other committee members.
((laughter))

It is possible to reply "yes" to the 3-K's question, as far as the access guide for foreigners is prepared, even if it is written in Japanese. But 3-K is, under a taken for granted presupposition , asking whether the access guide "F" is well prepared for foreigners to read it. As far as it is written in Japanese, foreigners can not read it. If this implicit presupposition were taken for granted, S should have answered "No" to 3-K's question. Anyhow, adding "but written in Japanese" after a short pause to "Yes, we did", S succeeds in answering simultaneously "Yes but No". We can not judge if S's answer is witty talk or unintentional prompt answer of a faithful administration member. There we can find two possible congruous readings each negating the other. After such double meaning talk, recipients strongly laugh. So, as far as we refer to such example of laughter, the incongruity theory seems valid.

But if we look at other kinds of current speaker's laughters which occur in conversation, we can easily discover that the incongruity theory has not a general validity. In the next examples of conversation, current speakers laugh, but we can not find any incongruity in his talk.

3 Current Speaker's Laughter

Example 3: After playful self praising talk

A professorois talking with a house master M of a merchant family at M's house in a village in Omi province. They begin to talk about the difficulties of the ongoing economic recession in Japan. In order to explain how he has been working hard to overcome the crisis, M says as follows

M1: *Sorede wate asa hayaoki shiterun desu wa **omi shounin no konjou wo hakkisite** HAHHAHHAHHAHHAH* (boldface means stress)
So, I do get up early in the morning and work hard **with the true spirit of an Omi merchant**. ((laughter))

Omi people were famous for being hardworking and clever merchants in Japan. He underlies the phrase "with the true spirit of an Omi merchant" by saying it with emphasis and laughs aloud. If we pay attention to this emphatic tone, we may characterize this talk not as just self praise but as a playful self praising talk. Self praising in itself doesn't contain any incongruity.

With regard to this playfulness, we know that Gregory Bateson, in his well-known article "A theory of play and fantasy", pointed out that many high evolved animals can play by mutually acknowledging <this is a play>[2]. Under such a playful interaction, for example an ongoing mocking bite is produced in the following way: it seems <bite>, but is <non bite> and seems <non bite>, but is {non (non bite)}. Players can continue to play as far as they mutually recognize that they are lodging together between the presented self (serious) and the self-presenting self (non-serious). He says that this competence in playing must be obtained as an evolution of communicational competence of animals.

Moreover, it is well known that playing chimpanjees utter playful pants which are similar to the sounds of human laughter. A primatologist, Dr. Toshisada Nishida, taught me an interesting example of playful pants utterred during mother-infant playful interaction:

An infant chimpanjee was eating fruits on top of a tree. His mother, going under the tree and looking up at him, shook the trunk of the tree and uttered playful panting sounds. The infant meanwhile went on eating fruits without any expression of fear.

We can say that with palyful pants she is sending a metamessage: it seems <menace>, but is <not menace> and the infant takes this menace as play. After the stage of chimpanjee, we may have developed not only the ability to distinguish between serious and playful acts, but also may have obtained a competence to invite others into a playful interaction by laughter .

As far as we characterize the merchant's self praising talk as playful, we may say that the merchant's laughter is also representing the same playful participation stance by laughter as the mother chimpanjee's playful pants. And by laughing aloud, he is demonstrating that his talking seems serious self-praising, but it isn't serious and in fact he is soliciting the recipient not to take this self-praising talk at its face value.

However laughter is utterred not only in playful situations, but also in non playful situations.

Example 4: After a self depreciating talk on her ongoing act

It happened at the house of the above mentioned merchant M. Two researchers from Kyoto A and B passed the night there. The next morning they are sitting in the dining room for breakfast. Most of the dishes are already served on the table. Just before starting eating, the merchant's wife W comes to the table with a bowl of homemade salted pickles and says;

W: *Uchide   tsukutta   tsukemono   desuga.*   hohhohhoh
ko(h)re(h)yo(h)ka(h)tta(h)ra sansho no hou mo
Even though these are just homemade salted pickles, (abbreviated <if you pleases, help yourselves>) ((laughter)) *And if you please*, (abbreviated <please take>) also a sansho dish. (slight laugh sounds are superimposed on the phrase written in italics)

A Japanese lady demonstrates to be a good wife by showing her humility. Wife W is offering a homemade dish uttering the phrase; "Even though these are just homemade salted pickles". This talk can be taken as self minimizing of her ongoing offering act. She may be showing her anxiety about her homemade pickles which may not meet the Kyoto guests's tastes, because Kyoto is well known for refined salted pickles. From this self minimizing talk, we can recognize that she is afraid of being misunderstood: her offering act could be interpreted as self praising. She produces slight laugh sounds during her offering act accompanied with a self minimizing phrase.

By the way, any voluntary act is likely to be interpreted by others as done by someone because he/she thinks it something worthwhile doing. Especially when someone is offering something self-made, his/her offering act can be interpreted as self-praising. But in this example, the lady intends to avoid such an interpretation by accompanying self-minimizing words("just homemade") to her offering act. She is afraid of being misunderstood as a self-praising offerer, but in the same time she is potentially presenting herself as a self-praising offerer. She finds herself standing in between a presented self-praising self and a presenting self-minimizing self: in fact she is not what she is presenting now as self. By superimposing light laugh sounds on her talk, she may be soliciting the recipients not to take her offering act at its face value.

The next laughter is also utterred in a non-playful interaction.

Example 5: Reporting somebody else's request with a role distance

In each Japanese village, there is a Shinto shrine where traditionally people dedicate a kind of wooden ex-voto <ema> when they want to receive some favour from protective divinities. Usually the ex-voto is hanged on a wodden hanging board in the shrine court. A villager who dedicates the ex-voto usually pays some amount of money as a thanksgiving fee to the shrine priest.

The following conversation was recorded in a community meeting of a village in Shiga province where representatives of every family are present. In the second part of the meeting, a person for the village community H begins to report a request of the shrine priest.

H: *Sorekara gankake no emakakede gozaimasuga, korewa saikin yashirono higashini nijuugosai no kataga hoonoo shite itadaki mashita. Sokode jousetsushite gozaimasu node, hoonoo wo shite itadakitai to iukotode gozaimasu. Kokorozashi to moushimasuka daitai sa(h)n(h)bya(h)ku(h)enkara gohyakuen toiukotode. Anoo gujisan nohou, (?) kingakuwa otagasan no ema ga gohyakuen ya toiukoto de gozaimasu node, ichiou maa sa(h)nko(h)nota(h)me(h)ni(h) hiroushite oite ku(h)re(h)to(h) iukotode gozaimasu node.*

By the way, about the hanging board for ex-votos (of our shrine), the shrine priest asked me to convey to all villagers his following message: "A 25years old villager has recently offered a new board on the east corner of our shrine. Villagers will be welcome to dedicate ex-votos on this board. As for the thanksgiving fee, it would be suitable *from about three hundred yen* to five hundred yen". Er, and the shrine priest said, "The thanksgiving fee of Taga shrine is five hundred yen. *Please inform villagers of this fact too as a comparative data*". (slight laugh sounds are superimposed on the phrase written in italics)

While H is reporting the priest's request to villagers, he superimposes light laughing sounds on several syllables of two different phrases. The first one is utterred when he is reporting the figure for thanksgiving fee proposed by the priest. The second one is uttered when he is just ending his literary reproduction of the priest's request in direct narrative form after giving the fee of another higher ranked shrine as a comparison price.

Why does the reporter H superimpose a laughing voice on these phrases, even though his reporting act has no playful intention? Later when I asked H the reason, he said that it is unsuitable to propose thanksgiving fees demonstrating comparative sums of other shrines. The amount of a thanksgiving fee should be freely decided individually and spontaneously. That means that such a thought had emerged in his mind while H was reporting the presumptuous request of the priest.

We know that a radio or TV announcer sometimes adds his critical comment immediately after he has reported someone's words. Of course, an announcer should carry out his professional role by faithfully conveying other people's words as a messenger, but it may happen that some critical thought comes to his mind. Goffman qualifies this kind of comments as talk with a role distance. In the same way, the reporter H is also carrying out his role in faithfully reporting the priest's presumptuous request, but at the same time, even if momentarily, he indulges in a critical thought on the priest request. At this very moment, he takes a distance from his ongoing role achievement. Even though he is presenting himself as a reporter, he finds himself in between the presented self (role achieving) and the presenting self (role distancing). He is not what he is presenting now as self in the public place just as the housewife W in the previous example. And he also utters slight laugh sounds as a current speaker.

Now let's go back to example 4 in which the Omi merchant M laughs after a playful self praising talk. We have interpreted his laughter as being uttered to convey his self-praising as not serious but playful. However, we can also say that he laughs just when he is not what he is presenting now as (serious) self. So, we can generalize all the laughters in examples 4, 5 and 6 as follows: independently from a playful or a non playful situation, any laugher laughs when he finds himself standing in between the presented self x and the self-presenting self non(x) each self being incongruous with the other. And by uttering laughter, he is suggesting that he is not what he is presenting or has presented as self x and solliciting the recipients not to take his ongoing act at its face value.

With this regard, I would like now to cite the following phrase of E. Goffman in his "Forms of Talk": "Talking interaction is an arrangement by which participants come together and mutually sustain matters having a ratified, joint, current, and running claim upon attention, a claim which lodges them together in some sort of intersubjective mental world"[3]. In talking interaction, as far as a participant doesn't correct other people's misunderstanding on his self presentation without correction or deliberately manages to invite other people's misunderstanding, he can't expect to lodge together in an intersubjective mental world; therefore if he intends to collaborate for a common intersubjective mental world, he must take measures to avoid others people's possibile misunderstanding, when he is not what he is presenting now as self and there is a possibility to be misunderstood. Owing to a default inference, he must send a sign to reframe his participation stance in order to avoid misunderstanding.

In all previous examples 4, 5 and 6, the speaker's laughter may be uttered not only as a self referential metacommunication to solicit the audience to negatively qualify his presented self, which is incongruous with the self-presenting self, but also as a collaboration in the mutual ratified claim to lodge together in a common intersubjective mental world.

4 Recipients' Laughter

As far as the current speaker's laughters are concerned, we could give a general answer as to the situation in which laughter is produced and to its interactional function. Nevertheless we know that there are many other cases in which the hearer laughs during or after a current speaker's talk. It seems the hearer has no reason to solicit other people to negatively qualify the current speaker's talk. He is only a recipient of the speaker's talk. Now we need to ask why a recipient laughs and in what situations he laughs.

Let's examine the next example in which the hearers laugh after a playful talk.

Example 6: Mocking menace in response to a shocking experience story

After lunch time, three people A (Akiyama), H (Hirota) and C (Chou) are chatting. At some point, A begins to tell about his shocking experience he had one night while he was sitting at his desk writing. The story may be summed up as follows:

He felt something moving inside his trousers and thought that some small insect was creeping up his leg inside his trousers. So, he softly patted his leg. At his surprise, he saw a centipede about 15 cm long fall down on the floor. He knew that the bite of a centipede is excruciatingly painful but fortunately he hadn't been bitten. Fearing that the centipede would hide again in the room, he quickly took a pair of scissor and cut it into two parts.

After reporting this experience, A makes the following retrospective comment; "*Are motto tsuyoku tataite itara sasareteta neh* (Had I hit it more strongly, I might have been bitten)". Those words provide a proper transition relevant cue to the participants. Now C takes the next floor and for a while they talk about the usual way of killing centipedes in Japan whenever they find them. After such an exchange, A finally regains his conversation floor in order to conclude his interrupted story and says;

1-A: *Iya sorede sasarete itara hitobanya futaban itakute jikan wo bouni futta to omottara hotto shita*
Nay! I thought at that time; Had I been bitten, I would have suffered strong pain for more than one or two days and I would have wasted lots of working time.

2-C: *Sonnanoni sasaretara itai de sumanai desuyo!*
Had you been stung by such a centipede, you would have suffered more serious effects than just pain.

3-A: *Rashii desune. Bikkuri shita*
So they say. I was really shocked.

4-H: *hohhohhoh*
((laughter))
(short pause)

5-H: *Ima haitte inai ka nah* ((finger pointing at the lower part of A's trousers))
Careful, you may have it inside, now! ((finger pointing at the hem of A's trousers))

6-A: *hahhahhah [hah*
((laughter))

7-C: [*hahhahhah [hah*
((laughter))

8-H: [*hahhahhah*
((laughter))

Laughters 6-A, 7-C and 8-H are an example of shared laughter. The initiator of laugh is the addressee A of the previous talk 5-H: <Careful, you may have it inside, now!>. In Japanese, 5-H is a negative questioning and it is taken for a claim of positive assumption. By presuming a fearful situation at present, 5-H is menacing A. Of course, it is an unbelievable assumption. Participants can easily understand that 5-H is a playful mocking menace. At this moment menaced A at first laughs and C follows. Why do they break into laugh?

In this case, it is clear to the recipients that the current speaker's talking act is playful. The recipients can recognize that the speaker's self presentation should be negatively qualified. In such a situation, it is better for the recipient to give a responding sign in order to convey acceptance of the speaker's act as play. Otherwise, the invitor of playful interaction cannot recognize whether the recipient has taken his talk as serious or playful and he would assume that the recipients have taken his playful talk as a serious attention call. Following such a default inference, a recipient intending to avoid mutual misunderstanding ought to show that he accepted the speaker's talk as playful. Because he is not what he has presented until now as a serious listening self x, but a non (x) self accepting the speaker's talk as a play invitation. We can interpret that by uttering laughter A and C may be soliciting the playful speaker to negatively qualify their presented selves at their face value and be suggesting that they have accepted the speaker's talk as play.

However, how can we characterize the recipient's laughter in the following example?

Example 7: We can't see anything except for the monkey's buttocks

In an academic informal meeting, several colleagues of different specializations are listening to a primatologist's talk on his field survey. After the primatologist has explained how difficult it is to work and get reliable data using binoculars in a primatological field survey, someone in the audience breaks into laughter.

Lecturer: *Iyaa, jyujo no saru to iumonowa bouenkyou de mitemo oshiri shika mienai nodesu*
Nay, monkeys on trees, even if we try to observe them by binoculars, we can't see anything except for their buttocks.

Someone in
the audience: *hahhahhahhah*
((laughter))

The lecturer's phrase is uttered in order to convey a common experience which primatologists encounter during their observation of tree living monkeys. To a field observer of monkeys' behavior, it is a familiar and taken for granted experience. It is almost certain that he has uttered this sentence without any intention to invite the audience "to play together". Nevertheless, someone in audience laughs. Why is he laughing?

In this talk, there is a potentially sexy word "buttocks". Even though the current speaker has no intention to invite the audience into joking interaction, it happens that one recipient misunderstands it as a playful invitation from the speaker's side. We can take the above laughter as an example of a recipient's response to a misunderstood invitation to play.

But we could also give a different possibile interpretation. Though the primatologist's reporting fact: <even if we try to observe them on trees by binoculars, we can not see anything except for their buttocks> is a familiar and well known fact to primatology experts, this fact could be taken as an unexpected remarkable experience by non-specialists. Of course, in such an interpretation, the question why someone in the audience laughs remains.

We can find similar recipient's laughters in the following examples 8 and 9 which are uttered in example 6: the story telling of a shocking experience. The previous speaker has absolutely no intention to make fun. Nevertheless a recipient laughs just after the previous speaker has finished talking.

Example 8: I have acknowledged your talk as a remarkable unexpected experience

1-A: *Sorede awatete hasami wo motte 'chon' to kitte yatta*
   Then in a hurry I took a pair of scissor and cut it into two (with the onomatopeic adverb "chon")
2-H: *hohhohhoh*
   ((laughter))

The light laugh is produced when the story telling of the centipede ends with an unusual method of killing. If you ask anybody how they kill a centipede in Japan, he will have in mind the method of hitting it hard with something. The method which A adopted, scissors cutting, may be seen as an remarkable unexpected experience by H.

The second laughter is uttered when the story teller A concludes it with his retrospective thought on his shocking experience (3-A).

Example 9: I agree with you with compassion

1-A: *Iya sorede sasareteitara hitobanya futaban itakute jikanwo bouni-futta to omottara hotto shita*
   Nay! I thought at that time; Had I been bitten, I would have suffered strong pain for more than one or two days and I would have wasted lots of working time.
2-C: *Sonnanoni sasaretara itai de sumanai desuyo!*
   Had you been stung by such a centipede, you would have suffered more serious effects than just pain.
3-A: *Rashii desune. Bikkuri shita*
   So they say. I was really shocked.
4-H: *hohhohhoh*
   ((laughter))

2-C and first half of 3-A can be taken for the adjacent pair of statement and response type. But in the second half of 3-A, A returns to his conclusive talk and defines his narrated event as a shocking experience. 4-H's laughter is produced just after that. Even if in A's talk there is no suggestion of an invitation to a playful interaction, nevertheless a recipient laughs.

This kind of story telling about a thrilling and fearful experience usually has a power to solicit either compassion or at least interest from the hearer. So after a conclusive confession of his experience ("I was really shocked"), the story teller expects some response from the hearers. The hearer may have accepted the talk as a remarkable experience to share compassion. At this moment, he is not what he has until now presented as mere story listening self. In such an occasion, as far as he keeps silence without any response, the story teller can not learn how the hearer has accepted his confession. If the hearer has a collaborative intention to share his experience as hearer, he may worry about being misunderstood by the story teller, lest he demonstrates response in a certain way. Without response, the story teller could take the hearer's silence as an evidence of his indifference to the emotional confession. Laughter is uttered just at this moment. This kind of laughter is sometimes qualified as flattering laughter or follower's laughter (osejiwarai or tsuishou warai) in Japanese. This kind of laughter, even though light, can be taken by the listner for a sign to inform that he has accepted the told event as an remarkable unexpected experience compassionately.

To sum up, any laugher in examples 7, 8 and 9 produces laughing sounds at the moment when he takes the told story as an unexpected remarkable experience and when he is not what he had presented as a mere listening self. And as far as he doesn't reveal his experience as such, he remains one who knows what others do not know. The next example is a typical laughter produced in such a situation.

Example 10: Now I know what he doesn't know

This example was collected at a home in northern Kyushu. The interlocutors are a mother and her child. The mother is of Kanto (Eastern Japan) origin. Instead, her son was brought up in Kyushu (Southern Island of Japan) and is accustomed to Kyushu dialect. You will find a misunderstanding happening because of a dialectical differnt usage of a word (the verb "naosu") between them.

It is afternoon; the son comes home from school and in the living room he shows his mother a sheet of arithmetics test already checked by the teacher. After a superficial glance, she says to him: "Chanto <naoshite> okinasai! (<Correct> it thoroughly)", meaning to ask him to correct the mistakes. He nods showing his willingness to do as she has told him and goes to his room. Soon after, he dashes from his room to the front door to go out to play as usual. The mother who thought he would stay in his room to correct the text, asks him, "Chanto <naoshita> no? (Have you already corrected it?)" in a slight tone of suspect. He answers, "Un, chanto hikidashini <naoshita> (Yes, I have <put it in> the drawer". At this moment, she breaks out into a slight laugh.

According to the Kanto usage, the verb "naosu" means <to correct>, while in the Kyushu area it means <to put something back into place>. When she heard her child's answer to her question, she was reminded of the Kyushu usage of the verb by what the child had understood and realized the consequent mutual misunderstanding.

Anyway, she asks a question to know whether he has done the corrections and he answers by reporting what he has done, though misunderstanding what she meant. In this example, both the interlocutors exchange thier talk without any intention to play. Nevertheless, at the boy's answer, the mother, as recipient, breaks into a slight laughter.

If there is something to be pointed out here, it is that she has realized the mutual misunderstanding. We may define this experience as an unexpected remarkable experience similar to the laughers' experience in the previous examples 7, 8 and 9. But what is more interesting here is that her child who doesn't know the Kanto usage of the verb cannot understand what she really means in her questioning and the following mutual misunderstanding. On the contrary, she unexpectedly learns not only that a mutual misunderstanding has occurred, but also that he didn't understand what she meant in her request.

A talk not only gives the hearer informations about what a speaker intends to convey, but also it sometimes reveals to him informational cues on what the speaker doesn't know. This case is a good example of it. Just after accepting her son's answer, she can not only learn what he doesn't know (meaning of her request and following mutual misunderstanding), but also she realizes that he can't realize that she has come to know about what he doesn't know. We may define such kind of cognitive experience as a unilateral cognition of asymmetrical distribution of interactional information. After she unilaterally finds out that a mutual misunderstanding has happened, she is no more the self she has presented until now. As far as she doesn't reveal her unilateral cognitive experience, she can not recover a common intersubjective mental world with him. Just at this moment she laughs.

Now, let's recall the laughers in the previous examples 7, 8 and 9. Any laugher, as a recipient of a current speaker's talk, receives it as an unexpected remarkable experience. But the current speaker can neither know nor imagine if the recipient has acknowledged his talk as such without any response. As far as a recipient receives a current speaker's talk as an unexpected remarkable experience, he, even if momentaneously, can unilaterally recognize that he is under an asymmetrical distribution of information with the current speaker. At this moment he is not what he has presented until now as self x, but is non(x). Without revealing this fact to the previous speaker, a misunderstanding may occur. According to such a default inference, the recipient's laughter also is produced just in the same situation where the current speaker laughs.

The recipient's laughter as well as the current speaker's laughter are a meta-communicational sign to solicit listeners to negatively qualify their ongoing selves in such a manner as non (x), in order to lodge together in a common intersubjective mental world avoiding mutual misunderstanding among participants.

To sum up my discussion on the basic nature and function of laughter, I must say that the basic ground for producing laughter resides not in some external laughable event, but inside a laugher's mind when one recognizes that he is not what he is presenting now as self, even if the <laughables> as triggers of laughter are various: play invitation, self praising, role distance, impropriety, error, confession of a shocking experience, misunderstanding and so on. The mother's laughter in example 10 symbolically provides clear evidence for that. She laughs, when she realizes that she knows what her child doesn't know and that she is not what she has presented until now as self. Now I would like to ask where this knowledge about the son's ignorance lies. This basic trigger of laughter resides neither in the son's ignorant mind nor in her mind from the beginning. She unexpectedly picks up this knowledge about her child's ignorance in the course of a talking exchange. She is no more what she has presented until now as self x. On the contrary, the others don't know this fact. This kind of unexpected unilateral cognition of asymmetricity is crucial. As far as a laugher judges that the ongoing presenting self is incongruent with the presented self x, he/she laughs showing willingness to avoid potential mutual misunderstanding. All laughers are leaking a minimum but pinpointing hint for others to negatively qualify an ongoing self now and here in such a manner as a non (x) self inserting it in the proper position of the swiftly shifting converstaional flow. And laughter has a power not only to suggest a laugher's collaborative attitude to lodge together in a common intersubjective mental world, but also to suggest another possible mental world where his ongoing self presentaion would not be interpreted at its face value. Shared laughter gives, even if momentarily, a sure evidence for laughers to be lodging in the same mental world. Laughter makes participants recognize that a laugher intends to lodge in a wider and tolerant world different from the world where only serious and formal statements and responses are mechanically exchanged.

Before ending my point, however, I need to underline an important reservation on my conclusion. I said that when one has accepted an ongoing (talking) event as an unexpected remarkable experience and realizes that only he knows that others don't know the fact, he laughs. But most events that appear one after another in front of a person can be unexpected and remarkable to him. If so, we might have to laugh at each eventual unit to come, but in fact we don't always laugh. It means that we don't take all these inner experiences as worthwhile and tolerable to reveal in public. What new subjective experience one deems worth to reveal depends on the subject to judge. They say that young Japanese girls laugh every time chopsticks are dropped. Young girls in Japan tend to coquettishly show themselves more sensitive than boys. When they are at a village festival banquet, they are easy to laugh to share together communality. Judging criteria vary depending on relational situations.

Moreover laughter is socio-culturally controlled. When we hear unhappy news, we don't laugh even if it is an unexpected remarkable event. Why? In such an occasion, we are requested to express condolescence as first. At school, students are requested not to laugh during a principal's lecture and maintain a talking-listening relationship with the lecturer. This is the intersubjective mental world which students should sustain. Even if light, a student's laughing suggests that he is not what he is presenting now as lecture listening self.

Now, ending my analysis on the basic nature and function of laughter, I would like to point out the background of variability and equivocality of its impression.

5 Variability of Laughter's Impression

To initiate this discussion, I want to remind you the basic nature and function of laughter. Laughter was a minimum but pinpointing metamessage to solicit others to negatively qualify a self presentation at its face value. Laughter is uttered at the moment when one realizes that he is not what he is presenting now or has presented as self x and worries about possible misunderstanding, but this kind of negative metamessage, even if it informs that a laugher is not what he in presenting now as self, it doesn't give any exact information about how he has arrived at such a stance and where he is. The message <it is not x> doesn't specify what is <non x>. Identification of <non x> relies on a recipient who infers the laugher's position with reference to contextual informations available to him. The original reason for equivocality of laughter is hidden here.

Of course, we know that there is a variety of laughing manners: loud laugh, light laugh, grin laugh, smirk laugh and so on. We change its sound tone, volume, pitch and facial expressions. These micro varieties give cues to interpret the laugher's attitude. But there are other factors to orient the impression of laughter.

I pointed out at the beginning that there are oppositional qualifications of laughter such as sarcastic and embarassed. Some improprieties provoke an unexpected remarkable experience that can trigger laugh. When one laughs at some other person's impropriety, it may be interpreted as sarcastic, while it is taken for a sign of embarassment when it is triggered in front of one's own error. The impression varies according to whom the laughable belongs.

Moreover, another factor orienting a laughter's impression is the availability of background information about what kind of unexpected remarkable experience a laugher has. In example 10, the mother produces laugh sounds when she realizes that her son misunderstood her request. But he who is not accustomed to the Kanto usage of the verb can't understand why she laughs. Her slight laughter may sound to her son enigmatic. In the same way the reporter of the priest's request in example 6 also superimposed slight laugh sounds on his reporting talk while he was indulging in a critical thought of the priest's request. Nobody else could infer why he is laughing. That laughter may also sound enigmatic and equivocal. Had he revealed his critical thought to some participant before the village meeting, that person might interpret his laughter as sarcastic.

On the contrary, about the shared laughter in example 2: Yes, we did, but in Japanese, the recipient of laughter can infer that the museum staff's answer has a double meaning <yes but no>. If we interpret that the laughers accepted the staff's answer as a witty one, we take it as fun laughter, on the other hand, if we interpret that the laughing recipients found a careless mistake on the part of the museum, we interpret the laughter as a kind of sarcasm laughter. We can not see through a laugher's mind, therefore whether interpretation is correct or not is impossible to determine. However we can name the two possibilities above mentioned as a background of laughter by referring to contextual informations which are shared between all participants. Because of this transparency shared laughter may give an impression of open laughter.

When someone listens to a canned joke, all the contextual cues to interpret it are provided inside the talk. The hearer, consulting his "encyclopedic" knowledge, finds something curious, and acknowledges that it is intentionally fabricated as a joke and laughs. It is a moment when not only the laugher but also the teller can believe that they are sharing a common intersubjective playful world. In such a situation laughter gives an open and mirthful impression.

Summing up, the equivocal impression of laughter derives not only from the laughter's basic message: <now he is not the presented self x>, but also from the various environmental contexts and availability of relevant informations.

References

1. Milner, G.B.: Homo Ridens: Towards a semiotic theory of humour and laughter. Semiotica 5(1), 1–30 (1972)
2. Bateson, G.: A theory of play and fantasy. In: Step to an Ecology of Mind, pp. 177–193. Ballantine Books (1972)
3. Goffman, E.: Forms of Talk, pp. 70–71. University of Pennsylvania Press (1981)

Author Index

Araki, Kenji 5, 306

Bary, Corien 146
Bekki, Daisuke 193
Butler, Alastair 119

Enomoto, Mika 275

Hagiwara, Gaku 48
Hagiwara, Masato 213
Hatano, Akira 5
Hosoma, Hiromichi 288

Ichise, Ryutaro 15
Iida, Hitoshi 273, 275
Ikeda, Kokolo 48
Ishida, Toru 73
Iwahashi, Naoto 62
Iwanari, Yuki 26

Jimbo, Kazuki 39

Kido, Hiroyuki 228
Kimura, Yusuke 242
Kita, Hajime 48
Kobayashi, Masahiro 103
Kurihara, Masahito 228
Kusui, Dai 87

Maier, Emar 133, 146
Matsuhara, Masafumi 5
Mizuguchi, Hironori 87
Mori, Mikihiko 48
Mori, Yoshiki 103
Murakami, Yohei 73
Murata, Kazuyo 294

Nakamura, Chidori 119
Nakamura, Hiroaki 103
Nakamura, Makoto 242
Nakayama, Yasuo 101
Nitta, Katsumi 211, 254
Nitta, Tsuneo 62

Ogawa, Yasuhiro 213
Ohba, Masato 275
Okamoto, Masashi 273, 275
Okumura, Manabu 39

Saga, Masaki 48
Satoh, Ken 211
Shimazu, Akira 242
Sjöbergh, Jonas 306
Suzuki, Satoru 177

Taguchi, Ryo 62
Takamura, Hiroya 39
Takanashi, Katsuya 273
Tanaka, Rie 73
Tani, Yutaka 314
Tasaki, Makoto 26
Tojo, Satoshi 211
Toyama, Katsuhiko 213
Tsuchida, Masaaki 87

Uehara, Tetsutaro 48

Wakaki, Toshiko 254
Winterstein, Grégoire 161

Yabu, Yuichi 26
Yokoo, Makoto 3, 26
Yoshimoto, Kei 103, 119

Printing: Mercedes-Druck, Berlin
Binding: Stein+Lehmann, Berlin